SOCIAL POLICY IN CHALLENGING TIMES

Economic crisis and welfare systems

Edited by Kevin Farnsworth and Zoë Irving

First published in Great Britain in 2011 by

The Policy Press
University of Bristol
Fourth Floor
Beacon House
Queen's Road
Bristol BS8 1QU
UK

t: +44 (0)117 331 4054
f: +44 (0)117 331 4093
e: tpp-info@bristol.ac.uk
www.policypress.org.uk

© The Policy Press 2011

North America office:
The Policy Press
c/o The University of Chicago Press
1427 East 60th Street
Chicago, IL 60637, USA
t: +1 773 702 7700
f: +1 773 702 9756
e: sales@press.uchicago.edu
www.press.uchicago.edu

British Library Cataloguing in Publication Data
A catalogue record for this book is available from the British Library.

Library of Congress Cataloging-in-Publication Data
A catalog record for this book has been requested.

ISBN 978 1 84742 827 1 paperback
ISBN 978 1 84742 828 8 hardcover

The rights of Kevin Farnsworth and Zoë Irving to be identified as editors
of this work has been asserted by them in accordance with the Copyright,
Designs and Patents Act 1988.

The statements and opinions contained within this publication are solely
those of the editors and contributors and not of the University of Bristol or
The Policy Press. The University of Bristol and The Policy Press disclaim
responsibility for any injury to persons or property resulting from any material
published in this publication.

The Policy Press works to counter discrimination on grounds
of gender, race, disability, age and sexuality.

Cover design by The Policy Press.
Front cover: image kindly supplied by Robert Proska.
Printed and bound in Great Britain by Hobbs, Southampton.

FSC
www.fsc.org
MIX
Board from well-
managed forests
FSC® C020438

Contents

List of figures and tables

Figures

Tables

Notes on contributors

Armando Barrientos is Professor and Research Director at the Brooks World Poverty Institute, University of Manchester, UK. His research interests focus on the linkages that exist between welfare programmes and labour markets in developing countries, and on policies addressing poverty, vulnerability and population ageing. His most recent books are *Social Protection for the Poor and Poorest* (Palgrave, 2008) and *Just Give Money to the Poor* (Kumarian, 2010).

Daniel Béland is Canada Research Chair in Public Policy and Professor at the Johnson-Shoyama Graduate School of Public Policy, University of Saskatchewan Campus, Canada. A student of politics and public policy, he has published eight books and more than 60 articles in scholarly journals, including *Comparative Political Studies, Environment and Planning C and D, Governance, Journal of Public Policy, Journal of Social Policy, Political Studies, Social Policy & Administration* and *Sociological Theory*.

Mairéad Considine is Lecturer in Social Policy at the School of Applied Social Studies, University College Cork, Ireland. She is co-author, with Fiona Dukelow, of *Irish Social Policy: A Critical Introduction* (Gill and Macmillan, 2009). Her current research interests include pensions policy and pension system reform, social policy and older people, and the impact of the current economic crisis on the Irish welfare state.

Sarah Cook is Director of the United Nations Research Institute for Social Development (UNRISD), Switzerland. Formerly a Fellow at the Institute of Development Studies, University of Sussex, UK, she has also worked for the Ford Foundation in China. Her research has focused principally on the social aspects of economic reform in China, including recent work on informal employment, gender and social protection.

Bob Deacon AcSS is Professor of International Social Policy, University of Sheffield, UK. He is Associate Research Fellow at UNU-CRIS and holds the UNU-UNESCO Chair in Regional Integration, Migration and the Free Movement of People. He is author of *Global Social Policy and Governance* (Sage, 2007), co-editor of *World Regional*

Social Policy and Global Governance (Routledge, 2010) and founding editor of the journals *Global Social Policy* and *Critical Social Policy*.

Fiona Dukelow is Lecturer in Social Policy at the School of Applied Social Studies, University College Cork, Ireland. Her current research interests include the impact of globalisation on the Irish welfare state, and welfare retrenchment and economic crisis. Recent publications include *Irish Social Policy: A Critical Introduction* (Gill and Macmillan, 2009), co-authored with Mairéad Considine, and *Mobilising Classics: Reading Radical Writing in Ireland* (Manchester University Press, 2010), co-edited with Orla O'Donovan.

Kevin Farnsworth is Lecturer in Social Policy at the University of Sheffield, UK. His research interests include the politics and economics of comparative social policy and the multiple functions of welfare. He has written widely on business influence on social policies and welfare. His latest research examines corporate welfare state provision that is designed to meet the needs of private corporations. He is the author of *Corporate Power and Social Policy* (The Policy Press, 2004).

Ian Gough is Professorial Research Fellow in CASE (the Centre for the Analysis of Social Exclusion) at the London School of Economics and Political Science, UK, and Fellow in LSE Global Governance. Until summer 2009 he was Professor of Social Policy at the University of Bath, UK, where he is now Professor Emeritus. He is currently researching climate change and social policy, funded by the UK ESRC.

Michael Hill is Professor Emeritus of Social Policy at the University of Newcastle, UK. He has written on many aspects of social policy and the policy process. He is co-author with Peter Hupe of *The Public Policy Process* (fifth edition, Pearson Education, 2009) and *Implementing Public Policy* (second edition, Sage, 2009), and co-author with Zoë Irving of *Understanding Social Policy* (Blackwell Wiley, 2009).

John Hudson is Senior Lecturer in Social Policy and Head of Social Policy at the University of York, UK. His research interests include comparative political economy of welfare, analysis of policy-making processes and the implications of the knowledge economy for social policy. He is co-author of *The Short Guide to Social Policy* (The Policy Press, 2008) and *Understanding the Policy Process* (The Policy Press, 2009) and is a member of the East Asian Social Policy Research Network's Executive Committee.

Zoë Irving is Lecturer in Comparative Social Policy at the University of Sheffield, UK. Her current research interests are in the social policy of small island states and the place of national biography in theorising welfare states. She has previously published in the area of gender, work and employment and is co-editor with Susan M. Hodgson of *Policy Reconsidered: Meanings, Politics and Practices* (The Policy Press, 2007), and co-author with Michael Hill of the eighth edition of *Understanding Social Policy* (Blackwell Wiley, 2009).

Pekka Kosonen is Lecturer in Sociology at the University of Helsinki, Sweden. He has studied structural changes in Finnish society and has compared Nordic welfare states in several articles and books. His other areas of research interest include the challenges presented to welfare states by European integration and globalisation.

Stefan Kühner is Lecturer in Social Policy and Director of the MA Social Policy Programmes at the University of York, UK. He has published on topics including the dependent variable problem within comparative social policy analysis, partisan and new institutional explanations of welfare reform, productive and protective welfare and, more recently, the global welfare regime debate. He is co-author with John Hudson and Stuart Lowe of *The Short Guide to Social Policy* (The Policy Press, 2008), which has been translated into Korean.

Wing Lam is a development policy researcher based in Hong Kong. As part of her studies at the Institute of Development Studies, University of Sussex, UK, she conducted field research in China on poverty and food security policy in the country. After her graduation, she affiliated with development non-governmental organisations and specialised on policy research and advocacy programmes. Her research interests include the intersection of social policy, economic crisis, and closing the rich–poor gap in China.

Eunna Lee-Gong obtained her MA in theory and practice in human rights at the Human Rights Centre, University of Essex, UK, and has recently completed her PhD in the Sociology Department at the University of Essex. Her research interests include social justice, implementation of economic and social rights, rights claims and social movements.

Adrian Sinfield is Professor Emeritus of Social Policy at the University of Edinburgh, UK, and has worked on social security, poverty, unemployment and the social division of welfare. He has been both Chair and President of the UK Social Policy Association and received its first lifetime achievement award. Co-founder of the Unemployment Unit and Chair for its first 10 years, he was also Vice-Chair of the Child Poverty Action Group for eight years.

Alex Waddan is Senior Lecturer in Politics at the University of Leicester, UK. His research focuses on US politics and social policy. He has published two books and various chapters on these subjects. His publications include articles in scholarly journals, including *Political Studies*, *Political Science Quarterly* and the *Journal of Social Policy*.

Acknowledgements

This book emerged from a study day held in Sheffield in the UK in September 2009, organised by the International and Comparative Social Policy Group, with assistance from the UK Social Policy Association. We are grateful to all those who attended this event and who contributed to the ideas and discussions informing the chapters presented here. As editors we would like to thank all the contributors to this volume for their intellectual support for the notion that it is not necessarily 'too soon to tell' what the impact of the economic turmoil in 2008 will be on the progress of social policy, and for their practical support in producing their analyses of the impact so quickly and painlessly. Finally, we would like to thank Emily Watt, Laura Vickers and all at The Policy Press for their support and patience in the production of this volume, which has been much appreciated. The current period is one of deep concern for all those working in social policy and social development, and we hope that while exposing the negative impact of entry to the 'age of austerity', the contents of this book also provide some grounds for optimism with regard to its spread and endurance.

ONE

Varieties of crisis

Kevin Farnsworth and Zoë Irving

Scoping the crisis

The evolution of social policy is punctuated with key dates. All of the major developed welfare states have their own chronological milestones and some share key historical 'moments': the economic crisis of the 1930s, the Second World War and the 1973 oil crisis all stand out. However, no period in history is likely to prove to be quite so significant for quite so many welfare systems as is the late 2000s. The body of literature built around welfare state development suggests that the golden age gave way to an age of 'limits' followed by retrenchment (see Palier, 2006, pp 358-41), and now, it seems, welfare states are embarking on a new age of welfare: the age of austerity. As this chapter and those that follow demonstrate, however, the extent to which the economic crisis will impact welfare states in the short, medium and long term, depends very much on the objective 'facts' of the extent of economic collapse, and the more ideological dimensions of crisis management, which concern the ways in which the crisis has been defined, understood and responded to.

To comprehend what makes the post-2007 crisis more significant than any that preceded it, we must first understand its context. To begin with, it took place at a time of unprecedented international financial interdependence, most obviously illustrated by the impact of bad lending practices in a relatively small financial market – the United States (US) sub-prime mortgage market – on the subsequent financial bankruptcy of a relatively wealthy nation – Iceland. In the advanced economies, it also took place against a backdrop of relatively high levels of national social expenditure within mature welfare systems. Modern welfare states were barely formed during the 1930s and the British welfare state was less than 30 years old in 1973. Significantly, then, these financial crises were less deep than today's, the devaluation of financial assets less significant and, crucially, the significance of state provision in the social and economic life of individuals far less universal.

Historically speaking, there have been many crises, the *Financial Times* noting that even in the short period between 1980 and 1996, the International Monetary Fund (IMF) reported 132 countries as having experienced 'macroeconomic or financial crisis' (Bevins and Cappitt, 2009). Nevertheless, there is no precedent to the crisis of 2008-10, which looks set to redefine social policy debate throughout the globe. The severity of the post-2007 economic collapse compared to crises since the 1970s is illustrated clearly in Figure 1.1. Notwithstanding its global reach, however, its actual effects are variable between nations. The argument presented through the contributions to this volume is premised on the belief that in understanding the implications of the present economic crisis for social policy, it is necessary to question both its nature and its scope. Analysis, therefore, has to consider the historical record and revisit political economy, as well as account for the various national and international dimensions of policy making. The chapters included here in Part One reflect these concerns.

The distribution of the 'pain' now associated with the crisis is differentiated among nations, reflecting existing political and economic conditions and institutions. The nature of these differences has been established in both the 'welfare regime' and 'varieties of capitalism' literature and these models, both separately (Esping-Andersen, 1990, 1996b; Hall and Soskice, 2001) and in combination (Schröder, 2009), provide a useful framework within which the shaping of national responses to the crisis can be explored. While the chapters in Part Two of this book give a clear indication of the breadth and depth of impact on social policy in national contexts, this chapter aims to provide some initial commentary outlining the ways in which the crisis has motivated change at the international level and what patterns of national response are emerging. Clearly, contemporary policy development has a greater sense of urgency than in times of economic stability but at the same time, as history tells us, policy is rarely more than incremental and while emergency economic measures can be introduced with some speed, the same cannot be said of welfare reform. Thus, while it is possible to present analysis of the initial impact of a redistribution of public funds and its likely consequences for social policy, discussion of the long-term developments will always be more speculative. Crises, or 'black swans' as Castles (2010) terms international emergencies, are not necessarily universal, even when they have obvious global repercussions. The questions arising for welfare states concern the extent to which their true colours are revealed – if they have veered off path during times of relative plenty, do they revert to type in times of hardship, for example? To what extent can and will essential change take place and

Figure 1.1: Economic crises, 1973–2009

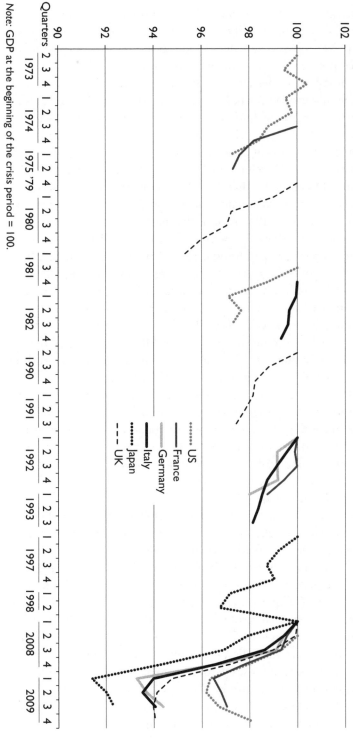

Note: GDP at the beginning of the crisis period = 100.

to what extent does this reflect new social politics, a reversion to the divisions of old or more of the same? Writing in the late 1980s, Sherer's (1987, p 291) observation that '[i]ndications are that budget deficits have become the obvious difficulty encountered by the welfare state' seems somewhat understated in the current context, but the future challenges identified remain fundamentally the same. It is towards the consideration of these questions that the country-focused chapters included in Part Two are addressed.

Today, governments of countries of the Organisation for Economic Co-operation and Development (OECD) typically spend 30-40% of their Gross Domestic Product (GDP) on welfare programmes and this level of expenditure has remained stable over the past 30 years or so. But this fact belies the transformations that have occurred within welfare systems over that period. To begin with, mature welfare systems spend far more on pensions and healthcare than they have in the past. They have also become more restrictive, more commodifying and more market orientated, and the private markets that, in the final instance, fund them, are leaner, more global, less stable and less predictable, even discounting the events of 2008-10. Thus, the impact of major economic upheavals such as the most recent one is different and arguably more severe. As O'Connor (1973) pointed out in his influential work on the last 'global' economic crisis of the 1970s, capitalism is full of contradictions, and deep economic crises, such as the one striking global capitalism today, reinforce the severity of such contradictions. It is fast becoming a cliché employed by economists to state that we need a new economics to understand and explain what went wrong in the present phase of capitalism; and it is even faster becoming a political cliché that we need a new social policy to understand the current phase of welfare reform.

What appears to have so thrown economists in the current crisis is the lesson that most disciplines outside the 'dismal science' have been aware of for some time: markets are not inevitable, objective, predictable or rational. As a recent text by Stiglitz (2010a) points out, markets are often self-destructive. Political economists, from Adam Smith to Marx and Polanyi to Galbraith, also understood this of course. The collapse in capitalist markets has resulted in a popular search for new ideas and this does create a window of opportunity in which to revisit old ideas and test new ones. In so far as it confirms what many social policy thinkers have asserted for some time, that social welfare is essential for sustainable capitalism, it may increase the confidence of social policy and could put the discipline on the offensive. But such opportunities must be weighed against the first real tension of post-crisis social policy. Any opportunities offered by the economic crisis to engage in more progressive theoretical debates on welfare will take place within the context of significant, perhaps unprecedented, levels of hardship and insecurity for many millions of people and, as always, the poorest will pay the heaviest price as the country case studies in this volume illustrate. Before moving on to discussion of some of the opportunities and risks for social policy that have emerged as a result of the 'crisis', by way of a reminder, the following section briefly sketches its origins and evolution.

What happened?

The crisis began around April 2007 with the collapsing sub-prime mortgage market in the US. US banks had provided credit to many individuals and households whose repayment prospects were far from secure, in the belief that rising house prices would offset any risks to the financial institutions (Stiglitz, 2010a). Thus, the relative risk of such lending appeared to be low. In addition to this, banks covered their exposure to risk by effectively reselling mortgages (and the risks attached to them) to other brokers around the world. In this way, debt was kept off the books and investors made huge gains. Other new difficult-to-comprehend market products were released by ever-more imaginative financial wizards, which were too complex for most people, including the regulators, to understand (Kaletsky, 2010). The collapse came when these products began to unravel. In the US in 2006, housing markets began to fall, borrowers defaulted in ever-greater numbers and smaller financial institutions were unable to cover the losses they had underwritten. As a result, large banks could not recoup their losses and they, in turn, found that they were suddenly harbouring huge amounts of increasingly worthless collateral in the form of property stocks and 'toxic debt'. Their only hope of survival was to try to recapitalise through a swift build-up of reserves, and this meant withdrawing lending facilities to consumers, businesses and other banks.

By August 2007, major problems in liquidity were beginning to appear in most banking systems. National LIBOR (London Interbank Offered Rate) (inter-bank lending) rates increased exponentially where inter-bank lending continued at all. The European Union (EU), US and Japan in particular all began pumping hundreds of billions into their banking systems to improve liquidity, but by the end of 2007, the first victims of the financial crisis began to emerge: Northern Rock collapsed in the UK, while Swiss Bank UBS, Citigroup and Merrill Lynch all reported massive losses. Towards the end of 2008, the knock-on effects of the mortgage crisis, which had become a banking crisis, were felt worldwide as huge financial players folded: Lehman Brothers declared bankruptcy, the US government took over American International Group (AIG) and numerous others and introduced the Emergency Economic Stabilization Act. In the UK, the government brokered the takeover of HBOS by Lloyds TSB and brought both the new superbank and Royal Bank of Scotland into part public ownership. In 2009, the financial crisis had become an economic crisis with all the concomitant recessionary features, and a number of countries embarked on strategies to boost economic demand and mitigate the effects of what has been referred to as the Great Recession (*Financial Times*, 2010).

The losses incurred in many advanced economies during this period cover, not only those of the private sector, and not only the interventions of the public sector – interest rates on government debt and a diversion of public financing away from state services towards propping up private institutions – but also those of individual households as housing markets continued to decline (spurred by the collapse in bank lending), the cost of credit soared, pensions and other financial assets collapsed and workers lost their jobs. In 2010, the crisis was reframed as one of 'sovereign debt' in several countries, including the eurozone and, more specifically, Greece (although Portugal and Spain were also under scrutiny). Following some rigorous EU debate, the European Financial Stability Facility was established in May 2010 with the European Central Bank also set to provide backing for debt-stricken eurozone countries. In the 2011 report released by the US Financial Crisis Inquiry Commission (FCIC), it is suggested that given its causes – poor and ill-informed regulatory oversight, weak corporate governance and reckless lending and risk accumulation – the crisis was entirely avoidable. Unsurprisingly, the report's conclusions are not supported by all Republican members of the Commission who are uncomfortable with the failure of regulation thesis, but the evidence is incontrovertible (*The Guardian*, 2011a). Yet, while citizens in Iceland, Ireland, Greece, Japan, Spain, the UK and the US experienced huge economic shocks, many other countries of the world suffered no more than very difficult and turbulent economic periods. The 'crisis' in the BRIC countries – Brazil, Russia, India and China – was, on paper at least, hardly perceptible. China and India continued to grow – albeit more slowly – and Brazil and Russia suffered deeper recessions but recovered quickly. Over the period of the crisis, these countries continued to grow at rates that far outstripped any of the major economies even during their most buoyant economic phases (see Table 1.1). They also had strong overall fiscal balances and the lowest levels of gross debt.

Table 1.1: Key economic indicators

	Finance, insurance, real estate and business services (% of gross value added to the economy)	Unemployment rates			GDP					Fiscal balances		General government debt (gross)	
	2005	2000	2005	2010	2007	2008	2009	2010	2011	2007	2010	2007	2014 (projection)
Australia	24.0	6.2	5.0	5.2	5.0	2.1	1.2	3.3	3.6	1.5	–2.4	9.8	27.8
Belgium	28.4	6.9	8.5	8.6	2.8	0.8	–2.7	2.1	1.8				
Canada	28.4	6.8	6.8	8.1	2.2	0.5	–2.5	3.0	2.3	1.6	–4.1	64.2	68.9
Denmark	16.8	4.3	4.8	7.2	1.7	–0.9	–4.7	2.2	1.6				
Finland	23.9	9.8	8.4	8.6	5.3	1.0	–8.1	2.7	3.0				
France	21.6	8.6	8.9	9.3	2.3	0.1	–2.5	1.6	1.6	–2.7	–8.6	63.8	96.3
Germany	32.7	7.4	10.5	6.9	2.8	0.7	–4.7	3.5	2.5	–0.5	–4.6	63.4	89.3
Greece	29.3	11.4	9.8	12.2	4.3	1.3	–2.3	–3.9	–2.7				
Iceland	27.2	2.3	2.6	7.5	6.0	1.0	–6.8	–3.6	1.5				
Ireland	22.1	4.3	4.3	13.6	5.6	–3.6	–7.6	–0.3	1.5				
Italy	33.5	10.1	7.7	8.6	1.4	–1.3	–5.1	1.0	1.3	–1.5	–5.6	103.5	128.5
Japan	26.9	4.7	4.4	5.1	2.4	–1.2	–5.2	3.7	1.7	–2.5	–10.2	187.7	245.6
Korea	26.6	4.4	3.7	3.7	5.1	2.3	0.2	6.2	1.7	3.5	–2.7	29.6	35.4
Mexico	45.5	2.6	3.6	5.2	3.3	1.5	–6.6	5.0	4.3	–1.4	–3.7	38.2	44.3
Netherlands	20.8	2.8	4.7	4.1	3.9	1.9	–3.9	1.7	3.5				
Norway	20.8	3.4	4.6	3.6	2.7	0.8	–1.4	0.5	1.7				
Spain	29.8	10.8	9.2	19.8	3.6	0.9	–3.7	–0.2	0.9				
Sweden	21.3	6.9	7.7	8.4	3.4	–0.6	–5.1	4.4	3.3				
UK	21.1	5.5	4.8	7.9	2.7	–0.1	–5.0	1.8	1.7				
US	28.7	4.0	5.1	9.7	1.9	0.0	–2.6	2.7	2.2	–2.6	–13.2	44.1	98.3
OECD – total	30.4				2.7	0.3	–3.4	2.8	2.3	–2.8	–10	61.9	108.2
Brazil					6.1	5.1	–0.2	7.5	4.3	–2.8	–1.2	66.8	58.8
China					14.2	9.6	9.1	10.5	9.7	0.9	–3.9	20.2	20.0
India					9.9	6.3	5.8	9.9	8.0	–4.4	–10	80.5	78.6
Russian Federation					8.5	5.2	–7.9	3.7	4.2	6.8	–3.2	7.4	7.2

What is clear, then, is that these economic events constitute not one 'crisis' but various crises impacting in a variety of ways with international and national variations. In the light of this, the following sections consider what is shared and not shared in the experience of crisis, how divisions and coalitions have emerged at the global, international and national levels, the ways in which these patterns might be understood and what this might mean for social policy.

A re-ascendance of multilateralism?

One of the more immediate effects of the events unfolding from 2007 was to signal a radical shift in global political thought and a reconfirmation of multilateralism. Gordon Brown stated in April 2009 that:

> The old Washington consensus is over. Today we have reached a new consensus – that we take global action together to deal with the problems we face; that we will do what is necessary to restore growth and jobs; that we will take essential action to rebuild confidence and trust in our financial system, and to prevent a crisis such as this ever happening again.[1]

A number of governments, the EU plus the G8 countries in particular, began to come together in late 2007 in order to try to stem the crisis in international financial markets and to devise a strategy for avoiding a global recession. A number of high-level international agreements were brokered, including a multi-billion dollar cash injection into banking markets by the EU, Canada, Japan, the UK and the US, coordinated by the US Federal Reserve in December 2007. The first properly coordinated multi-state meeting on the crisis was not to take place until a year later, however, in October 2008, when G7 ministers, Heads of State and the IMF held a series of crisis meetings in Washington. In November 2008, the G20 gathered to discuss ways out of the crisis and there were a number of formal meetings and behind the scenes negotiations between governments, especially within the G7 countries, to coordinate action on banking liquidity and interest rates, and to try to suppress growing signs of unilateralism in some states, through reconfirmation of their commitment to global free trade and improved multilateral regulations in the future. These efforts were exceptional in the speed with which they were put together, and also their relative success in uniting a wide range of countries in coordinated efforts to halt the crisis. In this respect, the international response was the epitome of advanced political and economic globalisation. And yet, these moves were criticised for not being quick enough and international financial organisations, primarily the World Bank and the IMF, were also criticised for not having adequate structures in place to deal with the crisis at the outset (Jerry Seib, *Wall Street Journal*, 10 October 2008).

What is clear is that continued cooperation on questions relating to financial stability and regulation is essential to overcoming the immediate and long-term effects of the crisis. Within relatively free global trading environments, unilateral programmes aimed at stimulating demand in one nation clearly have only limited impact, resulting in increased demand for goods produced elsewhere. The crisis appeared to emphasise the fact that global governance mechanisms were needed to ensure that the global economy maximises benefits for all, and this included viewing public expenditure and public services as potential solutions to economic and social problems rather than their causes. In this new period, coordinated and more progressive multilateralism appeared to be less distant than before.

But despite talk of European moves to regulate banking bonuses and an international agreement on a global 'Tobin'-style tax on corporate financial transactions, tough international rhetoric appeared to diminish in line with the recovery of the global finance industry. Meanwhile, although the OECD argued that better regulation and corporate governance were necessary to the recovery, it remains uncertain what this means in reality. The G20 did announce in April 2009 that a new Financial Stability Board would be established to monitor the global economy, including hedge funds and institutional debt, but it is not yet clear whether it will have teeth other than simply reporting to the G20 and the IMF. The EU, led by France and Germany, did push for much greater regulation and control over finance, but it failed to win agreement from the UK and the US.

Thus, early enthusiasm concerning a new multilateralism was tempered by the survival of old-fashioned unilateralism where national governments moved in the opposite direction: towards protectionism and the preservation of national interests. The US$825 billion stimulus package agreed in February 2009 specifies that only US iron, steel and manufactured goods are to be used in the projects financed by the funds, although a later amendment to the Bill, introduced after international opposition, stated that 'international trade agreements should be honoured' (*The Guardian*, 2009a). New forms of 'corporate welfare', that is, assistance to private businesses (primarily in the form of subsidies), have been extended beyond financial capital to big producers.

With regards to corporate welfare, provision for the private sector has never been so high. The EU has abandoned its previous scrutiny and control of corporate subsidies and during 2008-09 effectively turned a blind eye to various state aid measures to assist corporations that previously would not have been allowed. Although this may be expected given the depth of the economic crisis, it is useful to note that, as Zahariadis (2008) puts it, subsidies are simply another form of state protectionism and the only remaining legal means by which states can support their own corporations. Regardless of the positive effect this will have on national economies in the short run, there is a risk that these moves will further slow trade, which could have a negative impact on other nations, especially developing economies. Moreover, as some economies begin to show signs of recovery, the multilateral approach already appears to be coming undone. Led by the UK and the US, concerns were expressed by governments and commentators regarding unilateral and uncoordinated moves (primarily those led by France and Germany) to withdraw economic assistance. Moreover, subsequent to the UK General Election of 2010, which precipitated massive cuts in public spending, the Toronto G20 meeting of July 2010 confirmed the US to be a relatively isolated voice arguing against rapid cuts and the risks such moves pose to the global economy. In other words, in a global-ideological about-turn, the US had espoused Keynes while most of the rest of the world promoted neoliberalism!

Related to the above, the regulatory questions regarding what might be done to avoid similar financial crises from occurring again are proving difficult to answer. One of the problems implicated in the crisis is large banking bonuses, which are argued to encourage dangerous levels of risk taking among bank workers. This was initially a key point of debate and popular concern but has since faded into the background as attention is now focused on the costs of the public sector. France and Germany led an international move to try to regulate bank bonuses, but so far, the UK and the US, in many ways the biggest victims of the crisis, have refused to sign up to global measures, although President Obama continues a vociferous criticism of Wall Street practices.

The more formally constituted international governmental organisations were much slower to act than national governments. As already noted, the G7 and G20 countries did meet regularly, but most of the concrete proposals for stabilisation came from G7 meetings that excluded the key economies of Russia, India and China. The OECD responses and recommendations to the crisis were not published until December 2008. Perhaps more surprising is the slowness of the IMF in formulating a response. The United Nations (UN) was also slow to respond, but this is probably more to do with the lack of international backing it has received. It did finally convene a world Summit on the Economic Crisis in June 2009, which included 192 countries. Critics, such as Richard Jolly,[2] have argued, however, that the summit was sidelined and not treated with the seriousness it deserved, primarily because it was called and convened by developing nations (see also Dearden, 2009; Deacon, this volume).

Given its constitutional remit, the IMF should not only have warned of the pending crisis, but should also have been one of the first international governmental organisations (IGOs) to act in formulating a rescue plan. It was late 2008, however, before it began to formulate a strategy and its first major loan to a developed nation, Iceland, was not put in place until November 2008, several months after the Icelandic economy began to experience real difficulties (Conway, 2008). Given the IMF's history, it is ironic that its key 'diagnosis' of the problems that led to the crisis was one of 'poor regulation' while at the same time it warned against 'a rush to regulate', which it argued could 'stifle innovation' and 'make the credit crunch worse' (IMF, 2009). That it did not begin to respond with any real authority and effectiveness until the end of 2008 says something of the inadequacy of the organisation in its ability to coordinate government actions but something more telling about the status of the IMF prior to the economic crisis.

With a seemingly diminishing status on the world stage, the IMF had transformed itself over the 1980s and 1990s to a bank of reconstruction within developing countries. Prior to the crisis, it was becoming increasingly marginalised: condemned for its neoliberal fundamentalism and conditional lending practices (culminating in the public 'resignation' of Venezuela in 2007). For some (Masson, 2007) it had become a 'victim of its own success' as the number of crises it was asked to respond to, including the number of loans governments applied for, declined. The reality is that its strict lending practices meant that it simply could not compete with the less conditional lending terms offered by private markets and fewer customers meant less revenue from interest payments. Moreover, although the IMF was initially set up in order to pool financial resources (effectively financial subscriptions) and lend these to nations as their needs dictated, asking for support from the IMF had become akin to writing an economic and political suicide note for economies and governments. Paradoxically, the structural instability of the financial system that facilitated alternative sources of financing is what has led to the current rehabilitation of the IMF as an important international financial institution, backed by an additional, internationally coordinated, injection of new capital and a tripling of its lending capacity to US$750 billion plus the establishment of a US$250 billion fund to support emergency 'special drawing rights' for nations. Its re-emergence, interestingly, spurred a policy rethink on its lending practices set out in 2009:

> As part of a wide-ranging reform of its lending practices … the IMF has redefined the way it engages with countries on issues related to structural reform of the economy. The IMF's intention is to do away with procedures that have hampered dialogue with some countries, and prevented other countries from seeking financial assistance because of the perceived stigma in some regions of the world of being involved with the Fund…. Starting May 1 [2009], structural performance criteria will be discontinued for all IMF loans, including for programs with low-income countries. Structural reforms will continue to be part of IMF-supported programs, but only when they are seen as critical to a country's recovery.[3]

This was backed by uncharacteristic support for social policy programmes, and together, these moves seemed to present a more positive environment for social policy development. According to the IMF, it has been 'outspoken during the crisis in pressing for a coordinated response to the crisis through cuts in interest rates, big increases in government spending, cleaning up the financial sector, and bolstering regulation'.[4]

What is still not yet clear, however, is whether this new 'unconditionality' will be applied equally to the developed North and developing South. An analysis of IMF loans by the Centre for Economic Policy Research (Centre for Economic Policy Research, 2009) in Washington since 2008 found that the same conditions tended to be imposed, at least in the developing world. Loans made as a response to the crisis, to Hungary, Latvia and Pakistan, but not Iceland, for example, have come with strict conditions, relating to spending cuts and curbing budget deficits and Christian Aid reports similar pressures applied to governments in sub-Saharan Africa (Stewart, 2009; *The Guardian*, 2009b). Given the IMF's revitalisation, a softer approach to the social impact is probably fleeting rhetoric rather than long-term reality.

In terms of what the new multilateralism means for social policy, although immediate needs for countries to converge on the pivotal elements of a rescue plan were apparent, the fact that the IMF rather than organisations that have historically been more favourably predisposed towards social policy, including the UN or International Labour Organization (ILO), has gained most as a result of the crisis does not necessarily bode well. A momentary and partial return to Keynes has not, so far, created the space for more Beveridge. Neither market failure, Obama's presidency nor the ascendance of softer neoliberal models or 'corporate-centred welfare' (Farnsworth, 2006) have seriously undermined neoliberal hegemony.

Varieties of crisis

What the crisis means for the relative power of state, capital and labour is an important question in terms of the likely impact on social policies. In the onset of recession, organised labour clearly took a defensive stance, protecting corporate interests above its own in the struggle to salvage something from the crisis for workers. Trades unions have been forced to accept pay cuts and lock-outs (BBC, 2008) and have fought hard for greater levels of state assistance for corporations (*The Guardian*, 2008). Of course, this has since changed in some countries with increasing unemployment levels, job insecurity and the inevitable cuts in welfare provision that followed. Turning to capital, at first glance, it might have been assumed that the financial sector was incredibly weakened by the crisis and capital in general lost some of its legitimacy. Several governments now hold major financial stakes in some of their largest financial institutions, investment has fallen sharply and state rescues of ailing companies have increased significantly.

Despite this apparent rebalancing of power in favour of the state, many banks have eagerly repaid debts to governments, where they have been able, in order to free them from state 'interference'. And while financial institutions have grown more dependent on governments, governments in turn have become more heavily dependent on corporations. The unprecedented levels of public money that have been poured into national economies by governments have been financed partly through borrowing from other governments, but also by raising money from private finance. The difficulties faced by the UK in selling government bonds on the international market in the summer of 2009 is testament to the fragile situation faced by governments and the extent to which states continue to depend on private capital (*Financial Times*, 2010). National collapse-avoidance strategies have led to the establishment of huge financial institutions. In the UK, Lloyds Banking Group has grown to incorporate the former banks of the Halifax and the Bank of Scotland and holds close to one third of the UK savings and mortgage market (see Farnsworth's chapter on the UK, this volume). The financial industry in the UK and the US is also having little problem in fighting moves towards heavy regulation. Thus, while there are many reasons to suggest that the crisis has changed things, there are rather fewer to suggest that these changes reflect a significant challenge to the hegemonic power of capital. State intervention has clearly been more concerned with protecting the economic 'system' than national welfare. This is illustrated by the fact that the biggest beneficiaries of internationally coordinated measures have been finance and the car industry rather than taxpayers or the environment. Nevertheless, national governments have choices and it is how these are made that will mediate the threats and opportunities for welfare that a reconfiguration of power represents.

A comparative perspective seems the most productive in understanding both the differential impact of economic crisis and the range of responses it brings forth. Of course, the classification of national systems and the demarcations between them is imprecise beyond their ideal types. But what the varieties of capitalism literature do in particular, along with other institutionalist approaches, is to highlight the interdependence of political institutions, economic structures and actors. Although welfare systems do not necessarily follow prescribed paths, they often follow incrementally logical ones where policies emerge out of particular contexts defined by, and mediated within, political institutions and economic structures. Welfare states develop according to the ability of actors to get their issues onto the political agenda and the relative success of opponents in keeping such issues off the political agenda, or their ability to veto political progress. In addressing transition during the 1990s and early 2000s, the welfare regime literature suggests that although incorporation of the general trends towards Ferge's (Ferge, 1997) 'individualisation of the social' and a marketisation of welfare has occurred, the essential core of values that divide regimes remains intact. This can be seen, for example, in the workfare versus activation approaches to labour market participation that have developed in policy during this period, the adoption or revision of New Public Management strategies and policy responses to the question of long-term care in ageing populations. The discussion that follows presents data relating to early national responses to the economic crisis in the form of financial sector bailout and stimulus strategies. The section concludes with some observations on where the patterns identified will take welfare states beyond the immediate aftermath of the crisis.

The costs of crisis

As well as providing a spur to unprecedented international efforts towards its management, the financial crisis has led to national interventions exceptional in their scale and scope. Table 1.2 illustrates the enormous costs of the various measures borne by governments in their efforts to rescue the financial sector. The actual costs of some of these measures are, as yet, unknown since governments will likely recoup some costs in due course. The amounts recovered from the sale of assets, such as shares, are unlikely to result in 100% reimbursement of initial layout, let alone recover the costs of servicing that layout even though some profits may accrue. The IMF estimates that layout recovery rates during economic crises tend to be around 51% in developed economies compared to a rate of around 13% in emerging economies (OECD, 2009a). Guarantees may also bring with them zero or only marginal costs since, in most instances, corporations will remain solvent and governments will not have to make good the 'insurance' policies they have effectively put in place. However, there is a value to the private sector in both the purchase of assets and the guarantees issued by governments even if the eventual net costs to the state are negligible, just as any form of insurance or temporary loan has value.

Taken together, the value of the support packages that have been put in place ranges from zero in several countries, to 267% of GDP in Ireland. The value of the packages in the UK and the US is over 80% of GDP. However, it is the upfront financing that is more meaningful in the short term. This represents actual amounts pumped into the economy by government. Again, in some countries the cost of upfront financing is negligible, but in the UK, it amounts to 19% GDP. This does not include the costs of liquidity measures, including making short-term loans to the banking sector or buying up treasury bonds by printing money. Again, the former has value as a subsidy to the private sector, equivalent to the difference between the 'market' rate of lending and the state's rate of lending. At times of the crisis this latter was only a fraction of the equivalent private sector LIBOR or the retail lending rate. What this meant was that banks were able to borrow from the government at rates close to zero while lending to their customers at vastly inflated rates. These 'subsidies' are not costed in the OECD's figures and they may never actually be known.

The impact of the economic crisis, the ensuing recession and these various rescue measures on the public finances has been huge. Fiscal balances (the difference between taxation and spending) declined sharply and are not set to recover for several years. Accumulated national

Table 1.2: Headline support for the financial sector, upfront financing need and the cost of discretionary measures, 2008-10 (% GDP)

	Finance and banking sectors						Upfront government financing	Non-targeted measures, total (2008–10)
	Capital injection	Purchase of assets and lending by Treasury	Central bank support provided with Treasury backing	Liquidity provision and other support by central bank	Guarantees	Total		
Argentina	0.0	0.9	0.0	0.0	0.0	0.9	0.0	1.5
Australia	0.0	0.7	0.0	0.0	8.8	9.5	0.7	5.8
Austria	5.3	3.5	0.0	0.0	26.6	35.4	8.9	
Belgium	4.8	0.0	0.0	0.0	26.4	31.1	4.8	
Brazil	0.0	0.0	0.0	1.5	0.0	1.5	0.0	1.1
Canada	0.9	8.8	0.0	1.9	13.5	25.1	9.8	3.6
China	0.0	0.0	0.0	0.0	0.0	0.0	0.0	6.2
France	1.4	1.3	0.0	0.0	16.4	19.2	1.6	1.5
Germany	3.8	0.4	0.0	0.0	18	22.2	3.7	3.6
Greece	2.1	3.3	0.0	0.0	6.2	11.5	5.4	
Hungary	1.1	2.2	0.0	4.8	1.1	9.2	3.3	
India	0.4	0.0	0.0	6.3	0.0	6.7	0.4	1.8
Indonesia	0.0	0.0	0.0	0.0	0.1	0.1	0.1	2.0
Ireland	5.4	0.0	0.0	0.0	261.0	267.0	5.4	
Italy	0.8	0.0	0.0	2.5	0.0	3.3	0.8	0.3
Japan	2.4	11.4	0.0	1.2	7.3	22.2	0.8	4.5
Korea	2.5	5.0	0.0	0.2	12.7	20.4	0.3	6.0
Netherlands	3.4	2.8	0.0	0.0	33.9	40.1	6.2	
Norway	2.0	15.8	0.0	0.0	0.0	17.7	15.8	
Poland	0.0	0.0	0.0	0.0	0.0	3.2	0.0	
Portugal	2.4	0.0	0.0	0.0	12	14.4	2.4	
Russia	0.6	0.5	0.4	7.6	0.5	9.6	1.7	5.4
Saudi Arabia	0.0	1.2	0.0	0.0	…	1.2	1.2	9.2
Spain	0.0	4.6	0.0	0.0	18.3	22.8	4.6	4.2
Sweden	2.1	4.8	0.0	15.4	47.5	69.7	5.2	
Switzerland	1.1	0.0	0.0	7.2	0.0	8.3	1.1	
Turkey	0.0	0.3	0.0	0.0	0.0	0.3	0.0	1.1
UK	3.9	13.8	12.8	0.0	51.1	81.6	18.9	1.7
US	4.6	2.3	0.7	41.9	31.4	81.0	7.5	4.9

Source: IMF (2010)

debt (gross debt) has also risen sharply. The average gross debt in the G7 countries in 2007 was 73% of GDP, increasing to 99% of GDP by 2009 (IMF, 2010). This is projected to increase to over 118% of GDP by 2018. The cost of borrowing to bail out corporations is also cumulative and long term. The total cost of the bailouts is unknown, but in the worst-hit countries, debt has more than doubled. In the UK, the various bailouts have added at least £40 billion to government borrowing and the cost of this to government, and taxpayers, is not just an immediate one where some forms of expenditure are traded off against another, it is also a massive and long-term increase in interest rates. Again, the impact is variable. National gross debt in the UK was around 116.8% of total annual government revenues in 2007, which is high, but this figure is set to rise to 267.4% by 2014. In terms of the net annual costs of servicing the debt, interest payments in the UK are projected to be 3.1% of GDP by 2014, or to put it another way, interest payments are projected to represent 8.3% of total expenditure in 2014, equivalent to roughly half the health budget if current spending levels are maintained (see Table 1.3).

According to the IMF, in order to balance budgets and pare back debt to a 'moderate level' equal to around 60% of GDP, governments need to impose very deep spending cuts over the next 20 years. Still, given that the crisis has not had an even impact on all countries, the remedial measures prescribed by the IMF are not universal either. Mirroring the finding relating to historical and recent patterns in state aid, those economies that have historically had lower levels of public expenditure have been hardest hit by the crisis. This is illustrated in Figure 1.2, which plots average public expenditure between 2000 and 2008 against the IMF's target fiscal adjustment rate. This target rate is the amount of adjustment needed in public finances between 2010 and 2020 in order to reduce national deficits to zero by 2030. The IMF-required adjustment is greatest in countries with lower levels of public expenditure: the US, Greece, Spain, Ireland, Japan and the UK where public expenditure would have to fall from around 43% to 30% of GDP. Of course, this is based on present-day figures, which do not account for the impact of inflation, higher than average growth and changes in taxation. Countries with historically high levels of public expenditure – Denmark, Sweden, Finland, France, Austria and Belgium – require relatively minor fiscal adjustments (indeed, Denmark can afford to increase its expenditure slightly). If followed, the result of such fiscal adjustment would be to place an even wider gap between the most comprehensive and the more residualist welfare states.

Table 1.3: G20 stimulus measures, 2008-10

	Argentina	Australia	Brazil	Canada	China	France	Germany	India	Indonesia	Italy	Japan	Korea	Mexico	Russia	Saudi Arabia	South Africa	Spain	Turkey	UK	US
Expenditure infrastructure investment	×	×		×	×	×	×	×	×	×	×	×	×		×	×	×		×	×
Support to SMEs and/or farmers		×	×	×			×				×	×		×				×		
Safety nets	×	×	×	×	×	×	×	×	×	×	×	×	×	×		×	×	×	×	×
Housing/construction support				×	×	×	×	×		×	×	×		×		×	×		×	
Strategic industries support			×	×			×			×				×				×		
CIT/depreciation/incentives		×	×	×			×		×	×	×	×		×			×	×		
PIT/exemptions/deductions	×		×	×		×	×		×	×	×	×		×			×	×	×	×
Indirect tax reductions/exemptions	×		×		×	×	×	×	×	×		×					×	×	×	×

Notes: CIT = corporate income tax; PIT = personal income tax; SMEs = small- and medium-sized enterprises.

Source: IMF (2009a)

Figure 1.2: IMF-required fiscal adjustment and average public expenditure, 2000-08

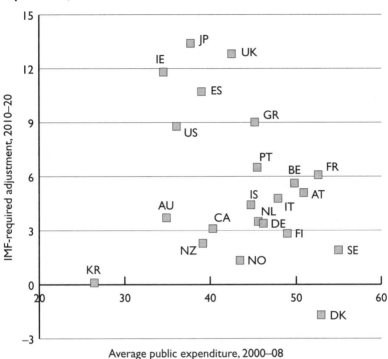

Average public expenditure, 2000–08

Source: Farnsworth (2011)

Table 1.3 provides more detail on the various stimulus measures introduced in a number of countries. In a demonstration of the centrality of social policy to the economy, the most popular measure employed by governments has been the use of social safety nets in support of workers. Beyond this, the majority of these countries reviewed by the IMF in 2009 increased capital expenditure on infrastructure investments (including road building programmes and housing development). Governments also cut taxation, both on personal incomes and expenditure (in order to increase consumption demand) and on corporations, as well as increasing depreciation allowances and other support including subsidies (in order to protect business profits, or at least cash flows, and to reduce insolvencies). These various measures have massively inflated national debt in many nations but they did stave off financial collapse.

Some of the largest multinational financial corporations have benefited hugely from the stabilisation measures put in place by government and by the collapse of some of their competitors. Governments, however,

Christian Democratic Union (CDU) gain most seats in the German elections, the conservative *Partido Social Democrata* (PSD) (Social Democratic Party) become the social democrats' coalition partners in Portugal after the latter's huge loss of majority, and the European socialist leader commenting on a 'sad evening for social democracy in Europe' following the results of elections to the European Parliament.[7] In 2010, Belgium, the Czech Republic, Hungary, Italy, the Netherlands and the UK all saw the election of rightist-led coalitions. Only in the 2009 elections in Greece and Japan were leftist governments returned, but given the scope of austerity measures planned in the former, there is little to suggest the preservation of a welfare-oriented social model.

In effect, most countries have a relatively limited range of options as far as expenditure cuts are concerned: some areas might have to be preserved for economic reasons such as compulsory education, which is core for business interests, some areas might have to be preserved for political reasons, and these vary according to national, historical and cultural predilections located in previous struggles and alliances. Examples of this might include the National Health Service (NHS) in the UK (the Department of Health was spared a cut in its budget, although tasked with efficiency savings) whereas in France health spending will be subject to lower growth. The question is where different states will turn to find necessary savings, whether pressure will require the relinquishment of core values and how states will present these changes as evolution in the national interest in order to garner popular support, or more actively use the 'crisis' as a tool to manipulate ideologically preferred social policy outcomes. Public sector wages and pensions are the most obvious casualties, but aside from these areas it is the detail of the direction of social protection and welfare service cuts that will illuminate the continuation of divisions between the varieties of social model.

Many governments have opted to rally their electorates around calls for 'national unity' in the face of adversity; the UK is a case in point where both Prime Minister and Chancellor continue to stress that 'we are in this together'. In one sense, a discourse of 'togetherness' is highly and historically significant for social policy since it requires refocusing on the fundamental questions addressed by Richard Titmuss and others and may permit the re-emergence of values of reciprocity and solidarity as core concerns of welfare development. There is evidence for this in the case of Iceland, for example.

However, the political turn in Iceland increasingly appears as an isolated case since the purpose of calls for national unity in other advanced economies is to quell disquiet arising from the austerity packages being developed and administered by both new and old governments alike. Nevertheless, the smaller European nations are more likely to achieve success in the use of 'national unity' as a means to ease the introduction of ostensibly unpopular welfare reform because, as has been shown (Katzenstein, 1985; Schmidt, 2003), the nature of coalition politics and closer, more direct relationships between state, business and labour allow greater policy flexibility, swifter change and more effective forms of communication between government and electorate. Literature relating to the capacity of welfare state types to deal with global pressures has more recently drawn attention to the greater problems of the Bismarckian states in coming to terms with deindustrialisation, defamilialisation and other unravelling traditional social and economic models (Esping-Andersen, 1996a; Andreß and Lohmann, 2008). Palier and Martin (2008), for example, show that reform has occurred, but in a way that continues to privilege standard male workers and the contributory principle, preserving the core values albeit in a more divided society. Thus, although the Bismarckian economies are likely to weather the current economic storm with less of a welfare battering, their routes back to growth will continue to be paved with model-defining social and redistributive questions such as the gender division of labour, immigration regimes and the transformation of work.

Countries within the social democratic model already benefit from a historically strong sense of togetherness and previous experience gained during the 'Nordic' crisis of the 1990s. There was negligible engagement in the international sub-prime market in Sweden, for example, and in April 2008 the Minister for Finance told Parliament that he was 'not concerned about events abroad'.[8] More recently, it is reported that the SEB Bank concludes that in 2010 Swedes were now richer than ever before.[9] Of course, Sweden and other Nordic countries have not developed immunity to 'events abroad'. Finland, for example, is facing a deep recession, with high unemployment at 8.6% in 2010; Sweden too has high unemployment (8.4% in 2010) but it is the policy response rather than the figures that is significant. In a recent address to UK public service finance directors, and reflecting on his experience in the 1990s, Swedish former Prime Minister Göran Persson noted that a fair distribution of the pain of spending cuts is a key component to successful crisis management and while much of the Swedish strategy has parallels in the recent emergency Budget in the UK, for example, the key difference is ideological – that Sweden wanted to become debt free 'because we do not want the market to run our welfare society' (*The Guardian*, 9 June 2010).

Liberal market economies (LMEs), on the other hand, are least well equipped in both economic buffers and social solidarity to deal with the impact of a crisis in welfare funding because interests are not shared corporately or between social classes. It will be revealing in the near future to consider the case of the UK compared with that of France (a CME although even within the varieties of capitalism literature, a relatively special case). In both the UK and France, 'togetherness' is a lever to force public sector workers to sacrifice jobs, wages and pensions for the greater social good and masks a deeply antagonistic wedge being driven between private and public sector workers particularly through public discussion of pension provision. Unemployment was high in both countries in 2010 (7.9% in the UK and 9.3% in France, see Table 1.1). Both countries also plan reductions in the support for low-income households, cuts in local authority transfers and the raising of the retirement age as part of their deficit control strategies. The UK has accrued a much worse fiscal position as a result of the crisis, but France has a much more recent history of social unrest and reform will thus be played out against a very different backdrop. The 'togetherness' discourse, and its use as a device to implement ideologically driven reform beyond that required by economic circumstance, is also apparent in President Sarkozy's recent speeches. Having declared the intention to cut local authority spending, his challenge to local authority autonomy is to suggest that they must comply with the same cuts that central government is applying to its own spending, that there is not a 'local taxpayer' and a 'national taxpayer' but a single 'French taxpayer'. Sarkozy is also keen to rally support around the future of the French social model, which is presented simultaneously as virtuous and at risk.[10]

While the imposition of spending cuts is a key source of welfare state variation, what is equally revealing is the distribution of cuts across policy areas and among social groups: where spending is maintained is as telling with regard to the essence of welfare commitment as where it is retrenched. In evaluating the immediate and long-term prospects for social policy, there are two core areas that emerge as loci of conflict and change: retirement and employment. Intergenerational solidarity is a particular target in governments' revival of the 'can we afford a welfare state?' question. The pension question is thus at the heart of most countries' austerity measures and the crisis has allowed governments in all countries to revisit the idea of insecurity in retirement, historically a central issue in the early development of welfare states and one that, in many countries, forms the core of organised labours' success. The demise of final salary pensions, particularly in the public sector, and the raising of retirement ages combine all manner of maximum participation, anti-poverty and productivity arguments presented in favour of working harder for longer. Clearly, however, the arguments do matter in terms of the welfare of older workers and the particular combination of responses to these retirement questions with other social policy reforms is what distinguishes welfare states from one another now and in the future.

A significant challenge related to this is the assumption that the private sector jobs market has the capacity to soak up both those ejected from the public sector and surplus employees in later life. Serious discussion of the impact of economic crisis and crisis measures relating to employment and unemployment has been conspicuous by its absence in public debate, and there are significant gender dimensions to these challenges that have also been ignored. Despite the huge amount of policy energy that has been devoted, at EU level at least, to the notion of 'making work pay' and 'activation', the long-term employment consequences of public sector cuts combined with recession have not been fully acknowledged. There is an argument that the employment consequences of economic downturn represent an opportunity for a wider and deeper transformation of work (see Gorz, 1999), one that allows the kind of 'occupational citizenship' more recently expressed by Standing (2009). Certainly in Europe, trades unions are engaged in battles over jobs and conditions of work but it remains to be seen whether labour market refugees in the 2010s can achieve the level of shared interest and organisation that evaded those of the 1980s. These kinds of struggles go beyond the resilience of core welfare values in the face of crisis to encompass a recognition of crises as systemic and it is this latter that seems unlikely given the developments discussed in this chapter.

More than any other crisis in history, the current one appears to illustrate that a complex range of factors has shaped its depth and its effects. No single factor appears to clearly explain the varying depth of the crisis in individual nations, although there are some important clues in the data. The relative dependence of nations on the financial sector appears to be one of the most important indicators. As Table 1.1 illustrates, the UK, US, Italy, Japan, Greece and Iceland have large financial sectors, but so too does Canada and Germany. Pre-crisis unemployment, GDP and debt levels rates are also important in terms of how well countries were placed to deal with the ensuing economic challenges. The early patterns, however, are not as might have been expected based on the conventional frameworks of comparative analysis. The contributions to this volume seek to reflect on how these patterns have come to emerge, suggesting both how they can be understood at a more general level of policy analysis and how they have formed at the national level.

Conclusions

What the preceding discussion points to is an understanding of 'the crisis' not as a single monolithic event but as a set of interlinked emergencies borne differently across the varieties of welfare state. Thus, while the impact of these crises is felt (almost) universally by populations, it by no means represents a common or uniting experience. Any sense of global togetherness that has been generated seems to be outweighed and thwarted by the resilience of dominant structures, and national difference. It is clear, however, that there is a continuing struggle over the redistribution of resources, albeit one that has changed most significantly within developed nation states, and most especially those that have been most exposed in terms of the volume of support required in the financial sector. This chapter demonstrates that with reference to theoretical frameworks established in both the varieties of capitalism and welfare regime literature, we can better understand what is expected to be a widening gulf between the social policy development of states with a commitment to welfare and those without.

Structure of the book

This book is set out in two parts. Part One sheds theoretical light on the political economy, policy and actor relationships forged and broken in the turmoil of economic failure, and the ways in which these intersect with core concerns of social policy: inequality and poverty and social security. Part Two tests the helpfulness of existing theoretical frameworks and models in explaining and understanding the impact of economic emergencies on social policy development in different countries. The chapters in Part Two do not follow a strictly defined format for description and analysis; nevertheless, they investigate the impact of the economic crisis, recognising that 'politics' as well as 'economics' matter. In presenting this collection of country studies, the book does not seek to set out a definitive list of possible welfare trajectories, but to select an illustrative and more unusual range of cases that provides a picture of what is possible in policy-making terms rather than what is not. The final chapter reflects on the nature of these welfare futures in the age of austerity.

As mentioned at the outset of this chapter, the current crisis has many historical precedents in previous financial and banking crises (see

Ferguson and Johnson, 2010) but at the same time is unprecedented in its particular effects on social policy, because public spending has never been so significant to national economies and so significant in so many people's ordinary lives as is the case today. In order to make sense of what is effectively an 'unsurprising' shock, then, and with reference to the wealth of past experience behind us and the uncertain future before us, the selection of essays contained in Part One are intended to address the questions of 'newness' and 'oldness' in the relationship between economics, social policy making and national economies in the world system.

To begin, Chapter Two takes the longer view, with Michael Hill's assessment of the significance of crisis for paradigm change, suggesting that despite the origins of the crisis, it has not as yet resulted in signs of reconstruction within the field of economics. In Chapter Three, Ian Gough also suggests that following the credit-fuelled propping up of consumption over the last two decades, and despite the culpability of the financial sector in precipitating recent events, response to the ensuing fiscal crisis remains wedded to the convention of deficit control and welfare cuts, rather than accepting more deficit-friendly investment and revenue-raising solutions, and that in the UK at least, there is little expression of public challenge to this orthodoxy. Adrian Sinfield's concern in Chapter Four is to take up examination of culpability in the City of London and the lack of sustained attention to its place in both the creation of an emergency and, more importantly, the structure of incomes. His account acts as a disturbing reminder that the seemingly passing problem of the 'bonus culture' is the tip of a hugely significant iceberg in the financial industries of particularly the UK and the US: namely their role in increasing wage dispersion and hence income inequality in these liberal market economies. In his discussion he points out that in the UK the most senior to average worker wage differentials have risen in the FTSE 100 from 1:10 in 1970 to 1:100 in 2009 and it is thus a question for debate why, despite this seemingly preposterous further enrichment of the richest, barely an eyebrow is raised in national discourse.

Chapter Five moves analysis to the level of global social policy and the extent to which these same issues of crisis-generated potential for economic change and social opportunity, set against entrenched and increasing inequalities, have been played out by key actors on the global stage. Bob Deacon argues that the initial outcomes of a contest of ideas at the global level are both encouraging and disheartening for those who support the worldwide development and expansion of universalist approaches to social protection. Headway has been made in the argument for a global social floor but, at the same time, global 'fiscal' (such that it is) tightening may prevent the argument becoming reality, particularly with the IMF's repositioning to centre stage. The final chapter in Part One, by Armando Barrientos (Chapter Six), also considers the global, international and transnational consequences: the costs to the global South of a crisis generated in the North, and more specifically its likely impact on the fragile developments in social protection policy. In assessing initial responses and future prospects, there are again positive developments in the expansion of some programmes but these are tempered by two key welfare concerns: first, the danger that a rush to respond to emergency conditions is at the expense of prior measures to address the conditions of chronic poverty; and second, that responses to acute problems are very much concerned with treating the symptoms and not providing long-term measures to address the causes. Having examined core aspects of the broader relationship between economic crisis and social policy, Part Two presents examples of how these dimensions are configured within individual nation states.

The selection of analyses in Part Two, although by no means globally representative, provides a picture of a variety of capitalisms all experiencing differentiated crises. This rich diversity of country case studies illustrates both the positives and the negatives for social policy development. These range from the expansion of US provision incorporated in the American Recovery and Reinvestment Act 2009, to the more moderate improvements in unemployment provision in Canada (Daniel Béland and Alex Waddan, Chapter Thirteen), to a raft of retrenchment measures enacted in Ireland, which, falling on a population already suffering relatively high levels of social insecurity, leads Mairéad Considine and Fiona Dukelow (Chapter Ten) to question 'how much deeper the cuts will go before the limits of austerity are exposed'. From the political 'revolution' in Iceland and experimentation with the engineering of fundamental social and economic change (Zoë Irving, Chapter Eleven) to the triumph of ideology over necessity in the UK with the punitive retrenchment of welfare (Kevin Farnsworth, Chapter Fourteen). Both of these latter countries were implicated in the emergence of crisis conditions through their tolerance of unregulated financial over-indulgence and yet the political and social outcomes could not be more different.

We can also therefore distinguish between countries that have suffered a serious trauma requiring major economic surgery, such as in the Irish, Icelandic and UK examples above, and those that have experienced little more than a slight and rapidly healed fiscal graze. Canada is the prime example of the latter, and while in social policy terms the crisis has not precipitated anything more than minor improvements to an already residual system of unemployment protection, in terms of its economic management, it is now the subject of admiring glances from its G20 partners (Hepker, 2010). Germany is also an example of a country that experienced the 'crisis' as something less than earth shattering. As John Hudson and Stefan Kühner (Chapter Nine) explain, Germany's contemporary welfare struggles around social security retrenchment began in the 1990s, and by 2007 the social market model had already been defeated in many policy battles. Added to this, Germany's much more limited reliance on the financial sector and increased power within the eurozone following the problems in the Greek economy suggest that, overall, the crisis has put Germany in a stronger comparative position than it has been for some years.

However, notwithstanding Germany's apparently exceptionally smooth navigation through the economic storm, it is China that stands out as *the* country that has lost least and gained most during this period of turbulence. Sarah Cook and Wing Lam show in Chapter Eight that although initially China was subject to the problems of falling demand, enterprise closure, rising unemployment and job insecurity that afflicted all developed countries, a rapid expansion of social protection and employment measures represents a new phase of development for the Chinese welfare state. Admittedly, China's success in stabilising its economy and preventing unrest partly lies in the colossal stimulus package introduced in 2008, but as Cook and Lam's discussion indicates, the social investment principle has also gained ground within China's competitive strategy.

Returning to the question of 'oldness' and 'newness', two chapters in this collection serve as a reminder that there is nothing new about financial crises. Sweden's banking collapse at the beginning of the 1990s was an early warning of future possibilities, and in Chapter Twelve, Pekka Kosonen assesses the ways in which events at this time inoculated the larger Nordic states against the effects of the more recent global meltdown. Eunna Lee-Gong (Chapter Seven) also considers the impact of past crises, specifically the impact of the 1997 Asian economic crisis on social policy in South Korea. It is fitting that this introductory chapter ends with a poignant reminder from Lee's chapter: that albeit an evolving 'welfare state', one of the lessons of South Korea's experience of crisis and response is that while chasing the neoliberal dream, the abject failure of wealth to trickle down only serves to increase the need for wider and deeper state intervention later.

Notes

[1] www.number10.gov.uk/Page18934

[2] www.ids.ac.uk/go/news/cold-shoulder-for-the-un-financial-crisis-meeting

[3] www.imf.org/external/pubs/ft/survey/so/2009/POL041309A.htm

[4] www.imf.org/external/pubs/ft/survey/so/2009/NEW040309A.htm

[5] A 20:80 ratio of tax increases to spending cuts has been effected in most nations.

[6] http://in.reuters.com/article/idINTRE5251VN20090306

[7] http://news.bbc.co.uk/1/hi/8088309.stm

[8] www.sweden.se/eng/Home/Business/Economy/Reading/Soft-landing-for-Sweden-in-financial-crisis/

[9] www.thelocal.se/16814/20090109/

[10] Conclusion to the 2nd Session of the Conference on the Deficit, 20 May 2010, www.elysee.fr/president/les-actualites/discours/2010/conclusion-de-la-2eme-session-de-la-conference-sur.8917.html and http://euobserver.com/9/28354

TWO

The economic crisis and paradigm change

Michael Hill

Introduction

This chapter will explore the politics of the response to the contemporary economic crisis in terms of Peter Hall's (1986, 1992) analysis of the significance of paradigm shifts for the explanation of policy change. Hall applied that approach to the analysis of the replacement of Keynesianism by monetarism in the 1970s. The obvious question now is: are we seeing, or likely to see, another shift, a reversal of that shift or indeed some new shift in the dominant approach to the management of the economy. Hall himself, in a comment for a news magazine, spoke of the crisis as 'bringing to an end the infatuation with market competition that gripped Europe and America in the wake of the economic crisis of the 1970s' but, without using the term 'paradigm shift', went on to speak of the waning of 'enthusiasm for market competition' in Europe (*Huffington Post*, 13 October 2008).

Care is needed both with the notion of 'paradigm' shift and with the concept of a 'crisis'. The word 'crisis' is used widely in popular discussions of economic and political problems. Indeed, it is one of those words like 'tragedy' that are ever on the tongues of journalists. *The Chambers Dictionary* defines a crisis as 'a crucial or decisive moment; a turning point'. So questions must be raised about whether we are really at a crucial turning point. But then there still remains a question about the extent to which such turning is likely to occur. There is a certain tendency, to which observers of economic problems of a radical frame of mind are prone, to see evidence of problems within capitalist economies as symptoms of an emergent crisis that will lead to a transformation of the existing order. Since economies are characterised by recurrent booms and slumps, there are difficulties in determining whether particular events are exceptional (a problem that has long generated pitfalls for Marxist-type analysis).

There is a related issue here about the terms used to describe an economic crisis. Hence, the contemporary crisis is alternatively labelled:

- a 'credit crunch', implying a very temporary disjunction;
- a 'recession', often given an entirely arbitrary definition among economists of two or more quarters of negative growth; or
- a 'depression', implying a deep and longlasting setback to the economy (note, for example, the title of Krugman's, 2008, book *The Return of Depression Economics*).

The problem about the notion of paradigm shift is that it sits within a body of institutional theory that has long struggled with the difficulty of explaining change within a theoretical approach that stresses continuity. The simple solution to that problem seems to lie in identifying exogenous shocks. That seems to be relevant to the explanation of change associated with the rather dramatic incidents – collapsing banks and other financial institutions – salient in the initial stages of the contemporary economic crisis. There are, however, two problems about this. One is that it may lead us into a determinist interpretation, giving little attention to agency in respect of the events that generated the crisis, and even more importantly as far as this chapter is concerned, ignoring the importance of the characteristics of the response to those events. The other is that this focus on the triggering 'shocks' takes our attention away from underlying events, away from the fact that – even in this situation – much of the relevant change has been much more gradual.

Nevertheless, the concept of 'paradigm shift' is useful since it directs attention to ideas, that is, to changes in the views of key actors. But such changes are likely to be gradual. While commentators on the present crisis have pointed with some glee to apparent 'confessions' from, for example, Alan Greenspan, former chair of the US Federal Reserve, that mistakes had been made, it is hopelessly naive to believe that dominant economic elites shocked by events will simply undergo some sort of dramatic ideological conversion. On the other hand, over a longer time span, changes will occur among the ranks of these elites. It is interesting to note, for example, observations that the education of economists should be broadened (Skidelsky, 2009) and that questions should be considered about the economic modelling techniques currently in use (Cassidy, 2009). An essential feature of Hall's analysis of the 1970s is the gradual waning of the influence of the Keynesian economists. We may now be seeing a comparable shift away from those espousing free market ideology and monetarism.

But in as much as the concept of 'paradigm shift' can be seen to embrace gradual change, this can be problematic for its explanatory value. It is relevant to note Streek and Thelen (2005, p 9) distinguishing between 'incremental' and 'abrupt' change, and also cross-tabulating this distinction against two alternative results of change: 'continuity' and 'discontinuity'. Pollitt and Bouckaert (2009, p 18) go on from this to an interesting classification (see Figure 2.1).

However, what this highlights is the extent to which the concept of 'paradigm shift' is one that essentially contributes to the analysis of change *after* it has occurred. From an interpretative point of view, institutional theory is of value. But its predictive value, like much else in policy theory, is severely limited. If, exceptionally, an earthquake is occurring, that may be evident right now, but if a stalactite is growing we will only be able to measure it in time to come.

It is in the sceptical spirit of those last remarks that the current events will be examined, asking:

- Have we experienced/are we experiencing a significant economic crisis in the strong sense of that term?
- Are we seeing/will we see a paradigm shift in ideas about how the economy should be managed?

To assist that process, some attention will be given to:

- the crisis of the 1930s, which seemed to have transformed Keynes from a rather eccentric academic only on the fringes of the 'establishment' to perhaps the seminal economic thinker of the 20th century, and a change in economic orthodoxy, which may reasonably be regarded as a paradigm shift;

Figure 2.1: Result of change

	Within path (incremental)	Radical/transformation
Gradual	Classic incrementalism **TORTOISE**	Gradual eventually fundamental change **STALACTITE**
Abrupt	Radical conservatism **BOOMERANG**	Sudden radical **EARTHQUAKE**

Source: Pollitt and Bouckaert (2009, p 18)

- the replacement (or rather, as will be suggested below, the partial replacement) of Keynes' ideas in the face of economy management problems in the 1970s (a topic on which we can make specific use of Hall's path-breaking paradigm shift analysis).

The crisis of the 1930s

Obviously, it is not appropriate to try, in this chapter, to provide a careful account of the events of the 1930s. What is important is the role that interpretations of those events have played in discussions of more recent crises, and particularly in policy discourses. The essential facts, in respect of the United Kingdom (UK) and the United States (US), was a stock market crash in the US in 1929, a sequence of stock market disturbances in both countries and elsewhere in the years immediately following it and then a severe recession to which the label 'depression' is commonly applied. In that pre-computer era there was not, of course, the detailed collection of economic trend data we have today but perhaps the seminal statistics – rendered particularly important subsequently by the Keynesian analysis of the so-called Great Depression – are those relating to unemployment.

Table 2.1 sets out official data on unemployment percentages in the UK and the US across this period. While, in the context of modern techniques for the measurement of unemployment, these figures must be considered very crude, they give a rough picture of the scale of the problem and the trend across the period. What they show, for both countries, is a very deep trough lasting for five or six years, followed

Table 2.1: Unemployment rates in the UK and the US, 1929-41 (%)

Year	UK	US
1929	10.4	3.1
1930	16.0	8.7
1931	21.3	15.8
1932	22.1	23.5
1933	19.9	24.8
1934	16.7	21.6
1935	15.5	20.0
1936	13.1	16.8
1937	10.8	14.2
1938	13.5	18.9
1939	11.6	17.1
1940	9.7	14.5
1941	6.6	9.7

Notes and sources: UK figures are percentages of the insured labour force provided by the Ministry of Labour, which are reprinted in Halsey (1988, p 174). US figures are from US Census Bureau (1960, p 70).

by a very slow recovery. Notwithstanding the extensive debate about appropriate government responses, and the suggestion that at least Roosevelt took the issue very seriously and enacted some measures – such as the support for creative arts projects – that have captured the imagination of subsequent generations, the fact is that it was only in the run-up to participation in Second World War that unemployment fell significantly. Indeed, Clarke (2009, pp 165-6) argues that the rise in the US employment rate around 1938 'was the result of a misguided plan by the Treasury Secretary, Henry Morgenthau, to balance the budget....'.

It fits therefore with the notion that paradigm shifts are slow processes that, while the 1930s saw a growing debate about alternative approaches to management of the economy, the impact of this on policy outcomes was slow (see Clarke, 1988). Keynes' groundbreaking contribution to that debate, *The General Theory of Employment, Interest and Money* was published in 1936, but he had of course been actively advocating new policies for some time before that.

It is probably wise to turn to Keynes' leading biographer, Robert Skidelsky (2009, p 97), for a succinct summary of Keynes' contribution to the analysis of the crisis. He argues that '[t]he *General Theory* advanced one main proposition: that a decentralised market economy lacks any gravitational pull towards full employment. Consequently, it is as likely to be in a state of underemployment as of full employment'. Elaborating, Skidelsky (2009, p 97) goes on to say: 'The collapse of optimistic expectations causes the economy to collapse; once established, pessimistic expectations cause unemployment to persist. This is Keynes's famous "underemployment equilibrium". Government should manage demand to limit fluctuations to the smallest feasible amount'.

That, in essence, is the Keynesian interpretation of what was going wrong in the 1930s and it is generally accepted that this became the dominant view of that period by the end of the 1940s, and in that sense the dominant paradigm. But in placing the dominance of the paradigm in the late 1940s it is important not to forget the transformative impact of the Second World War in 1939-45 in stimulating a debate about what went wrong in the 1930s. That debate occurred, moreover, at a time when a much more controlling role for government had been accepted as a necessity during the war.

It is important to acknowledge, viewed from a much later date, that the Keynesian interpretation is not the only interpretation of the events that occurred in the 1930s. What is, then, important to note is that the alternative – broadly speaking 'monetarist' – interpretation accepts the underlying 'deficient demand' assumption of Keynes' approach, but sees the mistake made by the governments of the time to be their perverse response to the undersupply of money (Friedman and Schwartz, 1963). In this respect, Gamble (2009, p 56) says: 'One lesson that Friedman, Bernanke and many others took from the Great Depression was that never again must central banks contract the money supply in response to a major crash and risk a major deflationary spiral'.

But this is not to say that in essence there is nothing to choose between the Keynesian position and that taken by Friedman and other monetarists. Obviously, there lies here a proposition that cannot be tested as to whether the events of the 1930s would have been very different if the central bankers had behaved differently. The Keynesian view is that such a response would have been inadequate. But there are here two other distinctions between the perspectives. One is about unemployment: it is important to note what a central place concern about unemployment takes in the Keynesian analysis. By contrast, we find the monetarists arguing at a later stage in history for something Keynes explicitly rejected: the pushing down of the price of labour. Second, where monetarism sees government (or even in more modern times quasi-independent central banks) simply needing to take measures to adjust the supply of money, Keynesianism gives a much more strongly interventionist role to government, particularly of course in relation to the creation of work. A distinction is drawn here between the former as 'monetary policy' and the latter as 'fiscal policy', involving much more explicit economic stimuli from governments. These differences are stressed here because of the continuation of this debate in modern times.

There is something else to be said here about Keynes' approach, which is of considerable importance for analyses of the contemporary crisis: this is his emphasis on uncertainty. Keynes' earlier work on probability theory may be seen as critical of the positivism that has come to dominate modern economics. Skidelsky (2009) emphasises Keynes' stress upon 'uncertainty' rather than risk. In this sense the *General Theory* can be seen as trying to arm policy makers to deal with the consequences of unpredictable crises rather than assisting them to prevent them. Skidelsky goes on to draw on this emphasis in Keynes' theory for a strong attack on modern economic modelling where variation is seen in terms of 'risk' and temporary deviation from market discipline in terms of the use of statistical ideas around the concept of the 'normal curve'. Skidelsky's analysis is interestingly echoed in a contribution to the modern debate by an economic journalist, John Cassidy (2009), who sees many of the assumptions about self-correcting markets, and the positivist modelling that reinforces, this as contributions to the contemporary crisis.

The counter-revolution: the 'rejection of Keynesianism'

Taking into account the ambiguity of what is today described as Keynesianism, in as much as this became a crude label for most attempts to manage levels of investment, even if only through controls over the money supply, it may be exaggerating to say that there was a complete rejection of Keynesianism. However, there was, from the mid-1970s onwards, a revival of classical economic ideas in a period in which inflation was seen to be a more serious problem than unemployment. Interestingly, in the UK it was a Labour Prime Minister, James Callaghan, who told his party's conference in 1976: '[w]e used to think that you could spend your way out of a recession and increase employment by cutting taxes and boosting government spending. I tell you in all candour that that option no longer exists....' (quoted in Cassidy, 2009, p 79).

However, the decisive change to the political climate occurred following the election of Margaret Thatcher in 1979 in the UK and of Ronald Reagan in 1980 in the US.

Any full explanation of how this counter-revolution occurred needs to embrace:

- consideration of the extent to which there was a 'crisis' in respect of economic management, exposing the inadequacies of existing policies;
- evidence that there was a coherent alternative waiting in the wings;
- and – here we reach a crucial issue about paradigm shift theory – powerful actors able to push that alternative.

The 'crisis' in question consisted of evidence of increasing difficulties in respect of the Keynesian approach to the management of the economy. There had been longstanding concerns about the difficulties in securing economic growth without inflation, manifesting itself in what were seen as 'stop/go' effects as governments shifted to and fro between economic stimulants and restraints. Then in the 1970s the phenomenon of stagflation emerged (recession and inflation at the same time, a phenomenon that Keynesian theory seemed to deem impossible). In retrospect (as we encounter a threat of the same phenomenon re-emerging now), hikes in oil prices at times when national economies were in recession seems to have been an important contributor to this problem. But at the time the main culprit was seen to be trades union power, pushing up wage costs regardless of the overall economic situation. In this respect – particularly in the UK – the new Right's commitment to curb union power may be seen as a central aspect of the new economic policy; the adoption of devices to unleash market forces were seen as key contributions to achieve this effect. We can thus explicitly see the counter-revolution as a re-run of the arguments between exponents of classical economics and Keynes, in which Keynes argued that letting the free play of the market reduce the cost of labour would have the perverse effect of increasing a recession.

Hence, in some respects, the alternative 'waiting in the wings' was a group of economists expounding classical theory, above all reviving the work of one of Keynes' opponents, Hayek. Peter Hall (1986, 1992) is not alone in demonstrating how this neoliberal movement in economics grew in strength and organisation and won the support of financial journalists and politicians in the 1970s (see also Parsons, 1989). We can thus see, in terms of Kingdon's (1995) policy agenda setting theory the coming together of a 'problem' and responding 'policies', from this increasingly effective group of 'policy entrepreneurs'. Need we then merely say that Kingdon's third ingredient for successful policy adoption ('politics') came in the form of the election of new, more ideological politicians of the Right?

Questions have been raised, in respect of paradigm shift theory, about the extent to which it does justice to concerns to explore the power of policy change advocates (Béland, 2005). Hall's analysis of the rise of monetarism addresses this problem. What he shows is that, at this time, the financial markets (in the City of London and worldwide) were changing: 'a series of changes in the institutional practices of the markets for government debt (the gilt markets) that happened to occur in these years substantially reinforced the power of markets vis-à-vis the government' (Hall, 1992, p 100).

These changes were partly induced by the removal of government controls. Interestingly also, they were reinforced by the arrival in the City of a new generation of experts with training in economics, and by the development of information processing capacity, which enabled the City to be better (and more quickly) informed about public policy and its impact.

The contemporary crisis: time for another paradigm shift?

Other contributions to this volume will have more to say about the roots of the present crisis. In the extensive and growing literature on this subject there is inevitably a strong focus on the extent to which those roots lie in aspects of the freeing of the markets in the 1970s. The analyses by Haseler (2008), Cassidy (2009) and Skidelsky (2009) are particularly interesting for their emphasis on the extent to which monetarism involves a dogma about markets, reinforced by the emergence of an economics profession whose theorising is trapped within assumptions about rationality in this context. Cassidy (2009) sees rational expectations theory in economics as leading to what he calls 'utopian economics' (the heading of his chapter 8, p 97). Keynes' argument about unpredictability (mentioned earlier) is a clear reference point here. Cassidy writes of 'rational irrationality' and quotes one of the actors caught up in the speculative boom saying 'As long as the music is playing you've got to get up and dance' (2009, p 296, quoting a *Financial Times* article by Chuck Prince).

Other analysts have given rather more attention to the roles of governments. A particular theme here has been, paradoxically given the origins of monetarist theory as described above, the readiness of the American government to respond to economic difficulties simply by reducing interest rates. Hence, Cable (2009, p 29) is one of a number of authors (see also Krugman, 2008; Stiglitz, 2010a) who writes of the response of US authorities to forerunners of the present crisis: 'that a major potential disaster could only be averted by applying – what they saw as the central lesson of the 1929-32 crash, which was the need to counter the deflationary effect of a financial crash by pursuing expansionary monetary policies'. Moreover, while the authorities in the US made light of evidence that their economy was prone to instability, the American (and International Monetary Fund; IMF) response to the succession of crises in other economies after 1980 was to make it difficult to initiate active responses by government going beyond the monetarist orthodoxy (see Reinhart and Rogoff, 2009).

However, Reagan, the American President who most explicitly identified himself with the monetarist camp, was quite happy to fund his costly military policies by running up public debt. It is pertinent that both the US and the UK authorities saw the liberation of financial institutions to make home loans to high-risk borrowers, the issue that was the key precipitant of the crisis in both countries, as a progressive policy, improving the housing and savings prospects of relatively low-income people. And in the case of the UK, the Blair/Brown governments were willing, until the crisis struck, to turn a blind eye to the activities of the City, which they saw as central to their economic growth strategy. In this way, the run-up to the contemporary crisis was characterised by a build-up of public and private debt in the developed economies, suggesting very different considerations to the stagnation

disappointing recoveries'. Of course, some might conclude from that view that there is little to be done – these recessions are endemic and have to be sat through. But more typically acceptance of this scenario leads to arguments for a more active response from governments. It is interesting to note Samuel Brittan (2009a) – one of the gurus of the earlier rise of monetarism – attacking those who saw 'green shoots' of economic recovery in spring 2009 and quoting Keynes on the need to encourage public and private investments.

By 2010, arguments like this about the role of governments had become very important. In the build-up to the crisis, both private and public indebtedness increased, as both sectors gambled with expectations of future growth. Since the crisis, two phenomena have shifted the debt burden towards the public sector. The one that has attracted most attention has been the bailout of the banks, but there is another: a fall-off in tax revenue, which is (as Reinhart and Rogoff, 2009, p 232, point out) an endemic feature of a recession. Hence, while blaming and claiming about the sources of the growth of UK debt have dominated political debate, there remain unanswered questions about what actually constitutes a dangerously high level of government debt and about how to reduce it without damaging the recovery. Again we may note Samuel Brittan still arguing in May 2010, despite his general support for the new coalition government, against its view that it inherited a fiscal crisis from Labour. He also suggests that the issues about UK government debt have been exaggerated, drawing on evidence about its long-run maturity (meaning that there is little pressure for rapid repayment) and cites the director of the IMF on the need to take care to ensure that corrective measures do not damage the recovery (Brittan, 2010).

In analyses that emphasise this second scenario, attention is given to the way in which both the interconnected international capital market system (world-wide repercussions from US sub-prime mortgage issue, fate of Iceland, Ireland and so on) and trade imbalances (US/China – see Hutton, 2007; Legrain, 2010; Stiglitz, 2010a) spread problems. Krugman (2008, p 177), among others, identifies how the 'rise of financial globalisation, with investors in each country holding large stakes in other countries', has contributed to the depth of the current crisis. This has provoked some consideration of the extent to which there can be measures that insulate individual economies from international pressure. These issues takes us right back to the problems Keynes sought to address. It is interesting to note how, around 1930, Keynes was willing to consider endorsing protectionism (see Clarke, 2009). He abandoned this after the shift from the Gold Standard but the thrust of his *General*

Theory still concentrated on a national response, in a context in which changes in exchange rates could protect the system from problems arising from outside. Skidelsky (2009, p 185) sets out evidence that 'he would not have been an enthusiastic globaliser'. In that sense, mainstream Keynesian theory does not offer much help. Worldwide underuse of human resources is a very different phenomenon to the national unemployment levels that so concerned Keynes in the 1930s.

However, at the end of his life, Keynes was a key actor in the setting up of an international economic system through the Bretton Woods settlement. These issues are still very much with us today, manifesting themselves at the time of writing in Greece's problems about trying to remain within the eurozone. The arguments about the repayment of government debt also centre very much on concerns about foreign creditors able to destabilise a national economy (although note Krugman's, 2010, argument that this problem is being exaggerated). Hence, while the core policy responses in respect of the second scenario are about some reversion to classic Keynesian policy – accepting fiscal measures alongside monetary measures and engaging in some efforts to stimulate employment – there are also suggestions that efforts might be made *either* to insulate national economies from international pressures *or* to try to restore ways of regulating international economic relations. The latter response seems to call for a new Bretton Woods settlement. This would move us away from the era in which the dollar has been the de facto reserve currency, establishing perhaps a 'global reserve currency' (Stiglitz, 2010a, pp 231-4).

The third scenario involves arguing that there are bigger things at stake, and that a reversion to Keynesianism (however international) will not do. Within this scenario, therefore, there are questions to be raised about the extent to which the credit crisis emerged from the masking of an imbalance between the expectations of consumers and competitive productive capacity in the US, UK and so on. Growth depending on borrowing, in a context in which there was little real new investment but rather a variety of ways of moving around other people's money, was illusory. The second scenario suggests that new ways of stimulating investment must be found. But are these feasible? The international dimension mentioned in connection with the second scenario highlights how the emergent economies (Chinese above all, but also India, Brazil and more to come) are transforming the world economic system. There are reasons for questioning the notion that it is simply a matter of finding new and better ways in which the established capitalist economies can compete with these new economies. An economics in which growth (in respect of GDP) is the yardstick of satisfactory national performance needs to be challenged. But what that means for the citizens of the hitherto dominant economies, and their governments, is finding ways of coping with relative decline (see King, 2010).

Coupled with these issues are two others: (a) global warming and (b) resource scarcities (oil, food and so on). Dominant opinion suggests that these issues can be tackled within conventional economic policies (green investment as a key element in growth, for example). An alternative view is that what is involved is a need to use existing resources more efficiently, in ways that will not generate growth (at least in the conventional sense). In any case, Jackson's (2009, p 11) observation may still be right: 'An economist commented to me in the middle of the credit crisis: "we didn't get the recession that many economists, looking at the commodity bubble, thought we'd get, the one driven by high resource prices". But one thing is for sure: that recession is coming'. While some caution is needed about the opinion of an anonymous 'economist', at the time of writing current price increases, particularly food and oil price driven ones, are pushing inflation up. While the governor of the Bank of England sees this as temporary phenomena, he has been over-complacent about the economy before! An alternative view is that this is an early sign of a return to stagflation.

To what extent do the alternative scenarios imply paradigm shifts?

Looking at these alternatives in terms of the notion of paradigm shift, the first scenario does not really imply a shift, while the other two do. However, in respect of the second scenario, changes in economic management, both national and international, are slowly occurring (the 'stalactite' phenomenon perhaps; only time will tell). At the time of writing, the strong responses in Greece and Ireland may perhaps be harbingers of further, more widespread change (see Considine and Dukelow, this volume). The third scenario also implies radical change, but as already noted, shifts in that direction are incremental and slight. It is in respect of this – and the ideas about changing international relations in the second scenario – that it is appropriate to go back to the questions (highlighted in Hall's analysis of events in the 1970s) about what would be likely to engender the sort of strong paradigm shift necessary for such change.

Ideological change is a slow process. In the 1970s, as was noted, the shift away from Keynesianism involved a shift back to earlier ideas, which had been kept alive and indeed increasingly strongly promoted in the early part of that decade. Obviously, similar points may be made about any reversion to Keynesianism now. But as already noted, what is perhaps happening is some fusion of Keynesianism and monetarism, which was in any case always going on. A related point concerns the quest for new ways of ordering international relations. Here, as noted, the reference point in the past is Bretton Woods, where Keynes had to compromise strongly with American dominance. The characteristic of the post-1970s order was the reinforcement of that dominance in a context of efforts to minimise constraints on markets. Here, critics are in evidence, with Stiglitz (2010a, 2010b) the key figure. As far as the third scenario is concerned, on the other hand, new voices are as yet weak (the New Economics Foundation, for example). They have a massive task on their hands challenging productivist and growth assumptions in conventional economic thinking (Jackson, 2009).

Central to radical change has to be something more than the imposition of constraints upon finance capital. We noted the rise of this interest in relation to the paradigm shift of the 1970s. There seems little evidence so far of a significant reversal here. On the contrary, the battles over bonuses and the continuing development of hedge funds suggest that nothing much is changing. Implicit in change is that there has to be a changed relationship between government and the financial sector (the Treasury and the City in UK discourse). At the time of writing, the dominant view that government deficits must be cut for fear of market reactions does not suggest that much is changing. In a *Guardian* interview, Stiglitz (2010b) expressed this forcefully: '[c]risis policies were working – but now bankers are back in charge' (see also the expressions of dissatisfaction with Obama's policies in his book *Freefall*, Stiglitz, 2010a).

The issues about the third scenario imply more than merely a shift in the balance of power between Treasury and City. Facing up to issues about the need for, or even coping with, low growth calls for a change in political behaviour. While there are good reasons for challenging much of the logic of public choice theory (itself the political science equivalent of monetarism in economics), it nevertheless reminds us of the extent to which democratic electoral processes involve efforts to promise citizens maximum benefits with minimum costs. There are good grounds for alleging that some of our contemporary economic problems stem from that as well as from the behaviour of markets. In the long run, the emergence in the UK of a need for political coalitions could curb this tendency. Meanwhile, in the US, President Obama's political problems provide no grounds for optimism about a shift away from a crude political marketplace there.

This connection between politics and markets – echoing some of the things discussed above – raises a question about the extent to which any interpretation of the potential for change needs to consider whether there has been a peculiarly Anglo-American trajectory to the present crisis (embracing within that, of course, other nations such as Ireland that have been identified in comparative theory as sharing a set of political and cultural assumptions about the management of markets; see Hall and Soskice, 2001). However, while commentators have in this respect drawn attention to the quicker recovery in, for example, Germany (see Hudson and Kühner, this volume), the impact of the crisis has been widespread. Moreover, at the time of writing, attention is particularly on a group of nations not within the theorised 'liberal' or 'Anglo-American' regime group: Greece, Portugal and Spain. The underlying issue here is: to what extent is the Anglo-American model dominant, pulling those nations where liberal market doctrines are not so widely accepted into its mainstream? But on the other hand, the evidence that the Chinese economy is growing rapidly again, with 'knock-on' benefits to countries such as Taiwan, reminds us of the presence of emerging economies with rather different characteristics. These considerations then highlight the issue, given some attention above, about the feasibility of national strategies to manage economies, insulated to some extent from international forces.

Conclusions

This chapter has used paradigm shift theory to look at contemporary economic events, to ask can we see (or indeed will we see) shifts in economic policy comparable to those that occurred either when Keynesian ideas were first adopted or when there was a reaction away from them in the 1970s? In doing that, it suggested that it is important not to exaggerate the changes involved in those past events. It has also indicated some problems about the notion of paradigm shift. These concern questions about the real nature of such shifts, the extent to which they are fundamental in nature and the extent to which they involve radical as opposed to gradual change (earthquakes versus stalactite formation). They also concern the extent to which both older theory about the behaviour of key interest groups and later theory about the key role of actors as agents of change need to be embraced within the concept of 'paradigm shift'.

But above all, it has been argued that paradigm shift theory almost inevitably involves interpretation after the event. It is not easy to review a policy debate and proceed to predictions about changes that will occur. In that sense, the contemporary situation has been examined asking questions about what evidence there is that a shift is occurring or will occur. In such a situation it is not easy for an author to be detached. We have views about what we think should occur. In this respect this author believes that the radical shift implied by his third scenario needs to occur. But he would be stepping outside his comfort zone into macroeconomics if he were to try to justify that interpretation of trends in contemporary economies to try to argue that it will become inevitable or essential. Generations of radical analysts who have, at various points in history, argued that a fundamental crisis of capitalism is about to occur, offer a warning against such boldness. The theory used here, stressing the need to see policy change as a product both of crises and of human agency in response to those, suggests that the advocates and potential agents of fundamental change would need to get a great deal stronger than they are now for this to happen.

THREE

From financial crisis to fiscal crisis

Ian Gough

The financial crash of 2008 and the ensuing global recession have been widely recognised as the most decisive capitalist crisis since the Great Depression of the 1930s. The scale of the crash, the speed in which the circuits of finance capital unravelled, its origins within the heartlands of Anglo-American capital, the synchronised global slump in output and the gigantic scale of government reactions, marked it apart from all other post-war financial crises. Take just one authoritative real-time commentator, Martin Wolf (2009) of the *Financial Times*, and just one of his many interventions on the transformation in capitalism that will surely result:

> [T]he glory days of financial capital are behind it for decades, the hegemonic model of the market economy is past, globalisation may be fatally destabilised by present and future global imbalances, and the prestige of the US is damaged. The state has been strengthened, and decisive action by policymakers has staved off a severe global depression, but in the process states are becoming bankrupt. Moreover, there are major uncertainties, 'things we cannot know': how far unprecedented levels of indebtedness and falling net worth will permanently depress Western consumption spending; how long current fiscal deficits can continue before interest rates must rise; can central banks engineer a non-inflationary exit from the bank and financial rescues they have implemented?

This list indicates a systemic crisis of capitalism, and even this does not touch on the subsequent recession in the global economy – the most serious since the Second World War.

This chapter explores the consequences of the financial crisis and its aftermaths for the role of welfare states and fiscal regimes – the ways in which the financial crisis has been transformed into a fiscal crisis of the welfare state. It begins in the first section by providing a theoretical sketch, offering an endogenous explanation of the crisis in terms of the inner contradictions of the previous phase of capitalism rather than simply in terms of an exogenous shock or of such factors as 'irrational exuberance'. The second section details the reactions of and impacts on governments and public finances. The third section briefly describes the subsequent reactions of governments to fears of rising public debts, the switch to fiscal tightening and the targeting of welfare expenditures. In the fourth section some alternative policies for a sustainable and just economy and welfare system are sketched. The final section concludes the chapter.

The theoretical framework adopted is a modified version of the political economy perspective previously developed in 1979 (Gough, 1979). According to Caporaso and Levine (1992) and Gamble (1995), historically rooted political economy (not the public choice model so popular in economics) is characterised by two assumptions. The first is that political and economic processes, although analytically distinct under capitalism, are interlinked and should be studied as a complex and interrelated whole. The second is that the economy, the sphere of 'material provisioning', has a special weight in explaining and properly understanding polity and politics.

The chapter covers only the advanced capitalist countries and does not pretend to cover the rest of the world. Within this it focuses on the United Kingdom (UK), one of the hardest hit by the crisis and, not unrelated to this, having the second most powerful, and one of the most lightly regulated, financial centres in the world – the City of London. The 2008 crisis was unique in the post-war period in originating in the heartlands of financialised capitalism and in reflecting many features of Anglo-American capitalism. Its impacts then rippled or rushed around the world affecting countries exhibiting different varieties of capitalism. This is not a comparative essay on the crisis, although I do draw on cross-national data in places, mainly from the International Monetary Fund (IMF). My focus on the UK is in recognition of its central role in fostering the crisis, with the result that it is the major Western country most threatened by its aftermath.

On crises, conjunctures and contradictions: the political economy of financialised capitalism

Taking history seriously entails the idea of conjunctures – of interactions between distinct causal sequences that become joined at particular points in time. These conjunctures may initiate rare periods of *systemic* change, when institutions and regimes are shunted on to new tracks. Such transformative moments are commonly described as *crises*. But this word has been much overused and abused in the social sciences, so conceptual clarification is essential (Moran, 1988). One definition stems from the medical meaning of crisis: a stage in the course of a disease when the patient is expected to recover or die: 'The concept of crisis was familiar to us from its medical usage. In that context it refers to the phase of an illness in which it is decided whether or not the organism's self-healing powers are sufficient for recovery' (Habermas, 1975, p 1).

From this stem related definitions applied at the social scale: a crucial or decisive situation; a turning point; an unstable situation in political, social, economic or military affairs, especially one involving an impending abrupt change (www.thefreedictionary.com/crisis).

However, this does not sufficiently discriminate between an external blow, such as 9/11, and a more deep-seated *contradiction* within social and economic systems, which eventually blows up into a crisis. The latter points to 'underlying causes and conflicts which even in periods of relative calm ... have not gone away': a crisis 'of' capitalism, not just a crisis 'in' capitalism, of which there have been several in the past two decades (Gamble, 2009, p 40). Using Lockwood's (1964) seminal article, two forms of contradiction can be distinguished – a failure of system integration or of social integration. The former refers to the clash between incompatible features of social subsystems; the latter to conflicts between social actors pursuing incompatible goals (Lockwood, 1964; Gough and Olafsson, 1999; Rustin, 2009).

The idea of a system contradiction might suggest a return to a form of functionalist thinking, where objective 'problems' 'require' new solutions and policy responses. But, if this were ever an adequate stance, it is no longer so. Since the 1930s, governments have intervened to moderate the 'automatic' processes of capitalism in significant ways. Ever since Keynes, crises within capitalism have become intensely political events, influenced by the balance of social forces and dominant ideologies. This means that each is a singular event, in part decided by the resolution of the previous crisis (Gamble, 2009). Crisis resolution is a path of learning and collective action through historical time.

I turn now to interpret the crisis of 2008 in these terms, following the work of Glyn (2006). His work is relevant – and rather unusual – for paying attention to the key driver of accumulation and growth in the capitalist world – profitability – and the basic class divisions within capitalism. The underlying explanation of the crisis for him is the imbalance of factor incomes – the shares of total profits and wages in national income. Figure 3.1 shows that the share of wages and salaries in total incomes rose across the Organisation for Economic Co-operation and Development (OECD) world from 1960 to 1975 by six percentage points; since then it has fallen by almost 10 percentage points (Glyn, 2006). This is confirmed by another time series of the ratio of equity prices to average wages, which exhibits an inverse pattern. There is clear evidence here of a generational reversal in the distribution of factor incomes (Atkinson, 2009).

The trend since 1980 has been compounded by a surge in inequality of incomes, notably in the Anglo-American forms of capitalism (Lansley, 2009). Between 1978 and 2008, real median earnings in the UK rose 56%, those of the poorest 10th by 27%, while those of the richest 10th rose by more than 100%. By the end of the decade to 2008, the top 10th of earners received £20 billion more, purely due to the increase in their income share, of which £12 billion went to workers in the financial sector (almost all of which was bonus payments) (Bell and van Reenen, 2010).

This fundamental division of income exerts a contradictory effect on the dynamics of capitalism. In brief, profits drive capital accumulation and production but wages and income from employment are the major drivers of consumption expenditure, which is the largest component of aggregate demand. In Marxist terminology, profit-driven enterprise boosts the production of surplus value, but wage consumption is necessary to 'realise' the surplus thus created. It is possible to conceive, as did Robinson (1961, pp 93-9), a 'golden path' of capitalist development

Figure 3.1: Trends in Labour's share of GDP, 1960-2005; average of 17 OECD countries (%)

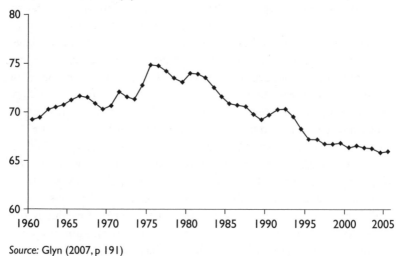

Source: Glyn (2007, p 191)

wherein these two aggregates grow in step. However, as we have seen, the pattern since the Second World War has been of two great waves: first of rising labour shares and then, after the counter-revolution of monetarism and neoliberalism, of rising profit shares. The latter trend over the past three decades, plus the surge in inequality, has threatened aggregate domestic demand in the OECD world.

The solution to this dilemma that emerged was the rise and rise of consumer indebtedness, notably again in the Anglo–American economies. The ratio of total household debt to income in the UK rose dramatically from 45% in 1980 to 155% in 2007. By 2008, the credit outstanding of consumers in the United States (US) exceeded US$25 billion. These trends permitted the growth of domestic demand to more than match the growth in domestic output, despite the falling shares of labour in national income.[1] They also provided a huge and growing market for mortgages, credit lines, hire purchase and numerous other financial products. This contributed to the explosive growth of the financial sector and further enhanced its profitability. And this in turn fed a speculative frenzy among the new rich wealth holders. The resulting unbalanced economic structure can be labelled 'financialised capitalism'. But of course these trends were not sustainable indefinitely. On the basis of these trends, and the underlying contradictions they reveal, Minsky (2008), Glyn (2006) and others predicted a bursting of the bubble, which duly arrived in 2007-08. As Keynes recognised in an earlier era, it was soaring inequality that generated the unbalanced economies of the 1920s and the crash at the end of the decade.

To provide a background for what follows, Table 3.1 reproduces Gamble's (2009) short chronology of the unwinding crisis.

From financial crisis to fiscal crisis

How has the financial crisis and ensuing recession affected the public finances? There are four distinct routes.

First, the scale and nature of the crisis required massive government interventions to stave off runaway banking collapses and a catastrophic loss of confidence in financial institutions. These programmes divide into those undertaken by governments and those undertaken by banks. The former consist of capital injections and Treasury lending and purchases of assets. The latter comprise loan guarantees and other central bank support and amounted to some US$6,000 billion (that is, US$6 trillion) in the advanced capitalist world by the end of 2009. But for our purposes it is the former, government assistance that is more relevant – see Table 3.2. This shows that the total amount pledged by advanced

Table 3.1: Chronology of the crisis, July 2007-April 2009

2007

July	Bear Stearns announces major losses on hedge funds
August	Severe tightening in wholesale money markets Federal Reserve cuts lending rate to 4.75%
September	Run on Northern Rock
Sept-Dec	Federal Reserve cuts lending rate to 4.25% Major international banks announce losses Credit ratings of bond insurers is reduced
December	Federal Reserve announces major loan package to banks

2008

January	Major falls in stock markets House prices start to fall
February	Federal Reserve cuts lending rate to 3%
March	Northern Rock is nationalised
April	Bear Stearns is taken over by JP Morgan Chase
July	IMF predicts financial losses will be $1 trillion
September	Collapse of IndyMac Bailout for Freddie Mac and Fannie Mae Collapse of Lehman Brothers Merrill Lynch is taken over by Bank of America HBOS is taken over by Lloyds TSB Numerous bank rescues, bailouts, nationalisations $700 billion bailout rejected by US Congress
October	Wall Street collapse Further falls in stock markets Further bailouts and rescue packages Further reductions in interest rates G7 proposes five-point action plan
November	Steve Forbes declares the worst is over
December	European Central Bank reduces lending rate to 3.25% IMF announces rescue package for Iceland Federal Reserve reduces lending rate to 0-0.25% US announces rescue package for Ford, GM and Chrysler

2009

January	IMF predicts worst recession for advanced economies since 1945
February	Bank of England reduces lending rate to 1%
March	Bank of England reduces interest rate to 0.5%
April	G20 Summit in London

Source: Gamble (2009, p 23)

country treasuries by end-2009 amounted to nearly $2 trillion, of which $1.1 trillion was actually utilised, equivalent to 3.5% of Gross Domestic Product (GDP). Part of the outlays will be recovered, but the IMF calculates that by end-2009, $882 billion remained outstanding.

Table 3.2: Direct government support for financial sector

% 2009 GDP	Direct support		Net direct cost
	Pledged	Utilised	
UK	11.9	6.6	5.4
US	7.4	4.9	3.6
Advanced economies	6.2	3.5	2.7
In $US billion	1,976	1,100	882

Source: IMF (2010b, tables 4 and 5)

Interesting here is the exposure of the UK government, which exceeds that of any other by a wide margin. The UK government directly pledged assistance to the banking and financial sector of almost 12% of GDP, of which just over half had been committed by mid-2010'. The maximum theoretical exposure of the Treasury and Bank of England combined is about one half of 2009 GDP (ONS, 2009).

Second, all states implemented large discretionary fiscal stimuli to prevent a major depression in the real economy; in the entire G20 these measures amounted to 2.0% of GDP in 2009 and 1.5% in 2010. Here the UK was not out of line and interestingly was the only major government to plan to cut back this fiscal stimulus to zero in 2010. This will switch to negative from 2011 onwards.

Third, several non-discretionary factors had had an impact on public finances. The 'automatic stabilisers' of increased spending on unemployment and other social benefits plus reduced tax receipts cushioned the recession, but widened the fiscal gap by more than 2% of GDP in many OECD countries in 2009. In addition, the 2008 financial crisis has entailed a sharp fall in equity, housing and other asset prices plus a decline in financial sector profits, all of which further reduce tax receipts.

Fourth, the worldwide crisis continues to drive down projected future growth rates, which, *ceteris paribus*, reduces tax revenues still further and expands expenditures. In July 2010, the IMF predicted a lower global growth rate for 2011 compared with 2010: down from 4.6% to 4.3% (IMF, 2010c). But forecast growth in the advanced economies is lower (2.6% and 2.4%) and for the UK much lower (2.1% in 2010, falling to 1.2% in 2011). This compares with a prediction of 3-3.5% growth in the 2010 Budget statement of the outgoing Labour government just three months earlier.

Yet, these growth forecasts may be optimistic. The IMF (2010c, p 1) went on to warn that 'recent turbulence in financial markets—reflecting a drop in confidence about fiscal sustainability, policy responses, and future growth prospects—has cast a cloud over the outlook'. A Bank for International Settlements report in March 2010 stated:

> In many countries, employment and growth are unlikely to return to their pre-crisis levels in the foreseeable future. As a result, unemployment and other benefits will need to be paid for several years, and high levels of public investment might also have to be maintained. The permanent loss of potential output caused by the crisis also means that government revenues may have to be permanently lower in many countries. (BIS, 2010, p 4)

The result of these factors was a surge in government deficits and in accumulated public debt. Figure 3.2 shows the dramatic deterioration of fiscal balances in 2007-09 in the advanced economies. The primary balance, which excludes interest payments, fell to –7% of combined GDP and the total to –9%. After cyclical adjustments, the primary balance fell to –5%. These are now projected to improve, although the overall balance is predicted to remain at around –6% through 2015.

These continuing deficits are driving up the stock of government debt and the debt:GDP ratio. As a share of GDP, average gross government debt in advanced economies rose by 20% of GDP from 2007 to 2009 and is now predicted to rise by another 20 percentage points up to 2015, reaching an average of 110% GDP by then. However, the predicted debt in the UK by then is lower than this – some 88% – since it started off from a low debt ratio prior to the crisis.

According to the IMF (2010b), the debt surge in advanced G20 economies is driven mostly by the last of the four elements above – the output collapse and the related revenue loss. Of the almost 39 percentage points of GDP increase in the debt ratio, about *two thirds* are explained by revenue weakness and the fall in GDP during 2008-09. The emergency fiscal stimulus – assuming it is withdrawn as expected – would account for about 11% of the debt surge and banking bailouts for about 8%.

In the UK, the combined fiscal impact of the financial crisis and economic recession is more severe than in any other major country. My own rough estimate, based on IMF (2010b, 2010c) for the impact of the above four factors in 2009, is presented in Table 3.3. These are rough calculations, but they show that the crisis cost the Exchequer over 10% of GDP in 2009 in the form of escalating expenditures and falling revenues, and it will continue to weigh heavily on public finances for many years to come.

Figure 3.2: Evolution of fiscal balances, 2005-15 (% of GDP)

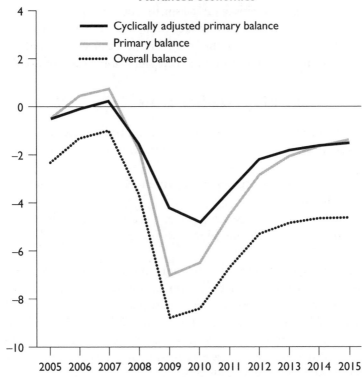

Source: IMF (2010b, figure 1)

Table 3.3: Financial interventions (%)

Financial interventions: bank nationalisations, bailouts and other pledged supports to financial sector less amounts recovered (table 2)[a]	5.4
New fiscal stimuli	1.6
Fall in taxation; rise in compensatory social benefits[b]	3.0
Structural deficit in public sector accounts due to lower growth[c]	1.8
Total	11.8

Notes:

[a] net direct costs to the Treasury = *utilised direct* supports to financial sector – amounts recovered.

[b] estimated automatic stabilisers = general government primary balance – cyclically adjusted primary balance.

[c] net expenditure on interest payments = general government balance – general government primary balance.

Sources: IMF (2010b, table 5, appendix table 1, statistical tables 1-3; 2010c, table 1)

Thus, a 'fiscal crisis of the state', much discussed in the 1970s, has returned as a central political issue in the UK and abroad. This is a direct result of the financial crisis of capitalism, the subsequent global recession and the (on the whole relatively successful) actions of governments to rescue the former and arrest the latter. It is most threatening in the UK because of the scale and economic centrality of the City of London.

From fiscal crisis to welfare crisis

The direct impact of these developments on the welfare state and on the welfare of citizens is affected by three things:

- the extent to and speed with which governments commit to reducing debt levels;
- the balance between spending cuts and tax increases in achieving this;
- the extent to which cuts fall on welfare state spending.

First, there is an ongoing debate about the need to reduce the size of planned government debts in the advanced capitalist world. This raises macroeconomic issues there is not space to cover here. What is an acceptable public sector debt:GDP ratio? Why is 60% of GDP the target accepted by the IMF? Will not a precipitate squeeze on fiscal balances threaten renewed recession? Why not accept a permanently higher post–crisis level of public debt?

Against these arguments, the IMF asserts, first, that with the US and other large economies moving beyond 100% debt levels (although not the UK), the world is moving into uncharted territory. Second, that 'the current crisis involves truly novel features compared with historical episodes: in particular it involves large contingent liabilities associated with guarantees of financial sector obligations; and it takes place, in many countries, in a context where pension and health care systems will give rise to large future spending increases' (IMF, 2010a : 34). Third, that future growth assumptions are uncertain. Fourth, that this might raise interest rates and risk premiums on bonds and thus debt service costs, although at present interest rates are at an historic post-war low.

Despite the numerous uncertainties involved in judging these issues, the British Labour government proposed a substantial debt reduction strategy to reduce the deficit over the lifetime of two Parliaments. The incoming coalition government adopted deeper and faster cuts in the emergency Budget in June 2010 and the October Comprehensive

Spending Review. Furthermore, the new government proposed that the bulk of the fiscal rebalancing should fall on spending, not tax increases:

> Tough decisions need to be taken in order to reduce the unprecedented deficit. The Government is committed to achieving the bulk of this through reductions in Government spending, rather than tax increases, while protecting the quality of key frontline services. This Spending Review is not just about cutting spending and setting budgets. It will be a *complete re-evaluation* of the Government's role in providing public services. (HM Treasury, 2010, emphasis added)

The 2010 cuts are summarised in Table 3.4, distinguishing between the three rounds.

The total fiscal tightening planned for 2014/15 amounts to £110 billion, equivalent to around one fifth of the total budget in 2010. The goal is to reduce the deficit to manageable levels in five rather than 10 years. The share to come from spending cuts rather than taxation has increased to 73%. The contribution of public services has risen, and that of welfare benefits has escalated from zero to £28 billion. These are unprecedented measures in the UK's post-war history. Figure 3.3 shows how this marks a qualitative shift, which will pull the size of the public sector below even that in the US by 2015, according to Taylor-Gooby and Stoker (2011). In their words, 'Britain will abandon the goal of attaining a European level of public provision' (2010, p 14).

Table 3.4: Fiscal retrenchment in the UK, 2010

	Composition of the tightening in 2014–15		
£ billion	**March 2010 Budget**	**June 2010 Budget**	**October 2010 Spending Review**
Tax	21.5	29.8	29.8
Spending	50.9	82.8	80.5
Investment spending	17.2	19.3	17.0
Current spending	33.7	63.5	63.5
Of which:			
Debt interest	7	10	10
Benefits	−0.3	10.7	17.7
Public services	27.0	42.8	35.7
Total tightening	72.4	112.6	110.3
% spending	70	74	73
% tax	30	26	27

Source: IFS (2010)

Figure 3.3: Public spending trends, selected advanced economies, 2008-15 (% GDP)

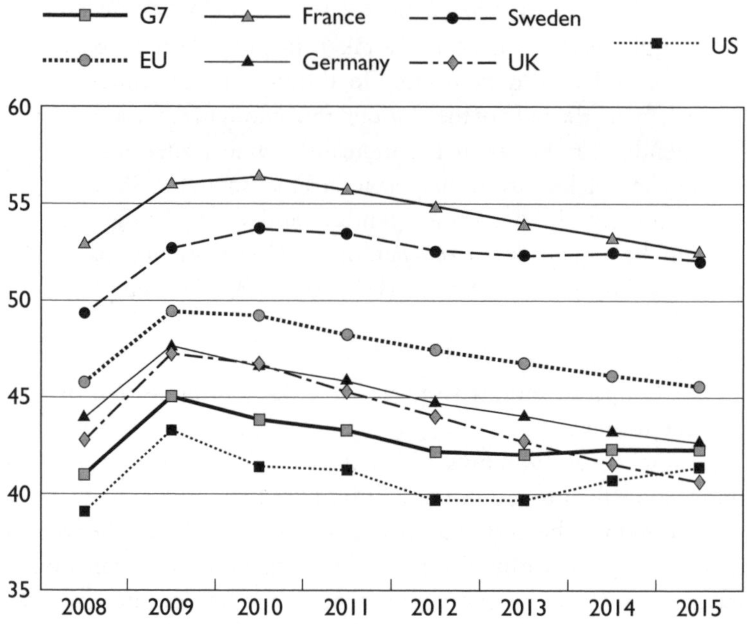

Source: Taylor-Gooby and Stoker (2011, Figure 1)

Although the taxation of higher-income groups initiated by the outgoing Labour government has been retained, the overall impact of the 2010 fiscal retrenchment will be regressive – see Figure 3.4 for the estimates of the Institute for Fiscal Studies. Apart from the richest decile, the cuts in social benefits and social services will reduce the living standards of the poorest and of children and women the most.

The upshot is that a crisis originating in the financial sector in which the City of London is deeply implicated will be rescued by a savage attack on the living standards of the majority of UK citizens, notably those with the lowest and least secure incomes. The Bank for International Settlements recently argued that the fiscal capacity of a country depends on 'how far the government can raise tax revenues without causing the tax base to shrink, and how far it can cut public expenses without causing major social and political disruptions' (BIS, 2010, p 20). The evidence from Europe suggests that major cuts in benefits especially in pensions can call forth substantial and coordinated opposition, which can topple governments. Will the current UK government's radical strategy generate new oppositional movements? As I write, the British public shows few signs of challenging this

Figure 3.4: The effect of all tax and benefit reforms to be introduced between June 2010 and April 2014, by income decile group and household type

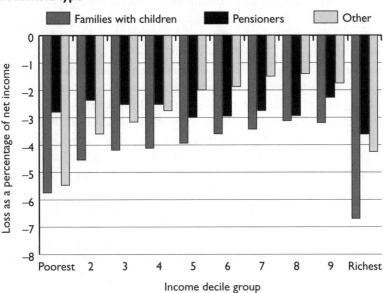

Source: IFS (2010, Table 4.4, p 14)

unprecedented attack, although prolonged student demonstrations in late 2010 may provide the seeds of a counter-movement.

Conceiving alternative futures and policies

There *are* alternatives. Some elements are as follows, although I restrict my attention solely to the UK in what follows.

First, the need to drastically cut the state deficit should be challenged (see also Farnsworth, this volume). This is not the place to discuss or even summarise the ongoing debate between expansionists and restrainers. And since this chapter is written in the autumn of 2010, the objective situation and the contemporary strategies may have changed wholly by the time this book is published. But this central debate is unlikely to go away. The government and its supporters, such as Niall Ferguson and economist Kenneth Rogoff, argue that higher debt ratios are unsustainable. They consider higher unemployment and lower growth a price worth paying. Those who argue against rapid cuts, such as economists Paul Krugman, Joseph Stiglitz and Martin Wolf, want to cut the deficit later when the economy is stronger. They recognise that such a policy would lead to a higher debt ratio but argue that the benefits to employment and growth now are so substantial that they outweigh this risk. The evidence from Ireland is that it is self-defeating to cut public expenditure in the middle of a deep recession.

Second, even if the expansionist view is challenged, the current desire to correct the fiscal imbalance via cuts rather than tax increases can be questioned. The political consequences of raising taxes on the mass of the population in a time of recession or stagnant growth are equally dire. But there is an alternative agenda of *fair taxation*. There is a strong case to tax the financial sector to at least cover the costs of the bailouts and other rescue operations by the state. A leaked IMF report argued that this would require new taxes equivalent to no less than 4% of GDP in the UK (IMF Direct, 2010). A report by the Institute for Public Policy Research (IPPR, 2010) showed how part of this might be achieved. UK financial profits and bonuses in 2011 are likely to total £90 billion (5% of GDP), of which c£20 billion will be paid in tax. The report shows that another £20 billion *per annum* could be raised by tackling tax avoidance, introducing a levy on financial institutions, taxing profits and bonuses on a permanent basis and introducing a financial transactions tax at a rate of 0.01%. The overall impact of this would be very progressive whether the burden ultimately falls on traders or their customers. In addition, the Green New Deal Group (2010) estimates that up to £70 billion per annum could be raised by clamping down on illegal tax evasion. If correct, these sums are large enough to render unnecessary all the extra cuts of the coalition government and most of those of the previous Labour government.

Third, there is a strong case to shift the role of public and social expenditure further from *compensation* to *investment*. Since the 2000 Lisbon Agenda and the New Labour Third Way strategy, the 'social investment' paradigm has prioritised policies such as investment in human capital from early childhood to continuing education, and removing obstacles to participating in paid work (IFS, 2009). The challenge of climate change is pushing governments into new investments in sustainable energy and lifestyles, although at a snail's pace in most countries. This could be radically extended to encompass investment in mass retrofitting of dwellings, transforming transport, redesigning urban and living spaces and 'eco-system maintenance', as argued in the Green New Deal (nef, 2008a, 2008b). There is also a strong case to use public control of the nationalised banks to invest in sustainable and socially just projects, as proposed by the World Development Movement (WDM, 2010). For example, transforming the Royal Bank of Scotland into a Green Investment Bank could release very large sums of money to kick-start the green energy revolution. It could bring an estimated 50,000 new green jobs a year, boost the UK economy, reduce the UK's carbon emissions and improve international competitiveness (although it may slow down deficit reduction slightly if green loans are made below market rates). At present the British public has incurred the costs of bank nationalisations with few of the benefits.

But to make these policies coherent requires new thinking and a new model of a sustainable social economy that would challenge both neoliberal and neo-Keynesian thinking. This would recognise the productive and reproductive role of much of the welfare state and of the emerging 'eco-state' to tackle climate change (Gough, 1979, chapter 6; 2010). To take one example relevant to this chapter, government and IMF calculations of public sector debt are typically of *gross* debt, not even subtracting financial assets let alone real public assets such as buildings and infrastructure. A first step to understanding that not all public debt is bad would be to create an integrated balance sheet of the public sector, as Hills (1989) proposes. Going further, we need to discriminate, as Jackson (2009, appendix 2) does, between types of public investment, building up public and public-guaranteed investment expenditures in human capital, climate adaptation and 'eco-system maintenance'. This will require a new conception of 'value' and new ways of calculating the social return on investment (nef, 2008a, 2008b).

The implication is that we need new economic-social-ecological models to comprehend these distinctions and to enable new priorities to be legitimised. The current crisis provides an opportunity to switch tracks towards an eco-welfare state. Past rates of growth are very unlikely to be restored, and they may well be undesirable anyway due to planetary constraints (Gough, 2010). Since the traditional welfare state has depended on the 'growth state' for its finance, a sustainable welfare state will have to be radically transformative. This is a major challenge in developing an alternative.

Conclusion

The 2008 world financial crisis resulted in large part from the soaring inequality generated since 1980 by the new phase of financialised capitalism, which fuelled consumer debt and unbalanced economies. The international capitalist system was saved by timely action by the major states, but these bailouts and the ensuing recession transformed the crisis during 2009 into a fiscal or sovereign debt crisis. The policy reaction to this in 2010 in much but not all of the advanced capitalist world was sharp fiscal tightening and welfare cuts.

The UK played a leading role in all three years. The City of London was one of the two epicentres of the crisis, and the finance-dependent British economy evinced both historic levels of debt and inequality. The fiscal situation of the British government remains peculiarly exposed and the speed, ruthlessness and regressivity of the cuts and restructuring of the welfare state are unmatched among the large economies.

Thus far, a crisis of financialised capitalism has not fostered an alternative economic and social strategy. Rather, it has resulted in its opposite – a renewed ideological onslaught on the welfare state and mass living standards and a redoubled effort to widen class inequalities. If this crisis marks a switching point, and if the above analysis of the link between inequality and crisis holds, this strategy is likely to fail. What follows will depend on ideas, politics and citizen involvement.

Note

[1] This was not the only mechanism at work. Real consumption in the West was also boosted by the growing import of very cheap commodities from low-wage countries, primarily China. Indeed, the other fundamental cause of the crisis has been the growing global imbalances, notably between the US and China. It is notable that Sir Howard Davies (2010), when surveying the still-unsolved causes of the crisis, put at the top of his list global imbalances and growing inequality.

FOUR

Credit crunch, inequality and social policy

Adrian Sinfield

Half a century ago, Richard Titmuss showed how 'the changing concentrations of economic and financial power' in *The Irresponsible Society* were impeding the creation of a fairer, more equal society (Titmuss, 1959, in Alcock et al, 2001, p 141). The credit crunch crisis that broke in 2007 and its repercussions make his reflections particularly relevant.

In its more ambitious moments, social policy engages with broader issues about the nature of society and the quantity and quality of life for all its members, even exploring this on a comparative and global scale. But often we fail to avoid 'the professional ideology of social pathologists' that C. Wright Mills criticised (Mills, 1943, developed in 1959b, chap. 4) and lapse into a context-stripped approach. This chapter identifies some key social policy issues that we need to address in the irresponsible societies of today. The change from individual to plural 'societies' is needed because the credit crunch crossed national frontiers with ease. With its immediate causes linked to problems of housing poverty in the United States (US), its longer-term manufacture can be found in growing concentrations of power and inequality that promoted and enabled financial market deregulation in and across many societies with continuing repercussions.

Social costs

The United Kingdom (UK) 'output loss' of recent 'banking pollution', to use the words of the Bank of England's executive director of financial stability, is likely to be 'between one and five times annual GDP [Gross Domestic Product]', that is, 'between £1.8 trillion and £7.4 trillion' (Haldane, 2010, p 4). Even this substantial amount probably omits knock-on social costs in increased unemployment, poverty, illness and their indirect costs, as well as the lost opportunities and long-term reduced standards of living that will result.

In his classic study of social costs, Kapp defined them as 'all direct and indirect losses sustained by third persons or the general public as a result of unrestrained economic activities' – a particularly apt phrase for the credit crunch. These losses or costs result in 'a redistribution of income' (Kapp, 1963, pp 13 and 15). The challenge is to ensure that these redistributed external costs are not left to lie where they fall (Titmuss, 1968, in Alcock et al, 2001, part 3:2), and much of what is regarded as the 'public burden of redistribution' is a response to these transferred costs.

Charting these costs and compensating those who bear them is only one part of creating a fairer society. The costs are 'part of the price we pay to some people for bearing part of the costs of other people's progress' (Titmuss, 1968, in Alcock et al, 2001, p 120). Because of his concern to challenge the conventional wisdom on economic growth as the solution, Titmuss focused on 'the losses involved in aggregate welfare gains' resulting from that growth. The credit crunch demonstrates that 'other people's progress' can also result in aggregate welfare *losses*, and that these losses make it harder to compensate social costs. This is not to oppose some people making progress, but a full account of the redistributive effects of change should consider not only the losers but also who gained, how and at whose cost (Walby, 2010, p 26). This is all the more important as the corrosive effects of greater inequality become better known (Wilkinson and Pickett, 2009).

The direct social and economic costs of high unemployment fall particularly heavily on those on low incomes who are already most vulnerable in the labour market as well as having a wider indirect – and unequal – impact across the whole of society (Sinfield, 1984). However, the redistribution of resources and power upwards from increased unemployment is rarely discussed (Kalecki, 1943; Reynolds, 1951, p 73), although workers may be well aware of this and ask why they should pay the costs if capitalism caused the crisis.

In the UK, not only have social costs not been picked up, but Labour's labour market policy changes penalising non-employment were continued through the crisis. While unemployment climbed sharply, welfare reforms designed at best for a tight labour market were pushed through with further restrictions and penalties, stigmatising 'the workless' at a time when protection against the recession was needed. The damaging effects of further shifts from rights to responsibilities with extra conditionalities and privatisation of employment agencies are likely to increase as governments have 'undermined the notion of citizenship and citizen's rights that should lie at the heart of the welfare state' (Green, 2006), leaving the social costs to fall on the most vulnerable in society.

Preventing this and maintaining demand to avoid a double-dip recession have not been given priority. The obsession with cutting the public deficit quickly is 'harmful nonsense, however often it is repeated and however bipartisan is the consensus' (Brittan, 2009b). A secure return to higher employment requires a more active state with more vigorous and thoroughgoing Keynesian policies, not the smaller state praised in a revival of Thatcherite discourse – 'Public expenditure is at the heart of Britain's economic difficulties' (UK, 1979). Maintaining demand also needs to avoid traditional growth strategies that exacerbate global warming and waste energy and requires public investment in sustainable energy and green jobs (Jackson, 2009; GNDG, 2010). Public spending cuts will jeopardise this essential strategy.

Differential compensation

Compensation of social costs through National Insurance (NI) has been intentionally weakened by UK governments over the last generation. For example, in 1961, 75% of those drawing benefits as unemployed received NI contributory benefits, but only 20% did so in 2010. The level of benefit has also fallen sharply. A generation ago, NI Unemployment Benefit was 20% of the average wage for 12 months, well below the European average. With cross-party opposition to uprating Jobseeker's Allowance (JSA), it is now even lower, only 10% and only for six months. Restoring the 1979 value would require an increase of some four fifths.

Social insurance now has an even more limited counter-cyclical effect, yet many believe that incentives to work are too weak, failing to recognise that low benefit levels contribute to continuing unemployment. A major study of labour market experience across Europe using the European Household Panel Survey revealed 'a vicious cycle of disadvantage.... Unemployment heightens the risk of people falling into poverty, and poverty in turn makes it more difficult for people to return to work' (Gallie et al, 2002, p 18). Raising benefits to reduce poverty would also discourage the trend towards low-paid and poor-quality jobs that is a greater problem in the UK than in most of its European neighbours (EC, 2003).

Recent Living Wage and Fair Pay campaigns have opened up debates on low wages and what is a 'fair' minimum. But differentials have been widening across the labour force, with those at the very top not only drawing further away from the average but also 'racing away' from the higher-paid (Brewer et al, 2008). Judgements on fairness cannot be confined to one end of a distribution. Half a century ago, Wootton (1962) raised searching questions in *The Social Foundations of Wage Policy* about desert and equity across the whole employment structure. The incomes and prices policies of the 1970s included restrictions on pay increases at levels that today are astonishing, even when suitably adjusted. Indexed to earnings, the £5,000 ceiling that stopped increases in pay under the 1976 incomes policies would now be around £45,000. Adjusted instead by the Retail Price Index, and so increasing in line with Unemployment Benefit/JSA, the ceiling would be well under £30,000, not far above average earnings today.

In analysing the banking crisis and inequality, Lankester (2009, p 151) identified 'remuneration structures and a "bonus culture" that encourages excessive risk-taking' among its causes. Lords Myners, the City Minister at the time (*The Guardian*, 2009c), and Turner, then chairman of the Financial Services Authority (FSA), condemned the scale of bonuses and challenged the case for their recent disproportionate growth. 'Inappropriate remuneration structures' meant that 'illusory profits were ... used as the basis for bonus decisions, and created incentives for traders and management to take further risk' (Turner, 2009a, p 47). Sir David Walker, ex-chairman of Morgan Stanley bank, appointed to lead the review on banks' corporate governance, included 'unsafe remuneration policies' among the factors leading to 'this calamitous state' and set forward specific proposals on bonuses (Walker, 2009, p 90).

However, the FSA's new code of practice on bonuses was much watered down under pressure from the City – eventually 'little more than a gentle entreaty to Britain's financial services industry to behave better' (Kampfner, 2009). By September 2009, 'BAB' was already being used as a City shorthand for 'bonuses are back'. Management consultants reported that 'any changes to remuneration are cosmetic' (Will Hutton, *The Observer*, 13 June 2010). A fall in visible bonuses was offset by significant increases in base pay, a practice reinforcing inequality even more: '"Fellas that might have been on £80,000 are getting more like £120,000" said a [City] trader' (*The Guardian*, 24 July 2010).

Although bonuses are not the only element of high remuneration, they are the most significant, comprising almost 90% of the £1 million or more paid to each of over 2,800 City bankers in 2009 (*The Guardian*, 30 July 2009). One investment banker remarked to a colleague as they decided on team bonuses in the mid-1990s: 'If the rest of the country knew what we were being paid, there would be tumbrels in the street and heads carried round on pikes' (Freud, 2008, p 307). He added that the pay for a junior banker increased almost fourfold from 1997 to 2000. The writer, David Freud, was ennobled as the last government's adviser on welfare reform (2007) and is now the coalition Minister for Welfare Reform (the role of bankers – Seebohm, Taylor, Turner, Wanless – in shaping social policy deserves closer examination).

The significance of bonuses is brought out in Bell and Van Reenen's (2010) study, 'Bankers' Pay and Extreme Wage Inequality in the UK', 'the first time it has been possible to measure the extent to which the financial services sector has contributed to rising inequality' (quoted in *Financial Times*, 18 April 2010). By 2008, the highest-paid 10th of employees received 30% of total annual pay, compared with 27% a decade earlier. Sixty per cent of that increase – some £12 billion – went to finance workers, and virtually all in bonuses (Bell and Van Reenen, 2010). Among the very top percentile, that proportion almost reached three quarters.

The value of a bonus varies greatly, from 1% of wages in the health service, public administration and education to 25% in finance, with an overall average of 8% (Bell and Van Reenen, 2010, table 4). To most workers it must seem strange that the chief executive of the Royal Bank of Scotland should be paid £1.2 million a year – a salary 100 times more than the national minimum wage – and should then be given many millions more in various incentives and bonuses so, presumably, that he really does his best, and it is almost invariably 'his' (*The Scotsman*, 11 May 2009 and 23 October 2009). This sceptical view has received strong support from a group much closer to that world. In calling for a windfall tax on bonuses, 14 professors of business studies across UK universities firmly rejected many standard arguments defending current bonuses (*The Guardian*, Letters, 12 August 2009).

Not only does the value of the bonus vary greatly up to large multiples of salary in finance, and increasingly outside it. In contrast to tough conditionalities at the lower end of the labour market, targets for entitlement to top bonuses can often be easily met or wriggled round. Guaranteed bonuses stray far from the *Oxford English Dictionary* meaning: 'a boon or gift over and above what is normally due'. Discussing what constituted 'legitimate inequality', Plant (1986, p 101 – see also p 105) identified an incentive as 'that sum of money which will get a job done without which society would be poorer'. The application of that criterion would demolish many of the peaks of the City's 'remuneration architecture', as business consultants call it.

But bonuses are only part of the towering monuments these consultants construct, with many more incentives, long and short term – share options, final-year pension boosts, expense accounts and so on (Main, 2004). 'Current levels of executive pay in the UK are strikingly high: a 2008 survey showed the highest earner as being paid £23m annually, with 34 receiving packages valued at more than £5m' (Higginson and Clough, 2010, p 3). The average FTSE 100 chief executive officer package was £2.9 million, over 100 times higher than the average salary of a FTSE 100 employee (£26,000). 'In 1970 this differential was approximately 10:1. The UK is reckoned to be second only to the US in executive pay' (Higginson and Clough, 2010, p 3). Compared with the 50% fall of Unemployment Benefit against average pay reported earlier, this 1,000% increase is even more remarkable – and yet it is the unemployed who, we are constantly told, need incentives to do better. Regular accounting of the full range of compensation might open up wider considerations of need, desert and fairness than keeping to narrower comparisons. 'Clearing oases in the jungle', as Wootton put it, does not lead to the more searching examination of how many are paid more than they earn, and how many earn more than they are paid, which is needed to tackle the sharp rise in inequality.

Even the director-general of the Confederation of British Industry, normally defensive of the City, has condemned 'corporate folly', making much of an Income Data Services report that 'the chief executives of the UK's 100 largest companies will have earned 81 times the average pay of all full-time workers in 2009, up from 47 times the average wage back in the year 2000' (Lambert, 2010). He added that '[f]or the first time in history, it has become possible for a manager – as opposed to an owner – of a large public company to become seriously rich'. He partly attributes this 'big change in corporate culture' to 'strictly short-term interests' of global shareholder value, giving executives 'another powerful incentive to maximize short-term profits'. If 'a small cohort at the top reaping such large rewards … seem to occupy a different galaxy from the rest of the community, they risk being treated as aliens' (2010).

By contrast, Lambert recalls that, in the past, business people spoke of the need to generate 'an adequate profit'. Similarly, the 14 professors of business studies mentioned above declared: 'we reject the notion of superiority fostered by some firms, and some business schools, that providing financial services to society is worth hundreds of times more than providing services in nursing or transportation or childcare' (*The Guardian*, Letters, 12 August 2009). Research by the Centre for Research on Socio-Cultural Change (CRESC) at the University of Manchester on the failure of banking to provide more than '3% of cumulative net lending in the decade up to' 2009 to manufacturing while most of the rest went to commercial real estate and residential lending strengthens that argument (Will Hutton, *The Observer*, 13 June 2010).[1]

'Obscene inequalities' in pay tend to be quoted with a 'never again' air of revelation as if their very exposure ensures change, but earlier exposés challenge such optimism. Lansley's (2006) *Rich Britain: The Rise and Rise of the New Super-Wealthy* provided similar 'shock and horror' examples before the credit crunch in 2006 (see also Lansley, 2008). In 1997, *A Class Act: The Myth of Britain's Classless Society* by Adonis and Pollard (1997) revealed 'The super class: Britain's winner-take-all elite' (1997, chapter 3), 'a recognizably new phenomenon … its size and character are shaped by extraordinarily rapid growth in one industry, financial services: an industry concentrated in the City, truly international, largely foreign-owned and heavily US-influenced in ethos, regime and remuneration' (1997, p 67).

The widening of differentials in income and wealth has probably been developing for a generation (NEP, 2010). 'The Thatcher years legitimised a grasping philosophy, ruthlessly applied. The proliferation of adventurous pay packages, festooned with massive bonuses and pain-free escape clauses, was one of the wonders of the age, not least in the inventiveness applied to disconnecting performance from reward' (Hugo Young, *The Guardian*, 23 June 1992). Such attacks were dismissed as 'the politics of envy', a counter-charge successfully suppressing sustained debate of rising gross inequality. New Labour's relaxed attitude to inequality at the top combined with the Thatcher–Reagan project of deregulation, underlining the need to analyse these societal changes in their global context.

As Tett (2009, chapter 2) shows in 'Dancing round the regulators', skilled lobbying by and through international bodies in the early 1990s kept regulators away from financial innovations that contributed greatly to the final credit crunch. 'An ideological fight of the highest order … one of the most startling triumphs for a Wall Street lobbying campaign in the twentieth century … informed the thinking of policymakers outside the US too' (Tett, 2009, pp 45, 46-7; see also Ho, 2009a, 2009b). Similar powerful influences may explain why the Bank for International Settlements 'diluted earlier proposals' so that 'all the regulatory resolve' in 'the 2008 consensus on the need … to tame the financial leviathans' has been reduced to 'pious aspirations' (*Financial Times*, 31 July and 1 August 2010).

architecture. 'Fiscal efficiency' dominated economic efficiency, leading to 'socially' or 'economically useless' trades that exploited tax differences across frontiers and took advantage of loopholes (Turner, 2009b; *The Guardian, Tax Gap* series, 2009). Tactics designed to reduce solidaristic contributions to public resources have been regarded as both smart and desirable, and not only by those using them, with little understanding of, and regard to, the losses to the common wealth.

Meanwhile, most debates about taxing and spending presume that the richer contribute and the poorer benefit. This gap between perception and reality of tax and welfare deserves closer attention in policy analysis (as do the ways in which distorted views are fostered). The overall impact of UK personal taxation has remained fairly stable at around 35% of total income, although it dropped slightly in 2008-09. Despite widespread assumptions about its progressiveness, overall tax is broadly proportional, but regressive for the poorest. Even after Council Tax relief and tax credits, the poorest fifth of households pays a larger share of income in all taxes than average. In 2008-09, the proportions were 36.2% for the poorest fifth, 33.5% for all and 33.9% for the richest fifth (Barnard, 2010, table 3).[2]

Redistributing upwards through tax welfare

Significantly for this analysis, it is taxation, the government system designated to control growing inequality, that also helps to maintain it by redistributing upwards as well as downwards. Tax reliefs mainly benefit the higher paid, enhancing their privileges in ways that still escape public scrutiny, despite Titmuss' early analyses of fiscal or tax welfare (Titmuss, 1958, 1962). Companies arrange financial counselling for directors and top management to maximise 'tax mitigation' and reduce what professional advisers term 'tax wastage'. By contrast, Smith ([1776] 1996, pp 324, 307) not only made a clear case for progressive taxes but also emphasised the importance of contribution in return for 'enjoy[ing] the protection of the state'.

The poorest fifth of households have to pay a much higher proportion of their income in indirect taxes than the richest, as they need to spend their income, while the richer can not only save but are also actively helped to save more by valuable tax reliefs. For example, net subsidies to non-state saving for retirement are equivalent to 2.2% of GDP if other special support is included with the substantial tax reliefs (PPI, 2010, table 29). Revenue lost by not levying employers' NI on their contributions to company pensions exceeded £8 billion in each of the last five years – greater than tax foregone on both working and child tax credits (estimated at £5.5 billion for 2009-10; HMRC Statistics, table 1.5³).

These 'upside-down' benefits of pension tax reliefs redistribute upwards: 60% of tax relief on individuals' pension contributions goes to those liable for higher-rate tax (a fact revealed not in regular statistics but only by parliamentary questions, House of Commons, *Hansard*, 9 October 2008, column 796W). So those already best placed to support their retirement are generously subsidised by other taxpayers to achieve even better protection, while the revenue to fund state provision such as the NI pensions and Pension Credit is correspondingly reduced. Yet, exploiting higher-rate pension reliefs to the limit is generally treated in media and tax guides as a 'victimless' privilege, even obligation. The recent growth in tax reliefs since the new pensions tax regime in 2006 indicate a missed opportunity to tackle the problem vigorously.

The widening gulf between the 'two nations in old age' that Titmuss (1958) first identified in 1955 is reinforced by companies' different treatment of pensions for staff and for top executives and directors highlighted in the Trades Union Congress PensionsWatch annual surveys. Directors of the UK's top 103 companies will be able to retire on pensions of nearly £250,000 a year compared with the current average from occupational pensions of £8,320 – nearly 30 times more in 2009, compared with 25 times more in 2008. Directors' pensions increased by over 23% from the previous year (TUC, 2009), and most were generous defined-benefit schemes with retiral at 60. The Institute of Directors ignores the cost to society of these privileges while it campaigns to control the rising costs of workers' pensions: 'Raise retirement age to 70, say Business Leaders' (Institute of Directors, 19 October 2009, press release).

Over a century ago, differentiation between earned and unearned income was introduced into the British income tax system as part of creating a more 'modern' system (Daunton, 2001) on the principle of greater risk, and so lower tax, attached to earned income. Today, the more favourable treatment of unearned income through, for example, Capital Gains Tax receives little attention or analysis in its reinforcement of inequality.

Media coverage of tax changes deserves far more scrutiny. Conjuring up a world of harassed hard-working victims of the tax system, it serves to delegitimise the role of the state and the necessary collection of contributions to the common wealth. Presenting tax manoeuvrings at the top as modern Robin Hoods fighting on behalf of all taxpayers against the oversized and oppressive sheriff state conceals how 'smart' schemes and 'fiscal excitement' diminish the resources of the majority who then have to make up the tax lost or bear the public service cuts.

Tax reliefs that privilege and enrich private provision were called 'subterranean' by Hacker (2002) in his analysis of the American private welfare state. In the UK too their visibility is limited as they continue to fall outside the public accounts and the detailed scrutiny of parliamentary committees, despite their significant effect on the distribution of resources across society. By various tax reliefs the top 10% reduced their 2004-05 tax bill by nearly £12 billion over and above the basic personal allowance – some 70% of that extra tax relief (author's own estimates from Brewer et al, 2008, table 1). The top one tenth of the top 1% – some 47,000 people – were estimated to benefit by nearly £50,000 each. With a pre-tax income of 31 times the average, they benefited from tax reliefs 86 times the average, enabling those at the very top to 'race away' even further at considerable public cost.

The *Racing away?* evidence (Brewer et al, 2008) gives emphasis to Atkinson's (2007, p 39) observation that '[t]axing the rich cannot now so easily be dismissed as a revenue source'. Although little of this 'bottom-up' and 'upside-down' redistribution through taxes appears in the official statistics (almost as limited today as when Titmuss wrote *Income Distribution and Social Change* in 1962), limits on these disproportionate tax benefits to the wealthiest could help to cut the current public deficit more fairly than has been proposed. The Green New Deal Group argues that putting a limit of £5,000 a year in tax reliefs above the personal allowance for everyone paid more than £100,000 a year could bring in £14.9 billion (GNDG, 2010).

Institutional contributions to avoiding 'tax wastage'

The focus on contribution has so far been confined to individuals, but this ignores not only institutions with their tax responsibilities to support public provision, but also the ways in which those with economic power are able to move resources between individuals, companies and countries in ways that reduce their total contribution. Growing evidence on the more predatory corporate raiding of the common wealth has emerged throughout the credit crunch crisis. *The Guardian's Tax Gap* series (2009) benefited particularly from the detective work of Richard Murphy and colleagues at the Tax Justice Network: 'large corporations and wealthy individuals are increasingly avoiding their contribution to society through taxation. With the aid of governments, they are shifting the tax burden further onto ordinary citizens and smaller businesses' (Kohonen and Mestrum, 2008, p xiii).

Many devices used by banks and other businesses were specifically created to avoid the payment of tax in different administrations so the private gain was at public cost, with little social or economic value and very probably some harm.[4] Murphy (2009) estimated revenue losses from the 700 largest corporations to reach £12 billion: the developing study of tax havens and other offshoring opportunities (Palan, 2009) reveals multiple transfers generating multiple fees, increasing support for a Tobin tax or some form of 'financial transaction tax'.

Some professional critiques of the tax raiders have been particularly forthright: 'relentless economic warfare against normal, decent and hardworking citizens' waged through tax avoidance by 'banks, together with accountants and lawyers…. Banks want public handouts but have systematically destroyed the tax base' (Sikka, 2008). Described by Lord Myners as the most state-aided industry (Myners, 2010, p 4), banking has played a significant part in bringing about a greater reduction of the government revenue from which that aid can be paid. Both by its own tax-reducing activities and its assistance to others to do the same, it has reduced the public resources from which help to schools, those in poverty and even banks themselves can be paid, and yet this erosion of the tax base receives little attention at national or international level.

Compliance and control in taxation and welfare at an individual level have traditionally been the concerns of different professions and agencies. In *Rich Law, Poor Law*, Cook (1989) found regulation reducing in taxation while increasing in social security. A tougher stance on tax may be starting to emerge, but past policy responses have been much criticised for their weakness, the Public Accounts Committee criticising HM Revenue & Customs' 'kidglove treatment' of the wealthiest tax evaders and the 'usually relatively trifling' penalties imposed on the few prosecuted – averaging 3% of the tax due with no sanctions in half the cases. 'Just two out of a thousand' cases were prosecuted, against 60 per 1,000 for benefit fraud (PAC, 2008).

Tax agencies' practices, public and private, need to be included in the scrutiny of overall lightness of touch on the wealthy and powerful, both corporate and individual. Very different treatment of taxpayers, presented as 'givers' to the state, as opposed to benefit recipients, presented as 'takers', means that more has to be found in public spending cuts (Cook, 1989). This operation of double standards, not only of discourse but also of respect and reward, has continued to be little challenged. Far from reducing tax staff, government should be recruiting more 'to tackle tax avoidance and tax evasion' and the more humdrum work not being done – 'to scrutinise tax repayments before they take place' and 'to recover debt owing' (Murphy, 2010a, p 2). Requiring all taxpayers, including the 'best' advised and most powerful, to carry out their tax responsibilities in return for 'enjoy[ing] the protection of the state', as Smith ([1777] 1966) recommended, could help to reduce the public deficit.[5]

The implications for study and practice in social policy

The credit crunch has demonstrated anew that in irresponsible societies some become deprived and many more made insecure while others become better insulated both from sharing common risks and from contributing to the public resources needed to protect the quality of life for all. In the downward-looking discourse of recent governments, they exploit their rights and evade their responsibilities.

This is not a rhetorical point: it underlines the need for a broader approach to social policy that not only takes account of individual needs and the services and benefits that promote social welfare but also engages with the sort of community in which we live: what Marshall (1950, pp 29 and 68) referred to as the ongoing war between citizenship and the capitalist class system. Titmuss was concerned that we tend to lose sight of our common humanity and the things that unite us. The 'social division of welfare' was reinforcing sectoral advantage, nurturing privilege and contributing to exclusion and marginalisation with 'the demoralising effect of cumulative social rejection' (Titmuss, in Alcock et al, 2001, p 145). Similarly, Townsend argued against the double standards growing in society in 1958: 'The central choice in social policy lies … between a national minimum and equality … the source of confusion' in choosing 'is that the national minimum has been held to be the badge of equality.… The problem for the future is to refuse to tolerate two standards of social value and apply one' (Townsend, [1958] 2009, pp 154-5).

Multiple standards are promoted through contrasting language and presuppositions framing the different policy discourses on the needs of the City compared to the needs of citizens and, in particular, those portrayed as dependent on the state. The dependency of banks 'too big to fail', the conditions that might be imposed on them and the restraints and incentives that might work are discussed on a totally different plane from 'welfare state' discourse. Contrasting discourses not only shape the policy-making agenda but also close off particular policy responses that might challenge the existing distributions of power and resource.

To the Queen's question, 'Why did nobody see it coming?', the brightest and the best at the British Academy concluded: 'in summary,

Your Majesty, the failure to foresee the timing, extent and severity of the crisis and to head it off, while it had many causes, was principally a failure of the collective imagination of many bright people, both in this country and internationally, to understand the risks to the system as a whole' (British Academy, 2009).

One of these 'risks to the system as a whole', as even the dullest of us now knows, is that 'parts of the financial services industry have a unique ability to attract to themselves unnecessarily high returns and create instability which harms the rest of society' (Turner, 2009b; Kay, 2009). There could be no clearer example of what Mills (1959a, chapter 15) called 'the higher immorality' in 'organised irresponsibility'. The case for political economy analyses to engage 'upstream' with the societal context of social policies is strong – a classic use of the sociological imagination or, as Mills originally intended, the 'social science imagination'. To this, social policy can make a contribution.

'Any adequate "answer" to a problem … will contain a view of the strategic points of intervention – of the "levers" by which the structure may be maintained or changed; and an assessment of those who are in a position to intervene but are not doing so' (Mills, 1959b, p 131). The crisis of the credit crunch and the after-effects challenge social policy, by itself and working with other subjects, to take a broader, societal approach to problems if we wish to inform and influence debates on the quantity and quality of life and the distribution of welfare across the whole society.

'Inequality has a dynamic of its own' in 'the irresponsible society' (Titmuss, 1959, in Alcock et al, 2001, p 151). Who contributes to welfare and how are as important questions as who benefits and how (van Oorschot, 2008), so the fairness of contributions from all in society requires more scrutiny. That needs to take account of the ways in which some, both as individuals and through institutions, insulate themselves both from the social costs of change and from contributing to their compensation. Erosion of the overall tax base has reduced the common wealth.

'Inequality lies at the heart of the modern free market', concluded Augar (2006, p 214), drawing on his 20 years as an investment analyst. The ways in which the distribution of resources and power across individuals and institutions shapes social policy as much as the rest of society require more attention. 'To recognise inequality as the problem' rather than poverty 'involves recognising the need for structural change, for sacrifices by the majority' and acknowledging 'the limits of conventional welfare' (Titmuss, 1965, pp 132, 131).

In 1909, *The Minority Report on the British Poor Laws* (Webb and Webb, [1909] 1974) sought to anticipate those who believed nothing could be changed. 'Less than a century ago … half a million separate private cesspools accumulated each its own putrefaction', but 'a single main drainage system' effectively removed that particular problem (Webb and Webb, [1909] 1974, p 325). It seems a suitable reflection on which to end a chapter stimulated by what an executive director of the Bank of England calls 'banking pollution'.

Notes

[1] A deputy governor of the Bank of England told the Treasury Committee, '[t]oo much of the balance sheet growth was re-financing stuff within the financial system rather than financing stuff in the real economy' (Andrew Haldane to the Treasury Committee, Q 159, 26 January, 2010).

[2] Adam and Brewer (2010) have raised questions about the validity of this calculation.

[3] www.hmrc.gov.uk/stats/tax_expenditures/menu.htm.

[4] Super-injunctions removed reporting from the online *The Guardian* on a high-street bank's promotion of some tax avoidance schemes – see hard copy for *The Guardian*, 16 March 2009 (Kerevan, *The Scotsman*, 16 October 2009).

[5] The Association of Accountancy and Business Affairs' *Code of Conduct on Taxation* (AABA, 2007) proposes a General Anti-Avoidance Provision to bring in £5 billion. The Liberal Democrats manifesto claimed that £4.625 billion could be clawed back by a crackdown on tax avoidance. Quickly judged 'highly speculative' by the Institute for Fiscal Studies, it was dismissed by a leading tax professional: 'Accountants and lawyers will find ways round whatever rules are in place to help our clients…. It is a bit like picking up a bar of slippery soap – you think you've got it, then it slips away' (*The Guardian*, 15 April 2010).

Acknowledgements
Graham Room provoked me to write this chapter and I have been helped by seeing draft chapters of his new book (Room, 2011). My warm thanks to Jay Ginn for her detailed comments on an earlier version, to Neil Fraser, Brian Main and Kirk Mann for their advice and comments and to Dorothy Sinfield for enduring and commenting on yet more drafts and accompanying preparations.

FIVE

Global social policy responses to the economic crisis

Bob Deacon

Introduction: discursive struggle matters in global social policy

Global social policy (GSP) studies has emphasised the contest and conflict regarding advice given to countries about their social policy by a diverse range of global players, including intergovernmental organisations. Thus:

> The ideas about desirable national social policy carried and argued for by the international organisations ... reveals something approaching a 'war of position' between those agencies ... who have argued for a more selective, residual role for the state together with a larger role for private actors in health, social protection and education provision and those who took the opposite view. This division of opinion often reflected a disagreement as to whether the reduction of poverty was a matter of targeting specific resources on the most poor or whether it was a matter of major social and political-institutional change involving a shift in power relations and a significant increase in redistribution from rich to poor. (Deacon, 2007, p 171)

This analytical framework draws on the concept of '*global policy advocacy coalitions*' as, for example, used by Orenstein (2005, 2008) to analyse the development and selling to the world of the global pension policy preferred by the World Bank since 1990. Here, transnational actors formed coalitions linking scholars in a particular epistemic community, pension providers, international organisations, regional development banks and others to win governments to this view. GSP studies has at the same time argued for the importance of *international networks of knowledge-based experts* who play a part in helping international organisations shape the issues for collective debate. This chapter draws on this framework of analysis to address the current global economic crisis and the ideas about social policy being articulated by such global actors and networks.

During the 20 lost years of global neoliberalism, social policy in the context of development became relegated to a residual safety net approach (Deacon et al, 1997; Deacon, 2007; Mkandawire, 2004; de Haan, 2007). The dominant focus of the World Bank, the International Monetary Fund (IMF) and much of the aid industry, supported by the Millennium Development Goals (MDG) approach of the United Nations (UN), was focused only on the poorest of the poor, working with the erroneous assumption that the question of poverty could be solved without addressing issues of equity, social inclusion and the role of the state in fostering a developmental project for the benefit of all social groups. In the context of the global economic crisis, it has become imperative to break from this 'global politics of poverty alleviation' paradigm and (re)build developmental welfare states and a universal approach to social policy.

This chapter asks whether the crisis provides an opportunity for this to occur. For this to happen there needs to be a fundamental shift in *global* social policy thinking and practice. Although countries still have the capacity to shape, to an extent, their own social policy, the ideas about desirable social and economic policies articulated by international organisations and epistemic communities are instrumental in framing national decision making (Boas and McNeill, 2004). As was argued above, the analysis of GSP over the past 20 years has taught us about the relevance and importance of discursive/hegemonic struggle, including at the international level.

This chapter, therefore, examines empirically the nature of shifts occurring in *global* social policy thinking and practice, and assesses the extent to which the global crisis has facilitated a counter-hegemonic struggle against the previously dominant safety net approach to social policy; and explores how this may be playing out in practice. There are some signs that this is happening but also there are still major constraints and risks of perpetuating a narrow approach to social protection rather than more redistributive and universal rights-based approaches.

In order to examine these global ideational questions, this chapter takes as its focus the renewed energy engendered by the crisis to make the case for a 'Global Social Floor' or Minimum Social Protection Package. This had been argued for by a Global Social Policy Advocacy Alliance consisting of individuals in, among others, the International Labour Office (ILO), the UN Department of Economic and Social

Affairs (UNDESA), UNICEF and HelpAge International, and is now finding new institutional expression as one of the several urgent calls for action agreed on by the UN Chief Executives Board for Coordination (UNCEB) at its meeting in Paris on 5 April 2009. Item 6 of the communiqué refers to a 'Social Protection Floor', the details of which are now being articulated under joint ILO–World Health Organization (WHO) leadership. Of key concern here are two issues:

- whether the IMF in its renewed lending policy has been influenced by these ideas and is giving greater priority to increasing social expenditures in the wake of the crisis;
- whether the Global Social Floor goes far enough in itself in breaking the misjudged 'global politics of poverty alleviation' and replacing it with a more desirable 'global politics of welfare state (re) building'.

The chapter is structured as follows. First, more detailed consideration is given to the recent emergence of the idea of the 'Global Social Floor'. Its emergence is traced back to an informal global network or invisible college of experts working in and around the ILO, UNDESA, the International Council on Social Welfare (ICSW), HelpAge International and others. Second, the *desirability* of the Global Social Floor approach is then assessed in terms of whether it perpetuates or breaks with the 'global politics of poverty alleviation'. What would its likely impact be on social inclusion and equity, and on effective, inclusive social development in developing countries? If adopted, would it mean that this global economic crisis is ushering in a renewed period of state-led development within which social expenditures are central, equitable and a high-quality endeavour? Third, there is a review of the outcomes of *several significant global meetings* in the context of the global financial crisis. These include:

- G20 London meeting of April 2009;
- UNCEB meeting of April 2009;
- Commission of Experts of the President of the General Assembly;
- UN High Level Meeting on the World Financial and Economic Crisis, 24-26 June 2009;
- United Nations Conference on Trade and Development (UNCTAD) Symposium on the Global Economic Crisis and Development, 18-19 May 2009.

The question here is to what extent has all of this conferencing further shifted the global discourse in favour of either the Global Social Floor and/or a renewal of the idea of state-led social development? Fourth, the recent apparent *shifts in policy on the part of the IMF* and its recent lending practices are assessed against the benchmarks of its past practices and policies, of the idea of the Global Social Floor and of the project of state-led social development. A concluding section follows.

The emergence of the idea of the 'Global Social Floor'

A recent public presentation of the campaign for a Global Social Floor brought together Isabel Ortiz, then of UNDESA, now of UNICEF, Michael Cichon, director, Social Security Department, ILO, Silvia Stefanoni, director, HelpAge International and Gaspar Fajth, UNICEF on a public side event at the Doha Financing for Development Conference in December 2008. The publicity material for this event, 'A New Deal for People in a Global Crisis: Social Security for All', asserted that:

> The current global financial crisis is an opportunity to create a Global New Deal to deliver social protection in all countries through basic old age and disability pensions, child benefits, employment programs, and provision of social services.... Social security is a human right (Articles 22 and 25 of the Universal Declaration of Human Rights) and it is affordable, a basic package is estimated to cost from 2 to 5 percent of GDP [Gross Domestic Product] as an average. It is feasible if the international system commits to providing financial support for a Global New Deal to jump start an emergency response to the urgent social needs of our times.

Similar events have taken place in the context of different UN regional and global meetings, such as the UN's Commission for Social Development in February 2009, or the Cairo World Bank Conference on the Financial, Fuel and Food Crisis June 2009. There is no one clear starting point to the emergence of the policy ideas with which this Global Social Floor network is associated, and several strands of activity feed into the current rather more sharply defined 'campaign' for a 'Global Social Floor' or 'Minimum Social Protection Package'. First was the work of the ILO in its 'Global Campaign on Social Security and Coverage for All' (2003), initiated after the 91st Labour Conference by ILO director-general Juan Somavia. This was picked up by the work of the ILO's World Commission on the Social Dimension of

Globalisation, published in 2004, which called for a Global Social Floor (ILO, 2004b, p 110). The Socio-Economic Security work programme of the ILO culminated in a report entitled *Economic Security for a Better World* (ILO, 2004a), which argued for a range of policies, including a citizenship income and categorical cash transfers. Subsequently, Cichon, now director of the ILO Social Security department, argued for mainstreaming within the ILO, some elements of the legacy of the Socio-Economic Security work, by reconciling the idea of universal cash transfers with the extending social security campaign. Hence the call for a new Minimum Social Protection Package, and a new ILO Social Protection Standard (ILO, 2008). Other activities and coalitions contributing to the emergence of the 'Global Social Floor' concept include:

- the work of the Globalism and Social Policy Programme (GASPP);
- the work of individuals in the Organisation for Economic Co-operation and Development (OECD); the work of individuals in the Social Development Advisors Network of the OECD-DAC (Organisation for Economic Cooperation and Development: Development Assistance Committee).
- the drive by a team of like-minded colleagues in UNDESA to produce UN policy social policy advice to counter World Bank thinking (Ortiz, 2007);
- the campaigning work of the ICSW to shape the UN agenda on social issues;
- an experts meeting on 'Social Policies for Development in a Globalizing World' held in Kellokoski, Finland in November 2006 – this generated the document *Comprehensive Social Policies for Development in a Globalizing World* (Wimann et al, 2006), which asserted '[u]niversal policies, expanding coverage of social services, health insurance and social pensions are a crucial priority in efforts to achieve socially sustainable development' (Wimann et al, 2006, p 12);
- the campaign for a cash transfer approach to social protection and in particular for universal social pensions in Africa led by HelpAge International and culminating in the adoption of the idea at the first ever meeting of Ministers of Social Development in Africa in November 2008 (Deacon et al, 2010).

The crystallisation of this broader progressive global social policy stream of the specific campaign for a Global Social Floor can probably be dated to November 2007 when a bid was drafted for funds for a campaign to establish a coalition for a Global Social Floor. Then it was envisaged that there would be 'an alliance of organisations united in the common pursuit of a fairer globalization and the right to social security for all, driven by the conviction that a global social floor is achievable and essential to fast-track poverty reduction'[1]. It was expected that the core groups of the coalition would consist of:

- international organisations – UNDESA, the United Nations Development Programme's (UNDP) International Poverty Centre, the ILO, UNICEF, the United Nations Population Fund (UNFPA), WHO;
- bilateral aid agencies – the German GTZ, the UK Department for International Development (DFID), the Swedish International Development Cooperation Agency (SIDA);
- social partners – the International Trade Union Confederation (ITUC), the International Organisation of Employers (IOE);
- international non-governmental organisations – HelpAge International, Save the Children, ICSW.

No such funding was secured but the informal networking including public campaigning at the level of senior players in UNDESA, the ILO, UNICEF, HelpAge International and so on, took place, and has led as we see later, to the adoption of the policy by UNCEB of the UN System. More recently the concept was incorporated into the MDG targets at the September 2010 UN summit on the MDGs.

Assessing the desirability of the Global Social Floor

Before celebrating the further advance of the idea of the Global Social Floor made possible by the global economic crisis, we need to assess it in terms of whether it is a fundamental break from the 'social-policy-as-safety-net' discourse of the 1980s and 1990s. As argued above, a concern is that for the past 30 years the dominant discourse in international development has been the 'global politics of poverty alleviation', which focuses on the poor and seeks policies targeted upon them to lift them out of poverty, protect them from it or compensate them for it. As argued elsewhere (Deacon, 2009), this needs to give way to the 'global politics of welfare state (re)building' focused on the alliances that need to be constructed between the poor and non-poor (especially the middle class) to rebuild bonds of solidarity nationally and internationally.

The emergence of the newer global discourse on a Global Social Floor, on universal or conditional cash transfers and a Minimum Social

Protection Package does not yet appear to have shifted far enough towards the global politics of welfare state (re)building. The Global Social Floor or Minimum Social Protection Packages being argued for by Cichon for the ILO and Ortiz for UNDESA and UNICEF are still essentially packages for the poor. The issue to be addressed, which the Global Social Floor sidesteps, is the middle class and their historic role in state-led development. Effective functioning states, which meet the welfare needs of their citizens and residents, do so because they also meet the welfare needs of their state builders. In sum:

- A focus on the poor distracts from cross-class solidarity building.
- A focus on the poor undermines the middle-class commitment to pay taxes.
- Countries need higher education as well as primary, city hospitals as well as rural clinics, wage-related pensions as well as social pensions and cash transfers to the poor.
- Civil servants, judges and tax collectors need to be better paid to avoid endemic corruption.
- International aid to poor countries needs to fund not only social policy activities but also the normal day-to-day budgets of the state.

The question remains, the progressive aspects of the Global Social Floor not withstanding, whether a global politics of welfare state (re) building can be re-established within the context of globalisation and its economic crisis. In this global era, the middle class, who have been abandoned by their states, have become outward looking and aspire to have their needs met by attachment to global markets rather than national states and to transnational actors rather than national ones. Can this be reversed?

There has been some recognition of this issue in recent scholarly and policy-related publications. Cohen (2004, p 114), researching the global aspirations of the middle class in Morocco, notes:

> [T]he political goal of the global middle class would be to obtain access to services formerly subsumed within the province of the state, that now increasingly comes from the non-located, heterogeneous social relations that signify and support globalisation … [as a result] the social and political bond between elite and non-elite falls apart globally and locally leaving only economic benefit and exploitation.

Reflecting on Tanzanian and other African experiences, Finnish scholar Jeremy Gould (2005, pp 148-9) has demonstrated that the Aid business has played a major part in seducing the professional and middle class of developing countries from the developmental role they used to occupy:

> Seduced by access to the dollar economy, they prioritise acquiring skills for … the requirements of the aid cartel … at the expense of contributing to the development of domestic manufacturing and processing industries that would generate actual wealth within the national economy … the intellectual and entrepreneurial class must choose between a self-referential and parasitic post-developmentalism, and national(ist) development projects – enhancing domestic savings and productive investment, improving the productivity of land and labour, building the revenue base of the public economy.

Some policy documents have begun to address the issue. Policy analysts such as Birdsall (2007, 2008) have associated political stability with a large middle class. Like modernisation theorists before her, Birdsall makes the assumption that the middle class, educated and dependent on modern institutions and technologies, will engage in civic activism and support political liberalisation. Analysing the failure of relatively successful African economies to undergo political transformation, she remarks: 'Africa seems to be subject to a different kind of trap [in addition to the poverty trap] – that created by the lack of a healthy middle class and the institutions that support and reinforce the middle' (2007, p 3).

The DFID (2006, p 22) White Paper *Making Governance Work for the Poor* comments that 'a growing middle class, more educated citizens, and a greater willingness by civil society and media to speak out' puts pressure on political leaders to improve the performance of the state. It also guards against worsening the problem identified by Gould: 'It is essential that international partners avoid doing things that undermine a country's capability' (DFID, 2006, p 25). The White Paper cites as examples, AIDS projects that 'have recruited professional staff from government health services which are already struggling to provide health care' and the practice in fragile states, such as Afghanistan, of 'giving aid only through non-governmental organisations (NGOs) or private contractors [which] can actually hold back the process of building the capability of the state' (DFID, 2006, p 25). Birdsall (2007, p 4) too writes that a consequence of aid can be the 'diversion of talented, educated citizens from government and from small businesses to work for donor and UN agencies and international NGOs, where salaries are higher and more secure'.

What, then, would be a global social policy strategy after the crisis to overcome the problems of middle-class neglect, consequential inadequacy of services for the poor and the outward-looking global aspirations of the globalised middle class?

Cohen (2009) argues that a policy approach to fostering an educated, middle-income population identified with more vulnerable populations entails integrating international health, social, governance, infrastructure and environmental policies with national employment strategies. Broadly, this means connecting job creation and employment trajectories across the public, private and voluntary sectors to the achievement of global objectives, such as the MDGs, and to local social change. Essentially, this policy choice takes us far beyond the limited steps being taken to fashion a Global Social Floor.

Contending global meetings and conferences: returning to safety nets, consolidating the Global Social Floor or advancing to state-led social development?

The question therefore becomes what other shifts in thinking about social policy and social development have been engendered by all the conferencing that has taken place in the wake of the global economic crisis? Do the emerging ideas spell a return to the global policy of poverty alleviation with its focus on safety nets, because in a crisis governments cannot afford anything else? Do the ideas emerging give support to the rather more progressive policy, the criticisms above notwithstanding, of the Global Social Floor to protect people from the consequences of the crisis? Do they even herald a rediscovery of the central place of social policy as social investment in the context of a rediscovered Keynesianism, which understands the contribution of social expenditures to economic growth; a strategy of state-led development within which middle-class welfare needs are also met?

In terms of the first coordinated world response to the crisis, it fell not to the UN, not to the Bank, not to the IMF but to the first ever meeting of the G20 at Heads of State level at the G20 summit on 2 April 2009, to fashion global policy on the hoof. It committed US$1.1 trillion to support countries in crisis, as follows: US$750 billion to be used under the guidance of an unreformed IMF, US$250 billion for trade facilitation and only US$100 billion for development purposes (including social development), through unreformed multilateral development banks. The UN was only given a marginal role, to monitor the crisis, with no additional resources. So in April 2009 we were faced with an interesting paradox. The world's rich countries were embarking on huge fiscal stimulus packages involving often large social spending guided by long-forgotten Keynesian principles, while for the poorer countries, the equivalent task was being given to the IMF without a word of comment about the fact that the IMF historically was focused on forcing countries into neoliberal, short-term, pro-cyclical, budget-balancing macroeconomic policies, which were the total opposite of that now being prescribed for rich countries. The key question of whether the IMF was about to change its spots and policies and embark on a policy of encouraging poorer countries to invest in social expenditures to spend their way out of their crisis is addressed in a subsequent section.

This forefronting of the G20 and the IMF as *the* global agencies to address the crisis annoyed many in the UN System and, concretely, led to a meeting of UNCEB in Paris later in April, which generated the UNCEB (2009) Issue Paper *The Global Financial Crisis and its Impact on the Work of the UN System*. The meeting was able to draw on an earlier draft report considered during 26-27 February 2009 by UNCEB's High-Level Committee on Programmes[2]. The report called for coordinated action across the UN System in eight key policy fields:

* finance;
* trade;
* employment and production;
* environment;
* food security;
* social services, empowerment and protection of people;
* humanitarian, security and social stability;
* international cooperation for development.

In terms of specific policies, the ILO would lead on a Global Jobs Pact and, 'to help developing countries cope with the crisis, a counter-cyclical global jobs fund could be established' (UNCEB, 2009, p 14).

Most important from this chapter's point of view was initiative six, which was to work towards a global 'Social Protection Floor which ensures access to basic social services, shelter, and empowerment and protection of the poor and vulnerable'. This was subsequently elaborated in the June 2009 UNCEB document (UNCEB, 2009, p 20) as a 'floor (that) could consist of two main elements: (a) public services: geographical and financial access to essential public services (water, sanitation, health, education); and (b) transfers: a basic set of essential social transfers ... to provide a minimum income security'. The ILO and WHO would lead on this policy supported by a host of other agencies such as UNICEF and UNDESA. The Global Social Floor had become UN policy at least in terms of UNCEB.

On 4 November 2009, the policy was discussed[3] at the Second Committee of the General Assembly, at which it was reported that collaborating agencies and a group of supporting donor agencies had met in the ILO Training Centre in Turin in October, to develop a blueprint of a manual for joint country activities on the Social Protection Floor. The interagency meeting was attended by:

- United Nations Human Settlement Programme (UN-HABITAT);
- IMF;
- the Food and Agriculture Organization (FAO);
- the Office of the High Commissioner for Human Rights (OHCHR);
- the United Nations Development Programme (UNDP);
- the United Nations Educational, Scientific and Cultural Organization (UNESCO);
- the World Food Programme (WFP);
- UNAIDS (the Joint United Nations Programme on HIV/AIDS);
- UNCEB (video link);
- UNDESA;
- UNFPA;
- UNICEF;
- WHO;
- World Bank;

and the following observers:

- Asian Development Bank (ADB);
- BMZ (Federal Ministry for Economic Cooperation and Development);
- DFID;
- Finnish Ministry of Foreign Affairs;
- GTZ;
- HelpAge International;
- Save the Children.

The experts approved, in principle, a draft manual on the *Strategic Framework for Joint UN Operations for National Social Protection Floor*

Initiatives.[4] The manual brings the respective tools and competencies of different agencies together and establishes a comprehensive guide for UN regional coordinators/country directors and country teams who are expected to take the lead in organising the UN support for national Social Protection Floor initiatives (ILO and WHO, 2009).

It remains to be seen how this initiative translates into the practice of agencies. There are some positive signs. Even UNICEF, which has been reluctant to throw its lot in with a ONE-UN policy, seems to be on board. With Isabel Ortiz now responsible for economic and social policy in UNICEF New York, the agency is clearly putting effort into the need for social protection investments to smooth the experience of the crisis.[5] In November 2009, UNICEF hosted jointly with the UK's Overseas Development Unit (ODI), a conference entitled 'The global economic crisis – including children in the policy response'. It examined the ways in which food and fuel price volatility, financial market volatility and the global economic slowdown are affecting children and young people in both developing and developed countries and recommended policy responses. The conference was concluded with an address by Isabel Ortiz. Echoing the 1987 call by UNICEF's Giovanni Cornia, Richard Jolly and Frances Stewart (1987) for *Adjustment with a Human Face*, Isabel Ortiz (2009) called for a 'recovery with a human face'. An online email discussion has been initiated by Cornia, Jolly and Ortiz to pursue this theme. Helen Clark, new UNDP administrator, in a speech at the G20 meeting of Ministers in Pittsburgh,[6] also at least paid lip service to this new ONE-UN policy. While Michael Cichon, Head of Social Security at the ILO has been at the forefront of the global campaign for a Social Protection Floor, within the ILO this policy is still having to jostle for attention with the dominant Decent Work campaign[7] (within which, of course, social protection plays a part). The tripartite organisation is still finding it hard to address issues of human rights and overall poverty as distinct from workers rights and wages policy. It is hoped by ILO insiders that the International Labour Conference in June 2011, which will be focus upon social protection, will provide a boost to this work.[8]

It is hard to determine whether the World Bank's formal membership of UNCEB and its formal participation in the global Social Protection Floor UN initiative is changing its policies and practices on social protection. Its two flagship training programmes on pensions and safety nets are going ahead as before. The World Bank did sign up to the joint Statement with UNICEF and a host of other UN agencies and international non-governmental organisations (INGOs) on Advancing Child Sensitive Social Protection.[9] Interestingly in the wake of the impact of the global financial crisis on the sustainability and utility of private defined contribution pension schemes, the World Bank's current work is focused on social pensions. Its recent publication *Closing the Coverage Gap: The Role of Social Pensions and Other Retirement Income Transfers* (Holzmann et al, 2009)[10] captures well the reasons why contributory schemes of either the defined benefit or defined contribution kind have their limitations:

> A sustained expansion of the contributory system in the average low- or middle-income country would require fundamental changes in the productive structure of the economy and the functioning of its product and labor markets.... Against this background, social pensions and other retirement transfers emerge as an important instrument for bridging the coverage gap—at least for the time being—by focusing on individuals with no or limited saving capacity, who are more likely to be outside the contributory system. (Holtzmann et al, 2009, p 18)

Noteworthy in this context is the World Bank's belated concern that defined contribution pension schemes might not provide a decent pension for those forced to retire during the crisis. That this in turn might encourage countries to reverse recent reforms setting up private schemes, and return to state pay-as-you-go (PAYG) schemes, has prompted the World Bank to caution against radical reversal and to offer public subsidy for a short while to those affected![11]

So, answering the question as to whether the series of crisis meetings takes us back to safety nets, forward to a Global Social Floor or on to renewed state-led development, we can say that a step appears to have been taken in the direction of the ONE-UN lining up behind the Minimum Social Protection Package or Global Social Floor. However, at the same time, a further UNCEB initiative – 'Additional Financing for the Most Vulnerable' – would ensure that 'countries with limited fiscal space (would have) additional financing in the form of concessional loans'. This initiative gave support to the 'Vulnerability Fund' that had been initially proposed by the President of the World Bank when he called on countries to commit 0.7% of the funds being made available for 'fiscal' stimulus to be allocated to a Vulnerability Fund for developing countries for safety nets and other purposes. This particular initiative, UNCEB agreed, was to be driven by the World Bank–UNDP. So we should be aware that the outcome of the UNCEB meeting might not be so much a new step in the direction of ONE-UN with ONE (Global Social Floor) policy under ONE leadership with ONE budget, but just the old story of the ILO-WHO universal Global Social Floor approach with no funds behind it and a World-Bank–UNDP Vulnerability Fund to be used for, among other things, safety nets. An empirical question yet to be answered is whether there is any money donated by impoverished donors to any of these contending funds or approaches. Indeed, as McCulloch and Sumner (2009, p 105) conclude in their review of the likely impact of the crisis on the development paradigm: 'In short, the crisis may increase the leverage of advocates of social protection in developing countries, but in many countries, their success will depend on whether donors are able to support sufficient fiscal space for the budget reallocations involved'. Interestingly, the World Bank's Vulnerability Fund has been strengthened by a US$50 million donation from Russia, which far outstrips the £5 million from the UK.

After the G20 and UNCEB, all eyes (actually very few eyes given the press blackout) turned to the upcoming meeting that would really get to grips with the world economic crisis: the UN Conference on the World Economic Crisis and its Impact on Development, eventually held 24-26 June 2009. Here surely with G77 influence would be neither a retreat to safety nets, nor just a timid advance to the Global Social Floor, but the case shouted loud for renewed state-led social and economic development. This conference had been resolved upon at the December UN Conference on Financing for Development and had been pushed hard for by the President of the General Assembly, positioning himself differently from the Secretary General of the UN, who was much more inclined to work with the G20 as a centre of global power. In the words of a Trans-National Institute's spokesperson, Nick Buxton (2009), however, it was not to be:

> Miguel D'Escoto Brockmann, the avuncular Nicaraguan priest and elected President of the General Assembly of the United Nations ... had dared to inject huge energy into the process by pulling together a high level UN commission chaired by Nobel Prize heavyweight Joseph Stiglitz and calling for radical changes in the institutions and rules that led to the crisis. Western diplomats were soon briefing journalists that Brockmann was a 'radical socialist' trying to impose its vision on the world community. Then when it became clear that the largest block of countries, the misnamed Group of 77 (in fact made up of more than 130 nations) was also pushing forward many of the same

ideas, the rich countries played down the importance of the conference and refused to send high-level representation. Finally the rich countries went through the G77 declaration and removed anything that entailed any reform to either the institutions (such as the IMF, World Bank and World Trade Organisation) or the international rules and laws that enabled the crisis to spread and deepen. The result was an anaemic final UN document that does little to tackle the root causes of the financial crisis.

Table 5.1 compares some aspects of Brockmann's draft outcome document (UN, 2009a) with the outcome document after EU and other intervention (UN, 2009b) and the same final outcome (UN, 2009c).

In terms of the concerns of this chapter, the challenge to traditional IMF conditionalities was watered down. Meanwhile, UNESCO, in the form of the Social and Human Sciences Division's Management of Social Transformations (MOST) programme, examined the impact of the global financial crisis in its September 2009 meeting in Paris. The MOST programme, often overlooked by analysts, regards itself 'as the only United Nations programme in charge of contributing through social science research to the development of policies able to better respond to the changes of contemporary society'[12]. Unfortunately, its deliberations rarely reach detailed policy conclusions. Of note, however, was the contribution of the UNRISD spokesperson, Katja Hujo, who outlined the impact of the global financial crisis on developing countries. She (ICSW, 2009):

Table 5.1: Outcome of the UN Conference on the World Economic Crisis and its Impact on Development, 24-26 June 2009

	18 May draft	22 June draft after changes	OUTCOME
Causes of crisis	Concentration of income and wealth (para 10)	Systematic fragilities and imbalances (para 9)	Same as 22 June draft
IMF conditionalities	Without unwarranted conditionalities (para 20)	Streamlining conditionalities (para 17)	Same as 22 June draft
New sources of finance	Establishment of new innovative forms of financing (para 28)	Establishment, where appropriate, of voluntary innovative forms of financing (para 31)	Same as 22 June draft
Economic Security Council	Establish a new Global Economic Council (para 53)	No such recommendation	Same as 22 June draft

Sources: UN (2009a, b, c)

went on to look at four areas of social policy responses. The first area was health and education where she spoke of maintaining and expanding social infrastructure in health, education and care services which would create job opportunities for women who are suffering more than men in this GFC [global financial crisis]. The second area was investment in water, sanitation, transportation, housing etc. which all have beneficial impacts on health. The third area was social protection where governments should expand and create cash transfer and employment programmes with wider eligibility conditions, increased amounts of benefit or increasing their duration. Fourth was the expansion of labour market policies by combining short-term with long-term measures.

Finally, in terms of a shift towards the idea of state-led investment and development, the UNCTAD's (2009a, p 51) *Least Developed Countries Report 2009* argues the case that 'the developmentally orientated elite ... should establish a social compact through which broad sections of society support the developmental project'.

IMF changing policies and practices: advancing social protection and social development or a return to safety nets?

Is the IMF changing its spots? Strauss-Kahn, IMF boss at the time of writing, insisted it was a new IMF and the website under his leadership stated:

> The IMF tries to ensure that economic adjustments taken to combat the impact of the crisis also take account of the needs of the most vulnerable by developing or enhancing social safety nets. Social spending is being preserved or increased wherever possible. For instance, in Pakistan expenditure will be increased to protect the poor through both cash transfers and targeted electricity subsidies. About a third of programs in low-income countries include floors on social and other priority spending. Structural reforms are designed in a way to protect the most vulnerable. For instance in Hungary, low-income pensioners were excluded from benefit reduction.[13]

Even if we take this at face value, the drift of the argument is *not* for social expenditures as social investments to support a renewed state-led development project. It is not even for a global Social Protection Floor. At best it is for a targeted approach to poverty alleviation and a residual means-tested approach to social policy.

Indeed, while the IMF has led the argument for large-scale fiscal stimulus in the rich world to kick-start economic growth, the Center for Economic Policy Research (CEPR, 2009) finds that nine agreements that the IMF has negotiated since September 2008, including with Eastern European countries, El Salvador and Pakistan, contain some elements of contractionary policies. These include fiscal (budget) tightening, interest rate increases, wage freezes for public employees, and other measures that will reduce aggregate demand or prevent economic stimulus programmes in the current downturn. Similarly, Eurodad's analysis (Molina-Gallart, 2009) of 10 IMF agreements signed in 2009 shows that the IMF is still advising stringent fiscal and monetary policies to low-income countries as well as controversial structural reforms. The paper comments that '[i]f the Fund is to provide funding to poor countries to meet the financial gaps created by the crisis it has to change and it has to do it soon. Reacting poorly and reacting late may mean death and starvation for millions of people in poor countries' (2009, p 3). Other research on loans to El Salvador, Ethiopia and Latvia comes to the same conclusions (Molina-Gallart, 2009). Work by Lendvai and Stubbs in Central and Eastern Europe confirms that in that region the message of the IMF, now in alliance with the EU, which is faced with its own crisis in Greece, is uncompromisingly for public sector restraint and a targeted welfare approach (Lendvai and Stubbs, 2010). Lutz and Kranke (2010) go as far as arguing that the EU has come to the rescue of the Washington Consensus.

Similarly, UNCTAD (2009a), in its 2009 annual trade and development report, notes that '[i]n reality, the conditions attached to recent lending operations have remained quite similar to those of the past. Indeed, in almost all of its recent lending arrangements, the Fund has continued to impose pro-cyclical economic tightening'. The report (UNCTAD, 2009a, p 56) goes on to argue:

> The scope for counter-cyclical policies among smaller developing countries and countries in transition varies greatly. Many countries with current account deficits and a weak currency are pushed by their creditors to lean towards pro-cyclical macroeconomic policies with high interest rates and fiscal conservatism. However, a departure from the

traditional policy practices and policy rules is warranted, indeed indispensable.

Towards a conclusion

It was argued at the start of the chapter that discursive struggles about policy alternatives within and between international organisations were an important element in shaping global and in turn national economic and social policies. The chapter proceeded to illustrate this with a focus on contending policy ideas designed to ensure poverty alleviation in the wake of the global economic crisis. This policy debate became articulated in the context of a number of forums, including meetings of UNCEB, the G20 summit and a specially convened UN conference.

The chapter addressed the question as to whether the ideas emerging from the debate within and between intergovernmental organisations spelt a return to the global policy of poverty alleviation with its focus on safety nets because in a crisis governments cannot afford anything else. There is more than a hint of this in the approach of the World Bank's Vulnerability Fund and in the endorsement by the G20 of the strengthened IMF as *the* agent for injecting monies into troubled economies. This conclusion was strengthened by evidence that there was a reversion to type on the part of the IMF as it retuned to its pro-cyclical policies for poorer countries, requiring the cutting of public expenditures except those targeted on the most vulnerable.

The chapter asked whether the ideas emerging from this debate gave support to the rather more progressive policy of the Global Social Floor, the criticisms of it also made earlier not withstanding. At the level of global discourse it is evident that a strong global policy advocacy coalition has been constructed in support of it by INGOs and UN social agencies and this has been helped by the argument of the coalition that a global economic crisis requires a global social response. Certainly, the endorsement of this policy by UNCEB is an important indicator of the growth of support for this idea. Whether there will be global funds available to back this policy up in impoverished countries is another matter.

The chapter also asked whether the debate heralded a rediscovery of the central argument that social policy is a social investment and not an economic burden. Did this happen in the context of a rediscovered Keynesianism, which understands the contribution of social expenditures to economic stabilisation and growth? For developed countries, it clearly had this impact initially when fiscal stimulus packages were agreed by many in 2008 and 2009, although the global politics of retrenchment and public expenditure cuts seem to have rapidly replaced this. To the extent that the Keynesian ideas did resurface is a further nail in the coffin of a failed neoliberal project and it could lead in time to empowering those such as UNRISD researchers, MOST spokespersons, UNCTAD and others who put forward arguments for a return to a version of state-led development in the development context.

In sum, UNCEB endorses the Global Social Floor, the G20 and the IMF probably point back to safety nets and UNESCO's MOST programme, UNRISD and UNCTAD call for a state-led social investment strategy. The UN failed June conference might have supported this too if the Global North had not sabotaged it.

Thus, the impact of the economic crisis on thinking and practice at a global level about social policy and development reveals, as was to be expected, contradictory elements. On the one hand, those (ILO, UNICEF) wishing to advance a comprehensive and universal social protection agenda have found their corner strengthened against those who still favour a residual approach because of UNCEB picking up the banner of a Global Social Floor. At the same time, monies provided by the Global North to help countries in the Global South steer their way out of the crisis are still being channelled through an IMF that, despite its webpage makeover, still clings to conserving the social protection only of the most vulnerable. Those within UNCTAD, UNRISD and UNESCO-MOST who argue that we should advance beyond both residualism and a minimal Global Social Floor in the direction of a new wave of state-led social development, find little support for this among donors, although the message is more readily understood in much of the Global South.

Notes

[1] Personal communication from Isobel Ortiz, then of UNDESA.

[2] www.unsceb.org/ceb/rep/hlcp/CEB-2009-4-HLCP-17

[3] www.un.org/ga/second/64/0411summary.pdf

[4] www.socialsecurityextension.org/gimi/gess/RessShowRessource.do?ressourceId=14484

[5] www.unicef.org/policyanalysis/index_49072.html

[6] http://content.undp.org/go/newsroom/2009/september/helen-clark-implications-of-the-financial-crisis-on-sustainable-development.en

[7] www.ilo.org/global/What_we_do/Events/lang--en/index.htm

[8] Progress can be tracked at www.socialprotectionfloor.org or www.socialsecurityextension.org

[9] www.unicef.org/socialpolicy/files/CSSP_joint_statement_8.20.09.pdf

[10] www-wds.worldbank.org/external/default/main?pagePK=641930 27&piPK=64187937&theSitePK=523679&menuPK=64187510&sea rchMenuPK=57313&theSitePK=523679&entityID=000333038_200 9073023543&searchMenuPK=57313&theSitePK=523679

[11] http://siteresources.worldbank.org/INTPENSIONS/Resources/ 395443-1121194657824/PRPNote-Financial_Crisis_12-10-2008.pdf

[12] www.unesco.org/new/en/social-and-human-sciences/themes/ social-transformations/most-programme/about-most/ (accessed 13 June 2011).

[13] www.imf.org/external/about/onagenda.htm (accessed 5 November 2009).

Acknowledgements

This chapter is based on a paper originally presented at the UNRISD Conference on the Global Economic Crisis and the Implications for Social Development held in Geneva, November 2009, and since published in Utting et al (2011). It is reproduced here with permission of Palgrave Macmillan.

SIX

Poverty, the crisis and social policy responses in developing countries

Armando Barrientos

Introduction

The onset of the post-2007 financial crisis in countries of the Organisation for Economic Co-operation and Development (OECD), particularly the United Kingdom (UK) and the United States (US), and its subsequent spread on a global scale has raised concerns regarding its impact on developing countries, and more specifically the likely impact of the crisis on poverty, vulnerability and other social indicators. These concerns come on top of earlier concerns regarding the impact on poverty of the recent volatility of food prices, and of climate change. The crisis is widely expected to afflict the economies of developing countries, through the effects of sharp contractions in trade and investment (World Bank, 2009b). Although a great deal has been written about the size and importance of the crisis, with some commentators drawing parallels with the 1930s crisis, uncertainty remains on the likely scale and duration of the downturn. A prolonged downturn could have a deep and lasting impact on global poverty and vulnerability.

Concerns about the impact of the crisis in developing countries have drawn attention to the role of social policies in mitigating its worst effects. Over the last decade or so, large-scale programmes providing direct assistance to households in poverty have emerged in the South (Barrientos and Hulme, 2008). At the onset of the financial crisis, evidence on the positive impact of these programmes on poverty and vulnerability had accumulated into a strong knowledge base informing policy at national and regional levels (Rawlings and Rubio, 2005; Grosh et al, 2008; Fiszbein and Schady, 2009). There is, therefore, a well-founded expectation that social assistance programmes could play an important and positive role in tackling the adverse effects of the financial crisis. This chapter examines the role and significance of social policies in developing countries, and especially social assistance, against the context of the crisis.

In the work of the International Labour Office (ILO), social protection is associated with a range of public institutions, norms and programmes aimed at protecting workers and their households from contingencies threatening basic living standards. Broadly, these can be grouped under three main headings: social insurance, social assistance and labour market regulation. Social insurance consists of programmes providing protection against lifecourse contingencies such as maternity and old age, or work-related contingencies such as unemployment or sickness. Social assistance provides support for those in poverty. Normally, social insurance is financed from contributions by workers and their employers, whereas social assistance is tax-financed. Finally, labour and employment standards ensure basic standards at work, and extend rights to organisation and voice. These institutions have been fully established in developed countries, but in developing countries their evolution has been uneven. In the last decade or so, the expansion of social protection has been concentrated on social assistance, encouraged by a global focus on poverty and vulnerability reduction signalled by the Millennium Development Goals, but also in response to labour market liberalisation, which limits the extension of social insurance. Social assistance in developing countries is in sharp contrast to social assistance institutions in developed countries, particularly Anglo-Saxon countries. In developing countries, social assistance is not dominated by income maintenance. Instead, it consists of transfers to households in poverty aimed at improving consumption and basic service utilisation. This chapter will therefore focus on social assistance programmes.

To an important extent, the recent extension of social protection programmes in developing countries constitutes a response to earlier crises, especially the acute crisis in Latin America in the 1980s and the financial crisis in East Asia in the late 1990s. The design and orientation of recently introduced social assistance programmes in developing countries reflect learning from those experiences. It is hard to generalise across the wider range of conditions in developing countries, but it has often been the case that immediate responses to a crisis turn out to be less than satisfactory, and it is only in the aftermath that effective policies are designed and implemented. In Mexico, for example, the thinking behind PROGRESA[1] was shaped by the inadequacies of emergency programmes introduced in the late 1980s and early 1990s (Levy, 2006). In Brazil, the nationwide adoption of *Bolsa Escola*[2] reflected a process of learning and experimentation in response to the crisis of the early 1990s

(Pochmann, 2006). In Indonesia, the development of a social protection system was informed in large part by the limitations of the responses to the 1997 crisis, especially its reliance on petrol subsidies (Sumarto et al, 2008). Perhaps the main lesson to emerge from earlier crises is that emergency responses are unlikely to be as effective in reducing and preventing poverty and vulnerability as the establishment of solid, long-term, social assistance institutions. It is therefore essential for developing countries that attention is directed to the post-crisis world.

The next section outlines the rapid expansion of social assistance in developing countries. The chapter then focuses on the financial crisis and the role of social assistance. It considers what kinds of policy responses to the crisis are required. A final section speculates on the priorities for a post-crisis world and concludes.

The global expansion of social assistance: a quiet revolution?

In the last decade there has been a rapid expansion of social assistance programmes in developing countries, although it is important to note that in developing countries social assistance differs significantly from the income maintenance design common in developed countries (about more later). Social assistance programmes are generally focused on poor and poorest households and include some form of transfer in cash and/ or kind. There has been a great deal of discussion around the design of these programmes, for example around targeting or beneficiary selection, and on the use of co-responsibilities or conditionalities in some programmes; but perhaps the most important issue is scale. The introduction of these programmes has resulted in a very rapid rise in coverage. New forms of social assistance introduced in the last decade now reach in excess of 150 million poor households in developing countries, with around three quarters of a billion people benefiting from the programmes. Notable recent initiatives include:

- South Africa's *Child Support Grant*, implemented from 1998 and now reaching 7.2 million children;
- the *Minimum Living Standards Scheme* in China, initiated in the late 1990s and reaching 22.4 million by 2006;
- Mexico's *Oportunidades*, started in 1997 and now reaching more than five million households;
- *Bolsa Familia* in Brazil, with coverage of 12 million households;
- Indonesia's *Safety Net Programme*, introduced in 2005 and planned to reach 15 million households;

- India's *National Rural Employment Guarantee Scheme*, initially expected to reach 26 million households annually but now reaching over 40 million households.[3]

The emerging social assistance programmes have the capacity to reach large numbers of households in poverty in the developing world.

There is considerable diversity in the design and objectives of these programmes. Some programmes are pure income transfers. They are focused on improving the purchasing power of households in poverty. The *Child Support Grant* and the *Old Age Grant* in South Africa, for example, provide monthly transfers to children and older people in poverty. Another group of programmes provides income transfers in combination with services. *Oportunidades* in Mexico or *Bolsa Familia* in Brazil, for example, tie the receipt of the transfer with basic service utilisation. Households are encouraged to ensure that children attend school regularly and all household members make use of primary healthcare facilities. The *National Rural Employment Guarantee Scheme* in India and the *Productive Safety Net Programme* in Ethiopia provide transfers that require beneficiary households to supply labour in infrastructure or community projects. These programmes combine transfers with improvements in human development or productive and service infrastructure. Finally, a few programmes combine transfers with a wide range of interventions explicitly addressing the multidimensional nature of poverty. They are integrated poverty eradication programmes. *Chile Solidario*, for example, combines interventions on seven dimensions: health, education, employment, registration, income, housing and intra-household dynamics. The scope and orientation of social assistance programmes reflect national and regional learning and experience in poverty reduction.

The dynamics of these programmes are especially interesting. In many countries, the scope of the programmes has expanded over time, as separate interventions have come to be integrated within a single programme. The multidimensional design of *Chile Solidario*, on the one hand, and *Oportunidades* and *Bolsa Familia*, on the other, have been influential in Latin America and the Caribbean in demonstrating the effectiveness of an integrated approach to poverty eradication (Fiszbein and Schady, 2009). Another interesting point is that these programmes have, in the main, focused on the extreme poor, but can be gradually expanded to incorporate other groups in poverty. In fact, the financial crisis has led to the extension of existing social assistance programmes in many countries, including Brazil, Jamaica, Mexico and South Africa. In Brazil and South Africa, the crisis led to the inclusion of 16- and

17-year-olds as beneficiaries; in Mexico, beneficiary numbers and benefit levels were expanded; while in Jamaica, an effort was made to include non-poor households in acute vulnerability

In spite of the very rapid expansion of social assistance programmes in developing countries, which has been described as a 'quiet revolution' (Barrientos and Hulme, 2008), significant challenges remain. The expansion of social assistance programmes in low-income countries has been slowed down by existing deficits in capacity and financing. Middle-income countries have advantages over low-income countries in terms of their capacity to design, deliver and finance social assistance. In low-income countries, where the incidence of poverty is substantially higher than in middle-income countries and where the capacity of public agencies is very limited, putting in place sustainable social assistance programmes is an urgent challenge (Barrientos, 2009).

Low-income countries in Sub-Saharan Africa, for example, have found it difficult to emulate the successful expansion of social transfer programmes in middle-income countries in Latin America. Political elites in low-income countries in Sub-Saharan Africa have relied in the past on international aid organisations to finance and implement appropriate policies. The high incidence of extreme poverty, and the low differentiation among groups in poverty, contribute to making narrow targeting both technically and political difficult. Overcoming large capacity deficiencies in public agencies tasked with poverty reduction adds to the large set-up costs associated with initiating large-scale poverty reduction programmes. These factors have conspired to restrict the expansion of social protection in low-income countries in Sub-Saharan Africa to small pilot programmes, largely financed and delivered by international aid agencies. It is impossible to exaggerate the potential role of South–South cooperation in poverty reduction because it ensures that policy learning and diffusion do not have to go through Washington or European capitals. The Africa–Brazil programme, supported by the Ministry of Social Development in Brazil, is a very welcome initiative in this context and has proven to be highly effective on the ground. In low-income countries in Latin America, similar issues have emerged. The extension of social assistance programmes in Central American countries, and in Paraguay, has been slower than in South America and Mexico. Weak institutionalisation of the programmes and a dominant role of international agencies have undermined national ownership and political support for the programmes (Soares and Britto, 2007; Barrientos and Santibañez, 2009b). In a sense, these two factors go together, as international agencies feel compelled to take a more active role in driving the programmes because of a perceived failure of domestic institutions to provide leadership. Often, the direct intervention of international agencies creates agencies in parallel to existing institutions, and therefore undermines their policy formulation and delivery capacity. In middle-income countries, the challenges are of a different nature. In Latin America, the recent expansion of social assistance programmes has to an important extent evolved independently of existing social insurance institutions and labour market policies (Mesa-Lago, 2007). This raises the issue of the integration of social assistance and social insurance institutions. Conditional human development transfer programmes, for example, have largely developed outside social insurance institutions and have been framed as a separate response to poverty and vulnerability. In the main, these programmes are located in social assistance governmental agencies or ministries, or in quasi-independent agencies linked to these ministries. On the other hand, the strengthening of non-contributory pensions in the region has been motivated to an important extent by the limited coverage of social insurance pension programmes. The issue of the interrelationship existing between contributory and non-contributory pension programmes has attracted attention in policy debates, while the integration of other types of social assistance programmes with social insurance institutions has hardly been discussed.[4] The integration of social assistance and social insurance institutions in the region will become more urgent as social assistance programmes develop. The integration of social assistance programmes and labour market policy is also an urgent challenge, especially in the context of the global financial crisis. Issues around exit strategies from social assistance into employment are acquiring greater prominence, as are issues around the quality of jobs, skills and productivity. For middle-income countries, the challenges are mainly to do with the integration of the emerging social assistance programmes within broader social policies, including social insurance, basic service provision and employment. For low-income countries, the issues are around strengthening households' productive capacity, especially in agriculture. Successful policies require linking up social assistance with active labour market policies, and in rural areas with agricultural promotion policies and programmes.

In sum, the rapid emergence of social assistance programmes in developing countries will enable a more effective response to the global crisis. However, important challenges remain: extending the reach of social assistance programmes in low-income country contexts and integrating social assistance within broader social policies in middle-income countries. The crisis will make it more difficult to address these challenges, but it is essential not to be diverted from the objective of reducing global poverty and vulnerability.

The financial crisis, poverty and policy responses

As noted in the Introduction, there is considerable uncertainty regarding the scale and duration of the global economic crisis in OECD countries let alone its impact on developing countries. The crisis has been more acute in Anglo-Saxon countries, which is largely explained by the fact that the epicentre has been their closely-knit financial markets. Current predictions are that some European countries will climb out of negative Gross Domestic Product (GDP) growth in 2010, followed by the US and the UK. Opinions differ as to whether the predicted recovery is part of a 'V', 'U', 'W' trend, or indeed any other part of the alphabet. Nobel Laureate Joseph Stiglitz argues that returning to the solid growth rate levels seen before the crisis could take the US several years, even a decade.[5]

There is as much uncertainty around the impact of the financial crisis on developing countries (World Bank, 2009b). Few developing countries are sufficiently well integrated into the international financial system to be fully exposed to the direct effects of the crisis. Malawi and Sierra Leone, for example, are unlikely to be directly affected by the fall of Lehman Brothers. In the developing world, the impact of the crisis will be felt indirectly, through the reverberating effects on trade and finance. Even then, developing countries with large domestic markets, well-regulated financial markets and reasonably well-diversified economies, for instance Brazil, will be in a position to mitigate the effects of the crisis. As regards low-income countries, the impact of the crisis is more likely to be felt through migration flows and remittances. Unemployed migrants may find that they are unable to send remittances home, or are forced to return home, perhaps displacing other migrants in the process. However, falling prices might be beneficial for some countries; lower energy prices might reduce input price, and foreign currency flows, for non-oil-exporting countries. In all likelihood, the impact across developing countries will be very diverse, influenced by their relative exposure to the world economy but also by domestic factors determining fiscal space.

Overall, there is every indication that the crisis will lead to across-the-board growth slowdown, which itself will be responsible for less poverty reduction than would have been the case in the absence of the crisis. Chen and Ravallion (2009) estimated that, given then current growth projections for developing countries in 2009 and 2010, global poverty reduction will be significantly less than could have been predicted on the basis of trends before the onset of the crisis. They estimate that the financial crisis could be responsible for 'an extra 73 million people living under US$1.25 a day and 91 million people under US$2 a day by 2010' (2009).

For Latin America, it is possible to draw some rough order of magnitude of the effects of the growth slowdown on poverty based on recent trends. Estimates published by the Economic Commission for Latin America and the Caribbean (ECLAC) of the growth–poverty elasticity provide a useful starting point (ECLAC, 2008). These estimates suggest that for the period 2000-07, a 1% increase in GDP on average reduced the poverty headcount by 1.2%, and the extreme poverty headcount by 2%. Of course, this is an average for the region. The growth–poverty elasticity shows large variation across countries, ranging from −3 in El Salvador to +0.4 in Uruguay (that is, a 1% increase in GDP in El Salvador would have reduced the poverty headcount by 3% and increased it by 4% in Uruguay). This difference in performance reflects differences in economic conditions and especially the speed of labour market responses in the two countries.

ECLAC growth projections for Latin America were revised several times during 2008 and 2009, reflecting new information on the impact of the crisis. Before the onset of the crisis, growth was projected at 4.5% for 2009. This projection was then revised downwards to 1.9% in March 2009, which implies that, other things being equal, poverty reduction in 2009 will be less than one half of that expected on the basis of the situation prior to the crisis in March 2009, and then revised again to a contraction of GDP of around 0.3% for 2009. The growth slowdown means rising poverty and indigence in the region.

In this context, the role of social policy, and social assistance in particular, becomes central to a response to the crisis (CEPAL, 2009). Few developing countries have in place income maintenance programmes, which could perform the role of automatic consumption stabilisers. Indeed, few countries outside the most developed among middle-income countries are in a position to implement counter-cyclical fiscal policy. Social policies can help protect the more vulnerable groups in the population from the adverse effects of the economic downturn; and the recently established and expanded social assistance programmes become a key instrument in protecting poor and poorest households.

The spread of social assistance prior to the onset of the financial crisis suggests that developing countries that have introduced large-scale social assistance programmes are now in a better position to address the effects of the crisis, and to sustain poverty and vulnerability reduction. Indeed, preliminary evidence on policy responses to the earlier food price crisis and the later financial crisis from a range of countries demonstrates the effectiveness of social assistance programmes. In Mexico, the two frontline poverty reduction programmes, *Oportunidades* and *Apoyo Alimentario*, implemented a rise in the value of the benefits provided as a means of addressing the rise in food prices. These two programmes combined reach around a quarter of the population of Mexico in greatest need. In Jamaica, the initial response to the rise in food prices centred around food subsidies, which proved unsustainable and largely ineffective. As prices continued to rise, budgeted public revenues were shown to be insufficient to compensate households in full; and a large share of the subsidies went to better-off households. A more considered response by the government led to the extension of the coverage of the PATH Programme, a conditional human development transfer programme; and a rise in the value of the benefits provided. In Brazil, an important component of the policy response to the crisis has been the extension of benefits to young people (as already noted above), an accelerated registration of households applying to participate in the programme, and a rise in the benefit levels in line with an updated poverty line benchmark. These examples demonstrate that where social assistance programmes are in place, they can be expanded in a short time to address the impact of the crisis, and reach the households most affected. Well-designed social assistance programmes have the capacity to identify households in acute need, tried-and-tested procedures for application and assessment, and delivery capacity.

In those countries where large-scale social assistance programmes are in place, it makes sense to design a comprehensive response to the crisis around them. However, it is important to pose the question of whether the crisis, because of its potential scale and duration, might require alternative responses. In previous crises, governments have relied to an extent on emergency safety nets: public works such as Argentina's *Unemployed Heads of Household Programme*;[6] price subsidies to essential goods in Indonesia and Mexico; and social funds. Labour-intensive public works have the advantage that they can be implemented in a short time, and provide support for badly affected areas. They can also be scaled down in the recovery phase. Price subsidies, on the other hand, tend to be fairly indiscriminate as regards the population reached, and are hard to scale down in the recovery phase. However, for those countries with stronger and more effective social assistance programmes in place, it is important to avoid returning to an emergency response to the crisis, which proved ineffective in the past and took considerable time and resources to scale down in the recovery.

The uncertainties surrounding economic and financial crises usually make it difficult for national governments to design appropriate responses. In the fog generated by volatile conditions, the 'politics of insecurity' often leads to short-term responses, which favour those groups with the strongest voice. It is often the case that emergency responses to the crisis turn out to be dysfunctional in the medium term, but it takes considerable time and political capital to change course. In the context of Latin America and East Asian countries, short-term emergency safety nets often proved ineffective in the past, and countries that took the opportunity to set in place long-term social policy institutions are now in a better position to address the adverse impact of the new crisis. Korea's overhaul of its social protection system in response to the 1997 crisis is a case in point (Kwon, 2003), but see also Kwon and Holliday (2006) and Lee-Gong (this volume). The appropriate response to the crisis lies in developing and strengthening institutions that can address current problems and can mitigate the effects of both current and future crises.

It is also important to remain focused on poverty and vulnerability reduction, especially as the demand for public programmes to address the needs of other groups in the population increases. The crisis will inevitably generate poverty and increase vulnerability among groups that were not in poverty prior to the crisis – the 'new' poor, including workers recently unemployed, traders whose small businesses collapse and ancillary workers facing falling demand for their services. Addressing the needs for support among the 'new' poor should not be done at the expense of support for the 'old' poor, those in poverty before the crisis. Reliance on poverty headcount measures in determining policy responses can be problematic if they are not supplemented with measures of the depth and severity of poverty. One-sided reliance on the poverty headcount rate often focuses policy on the 'new' poor at the expense of the 'old' poor. Policy makers concerned to reduce headline poverty figures have incentives to focus policies on groups close to the poverty line. Attention to the depth and severity of poverty in addition to the poverty headcount rate would provide policy makers with more comprehensive tools to inform policy.[7] The beneficiary selection methods used by emerging social assistance programmes in many developing countries are based on rankings of households in poverty, from extreme poor to moderately poor. They have proved more effective in securing support among voters than alternative selection based on a simple poor/non-poor distinction.

An important feature of the emergence of social assistance programmes in Latin America has been their focus on extreme and persistent poverty, especially persistent intergenerational poverty. The design of an important number of programmes aims to combine interventions that reduce 'current' poverty and 'future' poverty; for example by improving the nutrition, schooling and health status of children. The need to balance these objectives acquires even greater importance in the context of the post-2007 crisis. The impact of a crisis is most severe and enduring where it undermines the productive capacity and resilience of those affected. Short-term responses to financial distress, such as taking children out of school, 'economising' on healthcare or 'fire-sales' of assets, are most likely to delay recovery and generate poverty persistence. Strengthening the long-term productive capacity of households in poverty, on the other hand, is an essential component of an effective response to the crisis in developing countries. Improvements in nutrition and schooling of children can lead to long-term exit from poverty. Interventions that enable asset accumulation and protection can improve economic inclusion. Most importantly, interventions that enable households to deploy their resources in the most effective manner are essential to long-term exit from poverty. Central to this objective are interventions that reduce and eliminate gender disparities within the household, strengthen women's voice and influence over households' decisions, and enhance the opportunities and status of girls.

In low-income countries lacking existing social assistance programmes, the response to the crisis will necessarily have to be adapted to the specific conditions of the country. In countries where pilot social transfer programmes are in place, it will be necessary to consider whether they can be scaled up sustainably. In Kenya and Zambia, for example, initiatives are under way to bring forward planned programme expansion. In low-income countries with agreed National Social Protection Strategies and plans to introduce social assistance programmes, international aid, in the form of budget support, sector-wide aid programmes or cash on delivery, could facilitate implementation (World Bank, 2009b).

While social assistance has an important role to play in developing an effective response to the crisis, it is important to take account of the impact of the crisis on government revenues, which in turn may restrict the resources available to address the impact of the crisis, especially in low-income countries. It is likely that pressure on available resources will coincide with a rise in unemployment and with greater vulnerability. The reach of social assistance programmes in developing countries is limited by budgetary restrictions, and spending on social assistance remains inadequate in the majority of countries in the South. The capacity of social assistance to address the social impact of the crisis is therefore limited.

In sum, it is important that policy responses to the crisis are sensitive to a range of poverty measures, and take account of the poverty gap and poverty gap squared measures in addition to the poverty headcount. By focusing on the poverty gap and poverty gap squared measures, policy remains centred on the objective of reducing poverty depth and intensity. Multidimensional indicators of deprivation are also an important input for policy design. There are no gains in refocusing programmes on the 'new' poor at the expense of the 'old' poor, nor in refocusing the mix of programmes on current poverty at the expense of a focus on reducing future poverty. It is therefore important to remain focused on effective policies that address extreme poverty and vulnerability and to strengthen and develop existing social assistance programmes that have been shown to be effective. In low-income countries, the challenge is to bring forward a planned introduction or expansion of social transfer programmes.

Social assistance in a post-crisis world

What are the challenges for the post-crisis world? The main challenge is to establish long-term institutions to eradicate poverty and vulnerability. In the past, responses to crises in developing countries often led to emergency and temporary programmes, which fell away quickly after the crisis, and did little to help develop institutions capable of responding effectively to the next crisis. Decades of emergency food aid in Sub-Saharan Africa has done little to help build effective food protection institutions there. In middle-income countries in Latin America, social funds introduced in the 1980s to address previous crises did little to strengthen the capacity of public agencies to address future ones. While emergency responses might well prove necessary to address acute and unexpected crises, strong social assistance and insurance institutions are required to help prevent and reduce the impact of crisis on poor and vulnerable groups in developing countries. This is the main lesson emerging from previous crises, but one that has not always been heeded by policy makers in the South. Social assistance programmes will be most effective in addressing poverty and vulnerability arising from a crisis if they are in place before a crisis occurs (Ravallion, 2008). In the context of the current stage of development of social assistance programmes in the South, a key challenge for the post-crisis world is to strengthen the institutionalisation of social assistance.

In low-income countries, institutionalising social assistance programmes involves introducing them in countries that lack them, and extending their coverage in countries that have limited provision. It involves providing the necessary financing so that developing countries lacking resources could overcome the large set-up costs involved in introducing new programmes. Improving institutionalisation involves strengthening public delivery capacity, and encouraging South-to-South cooperation. In those countries where pilot programmes are in place, the challenge is to ensure successful pilots are scaled up.

In middle-income countries, the issue is how to integrate the emerging social assistance programmes within their social protection institutions. The emergence and evolution of social assistance shows considerable diversity across middle-income developing countries, but few of them have successfully managed to integrate, from the outset, social assistance programmes within their social protection systems.[8] In the context of Latin American countries, social insurance institutions pre-dated the recent expansion of social assistance. It is interesting to examine the interrelation between social insurance institutions and the emerging social assistance programmes in the context of this evolution of social protection institutions (Barrientos and Santibañez, 2009a). Due to the segmented nature of social insurance institutions in the region, covering formal sector workers only, a number of governments in the region are aiming to shift public subsidies from social insurance to social assistance. The resulting increase in resources to support social assistance, although so far limited in scale, implies a different dynamic in the linkages between social insurance and social assistance in the region.

Until recently, social assistance had a residual role within social protection in most countries in the South. Aside from the rebalancing of public subsidies in some countries referred to above, the recent expansion of social assistance programmes in Latin America and elsewhere has taken place without direct reference to existing social insurance programmes. In some countries with well-developed social insurance institutions, there has been concern over whether social assistance programmes reduce the incentives for workers to contribute to social insurance plans.[9] But in the majority of countries in the South, social assistance programmes have no counterpart in social insurance, and in the main they reach workers in informal employment. The challenges involved in improving the coordination of human development transfer programmes with social insurance are to do with generating ladders so that beneficiaries can be integrated where possible into employment covered by social insurance. For example, the decision by the Mexican government to extend to beneficiaries of *Oportunidades* the financial incentives offered to workers in formal employment to contribute to pension plans (equivalent to a government contribution to workers' pension plans) demonstrates the kind of policies that could achieve this objective (Secretaría de Desarrollo Social, 2003). It could have the effect of providing ladders into covered employment for beneficiaries of social assistance, in addition to lifting differentials in the treatment of workers in formal and informal employment.

The situation is more complex in the case of non-contributory pensions, mainly because counterparts exist within social insurance institutions. Integration here requires that consideration is directed to the design of contributory and non-contributory pension programmes in order to enhance incentives for workers to contribute to social insurance schemes. In Latin American countries, at least, the development of non-contributory pension programmes has been largely motivated by the low coverage of social insurance schemes in many countries in the region. The integration of social assistance schemes with social insurance schemes in ensuring old-age income security is an urgent issue in the post-crisis period for middle-income countries.

Overall, discussion of the integration of social assistance and social insurance within broad-based social protection systems in developing countries must pay attention to the relative size and composition of public subsidies to social insurance and social assistance. Comparing a measure of net public subsidies[10] to social insurance and public subsidies to social assistance for selected countries in Latin America demonstrates the regressive impact of government subsidies. Average net public subsidies for social insurance beneficiaries in Mexico in 2002 were US$65, while average public subsidies to social assistance beneficiaries amounted to only US$9.6. Social insurance in Mexico covered 2% of the bottom quintile of the population, while social assistance covered 38% (Lindert et al, 2005).

In the context of the crisis, social assistance will be most effective in combination with other social policies, and labour market policy in particular. In the context of Latin America, labour earnings, and especially the minimum wage, have a direct and strong impact on poverty. The marked downward trend in poverty headcount in Latin America after 2002 reflects, to an important extent, parallel increases in the level of the minimum wage. However, data for 2008 show that this upward trend was slowing down. According to ECLAC (2008), the real minimum wage grew by 3.7% in 2008 compared with 5.0%

in 2007. Studies for Brazil show that the minimum wage acts as a benchmark for wage setting in the informal sector; this is usually referred to as a 'lighthouse' effect. Furthermore, in Brazil, and other countries, changes in the level of the minimum wage are also important because they constitute a benchmark for the level of the benefits provided by social assistance programmes (Saboia, 2009). In Brazil, for example, the benefits provided by the non-contributory pension programmes, as well as the minimum pension benefit provided by the social insurance programmes, are benchmarked to the minimum wage. The upgrading of the minimum wage, which serves to show the close interconnection that exists between social assistance and labour market policy, has enhanced the effectiveness of social assistance programmes in Brazil. There are other areas where this connection can be observed directly, as in policies that improve schooling and the transition from school to work among households in poverty. Social assistance will be stronger in the post-crisis world if combined with appropriate labour market policy.

Conclusion

This chapter has discussed the recent expansion of social assistance in developing countries, considered its role in the current global crisis and the challenges for the future. The crisis is widely expected to lead to economic slowdown, with implications for the reduction of poverty and vulnerability in the South. The rapid emergence of large-scale social assistance programmes in developing countries has been described as a 'quiet revolution'. There is considerable diversity in the design and scope of social protection programmes in the South, which depart in important ways from the income maintenance model of European countries. Some programmes provide income transfers on their own, other programmes combine income transfers with service access and utilisation and a few programmes adopt a multidimensional approach to poverty reduction. The crisis will provide a stern test of social assistance programmes in the South.

The experience from previous crises suggests that social policy making in the midst of a crisis often does not lead to effective and longlasting institutions to address poverty and vulnerability. The emergence of social assistance programmes in developing countries demonstrates that it is important to focus on programmes that address 'current' and 'future' poverty through strengthening the economic and social inclusion of households in poverty. Emergency safety nets might be a necessity in certain contexts, but often prove ineffective beyond the short term. Social policy responses to the crisis will need to be articulated around existing social assistance programmes and with a firm focus on the post-crisis world. Among low-income countries, the challenge is to provide a stronger institutional basis for incipient social assistance programmes. In middle income countries, the main issue is to improve the integration of social assistance with social protection, including social insurance and labour market policies, and with broader social policy.

It will be important to extract what lessons may emerge from this crisis. Regrettably, it is unlikely that this crisis will be the last one to be experienced by developing countries. The recovery phase should provide us with an opportunity to continue to build the institutions of social assistance needed for the permanent eradication of poverty.

Notes

[1] PROGRESA, or *Programa de Educación, Salud y Alimentación*, was introduced in rural Mexico in 1997 with the objective of breaking the intergenerational persistence of poverty. In 2002, it was extended to urban areas and renamed *Oportunidades*.

[2] *Bolsa Escola* is a programme providing transfers to households in poverty with children of school age in Brazil. In 2003, it was renamed *Bolsa Familia* and integrated *Bolsa Escola* and other social assistance programmes.

[3] Admittedly, these are countries with large populations but there is now widespread coverage in many smaller African, Asian, Caribbean and Latin American countries. Information on the programmes discussed in this chapter, and references to relevant literature, are available from the Social Assistance in Developing Countries database, version 5 (Barrientos et al, 2010), which is available at www.manchester.ac.uk/bwpi

[4] Levy (2008) is an exception.

[5] See the resources section at the Initiative for Policy Dialogue website: www0.gsb.columbia.edu/ipd/

[6] This was introduced in Argentina in response to the acute financial crisis in 2000/01, providing transfers to unemployed heads of households through municipalities and community organisations. At its peak, it reached around two million households (Golbert, 2004; World Bank, 2009a).

[7] The poverty headcount rate measures the proportion of the population below the poverty line; it does not tell us much about the depth and intensity of poverty. The poverty gap measures the extent of the shortfall in the income/consumption of poor households from the poverty line. It provides information on the depth of poverty. The poverty gap square weighs the poverty gap by the poverty gap itself, putting more emphasis on the poorest. It captures the intensity of poverty.

[8] See note 9 below.

[9] In Brazil, for example, the qualifying age for social assistance pensions used to be 67 years, whereas the qualifying age for social insurance pensions was 65, or earlier. The differential was justified in terms of strengthening incentives for contribution to social insurance. Over time, the qualifying age has been equalised.

[10] This measure excludes the social insurance contributions of government as employer and adjusts for patterns of saving and dis-saving of contributors to pay-as-you-go social insurance schemes.

SEVEN

South Korea after the 1997 economic crisis: a 'paradigm shift'?

Eunna Lee-Gong

Introduction

The modern Western welfare state has its roots in the notion of an entitlement deriving from the citizenship model as expounded by T.H. Marshall (1950). What thereby becomes a social right to welfare has deeply influenced the development of welfare systems in Western countries, although different countries have established different national standards of social rights and these have been expressed through different programmes (Marshall, 1950; Esping-Andersen, 1990). However, faced with recurrent economic crises and the resultant 'fiscal crisis of the state' (O'Connor, 1973; Gough, 2000), Western welfare states have, in general, shifted from concern with the amelioration of market inequalities, to a concern with the marketisation of public services and the individualisation of social risk. Welfare systems based on the idea of social rights are also moving away from welfare and towards 'welfare-to-work' (workfare) systems for those able to work, by shifting emphasis from rights to duties and by introducing more conditions and means testing on previously universally guaranteed welfare schemes. For example, the recent United Kingdom (UK) government's welfare reform White Paper, entitled *21st Century Welfare* (DWP, 2010), again confirms a direction towards workfare and concomitant enhanced individual responsibility: 'Work and personal responsibility must be at the heart of the new benefits system. This should provide support backed up by a strong system of conditionality that makes clear what is expected of claimants in return for the support they receive' (DWP, 2010, Chapter 1).

While Western welfare states, under the pressure of a globalised neoliberal economic order, are moving towards workfare systems characterised by the retrenchment of social rights, the South Korean welfare system, called the National Basic Livelihood Security System (NBLSS), already incorporated a workfare element as early as the late 1990s as a response to the effects of the 1997 Asian economic crisis (AEC). However, the establishment of workfare in South Korea appears to represent a case for neither the 'shrinking welfare state' under globalisation nor the shifting emphasis from rights to duties that currently dominates Western welfare state thinking. Rather than substantiating the expectation that welfare systems retrench in the wake of economic crises and the resultant economic restructuring that generally follows, the AEC and the resultant economic restructuring demanded by the International Monetary Fund (IMF) and the World Bank (WB) in the case of South Korea, was actually accompanied by an expansion of the welfare system in significant ways. This has been referred to as the 'paradox' of the South Korean case (Shin, 2000). Contrary to a shift from social right to social responsibility, the NBLSS was actually based on a shifting emphasis from individual responsibility to individual right, being the product of the enactment of the first South Korean law that legally guaranteed the social right to welfare provision. The move was regarded as marking a 'paradigm shift from the last 40 years' simplistic livelihood protection based on handouts, to a welfare system with enhanced responsibility of the state for the low-income group' (MoHW, no date).

While an economic crisis presents challenges and costs to welfare systems, it also presents a number of important opportunities for future social policy (see Farnsworth and Irving, this volume). In the case of South Korea, it was the AEC of 1997 that profoundly challenged its welfare system and presented an opportunity for a 'paradigm shift'. However, while the economic crisis exposed and challenged the limits of the welfare system prior to the crisis, it cannot be said that the 1997 economic crisis alone brought about the major welfare policy shift in South Korea. To understand the paradoxical move and the 'paradigm shift' in South Korea after the crisis, and to be able to draw conclusions as to its appropriateness as a means of responding to crisis, it is necessary to examine the sociopolitical conditions on which the South Korean workfare system was and is based. Through such an analysis, it is possible to see whether it represents a coherent, systematic, effective response or a contingent and necessary compromise.

This chapter first reviews the development of the welfare system in South Korea prior to the AEC by highlighting key ideas that made it possible to maintain minimal state welfare provision in the absence of guaranteed social rights. It goes on to examine economic and social conditions after the AEC, as well as the political change marked by the election of Kim Dae Jung as President in 1997 as a background to the 'paradigm shift', and the significant expansion of welfare systems, including the establishment of the NBLSS in 1999. In the context of the impact of labour market reforms after the AEC, the chapter goes on to show that even with the shift, the current welfare system has failed to mitigate the impact of neoliberal economic restructuring on many of those in need. By drawing attention to an internal factor, such as the demands of people made through democratic participation, and an external factor of global economic crisis, it opens up discussions on whether the direction towards enhanced individual responsibility can be said to be a way forward in an era of economic crisis.

Welfare systems before the Asian economic crisis

From the end of the Korean War in 1953 and until the AEC in 1997, South Korea had achieved rapid economic development, from being one of the poorest countries in the world in the 1950s to becoming a member of the Organisation for Economic Co-operation and Development (OECD) in the 1990s. Gross National Product (GNP) per capita had increased from US$82 in 1961, to US$10,610 in 1996, and the unemployment rate remained under 4% from the 1970s up until 1997, with full employment status being achieved in the early 1990s (see Table 7.1).

Over the four decades, South Korea had also established four major social insurance systems as well as a social assistance system called the Livelihood Protection System. However, what the AEC revealed was that the existing welfare systems, both contribution based and tax based, did not provide the necessary protection to those in need. This failure was largely due to the way social policy was viewed and developed in South Korea, especially under the military regimes of Park Chung Hee (1961-79) and Chun Doo Hwan (1980-87).

Table 7.1: South Korea major economic indicators, 1961-95

Economic indicator	Year			
	1961	**1976**	**1986**	**1995**
GNP per capita (US$)	82	650	2,023	10,076
Real GDP growth (%)	4.1	7.9	7.4	9.4
Unemployment rate (%)	8.2	3.9	3.8	1.8

Note: Real GDP growth is the average annual growth rate for the periods: 1954-61, 1962-76, 1977-86 and 1987-95.

Sources: Bank of Korea (2007); KNSO, cited in Kim and Son (2004, p 134)

Throughout the period of rapid economic growth, social policy in South Korea was viewed as an instrument for economic policy (Goodman and White, 1998). For example, the National Health Insurance System, introduced in 1963, only covered industrial workers in large firms. The National Pension Scheme, introduced in 1973, was also seen as an effective instrument to mobilise capital for economic development, rather than as a measure for social protection (Kwon, 2003; Rieger and Leibfried, 2003). The Employment Insurance Programme, introduced in 1995, was seen as a way to deal with problems relating to labour market flexibilisation that the government was pursuing under the slogan of 'globalisation'. Therefore, the Employment Insurance Programme was not designed to provide income support to the unemployed but to create a flexible labour force, focusing on the skills development of workers (Chung, 2001).

Social policy in South Korea was also used as a tool to gain political legitimacy and ease social unrest (Kwon, 2003). The main concern of the first South Korean government after the end of Korean War in 1953 was to gain political legitimacy. Therefore, the first beneficiaries of social assistance were powerful social groups such as the police and war veterans rather than the poor (Kim, 2008). Similarly, Park Chung Hee, who took power by a coup d'état in 1961, used the welfare agenda to legitimate the military regime rather than to meet the needs or demands of people (Holliday, 2005) Military personnel, civil servants and teachers, in addition to workers in large firms, were the first groups to be covered by the pension scheme and to be provided with health insurance. Chun Doo Hwan, who took power by coup d'état in 1980, also considered the welfare agenda as an effective instrument to reinforce the regime's legitimacy and ease social discontent (Kim, 2008). The first welfare provisions for older people and disabled people were introduced in 1981. In the same year, the coverage of National Health Insurance was extended to include workers at firms with more than 100 employees. During the 1990s, the government actively embraced neoliberal economic policy, including market liberalisation, joining the World Trade Organization (WTO) in 1995. However, this move was faced with nationwide resistance. As a way to ease the emerging social unrest, especially among those most likely to be affected by the WTO agreement, such as farmers, the National Pension Scheme was extended in 1995 to cover those living in rural areas.

Being shaped by economic and political concerns rather than the needs of people, the establishment and expansion of the welfare system was carried out despite a lack of any real financial commitment to welfare as a principle (Shin, 2000). As such, in reality the state played a minimal role in welfare provision, with the greater burden of providing welfare being placed within the private sector, mainly on the family (Goodman and Peng, 1996). Relying on a principle of the 'family as the best safety net' (Lee, 2005), and by promoting self-reliance and the avoidance of dependency on the state, public social expenditure in South Korea until 1997 was less than 4% of GDP (Gross Domestic Product). The financial commitment of the South Korean government shows a stark difference compared to that of Western welfare states such as Germany and the UK (see Table 7.2).

The precedence of economic policy and the emphasis on self-reliance and the avoidance of dependency on the state go a long way towards explaining the minimal public assistance available prior to the AEC. The Livelihood Protection Act that established the Livelihood Protection System was introduced in the early 1960s. However, not surprisingly, public assistance had strict means-testing criteria and the actual benefits available were minimal. People aged between 18 and 65, unless disabled or pregnant, were not eligible as they were automatically regarded as being able to work, regardless of their actual ability to work or severity of poverty. People aged under 18 or 65 and over were expected to be either without a responsible family member who could shoulder the burden of their welfare, or with a responsible family member who was unable to work, in order to qualify for assistance. The scope of what constituted a 'responsible family member' was so broad that a 66-year-old woman, for example, was ineligible if she had any one of the following family members: husband, children, children's spouse, grandchildren, grandchildren's spouse, brothers and sisters living together. Furthermore, the level of cash benefits made available to an individual recipient was set to half the official poverty line (Kwon, 2003). This official poverty line, based on the notion of absolute poverty, was largely determined administratively and according to the budget allocated so that, in effect, people on benefits received whatever was allocated by the government irrespective of their actual needs.

Table 7.2: Public social expenditure in South Korea, the UK and Germany (% of GDP)

Country	Year										
	1990	1991	1992	1993	1994	1995	1996	1997	1998	1999	2000
South Korea	2.9	2.8	3.1	3.1	3.1	3.3	3.5	3.8	5.2	6.3	5.0
UK	17.0	18.4	20.2	20.8	20.4	20.2	19.9	19.0	19.4	19.1	19.2
Germany	22.3	23.4	25.3	26.0	26.0	26.5	27.1	26.4	26.3	26.3	26.2

Source: OECD Social Expenditure Database

In essence, welfare benefits before the economic crisis were based on the notion of charity rather than either on the concept of a social right or on an individual's actual need. As a result, only 0.8% of the population was receiving livelihood benefits under the Livelihood Protection System in 1997 (MoHW, 1997). Overall, the biggest shortcoming of the South Korean welfare system, resulting from the way it had developed, was the exclusion of the most vulnerable from necessary protection (Kwon, 2009), a weakness painfully revealed during the economic crisis through the suffering of vulnerable groups.

The economic crisis: challenges and opportunities

The AEC in 1997 brought unprecedented economic and social problems across South Korean society, the magnitude of which went far beyond what can be captured by numbers. The biggest problem caused by the crisis was a sharp increase in the unemployment rate and the fact that those affected found themselves without social protection. Based on the Structural Adjustment Programmes imposed by the IMF and WB, South Korea went through a large scale economic restructuring process during 1998-99, which included corporate restructuring and the flexibilisation of the labour market. Before the economic crisis, male full-time lifelong employment in the formal sector was the norm, with women more likely to have part-time and temporary work. However, in 1998, a new labour law was passed, allowing companies to lay off their workforce. As was seen in Table 7.1, South Korea had apparently achieved full employment status with high economic growth by 1995. However, after the economic crisis, unemployment had nearly tripled by 1998. Although the unemployment rate calculated by the Korean National Statistics Office has been much criticised for not reflecting the reality of the situation, the figures in Table 7.3 show the severity of the negative effect of the 1997 crisis on employment, even compared to those of the current economic crisis.

The South Korean welfare system was not able to provide necessary protection in the face of rising unemployment, as it had developed minimal welfare provision premised on the notion of full employment and self-reliance. Employment Insurance, implemented in 1995, was

Table 7.3: Unemployment rate in South Korea, 1997-2009 (%)

Year	1997	1998	1999	2000	2001	2002	2003	2004	2005	2006	2007	2008	2009
%	2.6	7.0	6.3	4.1	4.0	3.3	3.6	3.7	3.7	3.5	3.2	3.2	3.6

Source: KNSO, http://kostat.go.kr/

too new to provide any meaningful protection (Ramesh, 2009) and the public assistance system automatically excluded people aged between 18 and 65, providing no welfare benefits to the unemployed. Therefore, the burden of coping with hardships was left entirely with individuals and their families through their incomes and savings.

Increases in unemployment and underemployment following the economic crisis all contributed to a reduction in individual and household income. However, during 1997-98, the lowest income group suffered the highest decrease, with a 17.2% fall in real income compared to previous years, and the highest income group experienced the lowest decrease, with only a 0.3% fall (Choi and Chung, 2002, p 8). In addition to higher vulnerability to unemployment, a reduction in real wages, accompanied by the near absence of any government welfare provision to cushion the loss, contributed substantially to the increase in the level of poverty in South Korea after the economic crisis. As sharp as the increase in unemployment rate, absolute poverty rose from 3.9% in 1997 to 9.4% in 1999 (MGHA et al, 2005).

The economic crisis was also accompanied by various social problems. Choi and Chung (2002) found, for example, that cases of divorce related to economic difficulties increased after the economic crisis, and the emergence of a particular type of suicide, given the name 'IMF suicide', was attributed to the sudden drop in socioeconomic status experienced by those becoming unemployed. This sometimes manifested itself in a form of collective 'familial' suicide, explained through a mix of Confucian culture and the lack of state welfare provision (Lee-Gong, 2010). Where there had been hardly any homeless people on the streets before 1997, the number of homeless people, for example in Seoul, increased to some 5,000 in 1998 (Joo, 2001, cited in Shin, 2003, p 123).

Against this backdrop of crisis, the South Korean ideal of 'economic growth as the best welfare policy, and the family as the best safety net' was no longer feasible or acceptable. The economic crisis, and the hardship it placed on individuals and their families, focused people's attention on the role of the state with regard to welfare provision and brought about growing social demands for such provision. A timely survey on Korean attitudes towards the role of the state regarding individual welfare showed that after the economic crisis some 83% of respondents considered the state as responsible for individual welfare, compared to a figure of 49% prior to the crisis (Shin and Rose, 1997, 1998).

The economic and social impacts of the crisis were also registered in the political realm, with the first legitimate transfer of political power coming about in the election to President of the long-time opposition leader Kim Dae Jung in December 1997. The immediate task of this new government was to carry out the structural adjustments required by the IMF/WB, while at the same time dealing with economic and social problems caused by the AEC. However, the new ruling party did not have a majority in Parliament until the end of 1998. As a way to mobilise the support and social consensus necessary to carry out its proposed neoliberal reform policy, a Tripartite Committee of government, business and labour was formed in January 1998 in which the Korean Confederation of Trade Unions (KCTU) also participated. From the government side, the participation of the KCTU was vital for successful labour market reform. When the previous government, before the onset of the AEC, bowed to business sector pressure to pass a labour law to make the labour market more flexible, the KCTU staged a historic general strike and forced the government to repeal the law in early 1997. From the KCTU side, which incidentally at that time had no legal status, the participation in the Tripartite Committee was an opportunity to enhance its status, and the status of labour rights in general, as well as influence the direction of the reform. Based on negotiations through the Tripartite Committee, the new government had to navigate a political landscape of conflicting demands and interests. On the one hand, the government was under pressure from the IMF/WB and concerted lobbies from the business sector to initiate labour market flexibilisation measures, resulting in the aforementioned 1998 labour law reform. On the other hand, it was forced to moderate this flexibilisation in response to labour demands, as well as to strengthen labour rights, including legalisation of the government employees union, and expand the welfare system to cushion the negative impacts of the AEC on those affected both in the labour market and outside of it.

The welfare system reform in South Korea did not face an outright objection from the IMF/WB. The initial conditionalities of the loan made by the IMF in December 1997 was a standard prescription that it had applied in Latin America and Eastern Europe, including tight monetary and fiscal policy, raising interest rates and maintaining a budget surplus. However, the IMF's application of its ready-made 'one-size-fits-all' prescription for South Korea that paid no regard to the historic development of capitalism in South Korea was much criticised (Chang, 1998; Shin and Chang, 2005). Within a month of the initial bailout, the IMF backtracked from its initial conditionalities, admitting the seriousness of the credit crunch that its policies were causing (Chang, 1998). By mid-January, the inflation rate target and the monetary growth target were revised upwards. The IMF also withdrew from its insistence on a budget surplus and agreed to increase government spending, mainly to provide a safety net for the unemployed. The WB also took into account the need to provide social safety nets to cushion the impact of the restructuring requirements in its first (March 1998) and second (October 1998) Structural Adjustment Loans.

While the IMF/WB promoted targeted social safety nets, South Korea reformed its welfare system in a much more comprehensive way. Behind such a comprehensive reform was the active participation of bodies with an interest in welfare reforms that had been allowed to grow up under the Kim Dae Jung government. Under the previous military regimes, and even during the democratisation period of the late 1980s and early 1990s, elite bureaucrats dominated welfare policy making, exercising a top-down implementation approach. However, under the presidency of Kim Dae Jung, trades unions, including the KCTU, participated in the Tripartite Committee and played a significant role in building consensus for welfare reform at the earlier stages of the AEC. The political environment created by the election of Kim Dae Jung also presented a window of opportunity for progressive civil society groups to also channel their welfare agendas. For example, during the AEC a coalition of civic groups came together under the coordination of the People's Coalition for Participatory Democracy. This alliance successfully lobbied Members of Parliament (MPs) to propose a Bill to establish the NBLSS (Kwon, 2003).

Overall, in the wake of the AEC, the Kim Dae Jung government established three pillars of government: market economy, democracy and productive welfare. Under the pillar of market economy, labour market flexibilisation was accelerated, while under the pillar of democracy the participation of stakeholders was enhanced. The 'productive welfare' model needs to be considered against the backdrop of this process of political change and balance. The aim under this pillar was to develop a welfare system that nurtures both growth and the equitable distribution of wealth, recognising social welfare as a basic human right, while at the same time promoting an active policy of welfare through work.

In light of this political and social change, a significant extension of the social security system took place; the 'paradox' of the South Korean case (Shin, 2000). The Employment Insurance Programme, established in 1995, was largely expanded in 1998 to deal with the increases in unemployment. The coverage was extended to firms with more than 10 employees in January 1998; to firms with more than five employees in March 1998; and to all firms with at least one employee in October 1998. The qualifying condition for Unemployment Benefit was also lowered, from a minimum 12-month contribution out of an

18-month base period, to a six-month contribution out of a 12-month base period. By articulating social solidarity and linking welfare as a human rights issue, the Kim Dae Jung government also merged what were separate health insurance schemes under a single health insurance scheme established through the National Health Insurance Act 1999. This new scheme was regarded as more inclusive and redistributive than the previous schemes. It also expanded pension coverage to the urban self-employed in April 1999. In addition to the achievement of universal coverage of National Health Insurance in 1989, the Employment Insurance Programme and National Pension Scheme achieved universal coverage of the population by 1999.

Where the previous public assistance system had failed to offer any meaningful livelihood protection, the new government initiated the Public Work Programmes to provide income support for the poor. Those unemployed but excluded from the Employment Insurance Programme could also participate in the programmes. The first round of a three-month temporary work programme started in 1998 and ended in 2002, having provided temporary income support to some 500,000 people (*The SBS News*, 2009). In line with the productive welfare model, the Kim Dae Jung government eventually established the NBLSS as a means of guaranteeing a minimum living standard for the poor. The introduction of the NBLSS is often referred to as the flagship of the social policy reforms of the Kim Dae Jung government because the founding National Basic Livelihood Security Act 1999, for the first time in South Korea, recognised the social right of every citizen to a decent living, and the state's responsibility for guaranteeing this right. The Act was interpreted to mean that 'social protection has become an integral social policy goal in Korea' (Kwon, 2003, p 69).

The impacts of the reforms after the AEC

The South Korean economy recovered rapidly from 1999, with a growth rate of 9.5% in 1999 and 8.5% in 2000. Economic growth averaged approximately 5.65 per annum between 1999 and 2007.[1] Unemployment decreased to 4.1% in 2000 and has since maintained a level below 4% (see Table 7.3). In 2001, the government announced that South Korea 'overcame the financial crisis rapidly and established a solid basis for a next leap thanks to successful implementation of structural reforms' (Ministry of Finance and Economy, cited in Shin and Chang, 2005, p 410).

However, problems created by the economic structural reforms implemented by the Kim Dae Jung government were only to unfold under the Roh Moo Hyun government (2003-07). In particular, the labour market flexibilisation policy that was pursued under the stewardship of the IMF/WB brought about a fundamental change in the labour market. The biggest change resulting from the neoliberal labour market policy has been labour market 'dualism', which has led to a rapid increase in non-regular workers, which include temporary and daily workers, workers on fixed-term and part-time contracts, dispatched workers, temporary agency workers, independent contractors, on-call workers and home-based workers. The number of non-regular workers increased from 7,370,000 in 2001 to 8,610,000 in 2007, making up 54.2% of the workforce (Kim, 2007). The largest share of non-regular employment is temporary workers, whose share of employment increased from 16.6% in 2001 to 28% in 2007, the second highest among the OECD countries (OECD, 2010f). According to an OECD survey, firms, particularly small- and medium-sized enterprises, have hired more non-regular workers, mainly in order to reduce labour costs and to increase employment flexibility (OECD, 2007). While regular workers in a large firm are unionised and relatively well protected from dismissal, unorganised non-regular workers do not enjoy such protection. There is also a huge income gap between regular workers and non-regular workers. In 2007, the average monthly income of a non-regular worker was 50.1% of that of a regular worker and the average hourly wage of a non-regular worker was 52.4% of that of a regular worker (Kim, 2007).

The increase of non-regular workers in the labour market and the wage gap between regular workers and non-regular workers had a serious impact on income equality. South Korea was said to have achieved rapid economic growth with a relatively good record of income equality (WB, 2004). However, income inequality in South Korea has worsened since the AEC. The ratio of income of the top 10% of households to the bottom 10% rose from 3.72 in 1997 to 4.74 in 2007 (Lee, 2009). As shown in Table 7.4, since the structural reforms of 1998-99, the Gini coefficient has never recovered to the pre-crisis level, showing a steady increase in inequality between 1997 and 2007.

With an increase in income inequality, the relative poverty rate has also increased from 9.3% in 1997 to 15.6% in 2007. In the context of the increase in poverty since the AEC, it is important to note the increase in poverty of older people in particular. According to the OECD, the 2007 relative poverty rate for older people in South Korea was nearly five times higher than the national average in 2000, while the average relative poverty rate for older people in the OECD, at 13% in 2000, was not far above the 10% average for the total population (OECD, 2007).

Table 7.4: Gini coefficient and relative poverty in South Korea (urban households/market income)

Year	1997	1998	1999	2000	2001	2002	2003	2004	2005	2006	2007
Gini index	0.268	0.295	0.303	0.286	0.299	0.298	0.295	0.301	0.304	0.313	0.324
Relative Poverty Ratio %	9.3	12.2	13.1	10.8	11.8	11.4	12.8	13.7	14.1	14.7	15.6

Source: MoHW (2009)

As a way to deal with these social problems, the Roh Moo Hyun government expanded and enhanced welfare systems in line with the welfare paradigm established by the Kim Dae Jung government. In *Vision 2030* (Vision 2030 task force, 2006), a government strategy paper published in 2006, the Roh Moo Hyun government emphasised the urgency of addressing problems, including increasing income and other inequalities, the ageing population and the need to avoid losing global competitiveness. The report called for expansions of public expenditure on social welfare from the level of 6% of GDP to 21% by 2030. Steps to include non-regular workers in the Employment Insurance Programme were taken. Mandatory participation for non-regular workers at a workplace with five or more employees was initiated in 2003, which was extended to cover non-regular workers at a workplace with one or more employees in 2006. A Bill to enhance the protection of non-regular workers passed the National Assembly in 2006 and was implemented in 2007. As a way to provide income support to older people who had not been covered by the National Pension System, the Basic Old-Age Pension Act was introduced in 2007 and implemented in 2008. The Long Term Care Insurance Act was also introduced in 2007 and implemented in 2008.

Despite further efforts to enhance welfare systems under the Roh Moo Hyun government, there are still significant shortcomings in the welfare system as it has been reformed since the AEC. The biggest shortcoming is its failure to protect non-regular workers who suffer the most in the case of economic hardship. Since the expansion of the Employment Insurance Programme in 1998, the number of people covered increased from 5.2 million in 1998 to 9.3 million in 2008 (Yun et al, 2009). However, this figure only represents 41% of total employed people, excluding the majority of self-employed, daily and temporary workers from protection. As currently only those with a minimum of six months' employment are eligible for Unemployment Benefit, only 0.4% of daily workers, compared to 17.6% of regular workers, could claim Unemployment Benefit between 2005 and 2008 (Lee, cited in Yun et al, 2009).

Similarly, the total number insured through the National Pension System increased from some 16 million in 2001 to 18 million in 2008. However, in the case of regional contributors, 5,025,503 people who were mostly self-employed, daily and temporary workers, were exempt from contribution in 2008, which accounted for 57% of regional contributors and 27% of the total insured (MoHW, 2009). According to a report by the National Pension Service, the main reason for seeking exemption was economic hardship due to a loss of job and income (Kim et al, 2008). There were also two million households (25% of total participant households) with overdue contributions in excess of three months in 2008 (Hwang, 2009). Between 2001 and 2008, the number of workplace insured increased from some 5.9 million to 9.4 million. However, the National Pension System has its biggest shortcoming with regard to the provision of social protection to non-regular workers. While it is a positive sign that the participation rate of non-regular workers increased from 25.7% in 2002 to 40% in 2007, the participation rate of temporary non-regular workers who compose the biggest part of non-regular workers in South Korea was only 14% in 2007 (Kim et al, 2008). It was also temporary non-regular workers in small firms who were most excluded from the pension system, with less than 5% participating in the National Pension System.

Turning to the National Health Insurance, the situation is similar: 99% of regular workers were covered in 2007. However, in the case of non-regular workers, only 47% were covered in 2007 although coverage had increased from its level of 28.8% in 2002. There were also some 1.6 million households who failed to pay their contributions for six months or more and therefore did not have access to health benefits (Byun, 2009). In addition, there is a requirement that patients should pay about 40% of medical fees, which creates a barrier for low-income families in access to health services.

While the social insurance system does not provide necessary protection to the vulnerable, the record of the new social assistance system introduced in 1999 is not impressive either. After the implementation of the National Basic Livelihood Security Act in October 2000, guaranteeing the social right to welfare for all citizens, the number of welfare recipients receiving livelihood protection increased from 0.37 million in 1996 to 1.4 million in 2001. However, the actual percentage of people protected under the NBLSS is not that large. Only 2.99% of the population was protected under the NBLSS in 2001 and the percentage had not much increased by 2006 when 3.18% received the allowance. This was largely due to strict means-testing criteria with regard to those categorised as a 'family member who is obliged to support'. Despite the 2006 relaxation of rules on who constitutes a 'family member who is obliged to support', the increase in take-up rates in 2007 was marginal, with 1,549,848 people, equivalent to 3.19% of the population receiving benefits. Even in the face of the current crisis, the number of people on the NBLSS has not much increased, with 1,529,939 people receiving benefit in 2008, which is about 2,000 fewer people than in 2007, and 1,568,533 people receiving benefit in 2009, equivalent to 3.2% of the population. According to the government's own figures, the NBLSS failed to provide welfare support for some 4.1 million poor people in 2009 (Ministry of Strategy and Finance et al, 2009).

It is also important to note that the number of 'conditional welfare recipients' who receive benefits upon the condition of work, either in the private or commercial sector or on government workfare programmes, is not large compared to the number of people working but receiving or generating insufficient income to bring them out of poverty. Based on the 2008 survey on working poor by the Korea Institute for Health and Social Affairs (KIHASA), Roh et al (2009) estimated the extent of the working poor in 2006 to amount to 2.86 million people. However, the number of NBLSS recipients with working ability was 409,645 out of a total number of NBLSS recipients of 1,549,848 in 2007 (MoHW, 2010). Among those with working ability, only 56,000 were on the government workfare programme in 2007, alongside 24,000 'near poor participants', that is to say, people whose income is between the poverty line and 120% of the poverty line. This raises a question over the effectiveness of the NBLSS as a means of assisting those poor people considered to have 'working ability'.

One of the problems with the NBLSS is its inflexible means for overcoming problems presented by real-life situations. For example, two thirds of the working poor are informal, part-time workers (Shin, cited in *The Weekly GongKam*, 2010). Their income is irregular and therefore difficult to assess. As a result, they are subject to a 'presumed income', allowed under the guidelines for implementation of the NBLSS in cases where it is difficult to ascertain the actual income of the claimant. Yet in imposing a 'presumed income', the very fact that a claimant is surviving leads welfare officials responsible for assessment to assume that the claimant in fact has an income higher than the legal minimum living expenses that would qualify them for benefit. Thus, the claimant faces a de facto exclusion from welfare protection merely by their presence. Imposing a 'presumed income' also reinforces the duty to work by setting out the minimum amount a person *should* be able to earn. Although this should set the presumed income at a reasonable and non-arbitrary level, it nonetheless bears no relationship to the claimant's actual situation.

While the NBLSS was regarded as a rights-based social assistance system, the current system is operating based on the principle of putting individual responsibility before that of the state. The consequence is that some 4.1 million poor people are left without welfare protection at a time of economic crisis. Furthermore, this individual responsibility also extends to the immediate family of a claimant; a legacy of its predecessor – the Livelihood Protection Act – and rooted in South Korean Confucian cultural values. It is said that 74.2% of poor people who applied for the NBLSS were rejected due to the family obligation element (KIHASA, cited in People's Solidarity for Participatory Democracy, 2010). There are also 1.03 million poor people whose earned income is below the poverty line but who are not receiving the NBLSS benefits (KIHSA, 2009).

Effect of the current economic crisis and other challenges

The welfare reform that followed the AEC can be seen to be incomplete, leaving a majority of non-regular workers and the older population outside the welfare system. While barriers for trade and capital movement have been removed through the structural adjustments following the AEC, South Korea was directly affected by the recent economic crisis of 2008-09, resulting in a sharp economic downturn for the country. According to Table 7.3, an increase in the level of unemployment after the current economic crisis does not seem to be significant when compared to the one after the AEC. However, this should be understood in the context of the changed characteristics of the labour market described above. While the number of unemployed, through the structural adjustments after the AEC, was easily captured in statistics, under the current crisis the main group of unemployed are self-employed, temporary/daily non-regular workers whom the unemployment statistics fail to capture. Korea's output fell by 17% at an annual rate in the fourth quarter of 2008, which is more than double the decline experienced in the OECD area (OECD, 2010f). Although South Korea has been affected severely by the current global recession, it has managed to achieve one of the fastest recoveries from the crisis, driven by its robust export performance and the largest fiscal stimulus among the OECD countries (OECD, 2010f). Behind this rapid recovery was a return to an 'economic growth first' policy under the Lee Myung Park government, which took office in

February 2008. During the election campaign in 2007, Lee Myung Park, who represented the opposition party, urged the population to escape from the 'lost decade', an attack on the previous progressive governments of Kim Dae Jung and Roh Moo Hyun, while presenting himself, with a chief executive officer background, as one who will save the economy. His view on economy and welfare was summed up in repeated comments made by him during the election campaign:'if the economy grows, so does jobs, therefore demands for welfare will be reduced' (Lee Myung Park, cited in *The Weekly Kyunghyang*, 2008). With the election of Lee Myung Park, South Korea saw the revival of the 'growth first, redistribution later' paradigm. Accordingly, Lee Myung Park's government presented a market-friendly welfare model; the so-called 'active welfare' that aimed 'to secure welfare finance and curtail welfare demand by economic growth' (Kim, 2009). The government is said to be working 'to build an effective and efficient social safety net that will speed up social integration based on growth-friendly policies for supporting market' (Byun, 2009).

However, in utilising the old economic social policy paradigm, what the new government did not foresee was the ripened democratic attitude of the population and the enhanced mobilising capacities of civil society that occurred during the 'lost decade'. In early 2008, there were extensive 'candlelight vigils' by the people to protest against the government's economic policy, including its Free Trade Agreement with the US, issues over American beef imports and increases in oil prices. The government's heavy-handed crackdowns on the candlelight vigils led to a large-scale protest against overall government policy. Faced with the protest, a Grand Canal project, one of the major elements of the government's economic policy, was withdrawn and the 'market-oriented welfare' policies were excluded from the *100 Major Political Issues of the Lee Myung Park*, a government White Paper published in October 2008 (Kim, 2009). Meanwhile, the severity of the current economic crisis experienced worst by the most vulnerable brought the issue of non-regular workers and the large shortcomings of the welfare system into the public light (*The Ohmynews*, 2009; *The Hankyoreh*, 2010). Since the onset of the current economic crisis, the response of the government has taken a somewhat Keynesian turn in its welfare policy, focusing on temporary measures, such as Emergency Income Support for the poor, and various job creation programmes, including public work programmes for the working poor, youth internships in the public sector and care work programmes. The jobs created by the government are by their very nature temporary and do not provide a solution for job insecurity and vulnerability faced by non-regular, temporary workers. The current crisis has not brought a welfare reform as comprehensive as the one emerging from the AEC. However, there has been growing debate over the shortcomings of the existing welfare system and proposals for enhancing the social protection of the vulnerable. Following growing public attention to the weaknesses of the welfare system, a Bill aiming to reduce the employment insurance contribution period of non-regular workers from the current six months to five months was also proposed in July 2010. In order to make the NBLSS better provide welfare support to the poor, in September 2010 a coalition of MPs submitted a Bill aiming to revise the National Basic Livelihood Security Act, including the relaxing of the criteria for family support and the introduction of a relative rather than absolute poverty line.

Implications of the South Korea experience

What might be concluded from the above is that the South Korean state is wrestling with conflicting conceptions and demands of what is required of the modern state and its citizens. This is analogous to the disparity between conceptions of citizenship and what it requires presently found in Western welfare states. Where in Western states, the focus is moving from the notion of citizenship as a rights status to the idea that citizenship carries within it a heavy dose of individual responsibility to society, South Korea has its own tension between, on the one hand, the cultural, traditional Confucian legacy of family obligation as a source of welfare and, on the other hand, the emerging notion of welfare as a right to be provided by the state.

In many ways, the movement towards welfare as a right reflects successive governments' utilisation of welfare as a means to gain legitimacy. In effect, the government made a rod for its own back in that when the AEC hit and the social welfare need became greater, the continuing legitimacy of the state became predicated on an appropriate welfare response. At the same time, however, the credibility of the government to outside lenders and donors, such as the WB and IMF, seemed to require austerity measures that would least favour welfare reform at this time. A similar situation arose for the government in the recent crisis.

After the AEC, the government response was to try to appease everyone at the same time. Its welfare reform extended its reach but without removing entirely the ethos of 'family first, state later', as can be witnessed in the NBLSS, while its neoliberal economic reform created incentives for business to develop more flexible labour opportunities.

In the recovery and growth period in the wake of the AEC, this model, although failing to address the needs of certain very poor groups, appeared to be a reasonably functioning and successful approach to overcoming the AEC. However, those people who were left out not only reflected the failing of the system at that time, but were also a reflection of a weakness in the response that would have greater impact should a new economic crisis arise. The reason for this is because the flexibilisation of the labour market increased greatly the number of people potentially at risk of falling out of the welfare provision through the fact that they no longer had the security that a more traditional employment structure offered. As a consequence, the recent economic crisis has left more people vulnerable, as much entitlement to welfare provision relies on one being in permanent employment, as it does in Western countries. Where those in non-permanent employment were unable to benefit from Unemployment Benefit, in a functioning welfare system another layer of social protection would kick in. However, the construction of the South Korean social welfare system, following the AEC, has been shown to have several shortcomings in its bottom-line welfare provision, the NBLSS, partially as a consequence of trying to combine what can be seen to be two polarised objectives: individual responsibility and social rights.

Confronted with the effects of the recent economic crisis, the South Korean government's response has been to tinker with the details of the NBLSS, through introducing a relative poverty line baseline to replace the absolute poverty line for example, and relaxing the criteria for family support obligation among other things. In addition, it has introduced a number of new public works programmes. At the same time, the government has retained its intention of economic reform. In effect, just as has been seen in Western countries, there is degree of vacillation between neoliberalism, on the one hand, as demanded by business and the world of finance, and a Keynesian-style welfare response being called for by the people through the democratic voice, on the other, as seen in the way the present South Korean government was recently constrained in its economic policy.

The problem that South Korea may be experiencing, and from which other countries might take heed, is that trying to achieve a balance between neoliberal economic policies, on the one hand, and social rights, on the other, may present irreconcilable tensions, which inevitably lead to weaknesses that most greatly affect those whose need is the most. Furthermore, pursuing economic growth through appeasing the global economic model further adds to the burden by creating larger groups of vulnerable people requiring social welfare in times of economic crisis when the global business model fails. This can be seen from the South Korean example. What can be learned, it would seem, is that the South Korean model suggests a need to draw back from the extremes of neoliberalism. In doing so, its opposite – extreme social need – will, as a consequence, contract. In this less dichotomous environment, where neither extreme is created, the idea of citizenship both as a rights status *and* as requiring social responsibility has more credence.

Note

[1] http://kostat.go.kr/

EIGHT

China's response to crisis: what role for social policy?

Sarah Cook and Wing Lam

Introduction

The post-2007 financial crisis devastated the health of the global economy, leaving many advanced economies on the verge of financial collapse and later, in deep recession. It overshadowed even the impacts of the 1997 Asian financial crisis. Between 2007 and 2009, world growth contracted from 5.2% to –0.6%; world trade volume also plummeted from robust growth of 7.2% to a depressive figure of –10.7% (IMF, 2010f).[1] Although not at the epicentre of the crisis, China – along with many emerging Asian economies – could not remain unscathed by the fallout of such financial failure in the West (Chhibber et al, 2009; Liu, 2009; Athukorala and Kohpaiboon, 2010). The integration of the world economic system means that the economic problems of one country or group cascade through trade, foreign investment and other transmission mechanisms into the real economies of others. Thus, the idea that China, and possibly much of Asia, was sufficiently 'decoupled' from the global economy to be insulated from the impact of crisis was soon shown to be unfounded (Dunaway, 2009, pp 19-23).

China was one of the first major economies to respond decisively to the crisis. It quickly introduced a massive fiscal stimulus package in an effort to reduce the negative impacts on the real economy – jobs, enterprises and growth. A critical dimension of this package was a range of social policy investments, including interventions aimed at boosting consumption and protecting the vulnerable. Such emphatic endorsement by the Chinese government of the use of social policy instruments in economic crisis management was unprecedented (*Xinhuanet*, 2009; Wen, 2010b), and has attracted attention both domestically and internationally (Yang and Chi, 2009; Zhang, 2009; OECD, 2010b; Tang, 2010). Its impacts and implications deserve attention.

The stimulus package came as China was already embarking on significant expansion and reform of its welfare provisions. Over recent years, China has made significant, if somewhat patchy, efforts to expand social provisions and renegotiate the shattered social contract of the 'iron rice bowl' era. Major initiatives include the establishment of a major social assistance programme (the Minimum Living Standard Guarantee or *dibao*) and an ambitious plan to achieve universal health coverage by 2020. More expansive social policy goals continue to be set and substantial investment and reform in the social security system are under way (State Council, 2010; Wen, 2010a). While significant challenges persist, there is little doubt that political and social factors play a major role in sustaining the political commitment to a social policy agenda as part of a 'focus on people's livelihood' (Zheng, 2005; Liu, 2006). The crisis and China's response to it provides a significant moment to reflect on this process of state welfare restructuring, approximately a decade after China dismantled generous state sector welfare provisions to a privileged workforce. In particular, we can examine whether the crisis has been a catalyst to expedite the process of welfare restructuring; and whether China is able to use social policies in these circumstances to lay the foundations for more sustainable and inclusive growth, based on stronger domestic demand and greater socioeconomic security for the majority of the population (Wu, 2009).

The next section briefly reviews the social policy context existing as China was hit by the crisis. This is followed by a discussion of the impacts of crisis and China's response, in particularly its social initiatives. The chapter goes on to provide a preliminary assessment of the extent to which China has been able to use its social policy response to protect the vulnerable and achieve its economic objectives. While the expansion of social provisions and central government expenditures during the crisis have been impressive, and translate into long-term commitments by the government to universal and comprehensive social security, nonetheless a number of institutional constraints need to be overcome for effective and equitable implementation at the local level.

Social policies in China: a welfare system under reconstruction

China's social security system has changed dramatically since economic liberalisation policies were initiated in the early 1980s. In the first two decades of the reform period, the government partially withdrew from the social policy domain as market mechanisms emerged and welfare services became more commodified. This process was particularly detrimental to rural populations.[2] A major impetus to wholesale reform of the social security system followed the state enterprise restructuring of the late 1990s, although this had been preceded by incremental shifts towards employment-based and contributory social insurance programmes to replace the state-sponsored, enterprise-based welfare regime of the Mao era. The promotion of 'harmonious social development' as a major objective by President Hu Jintao in 2005 served to elevate social policy on the national policy agenda. In October 2006, the Chinese government openly committed to building a universal social security system by 2020 (CPC, 2006). Numerous social initiatives have subsequently been expanded or introduced, with a growing commitment of resources evident in the context of China's response to crisis. As Table 8.1 shows, these new initiatives must be seen as part of a longer process of constructing a new welfare system. Two issues can be noted here. First, insurance-based social programmes now constitute the core of China's welfare regime; in comparison with the pre-reform arrangement, the government's direct role in social welfare provision has declined drastically, a trend that is likely to persist. Second, the commitment to expand social programmes to rural areas as a way of promoting social fairness has been recognised, with major investments in rural healthcare and, most recently, a new pension initiative.

Table 8.1: Summary of major social policies and programmes: post-reform China

Social policy	In urban areas	In rural areas
Social security and assistance	• Five basic insurances covering: basic pension, medical insurance, work injury, maternity, unemployment • Minimum Living Standard Guarantee Scheme for urban residents and related subsidies	• Social assistance to destitute households • Natural disaster and social relief • Minimum Living Standard Guarantee Scheme for rural residents • 2010: rural pension programme
Education	• Nine-year free compulsory education	• Nine-year free compulsory education • 'Two exemption and one subsidy' programme for poor students
Healthcare	• Urban resident medical insurance covering non-salaried residents and children, and basic urban worker medical insurance	• New rural cooperative medical insurance
Employment	• Unemployment insurance	• None
Housing security	• Public housing fund • Affordable housing • Low-rent housing or subsidies	• None
Others	• Relief for urban vagrants	• None

Crisis, response and the role of social policy

The impact of the crisis

Because China's financial institutions were relatively sheltered from the global financial meltdown, the speed with which the knock-on effects passed through to the real economy was unanticipated. Growth, employment and trade plummeted in late 2008 and early 2009. Year-on-year Gross Domestic Product (GDP) growth fell to 6.2% in the first quarter of 2009. Exports reached a record low of –29% growth in January 2009. Contraction in exports and imports persisted for 13 consecutive months to November 2009. In Guangdong, the core of China's export manufacturing production, 4,900 export-producers reportedly closed down, went bankrupt or relocated out of the province by the end of 2008 with a loss of 490,000 jobs (*China.com*, 2009a). One senior government official was reported as stating that, by the end of 2008, 670,000 small-sized enterprises were forced to shut down with the loss of about 6.7 million jobs (*China Business Weekly*, 2009). Urban unemployment was estimated by some experts to have reached 9.4% by the end of 2008 (CASS, 2009). There is little doubt that migrant workers bore the immediate brunt of the downturn due to their flexible work arrangements. Sheng et al (2009) estimated that 12 million migrant workers made an early return home for Chinese New Year (February 2009) due to factory closures, redundancy and other crisis-related factors.[3]

The response to the crisis

China responded swiftly as the crisis hit its economy. Its massive 4 trillion yuan (US$586 billion) stimulus package introduced in November 2008 attracted global attention. This was supplemented by a range of measures with the overall objective being to stabilise struggling enterprises, maintain employment, and boost domestic consumption in order to sustain growth. Table 8.2 summarises some of the key programmes initiated during the crisis.[4] Among these measures are a significant number of social initiatives that deserve close attention.

The 4 trillion yuan fiscal stimulus package

The stimulus package, co-funded by central and local governments, comprises a range of investment projects, from basic infrastructure works to livelihood programmes (see Table 8.3). Between 2008

Table 8.2: Key programmes in response to the crisis

Strategic goals	Key measures	Expected outcomes
Maintain economic stability and growth through investment and social spending	• 4 trillion yuan stimulus package	• Create 22 million jobs 2009-11 • Contribute 1% GDP growth per year in 2009 and 2010
Reduce the economic burden on enterprises	• 'Five delays and four reduction' programme • Suspend minimum wage adjustment	• Retain 20 million jobs • Delay or alleviate a total of 2000 billion yuan financial burden of hard-hit enterprises
Prevent job losses and promote employment: through support to enterprises (above) and through employment training or other support	• Subsidise enterprises in difficulties to retain employees and provide retraining programme to workers • Retraining programme for migrant workers or unemployed • Fund to assists migrant or other workers/graduates to establish small businesses	• 15 million people to receive special vocational training
Boost domestic consumption	• Improve the social security system • Increase investment in social protection • Subsidies for rural 'white goods' • Consumption vouchers (mainly by local governments)	• 29 billion yuan for social spending • New rural old age insurance in 11% of rural villages, to cover 130 million rural residents • Universal medical insurance • Increase urban basic old-age pension
Maintain social stability through improved social protection	• Increase *dibao* standard and subsidy • Special one-off subsidies for specific groups • Raise unemployment insurance subsidy Introduce unemployment benefits for new graduates	• n.a.

and 2010, the central government committed to invest 1.18 trillion yuan, while the remaining 2.82 trillion yuan would come from local government finance, local government bonds, state loans and other finance sources (*First Financial Daily*, 2010). Planned investments by the central government were set at 487.5 billion yuan for 2009 and 588.5 billion for 2010 (*People's Daily*, 2009b). As of late 2009, the central government had disbursed only 384 billion yuan to local governments for approved projects (*Economic Observer*, 2009). However, little information on fund disbursement is reported in the public domain, making it difficult to scrutinise the progress and implementation of the stimulus package.

Table 8.3: Investment portfolio of the Stimulus Package (investment amount in billion yuan and share of the total investment [%])

Components of the Stimulus Package	November 2008	March 2009 (revised)	Change
Social welfare (healthcare, education, etc)	40 (1%)	150 (3.75%)	110
Technical upgrading and R&D	160 (4%)	370 (6.25%)	210
Public housing	280 (7%)	400 (10%)	120
Energy conservation and environment	350 (8.75%)	210 (5.25%)	−140
Rural infrastructure	370 (9.25%)	370 (9.25%)	0
Post-earthquake reconstruction	1,000 (25%)	1,000 (25%)	0
Transport and power infrastructure	1,800 (45%)	1,500 (37.5%)	−300
Total	**4,000**	**4,000**	

Note: Social initiatives were defined as including social welfare, public housing, rural infrastructure and post-earthquake reconstruction.

Source: Caijing.com (2009).

The investment portfolio was adjusted in March 2009 once the economy appeared to be stabilising. In response to criticisms that insufficient resources were targeted for social initiatives, allocations to social welfare and public housing increased by 230 billion, bringing the total 'social expenditures' as defined by the government to 48%.

Aggregate economic impacts of the stimulus package appear to be positive. Economic growth has returned to a promising trend. Trade flows have returned to double digit growth. In 2009, private consumption grew by nearly 17%, 3% and 4.5% higher than in 2008 and 2007 respectively.[5] The employment situation has also improved with new urban employment of 11.02 million, comparable with 2008, and new graduate employment exceeding 87.4%. Migrant worker employment increased 4.92 million between 2008 and 2009.

Five delays, four reductions, three subsidies and two consultations

The 'Five Delays' initiative announced in December 2008 aimed to provide a favourable policy environment to support enterprises hit hard by the crisis in order to prevent mass layoffs. To summarise, eligible enterprises (MoHRSS et al, 2008):

- were allowed to delay enterprise contributions to the 'five basic insurance' programmes for workers;
- were allowed to reduce worker contributions to four insurance programmes (excluding pensions);

- were allowed to receive subsidies for social insurance contributions, to retain employees or to provide on-the-job training;
- had to consult labour unions and workers in actions leading to laying off workers or flexible work arrangements.

The logic behind the measure was simple: by easing the burden on enterprises, enterprises would survive and retain workers for when the economy recovered. The programme was designed to alleviate the financial burden of such enterprises by over 200 billion yuan and secure millions of jobs (*People's Daily*, 2009a). The programme was originally set to expire at the end of 2009, but was extended to end 2010 due to its encouraging results as well as the continuing uncertain economic recovery.

While impacts are not easily attributable to one programme, the overall effect of these measures appears to be positive. The official unemployment rate stabilised and statistics of social insurance enrolment, an indicator of employment levels, showed signs of stabilising, falling in January 2009 after a year-long increase in numbers (see Table 8.4). Chinese officials estimate that as of September 2009, the measures had alleviated financial burdens on enterprises by 16.6 billion yuan and the measures that encouraged flexible employment and consultations over work arrangements secured over 10 millions jobs (Zheng, 2010).

Several issues are worthy of further note here. First, this programme primarily aimed to support enterprises and employers, leaving workers in a relatively passive position in the process although the role of the consultations deserves further investigation. Second, it had little impact on jobs for migrant workers who often lack contracts or are not covered by social insurance. The incentives offered under the scheme

Table 8.4: Change of social insurance enrolment in January 2009 and full year of 2009

	Jan 2009 (vs end 2008) (million)	End 2009 (vs end 2008) (million)
Urban workers		
Old-age pension	−0.23	+16.59
Medical insurance	−0.51	+83.25
Occupational insurance	−2.03	+11.09
Migrant workers		
Old-age pension	−0.93	+2.31
Medical insurance	−0.68	+0.69
Occupational insurance	−1.37	+0.94

Sources: Zheng (2010); MoHRSS (2010)

were also more likely to protect urban formal workers. Third, state-owned enterprises or large companies were more likely to benefit from the programme than smaller enterprises because of the larger impact of layoffs. Considering the core goal of 'maintaining stability', local authorities had more incentives to provide subsidies to ensure that large employers survived. Nevertheless, the programme was voluntary based and the definition of 'enterprises in difficulties' was not clear-cut, leaving flexibility for local authorities in implementing the programme, which also varied with local fiscal conditions. The initiative appears overall to have provided significant support to enterprises, possibly at some cost in terms of workers' terms and conditions in the short term, in the interest of maintaining jobs.

Employment promotion initiatives

In addition to the national programmes, local governments adopted a range of employment promotion initiatives designed to help the unemployed, migrant workers, informal workers and new graduates to get jobs or set up in business. Some examples include:

- cooperation between schools and enterprises to ensure the smooth employment of new graduates (Tianjin);
- subsidising interest payments on micro-loans for small businesses (Jiangsu);
- providing re-employment training subsidies (Yunnan);
- providing a one-off entrepreneurship subsidy (of up to 3,000 yuan) to new graduates from higher education institutions (Henan);
- prioritising employment creation as an objective and condition for new investment projects (Shanxi and Hubei);
- organising training programmes for returned migrant workers and providing funds for starting businesses (Hunan).

Overall, the government subsidised training programmes that benefited 21.6 million people, including:

- 11 million migrant workers;
- 2.6 million workers in enterprises in difficulty;
- 4.5 million urban unemployed;
- job preparation for 2.4 million workers;
- entrepreneurship training for 1.1 million workers (MoHRSS, 2010).

In addition, supplementary measures to the Five Delays programme announced in late 2009 involved suspending the annual minimum wage adjustment for 2009. In many provinces, the last adjustment had been in 2007, meaning that the suspension froze, if not reduced, the real wages of many workers during the financial crisis. The extent to which freezing the minimum wage contributed to retaining jobs is unclear. Between January and May 2010, as the economic outlook improved and the demand for workers rose, especially in coastal areas, 11 provinces raised the minimum wage (*Huaxia.com*, 2010). The first was Jiangsu, with an average increase of 12%. Guangdong and Zhejiang provinces increased by at least 10% over 2008. Some increases exceeded 20%, for example in Ningxia (24.9%) and Jilin (22.9%).

Consumption vouchers

Consumption vouchers were adopted in a range of cities (mostly better-off cities that could bear the cost), generally with the purpose of boosting consumption rather than directly helping the poor to cope with the crisis. A nationwide scheme to subsidise the purchase of home appliances (to support producers) in rural areas was also introduced, with similar objectives. Wealthier cities such as Chengdu, Chongqing, Hangzhou, Nanjing and others rolled out their own voucher schemes, largely to encourage citizens to buy home appliances, mobile phones or increased leisure and tourism (Table 8.5). Some programmes were targeted more directly to the poor to help them cope with the economic impacts of the crisis. One notable example was Chengdu.

Table 8.5: Examples of consumption voucher schemes in selected Chinese cities, 2009

City	Consumption voucher scheme
Hangzhou (February)	10 million yuan scheme initiated. Each citizen entitled to 200 yuan voucher; primary and secondary students received 100 yuan voucher. Mostly used in home appliances and mobile phone stores, leading to 4.42 million yuan consumption, a multiplier effect of 5.42, while the multiplier effect in four major department stores was 4 times.
Nanjing (February)	20 million yuan countryside holiday (leisure) vouchers on 16 February, expected to stimulate 50 million yuan consumption
Guangdong (February)	20 million yuan holiday/leisure consumption voucher, aiming to generate 40 million yuan consumption
Shanghai (February)	Holiday/leisure consumption voucher worth 40 million yuan

Chengdu was the first city to roll out a consumption voucher scheme, clearly targeted to the low-income population (*China Economic Times*, 2009). On 15 December 2008, the city government gave away vouchers each valued at 100 yuan to 379,100 local low-income residents. While the initiative was well received with a 100% utilisation rate, official assessments claimed that the initiative led to about 100 million yuan of final consumption but found that the multiplier effects were small, and the programme was not extended. This was in part due to the fact that most people spent the voucher on food and daily necessities, rather than consumer goods. However, the voucher certainly offered some assistance to the urban poor and to small food stores, which benefited from additional sales. According to a local supermarket chain, the voucher initiative boosted their sales by several million yuan between November and December 2008.

While the consumption voucher initiative drew considerable public debate, particularly over its potential for boosting consumption (*Beijing Review*, 2009; *China Daily*, 2009a), concerns were also raised about the cost and inflationary implications. Critics doubted the magnitude of effective demand that would be stimulated and questioned the financial viability of a large-scale, nationwide voucher scheme (*China Daily*, 2009b; *China.com*, 2009b). Others argued that the voucher scheme should be used as a welfare scheme, not as tool to boost consumption (CCTV, 2009). Overall, the voucher initiative turned out to be relatively short-lived and to have little impact on easing the impacts of the crisis.

Social security and assistance

As part of the stimulus package, and through a number of additional measures, existing programmes were expanded, new programmes introduced and benefits for the most vulnerable increased. It is often hard to assess what funding was within the stimulus and what subsequent measures involved additional allocations, or what was actually disbursed from central government and what had to be borne by local government. Nonetheless, the following key measures can be identified.

In terms of social assistance, in January 2009, the Ministry of Finance and Ministry of Civil Affairs announced spending of 9 billion yuan to provide a one-off living subsidy to populations in difficulty in urban and rural areas. One-off payments were to be disbursed by Chinese New Year to *dibao* recipients (150 yuan), rural '*wubao*'[6] (100 yuan) and state pension holders (180 yuan). It is estimated that 74 million people benefited from these payments (ifeng.com, 2009).

The *dibao* standard was subsequently raised.[7] At the end of 2008, the central government provided an advance disbursement of 27.6 billion yuan to local governments for the rural and urban *dibao* subsidy for 2009. By July 2009, the government had disbursed 54 billion yuan – an increase of 48.95% as compared with the full-year figure for 2008. In 2009, the government raised the *dibao* standard again by 15 and 10 yuan per month for urban and rural *dibao* holders respectively (*People's Daily*, 2009c). The raise has resulted in a significant increase of *dibao* expenditures. For instance, between 2007 and 2009, nearly all provinces increased *dibao* expenditure by at least 50%.

The urban basic old-age pension for workers also increased during this period, by an average of 100 yuan per month in 2008, 110 yuan in 2009 and 120 yuan in 2010, from the monthly pension level of 963 yuan (*Economic Observer*, 2008; *gov.cn*, 2009). This increase was on average 10% per year between 2008 and 2010. Some provinces were higher: Jilin, for instance, raised the monthly pension level by 13.3% on average for 2010.

Local governments also increased unemployment insurance benefits. For example, Suzhou raised the benefits from 450 yuan per month to 500 per month, effective January 2009. From July, other provinces raised the unemployment subsidy standard. For instance, Beijing, Hangzhou, Shanxi and Tianjin each raised unemployment subsidies by between 8% and 12%. The medical care subsidy and other attached benefits for the unemployed were also increased. In many provinces, some unemployment benefits also cover informal workers and migrant workers with a formal labour contract. Table 8.6 shows that unemployment benefit claimants fell while the total expenditure of the unemployment insurance fund increased significantly, indicating that

Table 8.6: Unemployment insurance fund, 2007-09

Year	Number of claimants (million)	One-off living subsidy for migrant workers (million)[a]	Enrolment of unemployment insurance (million)	Of which, migrant worker participants (million)	Expenditure of unemployment insurance fund (billion yuan)
2007	2.86	0.87	116.45	11.50	21.8 (up 9%)[b]
2008	2.61	0.93	124.00	15.49	25.4 (up 16.5%)
2009	2.35	1.08	127.15	16.43	36.7 (up 44.7%)

Notes:

[a] This refers to those whose labour contract was not renewed or terminated before the contract expired

[b] % growth on previous year.

Source: MoHRSS (2010)

per-capita benefits increased. Yet, a lower number of unemployment benefit claimants may not be attributed to the success of employment promotion measures. The most vulnerable among the unemployed, such as migrant workers, are often excluded from unemployment insurance or unaware of their eligibility for benefits.

Significant efforts have continued to be put into health system reform, building on initiatives under way before the crisis hit. In January 2009, the State Council endorsed the medical reform plan, which had been announced after public consultation in October 2008, and in April 2009, a three-year implementation plan was issued. The government committed to invest at least 850 billion yuan, including 331.8 billion yuan from central government finance, between 2009 and 2011 (an amount that was additional to the fiscal commitment under the stimulus package). These funds include resources to increase central government's subsidy to the Rural New Cooperative Medical Scheme. By the end of 2009, basic medical insurance had been extended almost universally to over 1.2 billion people in rural and urban areas. Over 94% – or 833 million – of rural residents are members of the scheme. The number of recipients of the basic medical insurance for urban workers and residents reached 400 million in 2009. While the level of reimbursements and other aspects of implementation remain problematic, in part due to insufficient funds, nonetheless significant improvements are being made, with the maximum coverage for medical expenses now at six times the annual average income of a local farmer.

In education, additional measures were taken in the crisis response period, building on earlier reforms to reduce the direct burden of education costs, particularly in rural areas. In May 2009, the government ordered schools to abolish boarding, book and other miscellaneous fees for students in compulsory education in rural areas. Central government allocated 17 billion yuan from the central budget to subsidise the public school operating costs of all rural primary and secondary schools, and continued fiscal support for teachers' salaries.

One of the most significant areas of social expenditure under the fiscal stimulus package is devoted to public housing, representing a dramatic increase in government spending on housing security. As a component of the stimulus package, central government spent 55.1 billion yuan to develop low-income housing projects in 2009, a twofold increase over 2008. The government claimed to have built, renovated or expanded two million low-income housing units of various types, and renovated or built 1.3 million housing units in different locations. Significant resources for earthquake relief also focused inevitably on housing. Housing construction is, of course, a major source of employment for migrant labour, with employment being a key motivation behind this programme. Data are not available to assess the direct employment creation effects of public housing or other fiscal stimulus investments. Nonetheless, housing security – having been left to the market since reforms in the 1990s – has clearly risen in priority during the crisis response as an important dimension of the broader social policy agenda, and one in which the government must again play a role.

Social policies in crisis – protecting the vulnerable and adjusting the economy

As noted above, the social programmes initiated or extended during the crisis and its aftermath represent ongoing reform efforts in various social policy areas. The crisis offered, and was used as, an opportunity for Chinese leaders to articulate a broader and more comprehensive vision of social security reform, supported by fiscal investment, even if the ultimate purpose of such investment is economic recovery and sustained growth. The responses represent a significant move towards recognising the critical role of social policies in the economy – in terms of their close links with effective demand and their role in enhancing capabilities and thus productivity gains necessary for further economic development.

The role played by social security in time of crisis is well recognised (OECD, 2010b; Zheng, 2010). It can provide transitional and anti-cyclical measures to protect enterprises, jobs and those affected directly by the crisis. It can act as an automatic stabiliser in maintaining consumption and effective demand in the economy, and smoothing a return to growth. It can also be used strategically – as in the case of Korea in the Asian financial crisis – to assist in the needed restructuring of its economy and to move on to a more socially inclusive development path (Kwon, 2004). Alternatively, moments of crisis may give rise to narrowly targeted safety net and relief responses, aimed at the protection of those most negatively affected, but with limited impacts on the wider economy and with short-lived effects.

The Chinese leadership has used the moment of crisis to strengthen its commitment to a comprehensive social security system covering the entire population.[8] While making use of the social assistance programmes already in place, and extending or increasing benefits where needed, the more significant developments involve the creation of new programmes and efforts to include previously excluded groups (migrants and rural older people, for example). The government has made use both of economic arguments including the recognised need to rebalance the economy and change the structure of demand, and of the need to maintain employment and incomes to ensure social stability, which is itself a prerequisite for a stable economy. Key government work priorities announced for 2009 were thus to improve people's livelihoods and strengthen efforts in employment and social protection. More concrete actions with fiscal support from the central government budget are noted in the two government work reports of 2009 and 2010 (Wen, 2009, 2010a; see Table 8.7).

The more difficult question to address is the extent to which the commitment to social security has actually helped in achieving the hoped-for economic objectives – to reduce unemployment pressure, lessen the economic impacts on the poor and assist in setting a new course towards a domestic-consumption-led growth model. Given the limited data available in the public domain and the short timeframe for analysing the impacts, it would be premature to draw any firm conclusions. Yet, some insights can be highlighted to map out the likely effects of the Chinese government's social policy agenda.

Table 8.7: Chinese government commitments to social security spending, 2009 and 2010

2009	• Social security: 293 billion yuan on the social safety net; 17.6% increase on 2008; to expand coverage of social security programmes and increase social security benefits.
	• Healthcare reform: an additional 850 billion yuan 2009-11, including 331.8 billion yuan from the central government, to ensure smooth progress in the reform of healthcare system.
	• Social security for migrant workers: to implement an old-age pension for rural migrant workers, including allowing portability of benefits
2010	• Speed up the expansion of social security system for both urban and rural residents.
	• Expand the coverage of the new rural old-age insurance system to 23% of Chinese counties.
	• Extend workers' compensation to the 1.3 million workers injured from previous jobs but yet to receive benefits.
	• Extend coverage of social security to rural migrant workers.
	• Gradually increase the level of subsistence allowances (*dibao*) in both urban and rural areas.
	• Build a social security and social services system for disabled people.
	• Increase basic old-age pensions for enterprise retirees by 10%.
	• Governments at all levels to spend more on social security, with central government to appropriate 318.5 billion yuan for this purpose.

Sources: The Government Work Report 2009 and 2010 (Wen, 2009, 2010a).

Easing unemployment – a question with no clear answer

As discussed above, official statistics on unemployment in China tell only a partial story so that the actual level of unemployment is unclear, making it difficult to assess the impact of initiatives aimed at smoothing the unemployment situation. Official urban unemployment rates showed a very mild increase in unemployment between 2008 and 2009, up from 4.2% to 4.3% over the period. Even compared with 2007, the unemployment rate was only 0.3% higher. Unemployment had then fallen by similarly slight amounts in 2010, to 4.2% in the first two quarters. Although the official measure is not the best indicator, the unemployment situation is generally viewed as having stabilised and gradually improving, although some groups (such as new labour force entrants and graduates) remain of concern. In Sichuan province, the provincial government reported its investigated unemployment rate to be 9.5% at the end of 2008, dropping to 7.5% by the end of 2009.[9] The labour authority in Guangdong province reported over three million migrant workers had returned to the province after the 2009 Chinese New Year, accounting for 45.7% of the nearly seven million migrant workers who had returned home before the holiday (*Caijing Magazine*, 2010). In fact, Guangdong enterprises, and those in other coastal regions, have reported a significant shortage of workers as orders have resumed. Official data on new employment and re-employment (see Table 8.8) indicate a stabilisation of the employment situation.

It is unclear to what extent these improvements can be attributed to the employment and social initiatives adopted during the crisis, or simply to the fact of gradual economic recovery. Further analysis would be needed of the direct job creation impacts of programmes under the fiscal stimulus, as well as better data on the actual implementation of the various measures put in place. At the very least, the rapid response by the government in the form of concrete subsidies and programmes

Table 8.8: New employment and re-employment, 2007-10*

	New employment	Re-employment of the unemployed	Re-employment of the group with employment difficulty
2007	12,040,000	5,150,000	1,550,000
2008	11,130,000	5,000,000	1,430,000
2009	11,020,000	5,140,000	1,640,000
2010 (January-June)	6,380,000	3,050,000	880,000

Source: MoHRSS (2010).

as well as its rhetorical commitments to assist enterprises threatened by the crisis were important in preventing panic responses that could have led to large-scale company closures and layoffs.

Impacts on the poor

The impact of the crisis on the urban poor came mainly through the loss of jobs and incomes. In rural areas, the impacts would potentially include both a fall in income from agriculture and a loss of remittances or income from migrant workers. As the global market slumped, the demand for agricultural products fell, negatively impacting agricultural prices in China's domestic market (Zhang and Wang, cited in Tang and Zhang, 2010). The prices of a number of major agricultural products reportedly stagnated from October 2008, possibly due to the combined effect of falling international food prices and the Chinese government's efforts to keep domestic food prices intentionally low after the food price rises in 2007.

These impacts in terms of rural incomes and poverty rates are not yet clear. Agricultural income is no longer the core income of many rural households, which depend on migrant family workers. The group most seriously affected by stagnant agricultural prices would be those not engaged in any off-farm work or benefiting from remittances from family members in urban areas. This group is more likely to include older people, those unable to work due to ill-health or disability, and family members who care for them, particularly women. The increased subsidy for *dibao* recipients and other temporary social assistance schemes should in theory have provided some assistance to these groups, although more local data will be needed to assess the actual impacts. Increased government expenditures (both central and local) on the *dibao* subsidy as well as for medical care and pension are notable. But the variation in coverage and benefits among localities, between wealthy and poor regions, and across urban and rural areas, means that often the poorest are less likely to benefit. Despite the significant improvements in the system, urban–rural and other divisions in social protection provision constitute an ongoing barrier to ensuring that those in greatest need are adequately protected. Nonetheless, the crisis demonstrates the potential for rolling out or scaling up existing social protection mechanisms as part of a wider response; it may also have exposed weaknesses in the response at local levels, and could thus potentially serve as further impetus to patch up gaps and reduce inequalities and problems in the system.

A bigger role for government in funding social security

Growth in social security spending has risen noticeable since the late 1990s. Government expenditure doubled from 59.63 billion yuan in 1998 to 119.74 billion yuan in 1999, as part of state enterprise restructuring. In the next 10 years, it increased over fivefold to 680.43 billion in 2008. Table 8.9 shows central government expenditure on social security and employment – including social insurance, *dibao*, unemployment, subsidies to pension funds, other social assistance and low-income housing – for 2007-10. Significant increased spending is associated with the stimulus programme, but much translates into long-term commitments. While the growth in expenditure slowed in 2010, the overall commitment remains high. Nonetheless, this still represents a relatively small share of total expenditure, from 3.7% of total fiscal spending in 2008 to 7.7% in 2009, of which a large proportion was transfer funds to local government. In 2009, central government's transfer payment to local government for social security and employment accounted for approximately 40% of the local government's total expenditure on this item. According to the Ministry of Finance (*People's Daily*, 2010), in the first half of 2010, 220.6 billion was disbursed to local governments for employment and social security. The central government's transfer payments for social initiatives thus

Table 8.9: Central government expenditure on social security and other social programmes (in billion yuan), and year-on-year growth, 2007-10

	2007	2008	2009	2010
Social security and employment	230.32	274.36	329.67	358.23
	(+13.7%)	(+19.2%)	(+24.1%)	(+8.7%)
Healthcare	66.43	82.68	127.32	138.92
	(+296.8%)	(+24.5%)	(+20.2%)	(+8.8%)
Education	107.64	160.37	198.14	216
	(+76%)	(+49%)	(+49.5%)	(+9%)
Earthquake reconstruction	n.a.	60	96.99	78.01
			(+60%)	(−18.65%)
Low-income housing	n.a.	18.19	55.06	63.2
		(+114.3%)	(+202.7%)	(+1.4%)
Subtotal	*404.39*	*595.6*	*807.18*	*854.36*
% of total central government expenditure	13.7%	16.4%	18.4%	18.3%
% of total national social expenditure	n.a.	3.1%	7.7%	n.a.

Note: 2010 data refer to the budgeted fiscal spending for 2010.

Source: MoF (Ministry of Finance) (2008, 2009, 2010)

provided an important source of funding to secure the provisions and sustainability of social initiatives at the local level.

Such central funding is essential, especially for the less-developed provinces, but draws attention to variations in standard and coverage among provinces. Fair access to social protection is not only subject to the rural–urban divide, but also to disparities among provinces. This raises concerns about the fiscal capacity of some local government's to provide matching funds as required by the stimulus package and other welfare programmes, or to significantly invest in social security. Well-off provinces such as Jiangsu, Shanghai and Zhejiang have announced vigorous plans to increase social spending, especially in the areas of pensions and medical subsidies. However, more in-depth assessment is required to examine the real efforts of local government in implementing these initiatives, the role of direct funding from central government and the impacts on improving people's livelihoods.

A 2009 audit report (National Audit Office, 2009) found that, among the 1981 projects involving stimulus investment, 46% failed to adequately match this with local fiscal investment. While the report did not reveal the nature of the projects, it is clear that lack of local funding will significantly impact on the progress of extending social welfare provision. The audit report also revealed that local governments had run up bank debts of 2.79 trillion yuan (US$410.3 billion) by the end of 2009, most of it for funding infrastructure construction and to help pay for government stimulus package projects. This may also indicate, in spite of the rhetorical commitment to social security, that public investment remains focused principally on infrastructure projects. The political will of local governments in boosting social security may be compromised by their growth agenda.

Consumption

As mentioned above, personal consumption as a share of GDP increased by 3% between 2008 and 2009. While such success in boosting consumption has been lauded by government, it is again unclear how much of this growth can be attributed to improvements in social security. Analysis by Wang (2010, p 11) suggests that extending social security coverage would produce significant impacts on per-capita consumption: for the lowest income quintile, a 1% increase of social security coverage would have a marginal effect of 13.4 yuan on per-capita consumption, while its marginal effect in the top income quintile was 10.4 yuan. Data to analyse the actual effects of programmes on consumption are lacking, but several researchers suggest that the current level of social spending is insufficient to boost consumption. Wang and Li (2010) suggest that government spending on social security as a share of GDP should not be less than 7% and its share of total government spending not less than 20%. Public spending on education and healthcare should account for more than 4% and 6% of GDP respectively. Although it is reasonable to argue that people are generally more willing to spend when they are confident in their social security entitlements, it may still take considerable time, particularly for the poor in rural China, to make the attitudinal and behavioural changes needed to shift consumption patterns. In this context, the impact of social security provision on consumption may be relatively limited in the short term. Nonetheless, significant social expenditures on health and education can directly reduce household expenditures on these items, freeing up resources for other forms of consumption.

Conclusion

The above discussion suggests significant areas of progress, expedited by the financial crisis, in central government's commitment to comprehensive social security, funded in part from central finances. The expansion of programmes to bring formerly excluded groups, particularly migrants, into the system suggests significant change, including recognition of the contribution of migrant workers to economic growth, and the need to facilitate smoother transitions of labour to meet changing demands. More generally, social security is being recognised as a key facilitator of economic restructuring in terms of its contribution to effective domestic demand. Thus, social policies are now more than a residual safety net, or a mechanism of social stability, but also a central part of a sustainable growth agenda.

The ease with which this vision can be realised in practice, however, is subject to a number of constraints. While central government has demonstrated a commitment to funding, this will need to be increased to meet the scale of needs and to ensure some degree of equality in provisions across a highly unequal country. Local governments will also need different incentives, and a different fiscal revenue structure, to ensure that local commitments to social expenditures are met. The variation between and within provinces necessitates some degree of flexibility in rolling out and scaling up such programmes; considerable experience has been gained through the *dibao* and rural medical schemes. However, local government fiscal as well as other capacities to adapt and implement complex programmes, particularly in less developed regions, remain limited. Programmes will increasingly need to be organised, and funding pooled, at higher levels in the administrative hierarchy. This will be necessary to achieve adequate risk sharing, for example for medical expenditures; and for the integration of migrants into pension schemes, requiring portability of benefits. While many implementation and financing challenges lie ahead, clearly the crisis has coincided, and in part been the impetus for, a major new step in the evolution of China's welfare system. It remains to be seen whether this can be rolled out quickly enough to make significant further contributions to the much-needed adjustments in China's economic growth path.

Notes

[1] This compares with a contraction of world growth from 4.1% to 3.3% between 1997 and 1999. World trade growth also fell from 9.8% to 5.1% in the same period (IMF, 2000, 2010f).

[2] China's social policy is highly segmented along urban–rural lines, whereby urban residents enjoy significantly greater welfare provisions.

[3] According to the National Bureau of Statistics, there were 225.4 million migrant workers nationwide in 2008; of which, 140.4 million worked outside their home county.

[4] Many of these initiatives are voluntary, require co-funding from local governments, and vary in implementation by province.

[5] The private consumption figure refers to the total retail sales of consumer goods, which is the commonly used indicator for private consumption. Total retail sales of consumer goods grew by 12.5% in 2007 and 14.8% in 2008 (NSBC, 2009, 2010).

[6] *wubao* literally means 'five guarantees' in Chinese. A form of social assistance predating the reform era, it provided food, clothing, medical care, housing and education or burial expenses to orphaned children and the elderly without other means of support.

[7] Prior to the crisis, the *dibao* standard was raised twice (in January and July 2008). On each occasion, the urban and rural *dibao* subsidies were raised by 15 and 10 yuan per month respectively.

[8] Central Economic Working Conference, December 2008.

[9] The investigated unemployment rate is an indicator generally used for internal reference only, but rarely publicised. This indicator is believed to better reflect true urban unemployment.

NINE

Tiptoeing through crisis? Re-evaluating the German social model in light of the global recession

John Hudson and Stefan Kühner

Introduction: the rise and fall (and rise again?) of the German model

To contextualise the German case, it is tempting to draw comparisons with the United Kingdom (UK) as perceptions of these two economic powerhouses of Europe have been locked into something of a Yin and Yang relationship in recent decades. This is particularly so when Germany is viewed through the lens of British political debate.

In the early to mid-1990s, it was a commonly held view that the UK had much to learn from the German 'model'. Indeed, in his bestselling *The State We're In*, Hutton (1995) argued that there were fundamental weaknesses in the British economy – too focused on short-term profits and too heavily driven by the interests of the City – and held up Germany as the key example of a successful alternative. The book's publication coincided with Tony Blair's election as Labour Party Leader and, as Driver and Martell (1998, p 46) note, 'the early days of New Labour saw many look to European, more particularly German, capitalism as offering an attractive model'. Most notably, the idea of the UK adopting some elements of the 'Rhineland model' (Hutton, 1995) as part of a move towards 'stakeholder capitalism' briefly caught the imagination of Blair (see Kelly et al, 1997) before New Labour settled on an Anglo-Saxon model inspired by the approach of centre-left governments in Australia and America (Driver and Martell, 1998, p 46).

Once Blair was in power, however, far from Germany being a model for the UK to follow, the roles and reputations of their economies seemed to progressively reverse as the UK's performance outstripped Germany's. With the dot.com boom symbolically marking the emergence a seemingly lucrative new knowledge-based economy, and increased global competition in the industrial sphere creating a challenging environment for European manufacturing, by the turn of the millennium Germany seemed to look old fashioned and out of shape, while the UK seemed the exemplar of a modern, flexible, knowledge economy. Indeed, when Gerhard Schröder became German Chancellor in late 1998, he looked towards Blair for ideas on modernising the German model. The two leaders (Blair and Schröder, 1999) published a joint manifesto for renewing European social democracy that drew heavily on Blair's 'Third Way' approach (Blair, 1998; Giddens, 1998). Talk shifted towards injecting UK-style flexibility into the German model and boosting the strength of its knowledge-based sectors (Hombach, 2000). The narrative was reinforced by key economic indicators over the late 1990s and early 2000s, the UK outperforming Germany in terms of jobs and economic growth (OECD, 2010c): in his 2006 Budget speech, Gordon Brown boasted that the national income per head in the UK had increased to such an extent that the country had risen from being the lowest ranked in the G7 on this measure to the second highest ranked as a consequence of its sustained economic growth (Brown, 2006).[1] Germany, meanwhile, appeared mired in crisis as Christian Democrats/Christian Socialists and Social Democrats, forced by the unclear outcome of the 2005 General Election, formed the first 'Grand Coalition' (*Grosse Koalition*) since the 1960s. This coalition was charged with the unlikely task of overcoming previous ideological differences in order to deliver the fundamental social and economic reforms deemed essential given the nation's persistently sluggish economic growth and high unemployment. Although never comfortable with this comparison (Clemens, 2007), Angela Merkel stood at the head of the coalition, billed by some commentators as a German Thatcher (Basham and Tupy, 2005). Driven initially by Merkel, the Christian Democrats had run an election campaign based on the 2003 Leipzig plan, which poised to unleash a radical pro-market agenda that would sweep away historic elements of the German model (Clemens, 2009).

Yet, within months of Brown assuming the Premiership of the UK, the tables had turned once again. The size of the financial services sector in the UK meant that the dramatic implosion of the global banking industry hit the UK economy harder than any other major economy; the City of London's central role in the global banking industry suddenly seemed as much a weakness as a strength. Indeed, with as much as 5% of the UK's Gross Domestic Product (GDP) estimated to be permanently lost by the downturn in financial services (Hutton, 2009), claims that over-reliance on the sector is a structural weakness became fashionable once again. The search for alternative economic models gained renewed attention and the incoming David Cameron-led coalition government stressed the desirability of reviving British manufacturing (Cameron, 2010a) while also adopting the fiscal orthodoxy of balanced budgets advocated by Merkel (Cameron, 2010b). Certainly, the much softer landing for the German economy in the aftermath of the credit crunch fuelled unfavourable comparisons of the UK with Germany: Germany suffered negative growth for just five quarters while, at the time of writing, the UK was still in recession and had already recorded six quarters of negative growth (OECD, 2010d).

These shifting narratives about the relative merits of the German model vis-à-vis more neoliberal alternatives provide an important backdrop for this chapter, not least because there has been considerable debate both inside and outside Germany – and both before and after the global economic crisis – about the extent to which a shift away from this model is necessary. Talk of a German 'model' does, of course, oversimplify the reality of the German case, but given that many key works in the political economy literature highlight Germany as an ideal type, there are perhaps stronger grounds than is normally the case for assuming that the models bear some approximation to reality. At the very least they provide a good starting point for analysis, so we want to briefly sketch out the key features of what we regard to be the core models before moving on to examine the empirical reality of recent policy reforms in Germany.

First, (West) Germany was long presumed to be a 'social market economy' (*soziale Marktwirtschaft*) in which a careful balance between a free market and planned economy was a stated goal of successive governments from the late 1940s onwards. Indeed, the reconstruction of post-war West Germany around a 'socially conscious model of market capitalism' was symbolically important for a nation whose 'national identity had been discredited' by the rise of fascism (Van Hook, 2007, p 1). Central to this model was a corporatist approach to economic planning in which the state shared power with social partners representing business and labour: indeed, in their classic text *Varieties of Capitalism*, Hall and Soskice (2001) described Germany as the classic example of a group-based *coordinated (Rhineland) market economy* in which there has been a high degree of economic planning designed to support and protect specialised industries through 'cooperative industrial relations, collective provision of vocational training and long-term oriented financial systems' (Menz, 2005, p 197). They contrast this with the *liberal market economy* in which economic coordination takes place primarily through (free) market mechanisms and where flexibility is prized over longer-term planning.

Germany's corporatist economic model interfaces with its model of welfare. Esping-Andersen's (1990) characterisation of Germany as the ideal type of his conservative/corporatist world of welfare – in which generous but status-maintaining earnings related social insurance schemes predominate and where para-statal organisations play a key role in the management of funds – is well known. Less commonly cited, but worthy of wider attention, is Estévez-Abe et al's (2001) suggestion that each variety of capitalism is supported by a complementary 'welfare production regime': in Germany's case, this sees strong employment protections in evidence in order to guard against the risks for workers associated with building up specific skills that the economy requires but that cannot easily be transferred from one industry to another.

Finally, these social and economic models necessarily build upon a particular model of politics: one in which much political power is located outside of the core executive, with multiple veto points – be it through a strong federal and/or bicameral structure, a strictly enforced written constitution or the independence of key social and economic institutions such as a constitutional court or an independent central bank – constraining the power of central government. Indeed, such are the checks-and-balances built into the constitution that Katzenstein (1987) famously described (West) Germany as a 'semi-sovereign state'. Added to this, Germany, as a member of the European Monetary Union, is also subject to nominal interest rates set by the European Central Bank for the whole eurozone,[2] meaning it has passed sovereignty over this key area of economic policy upwards (Busch, 2005, p 134).

Social policy until the mid-1990s: incremental adjustment of the *soziale Marktwirtschaft*

For the majority of its history, the *German model*, and in particular the German *soziale Marktwirtschaft*, was seen as viable and working: it was at the heart of the German economic miracle of the 1950s and 1960s and retained its symbolic power during the different oil and stagflation crises of the 1970s (Van Hook, 2007). While the first cracks caused by structural labour market inactivity, fiscal austerity and the slow erosion of the German male breadwinner model had already begun to appear by then, it was not until the mid-1990s, forced by the late Christian Democrat/Liberal coalition under Helmut Kohl (Seeleib-Kaiser, 2003), that the political discourse shifted towards a serious debate about Germany as a business and research location (*Standortdebatte*).

The period of stalemate over reform (*Reformblockade*) that followed has been widely debated in the academic literature and popular press and the relative stability of the German social pact in the face of pressures for change led to notions of a 'frozen landscape' (Esping-Andersen, 1996a) and a 'badly adjusting' welfare state (Manow and Seils, 2000a, 2000b) being employed as a caricature of the German reform trajectory.

As gridlock over reform intensified from the mid-1990s, it is telling that among the list of 'annual faux-pas words' (*Unwort des Jahres*) published by the *Society of German Language*, which tries to capture the most contentious debates of each year and typically attracts a significant amount of media attention, we find 'socially agreeable job cuts' (*sozialverträglicher Stellenabbau*) in 1995, 'flexibilisation', 'outsourcing', 'reconstruction of the welfare state' and 'healthcare reform' all in 1996, and finally 'blockade politics/politicians' (*Blockadepolitik/politiker*) in 1997. For the first time in decades, Germany was viewed, both nationally and internationally, as the 'sick economy of Europe': persevering with the status quo of the previously praised German model was not generally regarded as a viable response to the most pressing challenges of the time.

This shift in perception is astonishing if one considers that only a few years prior to this, Helmut Kohl had comfortably won the General Election of 1990, promising to transfer the *German model* to Eastern Germany as part of his plans to create 'prospering landscapes' (*blühende Landschaften*) across a unified Germany. There was at that time a belief and confidence in the *soziale Marktwirtschaft* among the political elites that was represented in a mainly incremental approach to social policy making. So, for instance, fiscal imbalances of the different social insurance schemes were mainly dealt with by raising revenues through modest increases in contribution rates (Hinrichs, 2010). The end of the 'economic miracle' in the late 1970s was tackled through 'labour shedding' (Esping-Andersen, 1996a), that is, policies to extend education at the lower end and, more particularly, to facilitate early retirement at the higher end of the age structure, to ease labour market pressures and address slowly increasing unemployment. So, 'flexible retirement' was introduced in 1992, which enabled retirement at the age of 63 without any reduction in old-age benefits; the so-called '59-rule' gave people aged 60 or over the right to retire if they had been unemployed for more than a year (Manow and Seils, 2000a). These changes at the margins kept the core institutions intact.

Social policy since the mid-1990s: moving beyond incrementalism?

By the mid-1990s, the full cost of unification became apparent as the promised economic recovery in East Germany increasingly became a *castle in the air*: no less than a third of all jobs in the former German Democratic Republic (GDR) disappeared (Hinrichs, 2010) as total unemployment rose from just over one million to just over one and a half million between 1989 and 2000 (Statistisches Bundesamt Deutschland). After gradually decreasing during the 1970s and 1980s, total social spending, driven by rising unemployment and a host of other social problems in the Neue Länder, shot up from around 24% in 1990 to just under 28% of GDP in 2000; this was the highest percentage of all countries of the Organisation for Economic Co-operation and Development (OECD) apart from Sweden and way above the OECD average of 20% of GDP at that time (OECD Social Expenditure Database: SOCX). At the same time, non-wage labour costs increased at an equal pace from just over 35% in 1990 to a peak of just under 42% in 1997 (Streeck and Trampusch, 2005).[3]

Not surprisingly, perhaps, political discourse started to engage more closely with the perceived inadequacies of the *soziale Marktwirtschaft*. In particular, questions were raised about the international competitiveness of the German model and its ability to sustain and create jobs: Germany's relatively generous employment protection system and the governance structure of the Federal Labour Agency (*Bundesagentur für Arbeit*), which were perceived to impede increased conditionality and a move towards more activation, were the subject of heated debates (Trampusch, 2003). The corporatist system of collective bargaining was targeted, together with labour market rigidities, as the cause of the relatively small low-wage sector in Germany at the time, which was where some commentators argued the biggest potential for job growth lay (Sinn, 1995). Claims that generous unemployment insurance benefits and unemployment assistance were creating relatively high non-wage labour costs and thus considerable poverty and unemployment traps gained credence against the backdrop of Chancellor Kohl's repeated employment of the 'handouts hammock' metaphor (*soziale Hängematte*). Finally, as Hinrichs (2010, p 56) remarks, 1997 was also the first time that the notion of 'generational equity' (*Generationengerechtigkeit*) came to the fore in the light of new estimates of future dependency ratios and in an attempt to justify reductions of old-age pensions 'in order not to overburden the younger generations'.

As hinted above, the second half of the 1990s featured an adversarial style of policy making, which was relatively new to many Germans and placed the incumbent Christian Democratic/Liberal coalition (together with the large employers' organisations) firmly on one side of the political spectrum and the Social Democratic and Green parties (endorsed by large parts of the trades union movement) firmly on the other (Häusermann, 2010). As a consequence, ideological deadlock, blaming and questioning of motives was the reality of day-to-day German politics. It was against this backdrop that towards the late 1990s the Christian Democrats/Liberal Democrats coalition unilaterally moved away from supporting the German welfare state outright. Retrenchment was very much the order of the day. Policy initiatives designed to retrench the welfare state cut across many pillars. The 1997 reform of labour law was symbolic as it stopped unemployment benefit claimants from rejecting 'unsuitable' employment on the basis of it being outside their occupation or qualifications: after six months' unemployment, claimants essentially had to accept any job offer. Further changes affected sick leave benefits (cut from 100% to 80% of previous income) and, as Seeleib-Kaiser (2003, p 11) points out, 'for the first time in German history', old-age pensions were reformed, through inclusion of a 'demographic factor' in the calculation of future pensions funding. This new indexation of old-age pensions was meant to take account of increasing life expectancies and was predicted to lead to a reduction of net old-age pension replacement rates for an average production worker from around 70% to 64% (Seeleib-Kaiser, 2002).

The Social Democrats, together with the Green Party, opposed all of these changes. Together with the Party of Democratic Socialism (PDS), the offspring of the Socialist Unity Party (SED), the former state-party of the GDR, they were able to block in the Upper Chamber of Parliament (*Bundesrat*) any further attempt to recommodify labour markets and retrench social insurances. Indeed, in the course of the 1998 General Election, they vowed to do away with the 'social atrocities' committed by the Christian Democratic/Liberal coalition as part of a renewal of the social market economy (*Erneuerung der sozialen Marktwirtschaft*) (SPD, 1998). The strategy proved electorally popular and the Christian Democratic/Liberal coalition, still under the leadership of Helmut Kohl, lost the General Election after being in power for a total of 16 years. The newly elected coalition government of the Social Democratic and Green Party (Red-Green coalition) under Chancellor Gerhard Schröder immediately reversed several of their predecessors' late policy changes, including the 'demographic factor'.

But, this success proved costly, as Christian Democrats and Liberals adopted a similar strategy of blocking any government proposal subsequently. Not unlike the previous Kohl government, this proved especially troublesome for Schröder when the opposition gained a majority in the *Bundesrat* in 1999. Partly as a consequence, the first term of the Red–Green government (1998-2002) was relatively modest in its approach to tackling many of the inherited problems of the German welfare state.[4] In its second term (2002-05), however, it adopted a bolder approach in many key areas. The progress of these reforms – and subsequent reforms introduced by the Merkel-led Grand Coalition from 2005 onwards – has led to a debate among scholars over whether path-breaking change was in progress.[5] Interestingly, findings of many of these analyses suggest that the German welfare state has moved away from some of its guiding *leitmotifs* of the past.

The Red–Green government's first major reform was to pensions in 2001,[6] when contribution rates were fixed at a maximum of 20% until 2020 (and 22% until 2030), a departure from the past in that it had previously been net replacement rates that were fixed at 70% to ensure status maintenance (Hinrichs, 2003b; Schmidt, 2003). The introduction of tax advantages for newly certified voluntary private savings schemes, and a new means-tested basic security for low-income pensioners were meant to safeguard against possible pension gaps created by this shift. Whether these measures will suffice to secure incomes for pensioners with careers in atypical employment is still not clear (see Hinrichs, 2008). However, we do know that the overly optimistic old-age pension projections underpinning the benefit formula agreed in 2001 were no longer sustainable as early as 2004. Therefore, a further reform introduced a 'sustainability factor' (not unlike the 'demographic factor' so heavily fought against by the Red–Green opposition in 1998), which takes into account annual increases in the number of pensioners in relation to contributors and leads to a gradual reduction of future pension payments as a consequence. The Grand Coalition later pushed through the least popular of all pension reforms: the gradual increase of the legal retirement age from 65 to 67 between 2012 and 2029.

With regard to healthcare, reforms remained highly contested until 2003 and left the hospital sector virtually untouched at first. Healthcare has remained the most problematic sector in Germany: similar to old-age pensions, the Red–Green government immediately reversed charges introduced by the Christian Democrat/Liberal coalition. Ambitious plans by the Schröder government to introduce tightly controlled 'health budgets' had to be abandoned (Hartmann, 2003) and gridlock was exacerbated by very different ideas underpinning the views of the Left and Right on how to address the underfunding of healthcare in Germany. The Christian Democrats together with the Liberals have supported the idea of introducing 'health premiums' (*Kopfpauschale*) of around €150 for every insured person to be paid on a monthly basis. Social Democrats have fiercely opposed this suggestion, labelling it regressive, and floated the concept of 'citizen insurance' (*Bürgerversicherung*), in which every German citizen would pay an equal share of their income (including wages, capital gains and rent income) towards healthcare, as an alternative. An agreement is not yet in sight, but as this fundamental debate continues to smoulder, some incremental changes have been agreed: many of these are concerned with the efficiency and quality of services. Maybe more importantly, the 'health fund', which commenced operation in 2009, standardised contributions across all health funds and introduced tax financing of healthcare (Lisac and Schlette, 2006).

By contrast, a paradigmatic shift is evident in terms of German labour market policy. Seeleib-Kaiser and Fleckenstein (2006) and Fleckenstein (2008) have forcefully argued that the various labour market reforms inspired by the Hartz Commission (Hartz, 2002), which were at the heart Chancellor Schröder's 'Agenda 2010', constituted a move away from Bismarckian ideals. The Hartz I-III laws changed the governance structure of the Federal Labour Agency and led to stricter rules of acceptability for jobs by placement officers. In particular, the reforms resulted in the restructuring of job centres, the introduction of controversial 'mini/midi-jobs' and new opportunities for self-employment through 'Me Inc.s' ('*Ich AGs*'). All were geared towards triggering more fixed-term and temporary work and ultimately attempted to enhance employment options, especially for older workers and the un(der)employed (Trampusch, 2005).

By far the most controversial part of the Hartz legislation was the merger of unemployment and social assistance benefits (Hartz IV), which came into effect in January 2005 (Hudson et al, 2008). Fleckenstein (2008, pp 178-9) offers a formidable summary of the main changes implemented with the Hartz IV legislation: previously both unemployment benefit (*Arbeitslosengeld*) and unemployment assistance (*Arbeitslosenhilfe*) were calculated on the basis of the last earned income. According to contribution record and age of the claimant, unemployment benefit was paid up to a maximum of 32 months. Once entitlements were exhausted, the unemployed were able to claim unemployment assistance, which was unlimited in duration, means tested, but still based on previous income. Social assistance was reserved for those who failed to accumulate a sufficient contribution record; means tests were much stricter as were the conditions applied to receiving payments. With Hartz IV, the second- and third-tier system of unemployment income protection merged into a newly created, means-tested and tax-funded Unemployment Benefit II (*Arbeitslosengeld II*). Importantly, this newly created benefit was much closer to the previous social assistance rather than the unemployment assistance in terms of the level of its benefit payments and eligibility criteria. What is more, the previous unemployment benefit, now factually 'Unemployment Benefit I' (*Arbeitslosengeld I*), was reduced to a maximum duration of 12 months (18 months for those aged 55 or over), making it the principal means of income protection for all long-term unemployed. It is in this context that Hassel and Williamson (2004, p 13, cited in Fleckenstein, 2008, p 179) saw the German welfare state shift a 'significant distance towards an Anglo-American model of largely, means-tested, flat-rate jobless benefits', while, as Fleckenstein (2008, p 179) adds, 'the core of securing social status and achieved living standards, a guiding principle of the conservative welfare state, has [...] been restricted to the core of the short-term unemployed'.

Seeleib-Kaiser (2002) has made a similar argument in that he too sees a gradual dismissal by the political elites in Germany of the principle of securing achieved living standards (*Lebensstandardsicherung*) as the 'interpretative' driver of shifts in social policy making since the mid-1990s. Beyond this, however, he sees a 'dual transformation' of the German welfare state in light of the gradual expansion of family policies since the mid-1980s. Thus, the introduction of parental leave benefits by the Grand Coalition in 2007 can be seen as continuing the line of concerted attempts to expand child allowances and child tax credits, of recognising the childcaring responsibilities of mothers (by way of treating contributions of mothers equal to monetary contributions to the old-age pensions system), of forcing the establishment of parental leave schemes (as a means to facilitate the reconciliation of responsibilities both in work and at home) and, finally, of expanding the provision of childcare. To summarise, Seeleib-Kaiser (2002, p 34) stresses that 'in the cases of disability, old age and unemployment, the state no longer guarantees the standard of living. As a consequence, wage earners increasingly have to rely on the market and means-tested benefits'. While he takes these developments as indicative of broad welfare recommodification, 'the new emphasis of social policy on the "needs" of the family underscores ... a [second] redefinition of state responsibilities (recalibration)' (Seeleib-Kaiser, 2002, p 35). Hinrichs (2010) adds to this interpretation by emphasising that in recent years, that is, since the mid-1990s, the German welfare state as a whole has been steered away from contribution-based, earnings-related benefits towards tax-financed, means-tested ones, but adds that these subtle changes in both structure and ideology have unlocked a previously securely fastened door and thus have the potential to unfurl much bigger changes in the future.

A shifting German economic model?

So, while the financial crisis of the late 2000s may have precipitated a crisis in the social and economic model of many of the other nations being examined in this book, for Germany the global credit crunch arrived after a decade of increasingly bitter political debate about a crisis in the German model that had served the nation so well for much of the post-war period. And while it is perhaps too soon to draw conclusions on whether the late 2000s' economic crisis represents a critical juncture for welfare systems across the OECD, should this prove to be a turning moment, then for the German case, historians will note that the unravelling of the social market model began long before the economic crisis unfolded and will point to the significance of strong endogenous pressures for reform that were placing stress on the social model long before the exogenous force of the economic crisis bore down on European systems. Indeed, having sketched above the detail of the key policy debates that have taken place (see Table 9.1 for a summary),

Table 9.1: Major welfare reform projects in Germany, 2001-10

Healthcare	Old-age pensions	Employment policies	Family policies
2000: Focused on governance structure; stricter monitoring of hospital activity	**2001:** Fixed contribution rate at maximum of 20% until 2020; introduced tax advantages for voluntary take-up of certified savings plans (*Riester Pensions*); established a new means-tested basic security scheme for low-income pensioners	**2001–03:** Hartz I-III: Changed governance structure of Federal Labour Agency; stricter rules of acceptability for jobs offered by placement officers; Hartz IV: Merged unemployment and social assistance into Arbeitslosengeld II (since 2005)	**2007:** Introduction of parental leave benefits (*Elterngeld*)
2003: Introduced co-payments for patients; end of equal share of employers' and employees' contributions			
2007: Established 'health fund' to collect contributions at uniform rate; tax subsidies expanded (operating since 2009)	**2004:** Changed benefit formula		
2010: Raised contributions; cut spending	**2007:** Retirement age to be raised to 67 between 2012 and 2029		

it is worth examining some of the headline data in order to emphasise the strength of the endogenous pressures for reform in the German case.

Figure 9.1 shows the real GDP growth rate for Germany – with the UK for comparison – since 1990. While in both nations, the dramatic slump in GDP following the economic crisis is clear, what is startling is that growth rates for the German economy have been below those for the UK for much of the past 20 years. Indeed, during the entire period that Schröder was Chancellor, the German economy grew by more than 2% on just one occasion (the year 2000), in the years 2001–05 it never grew by more than 1.2% and, in one year (2003), it shrank. Over this same period, the UK economy grew by an average of 3% per annum and never recorded growth of less than 2%.

It is a similar story with respect to unemployment (see Figure 9.2). While (West) Germany enjoyed lower unemployment rates than the UK for much of the 1980s and 1990s, by 1996 the roles reversed as unemployment rose in Germany and fell in the UK. This remained the picture until the global economic crisis hit the UK labour market hard in 2009. Yet, the picture for Germany is more curious than might first appear, for the story here also involves unemployment rates dropping as the global economic crisis took hold. In fact, Germany's unemployment rate since the crisis unfolded in late 2007 has been lower than the

Figure 9.1: Real GDP growth since 1990

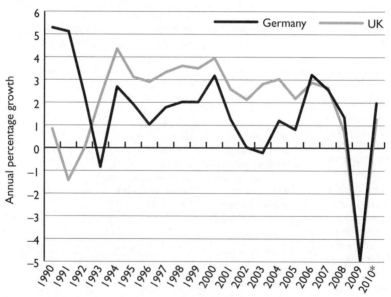

Note: *Estimated
Source: OECD (2010c)

Figure 9.2: Unemployment rate since 1991

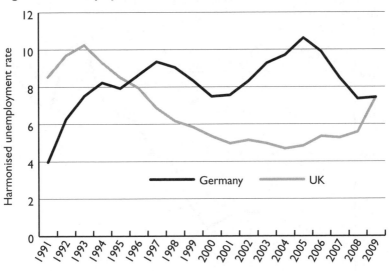

Source: OECD (2010d)

average rate during the years Schröder was Chancellor and, according to OECD projections, this will remain the case (OECD, 2010e). As discussed previously, high levels of unemployment over the course of the 1990s and 2000s have been a, if not the, key part of the endogenous pressure for reform of the German model. However, the headline figures alone do not provide the full story: youth unemployment has been consistently higher than the national average (reaching 12.5% of under 25s by 2005). Some stark regional variations exist too, many of the areas of former East Germany having suffered a difficult and only partially successful transition towards a capitalist market economy. In June 2010, the unemployment rate in East Germany went down to just under 12% (Bundesagentur für Arbeit, 2010) – a real improvement from its peak at just under 21% five years earlier (2005), but still almost double the rate of West Germany in the same year. The real extent of regional differences in unemployment becomes more pronounced when single federal states are compared: unemployment rates in Berlin and Sachsen-Anhalt, the two Eastern German federal states with the highest unemployment rates in June 2010, were at 13% and 12% respectively, while those in Baden-Württemberg and Bavaria, the two best performers in West Germany, were at or below 4.5% (Bundesagentur für Arbeit, 2008).

Figure 9.3 helps tease out a key element of the recent German economic 'recovery'. It has been widely trailed as an export-led

Figure 9.3: Trade balance (goods and services)

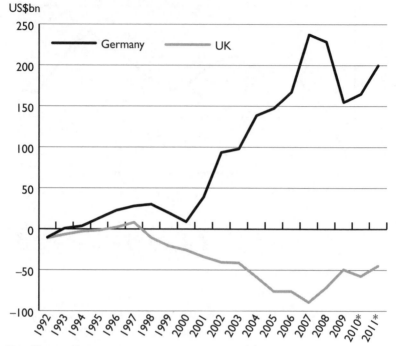

Note: *Estimated
Source: OECD (2010e)

economic strategy. Again the contrast with the UK is stark: since the turn of the century, Germany's trade balance has shown a strong surplus – exceeding US$150 billion even in 2009, despite the depressive effects of the global financial crisis. This not only represents a significant step change in performance compared to the 1990s, it also contrasts with the UK's record where a regular trading deficit featured throughout the New Labour years despite the strong record of growth in the UK at that time. While there has been some debate over how far Germany's record in recent years has been as a consequence of the weak euro (Stevens and Blackstone, 2010), the policy reforms documented above have also contributed to a significant reduction in the overall unit costs of labour in the German manufacturing sector at a time when the same costs have risen across the euro area as a whole (Figure 9.4), suggesting that domestic reforms have played a key role too.

There have also been some remarkable shifts in the overall composition of the German labour market over the past decade and, in particular, in the period since the Hartz reforms began. In common with other high-income OECD countries, industry has declined considerably

Figure 9.4: Unit labour costs in manufacturing

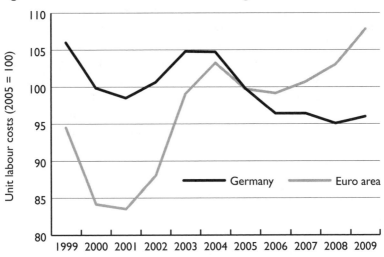

Source: OECD (2010e)

since the 1980s in terms of the share of total employment it accounts for. Yet, manufacturing continues to play a much more significant role in the economy than in most 'competitor' nations and is roughly twice the size of the sector in the UK or the United States (US) (OECD, 2009b). Germany's reliance on the traditional industrial economy was long seen as part of its traditional male breadwinner model. However, there are signs that the increasing size of the service sector is helping the economy to broaden its base of workers. Notably, after sticking at around the 65% rate for much of the past two decades, the overall participation rate in the labour market has steadily increased in the past few years and exceeded 70% by 2008 (OECD, 2010c). A key factor in this shift has been a rapid increase in female participation rates. While through the course of the 1980s (West) Germany rarely saw 50% of working-age women in employment, by 2008 the female participation rate stood at 64% compared with 59% just before the Hartz reforms began and 56% when Schröder came to office in 1998 (OECD, 2010c). Indeed, the rising participation rates and female participation rates left the German economy looking remarkably similar to the UK's in these two regards by the time the economic crisis began: a significant change by any account.

Unsurprisingly, these shifts in the composition of the economy and related changes to social and employment protections, have fuelled an increase in economic inequality too. In fact, the OECD (2008a) showed that due to a widening in the distribution of gross wages and an increase in the proportion of households without any market income to 19.4%, the highest rate of all OECD countries, income inequality increased more in Germany than in any other OECD country between 2000 and 2005. In those five years, income inequality in Germany increased more than in the previous 15 years taken together (1985-2000). While child poverty increased from 7% to 16%, the richest 10% accumulated around a quarter of the total disposable income and around 50% of the total net worth by the year 2005. The only bright spot in this gloomy picture was the fact that only 2-3% of the poor remained in poverty for more than three years and that Germany still did relatively well, and much better than the UK or the US, in terms of its social mobility.

In short, going into the global economic crisis, Germany had already undergone a period of considerable economic and social change that challenged many key features of the traditional German model. Perhaps in part because of this it has (so far) weathered the storm of the economic crisis better than many comparator nations, although this should not deflect from the not insignificant social impact of the crisis. Yet we might also add that luck perhaps played a part in Germany's relatively strong economic performance too. Certainly the depression in the value of the euro has helped Germany's export-led growth strategy. Added to this, its large manufacturing sector allowed it to adopt such a strategy, but a corollary of this is that Germany went into the global economic crisis with a much smaller financial services sector than is typical for a G7 nation. Indeed, in 2007 the value-added share of the financial intermediation sector was just 4% for Germany compared to almost 8% for both the UK and the US and an average of 7% across the G7. What is particularly interesting here is that what was often deemed a relative failure of the German economy over the course of the 1990s and much of the 2000s turned out to be a comparative strength by the end of the 2000s: the sector had grown in the UK, the US and across the G7 from a position similar to Germany's at the start of this period while in Germany the sector had remained flat (OECD, 2009b). Buoyed by the comparative robustness of its figures, the German response once the crisis hit was much less radical than that deployed in most other G7 countries. It is to the detail of the crisis package that we now turn.

Responding the global crisis: business as usual?

Despite the very similar extent of their cyclical deficits at the outset of the financial crisis, the reaction, fiscally and structurally, in Germany was relatively modest compared to other major economies, in particular the UK. In October 2008, the Grand Coalition passed the 'emergency package' for banks (*Rettungpaket*). The Grand Coalition made available €500 billion – of which €400 billion were debt guarantees and thus did not translate into new debts immediately – to stabilise the banking sector or, to use the government's rhetoric, to establish a 'protective screen' for banks. After some reluctance at the beginning, many land banks (*Landesbanken*) but also some private banks signed up to access this financial support, despite the fact that conditions applied. Indeed, in every case where support was received, an investigation of corporate policy had to be agreed, while managerial salaries were not allowed to surpass €500,000 and the payments of bonuses and dividends was discontinued.

The first of two stimulus packages (*Konjunkturpakete*), which included a total of 15 measures amounting to a total investment of €50 billion to secure up to a million jobs, soon followed in November 2008. Measures were fixed for two years and entailed: a waiver of motor vehicle tax for newly bought, low-emission cars; a reduction in the tax burden for some small businesses; and a €3 billion investment in green building developments aimed at reducing the carbon dioxide (CO_2) emissions of industrial plants. A further loan programme geared at medium-sized businesses had a volume of another €15 billion. Traffic investments worth another €1 billion were brought forward too. The second stimulus package, passed in January 2009, again had a volume of €50 billion: a large part of these funds was dedicated to the improvement of school buildings around the country, but reductions in the marginal tax rates down to 14% were also part of this plan to relieve some pressure on those on low incomes. It also saw the introduction of the 'car scrappage scheme' to help the struggling car manufacturers in Germany. Later, this scheme was relabelled 'environment scheme' since payment of the €2,500 premium for scrappage was tied to newly bought cars meeting strict CO_2 efficiency standards. A maximum of €1.5 billion was dedicated to this scheme providing scope to replace around 600,000 cars in total. Most importantly, however, as part of the second stimulus package, the German shorter working hours scheme (*Kurzarbeit*) was extended to 24 months initially (German Parliament has recently extended this scheme for another 18 months until March 2012). At its peak in May 2009, the scheme supplemented the pay of 1.516 million workers who had suffered a cut in working hours in the wake of recession. With the help of the €5.1 billion in federal funds, these workers have continued to receive 80% of their previous wages for working half time. Despite increased worries within Germany that the systematic government supplementation of wages has gone too far, the OECD (2009b) hailed the German shorter working hours scheme as a great success and advocated it as a model for other countries as it saved around 500,000 jobs during the recession, according to its calculations. The above measures caused some degree of political consternation as they went against the government's early commitment to achieve a balanced budget by 2011 – in fact the German government was right on course to achieve this overarching goal just prior to the financial crisis. Merkel was therefore keen to underline the necessary and temporary character of these measures. A more far-reaching push towards a Keynesian approach, and move away from the fiscal orthodoxy that characterised Germany, was never a serious option. Instead, after winning her second chancellorship and this time with her preferred partner, the Liberals, Merkel passed an 'austerity package' in June 2010. This package was criticised by parts of the media and the political opposition as 'socially unbalanced'; others dubbed it a 'mini austerity programme' that failed to go far enough. There is some truth to both these interpretations. At first sight, the envisaged savings do not compare well with the sums spent on the different emergency and stimulus packages beforehand: in 2011, the budget deficit will be reduced by €11 billion; by 2014, this figure is supposed to rise to €27 billion. Critical voices have warned that envisaged savings fail to correspond with the controversial 'debt-brake' (*Schuldenbremse*) regulation adopted in August 2009.[7]

The biggest single chunk of savings is envisaged through measures to 'adjust social policies'. The Federal Employment Office will have to save between €1.5 billion and €3.0 billion annually between 2011 and 2014; a further €1.8 billion annually is to be cut by abandoning state contributions to old-age pensions for claimants of unemployment assistance (*Arbeitslosengeld II*); parental leave benefit is also to be cancelled for this group. Although not insignificant in scale, these adjustments very much follow the line of policy reform already being pursued before the financial crisis, centring around a gradual erosion of social rights for the long-term unemployed. While the Christian Democrat/Liberal coalition has pledged to cut around 10,000 public sector posts, resulting savings are moderate at €2.0 billion to €2.5 billion annually until 2014, particularly in comparison to the savings to be generated by comparator nations, but also modest when compared to the saving to be generated by changes to Germany's energy and transport policies.

In gauging the thinking underlining this rather modest package of policies, Germany's role in shaping the international response to the financial crisis is also instructive. So, for instance, Germany played a key role in helping to stabilise the euro with the German Parliament authorising expenditure of some €750 billion to a fund for protecting the currency in May 2010 shortly after contributing some €22.4 billion to a package put together to bail out the Greek economy (Kollewe, 2010). However, it is widely acknowledged that in return for its reluctant contribution to these funds, Germany has gained considerable concessions in terms of future fiscal policy in the eurozone, be it in terms of insisting that Greece implements deep cuts in its public spending or in pushing a new European Union (EU) -wide toolbox for economic governance designed to penalise nations with seriously imbalanced budgets (Kollewe, 2010; Traynor, 2010). Interestingly, Germany's role in pushing the EU in this direction has opened up a divide among the G8 and G20 members that was barely disguised during the Toronto summit in June 2010. While the US – along with China and Russia – argued the case for a continuation of the Keynesian-influenced fiscal stimulus-based response to the economic crisis in 2008/09, Germany led the EU members in arguing the case for a more orthodox, balanced budget-based fiscal tightening from 2010 (Elliot, 2010; Pabst, 2010).

In many regards, the Toronto summit seemed to represent an odd state of affairs, with the US standing firm as advocates of a strong package of state-led intervention to ameliorate the social impact of an economic crisis, holding out against the strong advocacy of leading European nations for radical austerity packages required on economic grounds despite their potentially large social impact. However, from a German perspective, the emphasis on fiscal orthodoxy is not, perhaps, unusual. Indeed, Allen (2005) claims that Germany occupied an unusual position in post-war Europe in so far as apart from a brief period in the late 1960s, Keynesian ideas failed to gain any real traction in shaping economic policy. Allen's view is that fiscal orthodoxy has long formed the basis of Germany's long-run dominant political economy paradigm and that significant path-dependent pressures have prevented any serious moves towards an alternative model. All this suggests that far from the global economic crisis unleashing a new economic paradigm on German policy makers, it has merely allowed it – after implementing a modest and short-lived fiscal stimulus package – to return to its usual modus operandi and, indeed, push the case for tighter budgetary policy across the EU.

At the same time, as we have noted above, there are increasing signs that Germany has begun to dismantle some central aspects of its long-run social model. Indeed, some commentators even believe that some recent reforms can be regarded as path-breaking changes, although others are sceptical about this claim. However, irrespective of the outcome of that particular debate, a key observation to be made here is that the major social policy reforms that have taken place were *not* inspired by the global economic crisis. Instead, they arose from strong endogenous pressures, many relating to reunification, and the key reforms had been implemented *before* the global economic crisis begun. While social policy cuts have been a key part of the fiscal austerity package, they have been relatively modest in scale and, for the most part, merely followed the line of reform already being implemented pre-crisis.

Taken together, these two strands of thinking lead us towards what is, perhaps, a somewhat surprising conclusion. Our editors note in the introduction to this book (Chapter One) that '[t]he evolution of social policy is punctuated with key dates.... However, no period in history is likely to prove to be quite so significant for quite so many welfare systems as is the late 2000s'. But, while the impact of the crisis seems potentially path breaking in many of the countries examined in other chapters, for Germany the impact seems rather muted. The economic crisis hit Germany after it had already endured a long and often turbulent period of social reform over the course of the late 1990s and early to mid-2000s. The crisis itself was less significant for Germany, with its relatively small financial sector, than it was for the UK or the US and, indeed, perhaps even had a positive impact in so far as the depression of the euro aided its export-led economic plan. Merkel's governments tiptoed through the crisis and it already seems that, in Germany, it is now a case of business as usual.

Notes

[1] This is a carefully selected measure that spins the picture a little – although there is little doubt that the UK had managed to reverse a long-term position in overtaking Germany with regard to Gross Domestic Product (GDP) per capita.

[2] Busch (2005, p 134) notes that since inflation has historically been low in Germany compared to other European countries, its economy has been affected by some of the highest real interest rates in the eurozone as a consequence of this loss of autonomy over monetary policy.

[3] Data are downloadable from www.destatis.de/ and http://stats.oecd. org/

[4] Although we should note that disputes between 'traditionalists' and 'modernisers' within the Social Democratic Party of Germany certainly played a part as well (Egle and Henkes, 2003).

[5] For contributions to this debate, see Hinrichs (2003a), Leibfried and Obinger (2003), Seeleib-Kaiser (2003), Clasen (2005), Seeleib-Kaiser and Fleckenstein (2006), Hudson et al (2008), Zohlnhöfer (2008) and Oelschläger (2009).

[6] The government only managed to gain a majority in the German Parliament (*Bundestag*) by granting concessions to 'traditionalists' in the Social Democratic Party and some of the Christian Democratic members of the Upper Chamber of Parliament (Trampusch, 2006).

[7] The 'debt-brake' rule has made net borrowing in excess of 0.35% of Gross National Product (GNP) from January 2011 unlawful. This rule is an addition to the German Basic Law (*Grundgesetz*) and so compliance with the requirement of balanced budgets will be compulsory for the German Federation (*Bund*) from 2016 and for the *Länder* from 2020.

TEN

Ireland and the impact of the economic crisis: upholding the dominant policy paradigm

Mairéad Considine and Fiona Dukelow

Introduction

Ireland represents one of the more extreme cases of economic damage in the global economic crisis. The country became the first in the euro area to enter recession and, over the period 2008 to 2010, Gross Domestic Product (GDP) declined by about 11%. Ireland's banking crisis is, along with Iceland's, one of the largest of the advanced economies and the country also had the largest current deficit in the European Union (EU) by 2010. This situation poses near-impossible challenges and severe economic and social hardship. Such a rupture from the previous decade of high growth, for which Ireland was feted as a paradigm case of embracing neoliberal globalisation, would suggest potential for serious questioning of the model pursued and the level of economic and social risks it engendered. Perhaps paradoxically, however, the policy response to the Irish crisis has been characterised by a rapid and severe turn to austerity, with alternative proposals for economic recovery so far gaining little ground. While fundamental questions have been asked about the model of economic development pursued during the boom years, this has not translated into any radically different proposals in mainstream political discourse about how this might change. Instead, the idea that there is no alternative to the current policy trajectory weighed heavily in the debate as the crisis unfolded, and the EU/International Monetary Fund (IMF) loan deal agreed in late 2010 has further re-enforced the policy response of austerity and retrenchment.

Given this set of observations, this chapter aims to document the economic crisis and examine why, although the severity of the economic crisis might represent the conditions for what Hall (1993) describes as a third order change (when the dominant paradigm is challenged and changed to the extent that a paradigm shift occurs), there is little evidence of this occurring in the Irish case. As of late 2010, the crisis in Ireland remained far from resolved and in this climate, shifts can be difficult to confirm, being more easily identified after the event (see also Hill, this volume). However, if paradigm is taken to mean the 'cognitive background assumptions that constrain action by limiting the range of alternatives that policy-making elites are likely to perceive as useful and worth considering' (Campbell, 1998, p 385), it would appear that, so far, reaction has been heavily influenced by the policy legacy of the past, in particular, what are considered key components of the economic model that previously pertained and the need to attend to those in order to return to prosperity. While adhering to the pre-crisis economic model is a major element of the response, this is not a passive process; much policy action is needed to get back to 'business as usual'. The present situation may therefore be identified as a period of exceptional policy making (Hay, 2006), especially with regard to the unprecedented levels of state support for the banking system. Yet what comes with periods of exceptionalism, namely that 'the very parameters that previously circumscribed policy options are cast asunder and replaced, and in which the realm of the politically possible, feasible and desirable is correspondingly reconfigured' (Hay, 2006, p 67), does not appear to follow in this case. Instead, it may be suggested that what is being sought in mainstream politics is not so much a reconfiguration but a reinforcement of Ireland's pre-existing economic model.

The chapter proceeds in three sections. The first section sets the backdrop for examining the current crisis with reference to the evolution of the dominant economic paradigm and the position of the Irish welfare state in that context. The second section explains the specifics of the crisis, referring to the constellation of domestic and global factors that have had an impact on Ireland's problems. Attention is given to how the crisis is framed and responded to, demonstrating that this does not significantly deviate from the pre-crisis policy paradigm. The final section brings this analysis to bear on the impact of the policy responses on the Irish welfare state, where austerity and retrenchment measures to date suggest a certain reversion to type.

The evolution of Ireland's economic policy paradigm and its relationship to welfare state development

The dynamics at play in the current crisis indicate the significance of ideational path dependence in the Irish case. The background provided here maps the economic and social policy legacy in order to consider its bearing on the framing of, and responses to, the current crisis. Ireland has had a relatively long trajectory of opening its economy, triggered by waves of economic failure, and a welfare state settlement that has been tailored to the requirements of the dominant economic paradigm. The pursuit of a more open and expansionary economic model began after economic protectionism culminated in a crisis in the 1950s that Ireland seemed to suffer alone. Widespread unemployment and emigration contrasted with economic prosperity elsewhere in Europe (Kennedy et al, 1988; Jacobsen, 1994). A change in policy in 1958 signalled a major paradigmatic shift to a more open economy, an option that was constructed as an imperative given the failure of the previous model. This shift in strategy has been at the core of the subsequent institutional path followed. It marked Ireland as 'an early example of a state-orchestrated opening of the economy to the forces of globalisation' (Ginsburg, 2001, p 176), placing it 'well ahead of the field' (Ruane and Görg, 1997, p 20) in pursuing and attracting foreign direct investment (FDI). The strategy was reasonably successful in generating employment and economic growth, although it marked the emergence of a dual economy with negative consequences for indigenous industry and poor domestic policy choices that would return to trouble the macroeconomic landscape. Modest improvements were made in social services although living standards remained low; GDP per capita was 58% of the European Economic Community average when Ireland joined in 1973. The evolution of the welfare state to an extent reflects the limited nature of this economic development; focus centred on the political and economic legitimacy of the Irish state and a conservative approach to social policy dominated by Catholic social thinking (Fanning, 2003). In contrast to the expansionary period of welfare state development experienced in many European countries, Irish social policy developed later and in a more ad-hoc way, and social investment was predicated upon the economic model delivering the dividend from which such social policy could only then be developed (Considine and Dukelow, 2009).

Another wave of economic crisis was experienced in the 1980s, this time more evidently created by a constellation of international and domestic factors. This recession was long and more deeply felt in Ireland than in many other countries. Ultimately, a policy of fiscal retrenchment was implemented with a renewed focus on winning foreign investment under a new social partnership framework. Current spending was reduced by 10% in real terms between 1987 and 1989 although by 1991 expenditure levels were restored to their previous levels (Ó Riain and O'Connell, 2000). Cutbacks initiated at this time are often perceived to have been central to economic recovery, even if this policy response was damaging to social services. Significantly, key drivers of subsequent economic growth, including macroeconomic stability, access to European markets and to substantial EU funds, and improved external economic conditions are often sidelined in how the crisis and the policy responses of the 1980s are recounted in the current crisis, which tends to privilege the role that retrenchment played as a solution to the problems. The macroeconomic climate within which the Irish neo-corporatist framework evolved, changed from one of crisis to recovery and boom in the space of a decade, thus bringing into sharper focus what Boucher and Collins (2003, p 302) describe as 'a consensus among Ireland's elite to take the country in two apparently contradictory directions at once: towards European neo-corporatism and toward American neo-liberalism'.

As global trade and investment grew, Ireland became a significant site for new FDI, particularly from firms in the United States (US) wishing to gain a foothold in Europe, attracted by ongoing generous terms, including the lowest rate of corporation tax in Europe. In particular, investment in the financial services sector was won by promoting Ireland as an exemplar of the Anglo-Saxon business model (IDA, in Allen, 2009). Ireland gained recognition as a remarkable economic success story by the late 1990s, appearing favourably on various international indices that attempt to quantify constructs such as global integration, competitiveness and economic freedom. Economists such as Krugman (1997) and Sachs (1997) highlighted how Ireland's changing fortunes reflected the type of economic globalisation unfolding at that time, affirming Ireland's 'iconic status' (Jacobson and Kirby, 2006, p 26) as a successful globalised economy.

By the early 2000s, Ireland became noticeably feted by neoliberal apologists of economic globalisation, including 'globalisation guru' Kenichi Ohmae (2000) and the Cato Institute. The latter (Powell, 2003) explained Ireland's economic growth as a matter of implementing policies, which increased economic freedom and thereby enhanced growth and prosperity. Ireland's low-tax, low-spend model created market conditions for entrepreneurship and flourishing profit opportunities, which in turn proved a magnet for FDI (Powell, 2003). Similarly, Friedman (2005a, 2005b) eulogised the Irish growth model, in particular its innovative and flexible approach to labour supply. In a passage that predicted convergence to a minimal neoliberal model, he proclaims: 'it is obvious to me that the Irish-British model is the way of the future, and the only question is when Germany and France will face reality: either they become Ireland or they become museums. That is their real choice over the next few years – it's either the leprechaun way or the Louvre' (Friedman, 2005b).

External assessments of Ireland's success appear to have become a significant ideational influence in the evolution of the dominant policy paradigm over the 2000s and its internalisation in mainstream political discourse. The acceptance of globalisation as a beneficial force was not only part of the dominant policy paradigm but also the concept itself was beyond discussion, despite the reality that, as Antoniades (2007, p 314) explains, 'the main "objects" of economic globalisation (e.g. deregulation, privatisation, tax cuts) were ever-present in Irish politics. Yet, these objects did not define a new zone of contestation, but rather a set of taken-for-granted policies and practices'. Debates about the nature of globalisation and its impact were rare. Instead, the 'exemplar position' appears to have been subsumed into Irish political discourse about how economic wealth was created and how to sustain it.

The Irish approach demonstrates how 'neoliberalism is less a coherent totality, as is often assumed, than a loose conglomeration of institutions, ideas, and policy prescriptions from which actors pick and choose depending on prevailing political, economic, social, historical, and institutional conditions. The results can be either contradictory or complementary' (Campbell and Pedersen, 2001, p 3). Contradictions in the Irish approach were evident in the fact that substantial social investment and notable social policy developments (for example the establishment of the National Anti-Poverty Strategy and Equality Authority) took place at the same time as the overall level of welfare effort declined, relative income inequality increased and the dualistic nature of Irish social services became more deeply embedded (Kirby, 2008). While the Irish brand of neo-corporatism may have been perceived to steer Ireland from its liberal welfare tradition, with some social partners attempting to mediate the effects of the contradictions through concessions won on the social policy front, this was only made possible because traditional tax and spend trade-offs were not a fiscal necessity (given government surpluses derived from unsustainable sources, discussed in the next section), at the peak of the boom. Ostensibly, then, economic management assumed and internalised an idea that Ireland had found the 'winning formula': combining neoliberal economic policy, corporatist-style policy consensus and economic competitiveness with more explicit, although targeted, social policy commitments. Ireland appeared to be 'on an expansionary course' (Daly and Yeates, 2003, p 94) in respect of certain ground-breaking but ultimately short-lived social policy initiatives, and in making up for decades of underinvestment. However, these trends were not sufficient to mark a decisive break with the liberal welfare tradition. Greater social expenditure in the 2000s did not address the public–private divide in access to health and housing, market reliance to supplement social provisions grew and comparatively low rates of social welfare expenditure demonstrated a failure to break out of the liberal paradigm in any quantitative sense. The historical legacy of prioritising economic growth and limiting social policy development to what is politically necessary within the parameters of what is compatible with the overarching economic strategy, is significant in the Irish case. The extent and influence of ideational path dependency is now being tested in more difficult times. The evidence, thus far, points to a reassertion of the dominant policy paradigm notwithstanding the severity of the current crisis.

The evolution of the current Irish crisis and the framing of policy responses

Moving from the contextual outline of Ireland's crisis-prone economic trajectory and its policy legacy of limits to welfare development, this section spotlights Ireland's current economic crisis the root of which lies in the Irish property asset bubble originating in the mid-1990s. While similar property asset bubbles were forming elsewhere, and are related to the global economic crisis, these have been most severe among liberal economies. Within that subset, Ireland had the 'steepest and longest' (Honohan, 2009, p 209) of these bubbles with real house prices almost trebling in real terms in just over a decade, exceeding the UK's two and a half times increase and the doubling of house prices that took place in Australia, New Zealand and Spain (André, 2010). Much of the catch-up in Irish economic performance in the 1990s found expression in housing investment. Irish housing policy was not tenure neutral, but predicated on the idea that ownership was the tenure of choice for the majority of people. Policy actively created a material preference for home ownership as the commonsense financial option, the Irish housing regime being one of the least taxed in the OECD (OECD, 2008b). In addition, access to housing finance became easier following liberalisation of the Irish mortgage market in the 1980s (Conefrey and Fitz Gerald, 2009). Subsequent European and global changes during the 2000s, which saw growing integration of financial markets, high levels of global liquidity and a general loosening of monetary policy, continued this trend. Such conditions drove house prices further and the market became increasingly speculative.

Domestic fiscal and housing policy also played a role in these developments, creating a case of 'personal Keynesianism' (Blyth, 2008, p 391), fuelling growth in housing and consumption in the wider economy. Recommendations to curb house price growth via fiscal policy were made by transnational organisations such as the IMF (2003) and the OECD (2006). These recommendations, together with national public commentary, most notably by Kelly (2007), which warned of a house price crash, were treated as extremely contrarian positions in political discourse; it was dominated by the idea that the fundamentals of the housing market were sound and unlike conditions which caused property crashes elsewhere. The ideational path dependency effect of the emphasis on home ownership meant that policy discourse revolved around addressing affordability by assisting people with house purchases, constraining the use of fiscal policy, which on balance was inappropriately used to the effect of further stimulating the market.

Construction and property price inflation also had significant distortionary effects on government revenue; by 2006, for example, revenue from stamp duty on property transactions was three and a half times more than the amount derived from the same source in 2002 (NESC, 2009). Property-related revenue streams allowed a continuation of personal income taxation reduction into the 2000s, which seemed to confirm Ireland's success as a neoliberal business model. However, the shift in the composition of revenue left the Exchequer extremely vulnerable to a drop in tax receipts triggered by the house price crash.

The prevailing light-touch financial supervision and regulation regime also contributed to Ireland's economic vulnerability. This regime reflected the global shift towards less government intervention in this area. In the Irish context, the role played by financial supervision and regulation in allowing the credit and property boom spiral and heightening vulnerability to a general economic crash represents one of the more extreme cases of this shift. During the boom, however, concern about oversight or regulatory deficiencies were not part of public or political discourse. The Irish regime was promoted as a positive element of the economic model, integral to winning new foreign investment particularly in financial services. Policy emphasised the importance of a flexible principles-based regulation regime in maintaining competitive advantage in the midst of mounting competition for global financial services investment (Department of the Taoiseach, 2006). The perilous implications of this regime were highlighted in two reports published as part of a review of the role of banking and financial regulation in the lead-up to the economic crisis (Honohan, 2010; Regling and Watson, 2010). Both draw attention to weaknesses of the regulatory culture, which oversaw banks participating in increasingly risky property-based lending transactions.

Bringing these strands of the mounting imbalances in the Irish economy together, puts the relationship between the peak of the global and Irish crisis in perspective. Unlike many other countries, Ireland's banking crisis stems not from exposure to international bad debts but primarily from its high-risk Irish property debts resulting from the property market correction that began to occur in 2007. The crisis was therefore domestically triggered as opposed to being the product of an exogenous shock to a stable system. As Regling and Watson (2010, p 29) put it, Ireland's 'problems lay in plain vanilla property lending ... facilitated by heavy non-deposit funding, and in governance weaknesses of an easily recognisable kind'. These domestic vulnerabilities meant that the country had no buffer against the shock of the unprecedented global credit crunch and again domestic and global factors conspired in mutually reinforcing ways to produce a deep economic and social crisis.

Responding to the crisis

Recognition of the problems posed by domestically induced economic vulnerabilities were largely absent in mainstream political discourse at first. In July 2008, the Minister for Finance contrasted the soundness of the Irish economy with the problems being encountered elsewhere as the credit crunch began to spread:

> [T]he underlying health of the Irish economy remains solid. ... we have a low level of public debt; our markets are flexible allowing us to respond quickly to difficulties; we have a dynamic and well-educated labour force; and the tax burden on workers and businesses is low. Not many countries anywhere in the world are facing the present global economic difficulties from such an enviable position. (Lenihan, 2008a)

Despite the subsequent sharp decline in the economy, which quickly reversed the minister's portrayal of Ireland's 'enviable position', the economic policy paradigm pursued prior to the crisis has been consistently re-iterated as a principle of faith (Campbell, 1998) or a programmatic idea (Schmidt, 2008) at the core of the political response to the crisis. This policy paradigm holds significant influence in defining 'the problems to be solved...; the issues to be considered; the goals to be achieved; the norms, methods and instruments to be applied; and the ideals that frame the more immediate policy ideas proposed to solve any given problem' (Schmidt, 2008, p 306). The goal to be achieved is to return the economy to 'pole position' (Department of the Taoiseach, 2008, p 32). Consequently, discourse on what the crisis is, together with policy proposals and solutions, are constrained by the policy formula that is perceived to have produced the period of economic prosperity prior to the crisis. Past success remains the source of reference in navigating the crisis, as evident in one of the first speeches framing the crisis, made by the Taoiseach: 'Ireland ... has been a prime example of where an agile, small economy that focuses on the right strategies' produces full employment (Cowen, 2008). The role of government and business is one of 'agility and pragmatism', which 'keeps us ahead of the competition and demonstrates to the international business world that we are a place to come and do business' (Cowen, 2008) and crucially it entails a policy preference for retrenchment over other possible routes out of recession: 'we cannot simply borrow our way out of trouble or return to the days of punitive tax rates that stifled economic growth and resulted in high unemployment' (Cowen, 2008). This latter point has played a major part in the policy response as explored below.

The unfolding economic and fiscal contraction was presented as a largely externally generated crisis to which Ireland was especially vulnerable because of its small open nature, and which skewed what was acknowledged as signs of a 'downturn' into a much more serious crisis: 'as a small open economy, we are especially vulnerable to economic shocks beyond our shores. The international credit crisis has compounded and deepened the downturn in the construction sector....' (Lenihan, 2008b). This early attribution of the crisis to external forces creating a shock to the system shaped the terrain of what the crisis was about and marginalised counter-assessments. Attention to the economic and social risks of the Irish political economy model and the 'home-grown' nature of the property and banking crisis have latterly become more prominent in debates. However, these would appear to have gained attention too late to divert the action set in motion by the rapid attribution of the crisis to domestic shock generated by external forces. The construction of the scope and nature of the crisis has also been significant in limiting the definition of problems and policy solutions. Political discourse has coalesced around two core issues – a fiscal crisis and a banking crisis – and together these feed into a third issue identified as a 'reputational' crisis concerning the credibility of Ireland's 'economic brand'. Alternative analyses and policy actors have attempted to frame the crisis around other problems, most significantly the unemployment crisis and the wider social crisis (for example NESC, 2009). However, these have been marginalised in the mainstream definition of what is of 'systemic importance' and in the 'national interest', even if the dominant policy responses are based on contradictory ideas that become apparent when the fiscal and banking crises are examined.

The fiscal and banking crises

Ireland has the largest current government deficit in the eurozone. This deficit is underlined by a 30% decline in tax revenues between 2007 and 2010. Tax revenues have fallen back to 2003 levels while government expenditure has risen by 70% since that period. From the outset, the conceptual repertoire used to interpret the fiscal crisis has emphasised to varying degrees the problem of expenditure being too high over revenue being too low, frequently captured in the phrase 'living beyond our means'. Given the scale of the crisis, fiscal changes have involved expenditure cuts and tax increases, however the extent to which taxation is used has been circumscribed by the need to maintain a 'credible tax regime' as part of the policy response. Between 2008 and 2010, prior to EU/IMF intervention, tax increases and expenditure cutbacks amounting to €14.6 billion were implemented, with cuts in expenditure of €10 billion (8% of 2010 GNP) forming the bulk of this change (Government of Ireland, 2010). The notion of a credible tax regime was articulated in the 2009 Budget as part of the imperative of 'fiscal responsibility' needing protection:'Fiscal responsibility has been a cornerstone of our economic success ... we cannot put our reputation for fiscal responsibility in jeopardy. We must take the right decisions now to put the budgetary position on a path to stability' (Lenihan, 2008b). Such ideas have influenced a programme of retrenchment since the earliest acknowledgements of economic difficulty against which there has been little dissent in wider discourse, particularly economic discourse. Contest has tended to focus more on where the axe should fall rather than questioning the need for retrenchment. The notion of there being no alternative to retrenchment is justified with recourse to external sources of pressure that would push domestic problems into a sovereign debt crisis and economic catastrophe. This scenario and cost of inaction is captured in the Minister for Finance's speech concerning the introduction of 'Financial Emergency Measures in the Public Interest' in February 2009:

> [I]t is no exaggeration to say that this country is now fighting for its economic future. Unless we demonstrate the

will to restore stability to our public finances, there will be no economic recovery. The world is looking on. We need to persuade the international markets that we are capable of taking the tough decisions now to get our house in order. If we cannot do that, we are in danger of losing all the gains we have made over the last twenty years. (Lenihan, 2009a)

Other internal and external factors have contributed to this shaping of the response to the fiscal crisis. Factors notable for their lack of influence include the social partnership approach to policy making. The crisis has led to its demise as the government forged ahead with a public sector pension levy and pay cuts without social partnership agreement. Furthermore, the trades union movement has been unable to garner momentum around its alternative programme focusing on stimulus as an instrument of economic recovery (ICTU, 2009). By contrast, the *Report of the Special Group on Public Service Numbers and Expenditure Programmes* (McCarthy, 2009a) became highly influential in amplifying the idea of the political necessity of austerity. Chaired by economist Colm McCarthy, the group was commissioned to examine public expenditure and identify potential reductions in public sector numbers, and rationalisation of expenditure programmes and state agencies. Its identification of potential savings of €5 billion (approximately 10% of annual government expenditure) gained most attention and became a key part of the political shaping of public sentiment towards changes made in the 2010 Budget. This budget focused heavily on expenditure cuts as the effective solution and the obvious choice. These ideas were apparent in extensive debate preceding the Budget focusing on an over-sized public sector, and disparities between private sector pay and pension conditions versus those of public sector employees. The *Commission on Taxation Report 2009* (Commission on Taxation, 2009) garnered less attention but was significant in affirming views about the role of taxation in responding to the crisis. It focused on creating a broader and less volatile tax base and recommended the introduction of an annual property tax and environmental taxes. Yet its relatively modest proposals were heavily determined by terms of reference, which tasked it with conforming to government goals including keeping the 'overall tax burden low' and guaranteeing 'that the 12.5% corporation tax rate will remain' (Commission on Taxation, 2009, p 1).

The political use of these internal resources has been augmented by a 'symbolic translation' (Campbell, 2004, cited in Béland, 2009) of outside ideas. The overarching influence here has been the need to return the public finances within the limits set by the Eurozone Stability and Growth Pact. The urgency of austerity and the instruments used to reach this limit benefited from selective reference to transnational organisations and their observations about the Irish crisis. Prior to EU/IMF funding, the scenario of having to resort to IMF assistance and the pain that would engender, was frequently referred to in media commentary and this prospect was used to mobilise public acceptance of the government's budgetary measures. The Minister for Health (Harney, cited in McGee, 2009) suggested that '[i]f the Government hasn't the capacity to do what's needed, then others will come in, like the IMF, and overnight they will make decisions ... then they will immediately start cutting expenditure by maybe 30 or 40%, and that is a fact'.

Similarly, the OECD's (2009a) stark review of the Irish economic crisis, which recommended substantial cuts to public services as unavoidable, was described as 'compulsory reading' by the Minister for Finance (McArdle, 2009). As the government implemented its austerity programme, crisis discourse seemed at first to move from containment to stabilisation. Frequent recourse was made to external comments judged to affirm the government's tough but correct decisions, and the need to maintain tight fiscal discipline in order to sustain renewed, but still precarious credibility with international markets. Typical comments included the OECD's (2010a, p 148) observation that 'the overall emphasis on reducing spending rather than increasing taxes is appropriate' and the IMF's (2010e, p 1) reference to 'aggressive measures' being taken to restore credibility.

However, reflecting the contradictions and pragmatism of neoliberal ideas in practice, strong disparities are evident between the political responses to the fiscal crisis and the banking crisis. In contrast to the regime of tight fiscal discipline and the reference to risks surrounding borrowing too much or diverting from a low-tax economy model in order to fund current expenditure, no limits have been applied to the support that government has pledged to save the banking system. As the Minister for Finance has stated, 'whatever is required to be done will be done by the Irish state' (Lenihan, 2010a) and the borrowing required to fund that was not problematised. What was initially construed as a temporary liquidity problem created by international financial turmoil has gradually been revealed as a major bank solvency problem. In the process, the level of action required to maintain a functioning banking system has escalated and contributed significantly to the national debt, which has more than trebled from 25% in 2007 to 97% in 2010. The unprecedented move in September 2008 of introducing a blanket, system-wide guarantee of bank deposits and other liabilities for two years is valued at €365 billion, more than 2.5 times the Gross National Product (GNP). This guarantee, underpinned by a consensus 'that no Irish bank should be allowed to fail' (Honohan, 2010, p 119), paved the way for major state investment into the banking system as the gravity of the crisis grew. Since 2008, the actual cost of state liability for banking debt has continued to rise, reaching approximately 50% of GNP in 2010. This contributed greatly to the escalation of Ireland's borrowing costs on international money markets over the course of 2010, ultimately resulting in EU/IMF intervention with a loan package of €67.5 billion predicated on restructuring the banking system and implementing further fiscal retrenchment. Under the *National Recovery Plan 2011-2014* (Government of Ireland, 2010), which plays an important part in meeting the conditions associated with EU/IMF assistance, another €10 billion of expenditure cuts are planned along with €5 billion worth of revenue-raising measures with the aim of reaching the Stability and Growth Pact deficit rate of 3% of GDP by 2015. Essentially, the turn to external assistance has not altered the policy path taken prior to this point in the crisis. The conceptual repertoire used to justify this turn of events has continued to repeat ideas about taking credible action, the necessity of retrenchment and the certainty of catastrophe in the absence of such actions. Again, appeal to external actors and institutions plays an important role in justifying the actions taken, particularly with regard to state responsibility for banking debt and its austere repercussions. In this vein, the Minister for Finance (Lenihan, 2010b) has, for example, stated that 'there is simply no way this country, whose banks are so dependent on international investors, can unilaterally renege on senior bondholders against the wishes of the our [sic] European partners and the European institutions. That course of action has never been an option during this crisis'. However, it would appear that the crisis is far from resolved as questions grow about the ability of the state to repay the debt incurred.

Social crisis and social policy responses

In contrast to the response to the fiscal and banking crises, ambivalence surrounds the state's responsibility and capacity to address the social problems that the crisis has created and/or intensified, most notably evident in the rapid rise in unemployment, high levels of personal indebtedness and the poverty and hardship experienced. The Economic and Social Research Institute (ESRI, 2010a) estimated that over one quarter of a million less people would be in work at the end of 2010 than were employed in 2007. For a country the size of Ireland this represents a huge and rapid loss of employment, and unemployment has become one of the most intractable of the social problems arising from the crisis. At the time of writing (late 2010) the unemployment rate stands at over 13% and long-term unemployment has risen rapidly, accounting for 40.9% of total unemployment (INOU, 2010). While some modest policy initiatives have been taken to encourage employment, no overall jobs strategy has yet been published. In addition, approximately 120,000 people are expected to have left Ireland by the end of 2011 (ESRI, 2010b). The economic decline has had a major impact on the social welfare system. Social welfare expenditure rose by 14.8% between 2007 and 2008 and grew a further 15.3% in 2009 (DSFA, 2009; DSP, 2010). This represents an increase in gross current government expenditure, from 29.4% in 2007 to 36.8% in 2009 (DSP, 2010). Expenditure on jobseekers' supports has risen sharply as the number in receipt of Jobseeker's Benefit increased by over 170% between 2007 and 2009, while the number on Jobseeker's Allowance rose by 153% over the same period (DSP, 2010). With little sign of improvement in employment opportunities in the short term, demand on the system is likely to persist for some time. The policy preference for fiscal retrenchment bears most heavily on young unemployed people as evidenced by the stricter conditions and reduced rates of jobseekers' supports implemented since the onset of the crisis (see Table 10.1).

Table 10.1: Summary of cumulative cutbacks to the main social welfare payments 2008–late 2010

Working-age adults (including people with disabilities, one-parent families, widows)	• 8% rate reduction (on average) • Removal of double payment made in December to long-term social welfare recipients • Entitlement to illness benefit limited to 2 years for new claimants
Job-seekers	• 8% reduction (on average) for those aged 25 and over • 30% reduction for new claimants aged 22-24 • 51% reduction for new claimants aged 18-21 (except those with dependant children) • Limited entitlement for claimants failing to take up job offers or activation support • Social insurance contributions required to qualify for job-seekers benefit doubled and duration of entitlement reduced from 15 to 12 months (9 months where less than 260 contributions made)
Child benefit	• 16% rate reduction (based on 2 children) • Child benefit for those aged 18 years withdrawn on a phased basis (some compensatory measures introduced in respect of low income families)
Early Childcare Supplement	• Abolished and replaced with 1 year of free pre-school

The conceptual repertoire brought to bear on the framing of social policy options has concentrated in the main on the perceived 'generosity' of the Irish social welfare system, and that everyone must shoulder the burden of the pain while protecting the most vulnerable. The publication of the McCarthy (2009a) report was prominent in the shaping of the debate. In addition, the role of ideological entrepreneurs has been influential in framing current discourse, which is heavily informed by economic commentary, much of it of neo-classical persuasion. This dominance is not new in Ireland but its impact on policy debate has become more striking. As Lynch (2010, p 9) notes, 'economic analysis has been allowed to have hegemonic control over public debate' even if 'the discipline does not understand or analyse how social systems work'. Nevertheless, the evidence suggests that significant ideological entrepreneurs have been winning the battle of ideas on the response thus far, although counter discourses have been attempting to challenge this. The straightforward appeal to commonsense, no nonsense economic logic and rationality has held much sway in the policy prescriptions adopted. According to McCarthy (2009b), for instance, current measures are 'not being proposed for fun.... We are paying a substantial penalty rate of interest ... and it can't continue so we have to look at the big items of government spending'.

Justification for scaling back state agencies is put in equally direct terms: 'the whole government organisation chart has got incredibly cluttered over the last 8-10 years and it just needs ... a spring cleaning' (McCarthy, 2009b). While proposals to rationalise state agencies may have merit, failure to consider the impact of disbanding the organisations identified (for example, the Family Support Agency, the Law Reform Commission) reflects the lack of social policy insight sought in generating policy responses. In short, the crisis appears to have been framed in such a way as to sustain momentum around the logic of retrenchment to the extent that it has become normalised.

While the 'generosity' debate heightened following the McCarthy recommendations to cut social welfare rates, the 'communicative discourse' (Schmidt, 2003) of key political actors had already forged the way. The Minister for Finance has made reference to generous social provisions in all budgets brought forward since the onset of the crisis, stating that, cutbacks notwithstanding, 'It is the Government's firm intention to maintain the comparatively generous level of social provision we have in this country' (Lenihan, 2009b). That Irish social welfare payments compare well internationally has been a notable aspect of the argument: 'Over the last decade, we have been able to provide very significant increases in welfare payments. ... These payments compare very well internationally, particularly with payments in Britain and Northern Ireland' (Lenihan, 2009c).

This sentiment has been articulated widely, although the more comprehensive range of health and other services provided there is rarely acknowledged. Some civil society groups have attempted to challenge the veracity of the generosity argument, highlighting that '*Contrary to popular belief* – social welfare payments in Ireland are average to low compared to social welfare rates in the European Union' (EAPN Ireland, 2009, p 4). When compared with EU15 figures, the net unemployment payment in Ireland in 2007 (for a single person, no dependants) was 13th, with only Greece and the UK below (EAPN Ireland, 2009).

The manner in which the perception of generosity in social welfare is articulated contrasts with the concern that surrounds any move from the low-tax model. The argument is made that there are clear limits to the levels of personal income taxation that can be tolerated. According to Minister Roche (no date):

> International evidence and our own past experience make it clear that continuously increasing personal taxes is a disastrous policy. It provides a disincentive to work.... Most importantly of all heaping more tax on people working in Ireland will drive jobs elsewhere making the problem that raising taxes is intended to solve worse.

In the event, incomes taxes have been raised indirectly via new forms of taxation, while headline income tax rates remain unchanged. New income levies were introduced in 2009 on a broadly progressive basis. Their proposed replacement in 2011 is less so, with the introduction of the inappropriately titled Universal Social Charge (USC). The USC is effectively a form of taxation, collected by Revenue and has nothing to do with social benefits of any kind. It will be levied on those with an income in excess of €4,004 per annum, with only social protection payments exempt. This, combined with a proposed 12% cut in the minimum wage, will hit the lowest-paid workers disproportionately hard. Issues now arise about the implications for the working poor where 40% of households at risk of poverty in Ireland are headed by a person in employment (CSO, 2009). It is against this backdrop that the more challenging questions about the social goals and vision being pursued (that is, redistribution, social solidarity and the welfare state) are largely diverted by the dominant political discourse. It draws instead on the repertoire of collective effort to shoulder the burden, protect the most vulnerable and the belief that economic recovery is both the objective and the cure.

Reflecting on pre-crisis welfare rate increases has provided further rationale for the need to impose cuts and target benefits. 'It was right that when times were good, we increased payments to those who are vulnerable. Now that we are in recession, we must look at how we can use the … welfare budget to afford maximum protection to those most in need' (Lenihan, 2009c). The economic risk associated with not cutting back on social welfare was alluded to by the Social and Family Affairs Minister: 'If the Government doesn't take steps now to reduce overall public expenditure and restore stability to the public finances, we risk making the economic situation far worse for everyone – including welfare recipients – in the long term' (Hanafin, 2009).

The impact of this ideational pitch has been significant in preparing people for the reality of cuts. In this respect, as Fitz Gerald (cited in Barkham, 2010) puts it, the government has 'psyched the people of Ireland up to absorb huge pain'. How that pain is to be shared has been an integral component of the conceptual repertoire. The public is regularly reminded of the solidarity of effort required, in which 'we all have a responsibility to accept a proportionate share of the burden of adjustment needed in this economy' (Lenihan, 2009c). In addition, the minister draws on the collective memory of battling against economic crises in the past: '[i]n our short history as a nation, we have demonstrated our capacity to overcome economic adversity. We have worked together to build this economy into one of the most successful in the world. We must now work to save it from a downward spiral' (Lenihan, 2009c). Reference to and construction of national memory is, as Campbell (1998) notes, a framing strategy often employed to appeal for normative support for particular policy decisions.

The cumulative effect of policy decisions both prior and post EU/IMF intervention has been significant and broad ranging in its impact. All social service departments/agencies have experienced cuts in expenditure and the 'do more with less' approach has yielded significant savings. Increased conditionality of entitlement, reductions to the already limited universalist capacity in social services, cuts in social welfare rates, greater imposition of service-related charges and reductions in public spending have been the core features of the welfare retrenchment to date (see Table 10.1). This combined with some pre-existing shortcomings in the system has meant considerable hardship for many welfare recipients and service users (Harford, 2010). Considering that 14% of the population are living in poverty and that a quarter of all households have an annual income of €20,000 or less (The Poor

Can't Pay, 2010), the question now is how much deeper the cuts will go before the limits of austerity are exposed.

Conclusion

The trajectory of the Irish political economy since the late 1950s has been significantly shaped by the policy to successfully locate Ireland in an international matrix of trade, investment and enterprise. This, coupled with the rising influence of neoliberalism, further embedded the overarching policy paradigm of strategic economic positioning to fit the needs of a small, open and dependent economy. In the current narrative, the need to regain what has been lost, that is, to return to competitiveness and to restore reputation, by winning both the faith and the capital of international investors, has become the key element of policy responses to the current economic crisis. The amplification of neoliberal globalisation as the key to success in boom years now informs the mainstream policy domain as the solution to the crisis in the Irish case and has been further reinforced by actions committed to under the terms of the EU/IMF loan agreement.

The failure to take the opportunity of past economic prosperity to strengthen the capacity of the Irish welfare state has amplified the vulnerability of social policy development in times of crisis and the policy response to date accentuates the liberal trajectory of the Irish welfare state. Evidence thus far suggests a reversion to type, that is to say that institutional path dependency, coupled with paradigmatic reinforcement of *the* prescription for recovery, has left a weak Irish welfare state open to broad-ranging retrenchment largely without reform. The consequences of this may yet be the catalyst for exposure of the limits of the Irish approach. The relative absence of normative ideas and values in political discourse is notable although not necessarily inevitable in the long run; counter-discourses exist and offer a real challenge to the prevailing orthodoxy, should they succeed in mobilising support for their ideas.

ELEVEN

Waving not drowning: Iceland, *kreppan* and alternative social policy futures

Zoë Irving

Introduction

As a small island state with a population of less than half a million, Iceland does not generally feature as a country case study in comparative texts, even those with an interest in Nordic social policy (for example, Kautto et al, 1999). The place of small island states in the world order more widely has hitherto been of interest only occasionally: as pieces in larger geopolitical jigsaws put together in studies in international relations (Cyprus, Gibraltar and Malta for example); as examples of economic success against the odds in development studies (Singapore for example); or as wayward bastions of capitalism's less palatable underbelly, in the reporting of financial exposés (the Cayman Islands for example). Oddly enough, in the context of the present economic turmoil, Iceland exhibits all three of these dimensions of 21st-century 'islandness'. Both its geopolitical history and post-war economic growth strategy, as well as its more recent foray into the realms of international financial markets, make it a key player in, and a symbol of, the recent systemic collapse of global finance. However, in terms of its social politics, past, present and future, analysis of Iceland also demonstrates that there is little that is predetermined or predictable in responding to economic collapse, that it is political choices that govern social outcomes and that nation states are not victims of global circumstance.

Iceland is well known for having the oldest Parliament in Europe and the sagas that recount its distinctive medieval political history are an essential element of the island's cultural heritage and national identity. In order to understand the modern-day saga of Iceland's 21st-century history culminating in national bankruptcy, it is necessary to outline some significant aspects of its previous '1,100 years' (Karlsson, 2000). The temporal context is, as Pierson (2004) has argued, crucial to the fuller understanding of social processes, drawing our attention to mechanisms, sequencing and events that are lost in analyses of single moments. Citing Abbott's 'strict sense' of the meaning of context that concerns the use of 'defining locational information' (Abbott, 1997, p 1171, cited in Pierson, 2004, p 168), Pierson's methodological preference for thicker descriptions encourages historical analyses informed by the study of the multifaceted dimensions of political life. The story of Iceland's meteoric rise and equally dramatic and calamitous fall from financial grace demonstrates just how significant context is in political development and, relatedly, in the direction of social policy. Iceland's smaller population size and its islandness are crucial contextual factors in explaining its place in, and experience of, 'the crisis' or '*kreppan*' as it is referred to in Iceland. Despite the uniqueness of these features relative to the other country cases presented in this book, and *because* of its smallness, the Icelandic experience sheds considerable light on how the financial system failed, how this failure might be explained and, given existing welfare arrangements, what the possibilities for social, political and economic rehabilitation might be. The purpose of this chapter therefore is to explore how Iceland came to be at the centre of the financial crisis, and by locating Icelandic social policy in the existing frameworks of welfare regimes, to then consider what this seemingly unenviable economic position implies for the direction of its welfare future. The chapter begins by outlining some of the key features of Iceland's context and how these features have shaped the development of its welfare state. The discussion then considers how Iceland came to be at the centre of events in the autumn of 2008, what its national response has been and what these events mean for Icelandic social policy. The final section reflects on how this analysis of developments in Iceland fits within the theoretical literature on small states, and what it can contribute to the comparative study of social policy more generally.

Where social democratic east meets liberal west: social policy in Iceland

Iceland was a late European industrialiser and, since gaining independence from Denmark in 1944, its rapid shift from poor agrarian ex-colony to prosperous maritime economy has been of significant interest in anthropological accounts of the processes of modernisation (Pálsson and Durrenberger, 1996). Due to its colonial history first as a Norwegian outpost and from the 14th century as a Danish dependency, combined with its isolated geographical position,

Iceland's economy was relatively closed until the 1960s (Palmarsdottir, 1991) when a change in the direction of foreign economic policy and improved relationships with Western Europe allowed the development of crucial export markets, particularly for fish, and also the expansion of imports that had previously been the preserve of the American airbase at Keflavik. By the late 1990s, it is argued that Iceland had become a 'fishing superpower', not only in terms of its global ranking in the value of fishing exports, but also in terms of the growth of this industry through technological development and high productivity (Herbertsson and Zoega, 2003). As a corollary to its economic success (before 2008), from 1980 Iceland also consistently scored higher than the Organisation for Economic Co-operation and Development (OECD) average on the United Nations Development Programme (UNDP) Human Development Index (HDI), ranked at or near the top in its overall HDI score, on gender empowerment measures (25% of government ministers were women in 2003) and, by 2007, in terms of life expectancy (having the highest life expectancy among the 30 European Economic Area countries).

Iceland belongs to the Nordic family of nations in terms of its regional associations but propinquity to social democratic welfare regimes has not determined the shape of its welfare state. At critical strategic points in the 1930s and 1940s, sufficient strength of Left parties in coalition governments ensured the foundation of social and health insurance on solidaristic principles, but as both historical and gender analyses suggest, there are equally convincing political explanations for Iceland's subsequent lack of conformity to the principles and goals of social democratic social policy (Ólafsson, 1993, 2001, 2005a; Siaroff, 1994; Sveinsson, 1996; Jonsson, 2001). As is the pattern in small states more widely, coalition politics characterise the Icelandic system of government, and since independence, the centre-right Independence Party (IP) has dominated politics and policy. Thus, although as Katzenstein's (1985) study suggests there is an overall 'ideological preference for unity' in small states, this does not equate to a preference for universalism in social politics. Although the labour movement has been historically active, it has not been politically powerful and since the establishment of the post-war social insurance arrangements for health and social security, means testing has expanded while the value of social transfers has declined. Private provision and user fees in health and education, and the relatively more pronounced role of the voluntary sector in social care, all point to a welfare model more in tune with that of other 'settler states' such as New Zealand than with the risk socialisation that characterises Scandinavia.

Given the full-employment situation that existed almost continuously prior to 2008 and the means testing of state pensions, it is unsurprising that public spending on social security remained very low in comparison to the other Nordic countries and lower than the OECD average. The question of work incentives had also not been of policy concern in Iceland since it had the highest labour market participation rate among OECD countries (exceptionally high for those aged over 65), and a preponderance of second jobholding. Whether the low level of unemployment benefits, traditionally low wage rates or an island biography of 'self-help' were most important to the pre-crisis prevalence of individual 'one and a half earners' is debateable. Out of all the OECD countries, Iceland spent the least on active labour market policy in 2001, and throughout the latter 1990s to the mid-2000s, policy very much reflected a reliance on security through employment. Not only does this strategy risk failing those unable to work, but it carries substantial actuarial risk in a volatile global market where exceptionally low unemployment is not guaranteed. Prior to 2008, unemployment had peaked in 1995 at 5% following rates of less than 2% throughout the previous decades, and although it had risen to around 3% in 2003-04, it was back down to a barely frictional 1.6% in 2008, slightly higher for women (1.8%) than men (1.5%). Thus, although included in the foundational 1947 social security legislation, unemployment insurance only became operationalised following a general strike in 1955 (Jonsson, 2001) and, other than a minor concern with the creation of a 'disability trap' for long-term unemployed people in the mid-2000s (Ólafsson, 2005b), 'unemployment' as a public issue rather than a personal trouble had never been at the forefront of policy debate. Given the strength of employment, then, it is not surprising that in the other core area of social security – protection in old age – compulsory occupational pensions with approximately 60% replacement rates, represented a more significant element of retirement income than the state pension where receipt of the earnings-related supplement declined year on year from the mid-1990s.

The selectivist and relatively privatised architecture of the pension system and the implications of this for social inequality characterise the liberal elements of the Icelandic welfare state but there are also examples of policy dissonance in relation to this model. Extensions to unemployment benefit entitlements in 1989 and 1993, restriction of means testing in family benefits in 2001, and more obviously in the direction of housing policy in the 1980s, demonstrate Iceland's welfare hybridity and its capacity to respond to policy issues without the baggage of path dependency. Iceland's housing system is unique within Europe since, historically, low personal taxation has nurtured the development of self-built home ownership (Ólafsson, 1993, 2001), a tenure that has also dominated municipal housing through assistance for 'social owner occupation'. However, while liberal states such as the United Kingdom (UK) witnessed a residualisation of social housing from 1980, Iceland moved in the opposite direction with the development of state-supported housing cooperatives; 'nationalisation' of mortgage lending utilising the lending capacities of trades union-managed pension funds; and a substantial increase in the construction of social rented housing from 10.1% of all completed dwellings in 1980-82 to 32.6% in 1990. Although home ownership remained at 89%, by 1990 its status as the only socially valued form of tenure had been challenged and it is argued that a process of 'scandinavianisation' of housing had occurred (Sveinsson, 1992). Politics have mattered in the shaping of the Icelandic welfare state but equally there are contextual factors more related to size and biography that set the landscape for more recent developments, and these are set out in the following section.

Small island, world player

The broad context of the financial crisis in its global form is set out in the introductory chapter to this volume, but it is also necessary to outline briefly the pattern of events in Iceland that led to the collapse of its three largest private banks, national bankruptcy and a diplomatic incident. From the early 1990s, Iceland's eschewal of isolationism and adoption of the neoliberal agenda under the premiership of David Oddsson, a keen supporter of Thatcherism, led to a far-reaching programme of public sector privatisation and management reforms. Broadly informed by similar programmes that had taken place in the UK, New Zealand and also Denmark, New Public Management principles were introduced alongside Danish approaches to competition in public services and privatisation of tertiary education (Jonsson, 2001; Kristmundsson, 2003). National industries were privatised, and more significantly in terms of setting the conditions for a *kreppa*, a programme of liberalisation of financial markets and banking privatisation took place, which concentrated financial power within a small and closed elite, albeit one with significant internecine conflict. In presiding over these reforms and the pursuit of a low-tax international identity, Oddsson attempted to locate Iceland at the pivotal centre of the global market, to shed its semi-peripheral status and prove that size was not important in the world of financial capitalism.

Making banking and finance the sector of choice in the search for global competitiveness, between 2003 and 2008 Iceland's three biggest banks (Glitnir, Kaupthing and Landsbanki) saw the most rapid expansion in international financial history, and Iceland effectively became 'a gigantic hedge fund sitting in the middle of the North Atlantic' (Danielsson, 2009). Foreign direct investment rose by 500% between 1998 and 2003, and in 2005 in speeches to Danish and Icelandic bankers the-then Prime Minister, Halldór Ásgrímsson, proudly claimed that Iceland was the fifth most competitive economy in the world (Ásgrímsson, 2005a, 2005b). These speeches reflect expansionary zeal, and the widespread policy reforms in areas of tax and business[1] show the government attempting to locate Iceland as a key financial player (see Ísleifsson, 2009), a small state but not a 'micro state' as the Prime Minister was reported as emphasising (*Fréttabladid*, 27 September 2004). By 2007, the three banks had increased their consolidated assets to 880% of the Icelandic Gross Domestic Product (GDP), and having borrowed mainly in foreign capital markets, had increased Icelandic net external debt by 142% of GDP between 2003 and 2007. Combined with the credit-fuelled domestic housing boom, the banks were exposed to almost the full range of possible risks in both the global and domestic contexts (OECD, 2009d). The financial overindulgence came to a head in October 2008 when the three main banks collapsed with losses of over US$100 billion, and an International Monetary Fund (IMF) bail-out was required. Along with further foreign loans, the IMF 'Stand-By Arrangement' package stabilised the financial sector, but could not prevent the subsequent economic hangover with potentially serious consequences for solidarity. The unemployment rate was little over 1% in April 2008 but a year later reached 9.1%. Following intervention, the IMF (2009b) reported that Iceland's progress was 'broadly in line' with the recovery plan but OECD projections published later in the year (OECD Observer, 2009) and Iceland's own Ministry of Finance (14 May, weekly web release figures) suggested a picture of no growth, inflation at 10.2% for 2009, and interest rates into the teens, all of which were in direct contrast with the objectives of economic stability set out in the government's incoming policy statement in 2007 (Prime Minister's Office, 2007). In addition, spending on social security and welfare increased from 4.4% of treasury expenditure in 2008 to 46.5% in 2009.

Many commentators continue to argue that the banking collapse was foreseeable. As early as 2005, the OECD (2005) had begun to raise concerns regarding the level of household debt in Iceland, inflation was running at 12.8% by 2007 (compared to 3.8% in the UK and 5.0% in the United States; US), and in early 2008 the OECD (2008c, p 1) suggested that:

> The key challenge for policy in the near-term is to restore macroeconomic stability by ensuring that steady progress is made in unwinding imbalances. Additionally, steps need to be taken to strengthen the ability of both monetary and fiscal policy to moderate macroeconomic volatility and prevent the re-emergence of [internal and external] imbalances with a view to sustaining Iceland's favourable growth performance.

It was the feeling of action untaken and warnings ignored that was reflected in civil action and protest culminating in the 'pot and pan revolution', and the fall of the centre-right IP-led government, which had been in power more or less since independence in 1944. Although the IP had lost ground in the 2003 election, some of this had been regained in 2007, but the election in May 2009 witnessed a decisive shift to the left in Icelandic politics with a ruling coalition made up of the Social Democratic Alliance (29.8%) and the Left–Green Movement (21.7%). The latter had only polled 8% of the vote in 2003. In addition, in Johanna Sigurðardóttir Iceland had its first woman Prime Minister and one who pledged commitment to changing the gender balance in politics, and more particularly business. The Coalition Co-operation Statement released on the 10 May 2009 included the following:

> In the national elections just concluded, a majority of voters gave social democratic and left-wing parties a clear mandate to continue, and to prioritise new values of equality, social justice, solidarity, sustainable development, gender equality, moral reform and democracy in Iceland. The new government, guided by these values, aims at creating a Nordic welfare society in Iceland, where collective interests take precedence over particular interests. Foremost among its tasks is to revive confidence in the domestic community and rebuild Iceland's international reputation.[2]

In terms of social policy, Iceland faced a real dilemma in that the principles of state obligation and intervention, solidarity and egalitarianism had come to the fore exactly at the point where resources to support them had vanished. At the time, the new government's *First 100 Days Planned Actions* (Prime Minister's Office, 2009) included a 'cost-cutting drive launched in public administration, involving employees, managements and users of services'. Given that the Icelandic civil and welfare services had already been thoroughly made-over in the style of the New Public Management and that the previous government had also expressed a mission of 'focused government administration' with an emphasis on 'restraint' (Prime Minister's Office, 2007), it is hard to imagine how further cost-cutting exercises could deliver the welfare outcomes desired in a social democratic regime. More recently, the report of Iceland's Special Investigation Commission (SIC, 2010) has suggested that the dispersed structure of Icelandic public administration is its weakness. In fact, Minister of Finance (and Left-Green Movement leader) Steingrímur Sigfússon (2010) sees rationalisation of ministries and economy of scale as a strategy to *avoid* the worst excesses of public spending cuts and to safeguard services. The 2009 report of the government's Basic Services Taskforce also takes this view in advising that, at the local level, rationalisation should be undertaken 'within the executive system, while at the same time seeking to maintain and preserve the welfare system' (The Welfare Watch, 2010, p 9). Before examining in more detail the welfare outcomes and social policy developments relating to the crisis, it is important to consider briefly its explanation in the Icelandic context.

Following the events of late 2008, many accounts have been published, authored by both those involved in key positions (Jónsson, 2009) and those commentating from shorter (Boyes, 2009) and greater distances (Chartier, 2011). Unsurprisingly, given the particularly prescient national problem of *accountability* for Iceland's continuing economic disarray, and the more general neglect of analysis that recognises the systemic nature of the crisis and its ideological stimulus, there are competing explanations of the causes of Iceland's bankruptcy. Boyes (2009), for example, provides a persuasive actor-based thesis that the source of the problems lies in the longstanding oligarchy of wealthy families and their political connections, the feuding and corruption of the banks' owners and duplicitous government action and inaction in relation to financial deregulation, banking privatisation and the wider regulation of commercial activity. There is much popular support for this analysis in Iceland and also public recognition by the present government that cronyism has featured in national politics – hence changes introduced in 2010 to the process of judicial appointments.

Icesave, the online arm of Landsbanki used by thousands of British and Dutch small investors, is symbolic of the system collapse impacting at household, national and international levels. *Icesave* represents the interconnectedness of advanced economies but its collapse has highlighted how easily a retreat to national protectionism occurs. At the time of its collapse, the UK press was keen to sensationalise the losses to its local government and police authority depositors, amounting to some £21 million for the Sussex Police for example (*The Argus*, 10 October 2008), although not in the context of the potential effect on frontline services. In Iceland, David Oddsson (then chair of the Central Bank) gave Icelanders a televised assurance that they would not pay the 'foreign debts of reckless people' (*The Guardian*, 23 January 2011), which resulted in a decision by the UK government to freeze Landsbanki assets and utilise anti-terrorist legislation to prevent further Icelandic financial activity in the UK. Responding to the report of the UK treasury Select Committee, in a letter sent in 2009 to all UK Members of Parliament, the Icelandic Ambassador made it clear that not only was the UK government viewed by the Icelandic government as *implicated* in the worsening of the crisis, but also as creating a diplomatic incident further harming Iceland's international standing and the bilateral relations between the two countries:

> [W]e share the Committee's view that, by its use of the Anti-Terrorism, Crime and Security Act 2001 to freeze assets of Landsbanki on 8 October, 2008, the UK Government became an active market participant rather than passive observer in the unfolding financial turbulence in Iceland with potentially unforeseen consequences.... There is no doubt that the current situation has stigmatised a healthy and profitable economic and diplomatic partnership.[3]

Despite this initial response, Iceland's Special Investigation Committee (2010) report later suggested that the IP-led coalition did not listen to the advice of 'friendly' countries regarding its banking sector, and resolving the *Icesave* issue has thus become the measure of Iceland's international rehabilitation, not least with the IMF. It is assumed that sale of Landsbanki assets will eventually cover the costs of reimbursement for both the UK and the Netherlands' repayment of depositor claims. However, it is the fixed 5.5% rate of interest on the loans that the UK and Netherlands are charging Iceland that is the enduring source of hostility since this is passed on to Icelandic taxpayers who can ill-afford additional income reduction while British and Dutch citizenry profit from the debt. The angry perception outside the Icelandic political elite remains that the many are paying for the criminal actions of the few. Iceland has 'been tough with its creditors and disregarded some international norms' (*The Economist*, 2010) in its handling of *Icesave*, but the popular perception is not helped by the reality that many politicians who held central jobs at the time of the collapse were quickly appointed to new jobs both in intergovernmental organisations, and in Icelandic and regional government departments.

Geir Haarde, the former Icelandic Prime Minister (2006-09), is the only Head of State to face criminal charges relating to events surrounding the financial crisis, following his referral for prosecution for 'negligence' in a special court recommended in the report of the Special Investigation Committee (SIC, 2010). While several of those involved in the banks' collapse have been arrested or are involved in criminal proceedings both in Iceland and in other countries (Price Waterhouse Cooper is the latest agent to be placed in the legal spotlight in Iceland), it is the fact that the 'Reykavik 9', nine people involved in the protest at the Parliament building in December 2008, went on trial in January 2011, ahead of any criminal trials of members of government or the financial institutions involved, that symbolises the continuing disconnection in Iceland between those outside of political and financial circles and those within. The problem is summed up by one older respondent in Sigmundsdóttir's (2010, p 70) collection of biographies of *kreppan*, who states that '[w]hat we are experiencing now is not an economic recession. It's a recession caused by thieves'. Regular mass protests outside the Parliament building continued throughout 2010 and into 2011, as charitable food aid distribution remained visible and the cost of the crisis to individual households rose with inflation, unemployment and debt.

Where now for the Icelandic welfare state?

On taking office, planned government action in the welfare arena included a new social insurance system (originally set out in 2007), unemployment initiatives to address seasonal and youth unemployment and increase business start-up, services to assist highly indebted households and the collection of baseline data and monitoring of 'key indicators on economic and social issues', in much the same way that in the UK, Labour began to monitor social exclusion in the *Opportunity for All* reports from 1997.[4] In January 2011, the Ministry of Welfare was established, and this data collection and monitoring role is taken by 'The Welfare Watch', a committee comprising of 19 ministers and other representatives of the social partners and organisations with an interest in welfare issues. This group has set up a number of task forces and submitted its first report to the Althingi (Parliament) in January 2010. The report contains a series of policy proposals referring to various social groups. Some initiatives have been implemented swiftly such as the directive to local authorities and school committees that all children should receive a school meal, while others require long-term development and political negotiation such as activation measures for young unemployed people. The report, and the existence of the committee, evidences the government's desire to demonstrate its welfarist credentials but at the same time, there is a sense that what is required is harm reduction rather than the essential reform that would characterise 'regime change'. A 25%:75% ratio of tax increases to spending cuts is planned for 2011 in an effort to maintain the reduction in treasury spending (down from 44% in 2008 to 29% of GDP in 2010). The Minister of Finance states (Sigfússon, 2010): 'These actions will be difficult, even painful, but are unfortunately unavoidable. The good news is that this will mean the worst is over. Both 2012 and 2013 will be easier to deal with and the extent of cost-cutting required in those years should be considerably less, if the forecasts for economic recovery prove roughly correct'.

Although the evidence of crisis-induced 'diswelfare' appears more positive than had been anticipated (The Welfare Watch, 2010), as is recognised in comparisons with Finland's experience of recession in 1991, the social impact of economic disadvantage can take several years to manifest. The Welfare Watch report is also clear that in terms of safeguarding basic services, cuts will be implemented that privilege service users' interests and that with a view to economic recovery, all 'emergency measures' should be reversible. It is possible that the standard OECD advice around privatisation and competition in health services (OECD, 2008c, 2009d) will seem more attractive as a cost-saving option.[5] Healthcare accounts for 36% of social protection spending (9% of GDP) but the OECD's further suggestion for efficiency savings is the reduction of healthcare staffing levels and, given the unemployment situation, this kind of 'workforce rationalisation' is less welcome, although some changes to the structure of care employment have occurred.

The OECD has also been critical of the role of the publicly owned mortgage lending facility, the Housing Finance Fund, which it views as an anti-competitive obstacle to growth. Its recommendation is that once the recessionary period begins to wane, 'policy makers might have to reassess its role' (OECD, 2009d, p 10) and based on previous advice, this means residualising its scope of provision. As noted earlier, however, housing is the most 'Scandinavian' (socialised) pre-existing element of the Icelandic welfare state and as such it is an unlikely focus for a government wishing to expand this model. Housing is a critical dimension of *kreppan* and in an attempt to prevent the social crisis deepening, the government has introduced measures that are aimed at easing the financial pressure on mortgagees, including:

> suspension of forced auctions, the adoption of legislation to enable withdrawal of private pension savings, an agreement with financial institutions on co-ordinated debt relief remedies, temporary freezing of foreign-denominated loans, an increase in interest subsidies to taxpayers, the adoption of debt mitigation legislation and penalty interest reduction.... Major actions have been taken as well to deal with corporate debt and straitened financial circumstances, e.g. with adjustment of due dates and increased flexibility in settlement of taxes owed. (Sigfússon, 2010)

Sigfússon (2010) also reports that at least a third of the Icelandic population has used the debt assistance services put in place by the government, but public disquiet continues as the cost of mortgages and household debt rises unabated, and home owners lose any equity they held. Interest rates are indexed to the Consumer Price Index (CPI) in Iceland, and leaving aside the theoretical challenges to the calculation of this indicator, and its related use in the measurement of inflation in times of recession (Guðnason and Jónsdóttir, 2009), CPI indexation of mortgage interest, even within the state mortgage Housing Finance Fund, contributes to the unsustainability of repayments within households experiencing unemployment and other reductions in income. The Welfare Watch (2010) also report a 30% increase in the number of recipients of rent benefit and a 35% increase in the number of recipients of social assistance in the 2008-09 period. In the 2010 SILC Survey, slightly less than half of households reported 'struggling to make ends meet' and 10.1% reported being in mortgage or rent arrears during the previous year, with 13.3% reporting arrears in other loans. These difficulties were most concentrated among lone parents, a quarter of whom were or had been in arrears with housing costs over that period and within younger age groups, less able to cushion against unexpected expenses (Statistics Iceland, 2010). Household debt is even more precarious where money was loaned in foreign currencies and the exchange rate fluctuations and IMF requirement for regulation of currency exchange have hugely inflated the cost of repayments. The loss of jobs is also not straightforward in Iceland, where, as mentioned earlier, in previous times of full employment, many people worked in more than one job.

Measures to address unemployment are, of course, high on the agenda given the increase in numbers registering for benefit and expenditure on unemployment, which rose from 0.4% of GDP in 2008 to 1.7% in 2009.[6] Since this is a relatively undeveloped area of policy, the choices again will reflect battles of ideas between those promoting 'workfare' and those preferring 'activation'. Rates of unemployment actually compare favourably with other advanced economies – at 7.4% in 2010 the Icelandic rate of unemployment was less than the EU average (10%) and the lowest in the OECD (Sigfússon, 2010) – but is a far cry from the rates enjoyed before 2008. Long-term unemployment (12 months or more) increased from 14% of those registered unemployed at the end of 2009 to 24.2% at the end of 2010 (Statistics Iceland, 2011), and those out of work for six months or more accounted for half of all those registered in 2009 (The Welfare Watch, 2010). It is the groups affected by this, particularly young people, who feature most prominently in policy debate. The Welfare Watch is keen to promote study, and 'the moral responsibility of employers', including the state to supply employment in temporary and seasonal jobs. Partial unemployment benefits to support seasonal work and an increase in the support level of student loans have also complemented support measures for the young since 50% of those registered unemployed have no post-compulsory education in the context of Iceland's highly educated workforce relative to the rest of Europe. The state is the largest employer in Iceland and a programme of public works has been established, including the construction of a hospital and road-building. It is construction that has fared particularly badly in the post-crisis period, and it is construction companies that accounted for the highest proportion of corporate insolvencies in 2010.[7]

In an element of debate well established in liberal regimes, the structure of benefits for disability (which accounted for 14% of social protection expenditure in 2009) is also under scrutiny and in the Welfare Watch (2010) report the question of benefit 'dependency' is also noted although 'inactivity' is also presented as a condition that the state is obliged to prevent through the guarantee of opportunities for skill acquisition. Much policy space is devoted to the provision of counsellors and their role in steering unemployed people back into work as well as assisting debt-burdened households into manageable situations. This is a reflection of national concerns with mental health, identifiable from the National Health Plan published in 2004 (Department of Planning and Development, 2004). At that time, the plan reported that 22% of Icelanders over the age of five suffered from some form of mental disorder. Aside from the health dimension, the economics of this statistic are also apparent given that more than 25% of those in receipt of the full disability pension do so on grounds of mental ill-health.

If the new government is hoping to develop a Nordic social model then pensions are the most obvious area of reform. The committee appointed to develop the social insurance reforms in 2009 are indeed aiming to streamline pensioner provision and reduce the means-tested elements.[8] The pension funds, however, are regarded as Iceland's success story. In 2007, the question raised by the Ministry of Finance in its pension assessment concerned the future need for the pension funds to begin to increase foreign investment because they had run out of domestic investment opportunities (Jonasdottir, 2007). In 2010, the Minister of Finance reported that '[a]t year-end 2009, pension funds' net assets were equivalent to 119% of GDP. Iceland, the Netherlands and Switzerland are in a class by themselves in this regard, with pension funds' net assets of 120-130% of GDP. In Greece, by comparison, the figure is 0%' (Sigfússon, 2010).

One welfare concern where the situation has already changed is that of migrant labourers and their children. The need to import labour was hailed as an indicator of economic vitality earlier in the decade and by 2007, issues of discrimination, educational provision for migrants and cultural difference had made it onto the policy agenda (Prime Minister's Office, 2007). Despite assumptions about the homogeneity of Icelandic society, it has a higher population of foreign citizens than the other Nordic countries and migrants represented 8.2% of the population in 2010, 38.4% of whom were Polish.[9] However, although inward migration was (relatively) high and rising between 2003 and 2007 (2,607 people in 2003 compared to 9,217 in 2007), emigration also increased during this period and numbers entering the country decreased considerably in the first quarter of 2009 while the numbers of foreign citizens leaving Iceland increased. In 2010, emigration declined on 2009 figures but Denmark, Norway, Poland and Sweden continued to be the destinations of choice for those emigrating while the highest proportion of migrants came from Denmark. Both inward and outward migration are dominated by younger age groups.[10] Migration is clearly linked to developments in the labour market and minor changes have significant impact in small countries. Thus, there are likely to be shifts in patterns of labour market activity as jobs previously undertaken by migrant labour become available. Gender differences in patterns of inward and outward migration suggest that there is an association with the problems in the construction industry since male inward migration decreased while male emigration increased in the period between 2007 and 2010.

Iceland: recovery and future prospects

In his series of analytical pieces entitled *Rising from the Ruins*, Sigfússon (2010) paints a very positive picture of the Icelandic economy during 2010, with lower than predicted contraction, increasing domestic production, improvement in the balance of trade (now in surplus), inflation down to 4.8% (from 17.8% in early 2009) and an appreciating Icelandic *kronur*. With GDP growth estimated at 2.5-3% in 2011, it seems that Iceland has made an exceptionally speedy recovery without the need for unduly unpleasant IMF medicine. Sigfússon has been equally keen to point out publicly that the IMF is aware that it is dealing with a 'Nordic welfare state' and that it has adjusted its conditions accordingly – the joint recovery programme is expected to end, successfully and as planned in 2011. The deficit has been reduced from 15% of GDP in 2009 to 9% in 2010. However, optimism regarding the encouraging indications of these broad economic measures has to be tempered by the reality of what has happened to social welfare in the period between the collapse and the current recovery, and the social distribution of that recovery. Even at the general level of the HDI, Iceland has slipped to 17th place in the ranking of most developed nations.

It is perhaps unsurprising, then, that the Minister of Finance's upbeat analysis is not universally shared among the island's population. The 1980s ushered in a period of huge social change in Iceland where the hegemonic values of the global market were layered onto existing social relations characterised by a very different set of values. The dimensions of 'independence' previously represented by the IP were eclipsed by the political and business elites' desire that Iceland became a global player and the floodgates of advanced consumerism were opened. Icelanders took full advantage of their sudden exposure to the material excess available in other advanced economies. It is suggested that times have changed. Sigfússon (2010) concludes his analysis with a plea to:

> leave the greedification, the excesses and the arrogant conceptions of ourselves and our imagined superiority behind on the rubbish tip of history. What we want is a human, honest and moderate welfare society, open and democratic, based on power-sharing and in harmony with

> nature and other peoples. That is the direction to head for
> as we rise from the ruins!

But at the same time there is cause for caution as Sigmundsdóttir's
(2010, p 81) respondent reflects:

> If the IMF decides to cut off our aid because we don't want
> to pay for the Icesave debt, a private debt, then let them.
> We're fine up here on the rock. We're on our way back to
> the mud huts anyway. We'll just eat our fish guts and our
> potatoes and whatever else. We'll be destitute whether we
> take on the Icesave debt or not. I mean, it's not like there
> will suddenly be money trees growing here if we agree to
> take on the debt. If we agree to pay for Icesave, there will
> still be a kreppa.

It is interesting that a sense of self-sufficiency is apparent in the above
quote as the assumption that natural resources provide a survival strategy
is a clear element of Iceland's biography. Echoing the comfort offered
by Geir Haarde in his speech to the nation in October 2008, Sigfússon
(2010) also takes this approach, suggesting that with developments
in hydro and geothermal energy, water will soon be 'Iceland's oil'.
The OECD (2009d) also shares the view that energy projects offer a
route out of recession and Iceland's geographical advantage in further
exploration of the Arctic region is another element of the recourse
to natural resources in the quest for growth. The future development
of bilateral relations with Russia will be significant in this regard,
particularly since communication expressing US disquiet at the offer
of Russian financial assistance in the midst of Iceland's meltdown
was made available by Wikileaks at the start of 2011. There are two
further examples of Iceland's idiosyncratic approach to global survival:
nationalisation of industry and innovative competitive strategies.
Expressing 'little cause for anxiety about the future in Iceland', Sigfússon
(2010) argues that energy resources must be 'publicly owned'. In 2010,
there was public protest that a Canadian company had purchased HS
Orka, the geothermal energy production unit, and despite OECD
(2008c) advice that the 'divestiture' of the national power company
should occur, privatisation will be put to a referendum. To give an
indication of the result, in the 1990 World Values Survey, Iceland was
in complete contrast to all the other countries[11] with 38% in support
of nationalised industry (Inglehart, 1997). As for future competitive
identity, the BBC has reported (Vallance, 2010) that with the Icelandic

Modern Media Initiative (IMMI) developed by Member of Parliament (MP) Birgitta Jonsdottir in association with Wikileaks editor Julian Assange, the traditional tax haven island strategy was being replaced by plans to establish an 'international data haven' to counteract libel tourism, promote free speech and assist in rebuilding Iceland's economy (as modern media companies moved to this more favourable operating environment) and global perceptions of its integrity.

In many ways, Iceland has spent the years since independence expressing its resistance to conforming to the Scandinavian social model represented by its previous rulers, most recently by embracing the values connected to global neoliberalism. In his commentary on Icelanders as 'Scandinavian' or 'American', however, Ólafsson (2003b) suggested that there was a tilt to the 'east' and clearly, in hard times this tilt has become an historic swing. Disillusionment with the excesses of capitalism is obviously not the preserve of Icelanders; what is different in Iceland, however, is that its size, the accessibility of its political process and the effects of social proximity have made it possible to quickly reject the neoliberal agenda in favour of a new resistance operated via the 'welfare society'. How this resistance will continue to fare in the face of IMF borrowing remains to be seen, but Iceland has a history of making the 'wrong' choices at the 'wrong' time and its lack of a deeply furrowed path on which to depend means that it has policy versatility not enjoyed by big states. As the IMF (2009b, p 25) itself has noted:

> Iceland has dealt well with shocks in the past. One important aspect of this is the history of cooperation between the social partners in the labor market, not least when the economy is exposed to adverse shocks. A responsible wage agreement will be crucial for limiting the fallout from the current crisis. More generally, strong political and social cohesiveness and a tradition of mobilizing broad political support for difficult policies are among Iceland's great strengths. This, and the proven flexibility of the economy, augur well for the authorities' ability to tackle the daunting tasks ahead.

One dimension of Iceland's future ability to 'tackle the daunting tasks ahead' is its membership of the EU, which has been on and, most often, off the political agenda since the establishment of the European Community in 1957. In the immediate post-crisis period, with its promise of euro stability, membership of the EU had become so appealing that the Icelandic population was prepared to give up its fierce protection of its fishing rights, and more importantly its 'independence'.

In addition to the electorate (who have always been more pro EU than the politicians – see Palmarsdottir, 1991; Thorhallsson, 2002) and business organisations such as the Chamber of Commerce and Federation of Icelandic Industry, support for membership grew to encompass two thirds of MPs as well as the Confederation of Labour. Part of the Social Democratic Alliance's success in the 2009 election was thought to be due to its EU application plans. The alternative, a monetary union with Norway (or even the US dollar), did not seem so attractive. Clearly, Iceland would fare better in a regional organisation such as the EU where it has other small country colleagues (and a small island group) in addition to its Nordic neighbours Denmark and Sweden to assist in protecting its interests. The EU is a different organisation to the one that a one-time Icelandic opposition leader suggested would 'inhale' small states (Palmarsdottir, 1991, p 10). A so-called 'viking union' with Norway would see Iceland as a constrained junior partner in an unequal relationship with considerable historical baggage. Not only is EU membership a popular domestic policy choice but it is also a step that would be favourably regarded by both the IMF and other interested external actors according to the Prime Minister (Sigurðardóttir, 2009). An independent currency is argued by proponents of EU accession to be a liability in the international financial market and not a necessity for 'independence and vitality', but it is also possible that once the financial storm is weathered the appeal of being in Brussels will wear thin and the previously voiced disadvantages to membership will re-emerge in fortified form. Despite the OECD (2009d) view that joining the eurozone would provide 'credibility', the other eurozone countries experiencing difficulties have not found the EU to be as protective as they might have expected and Icelanders may hope to follow Denmark into union without the euro. Thus, although the application for EU membership was submitted in 2009, the Left-Green Movement is opposed and the final outcome, if the application is accepted, will be decided by a referendum. The idea that Iceland's good society hinges on its sovereignty has endured for a millennium and it is unlikely that it could disappear in a decade.

Conclusions

The Icelandic experience of the financial crisis shares many of the more general features of the crisis in other liberal economies such as the UK and the US where the finance sector forms a central part of the national economy. Unfortunately for Iceland, the financial sector had become *the* central part of the national economy and had become far more exposed than a population of 300,000 could ever guarantee, regardless of how well naturally resourced and economically successful. Iceland's rise to financial prominence came about as the result of a government-driven neoliberalisation of economy, politics and cultural values combined with happenstance in the form of a particular circle of commercial 'vikings' and their desires to make a mark in the global (and especially British) retail world. As with industrialisation, the process of development from maritime industry and its class-distinct patterning and resource-conscious approach to life, to aggressive financial capitalism and its associated new social risks, new social divisions and acquisitive materialism took place in a very short timescale in Iceland. All that has happened has greater intensity in a society with greater social proximity.

Iceland presents a revealing case in relation to the question of whether size matters in the development of a welfare state. Theoretical excursions in comparative social policy have led to a dismissal of population size as a key determinant of the principles underpinning welfare arrangements, preferring to focus on the nature and balance of political power. However, sociological approaches suggest that differences in the social relations of welfare could be expected between societies that exhibit communitarian forms of organisation with complex interdependencies and obligations between individuals and kin and other groups, compared to those which are large in size, ethnically and culturally heterogeneous and individualised (see, for example, Baumer et al, 2002, for a criminological investigation of this idea; and Irving, 2011). The personalisation of social interaction in a small state means that political decisions and street-level social policy practice can never be undertaken behind a veil of anonymity – although there is greater scope for clientelism, accountability may also have different qualities where decision makers are likely to personally interact with a significant proportion of those subject to the results of their decisions. The government in Iceland is certainly being held to account. The clear rejection of the domestic politics of neoliberalism and resistance to the 'business as usual' approach to which more powerful states have reverted indicates that paradigm change is possible, and that while 'exit' from the only game in town is not an option, 'voice' can be pursued in certain circumstances. In terms of vulnerability, all states are not Icelandic now and it may be that political risks are easier to take when there is nothing left to lose, but nevertheless it is clear that in responding to the crisis, there are choices. The fact that it is analysis of the most diminutive state that illustrates this is testimony to the argument that size matters.

Notes

[1] Among other substantial tax cuts, corporate tax was reduced to 18%.

[2] Prime Minister's Office: http://eng.forsaetisraduneyti.is/news-and-articles/nr/3706

[3] On behalf of the Minister for Foreign Affairs, Össur Skarphéðinsson, 30 April 2009, www.iceland.org/info/iceland-crisis/timeline/nr/7071

[4] See for example www.official-documents.gov.uk/document/cm66/6673/6673.asp

[5] Iceland spent 8.3% of GDP on public health expenditure in 2004, a global high (UNDP, 2008).

[6] Statistics Iceland figures at www.statice.is/Pages/444?NewsID=5912

[7] Statistics Iceland figures at www.statice.is/?PageID=444&NewsID=4970

[8] Personal communication, Office of Social Security, Ministry of Social Affairs and Social Security, May 2009.

[9] Statistics Iceland figures at www.statice.is/Pages/444?NewsID=5051

[10] Statistics Iceland figures at www.statice.is/Pages/444?NewsID=5406

[11] The highest percentage after Iceland was South Africa at 7%.

TWELVE

Experiences from two financial crises in the Nordic welfare states: 1990-93 and 2008-10 compared

Pekka Kosonen

Introduction

This chapter examines the 2008 economic crisis in three small Nordic countries: Denmark, Finland and Sweden. It compares the responses in these countries to the 2008 crisis with the financial crisis of the early 1990s. The structure of the chapter is as follows. First, the regulatory regimes of Nordic welfare states are explored. Second, the roots of the early 1990s financial crisis are analysed. Last, the economic and financial crisis from 2008 to 2010 is examined with a particular focus on the implications this has had for social policy.

On the basis that financial markets are inherent unstable, and given that the instabilities may be self-reinforcing and even self-devastating, *financial crises* are to be expected. These are even more likely if there is no, or very weak, public regulation of the markets. From 2007, these instabilities were strengthened in the financial (and housing) markets in the United States (US), leading to severe losses and even to a fall of big investment banks. However, as is argued elsewhere in the book, it soon became evident that the crisis was not restricted to the US, but was global in nature. The global financial and economic crisis from 2008 onwards extended also to the Nordic countries (in short: the Nordics). In these countries too, banks have faced difficulties; exports and Gross Domestic Product (GDP) levels have fallen dramatically and various rescue measures have been introduced. However, especially in Finland and Sweden, a deep recession and banking crisis had already been experienced in 1990-93. This was followed by mass unemployment and cuts in social entitlements. This chapter extends the analysis of 'varieties of crisis' between states by introducing a temporal dimension: looking at the impact of different crises over time.

National systems of regulation and the rise of the Nordic welfare states

The Nordics in the post-war period can be described, maybe paradoxically, as *open but regulated economies*. It is often the case that small states have relatively open economies; they generally have small home markets and large shares of imports and exports in relation to national product. Because of their relatively small production capacity and tendency to produce highly specialised goods, small states rely heavily on imports to support general consumption and high levels of exports to ensure a healthy trade balance. In addition, many small states have relatively high levels of inward and outward foreign direct investments. During this period of trade and investment liberalisation, however, many areas of the economy and society have remained highly regulated in these countries.

In the Nordics, as in several other small countries, relatively strong domestic economic and social political systems prevailed in the post-war period. These can be called *national systems of regulation*. Regulation dominated in foreign trade, international financial flows, agriculture and industrial development. Also, labour markets and working conditions were relatively tightly regulated, by the state and by the labour market partners. Several other areas of life were also regulated nationally, including broadcasting as well as the production and consumption of alcoholic beverages.

It is argued here that *the rise of the welfare states* can also be seen as a part of these national systems of regulation in relatively open economies. First, open economies tend to be vulnerable in the face of changes in the world market, and this calls for domestic social compensation represented by welfare systems (see Katzenstein, 1985). Second, the national system of regulation makes it possible to pursue independent economic and social policies. In particular, capital account controls, or foreign exchange regulations, can be seen as the foundation for post-war stabilisation policies in the Nordics. These regulations isolated the countries financially, thus allowing far-reaching interventionist and selective monetary and fiscal policies domestically. The controls served as a wall behind which the central banks determined the rate of interest and the distribution of credit flows. Since interest rates were kept low and the tax system allowed large deductions for the cost of borrowing (especially deduction for the payment of interest on housing loans), private sector demand for credit was always stronger than the available supply (Jonung et al, 2008, p 11).

The extensive Nordic welfare systems have been analysed in the light of specific political coalitions (for example Esping-Andersen, 1990), although the role of social democracy should not be overestimated. However, the connection to national regulation systems should not be forgotten. Independent economic policies, including the size of the public sector, formed the basis of welfare state decisions. The specific features of the welfare systems can be related to what has been called the '*Nordic normative legacy*'. This notion refers to a set of important objectives or goals that were institutionalised in the Nordics during the post-war decades. They were not necessarily all fulfilled, but they acted as legitimation pressures, as a constraint on political action. The following goals can be identified (see Kosonen, 2000, p 155):

* universal social rights;
* responsibility of public (governmental) power;
* equality (both income equality and gender equality);
* full employment.

Although these goals have been respected in all Nordic welfare states, we can also note inter-Nordic differences. Denmark and Sweden have had more extensive public service systems than Finland. The full employment commitment (Therborn, 1986) has clearly been stronger in Sweden than in Finland and also Denmark before the reforms in the mid-1990s. In relation to old-age pensions, these countries share the universal basic pension, but they differ with regard to occupational (earnings-related) pensions.

Financial deregulation: from boom to bust

The Nordic national systems of regulation, characterised above, changed radically when these countries were involved in the process of globalisation, as almost all countries were in the 1980s or 1990s. In this section, the boom in the latter part of the 1980s and the bust in the early 1990s in the Nordics (in particular in Finland and Sweden) will be assessed in relation to each other. My argument is that bust (financial crisis and deep economic recession) cannot be understood without consideration of the boom (deregulation and overheating of economies) years. The implication here is that the Nordic crisis of the early 1990s should be seen as predominantly homemade, which is not the case with the post-2007 crisis.

In line with many other nations, the *deregulation of financial markets* began to take hold in the Nordics from the mid-1980s. Prior to this, the view had held that the central bank should maintain low and stable interest rates and fixed exchange rates, credit should be rationed and monetary policy should be predominantly passive. However, during the 1980s, rationing and regulation were replaced by flexible interest rates and central bank operations within open markets, and the size and interest sensitivity of capital flows increased. Denmark led the way (among the Nordics) in the deregulation process: in 1982-83, it embarked on a hard currency option, and deregulation was already completed by 1987. This gave way to fast but stable economic growth in Denmark in the late 1980s and early 1990s. The deregulation of financial markets within Finland and Sweden since the mid-1980s spurred a rapid inflow of capital to finance domestic investments and consumption, triggering a rapid expansion of credit and resulting in a financial or speculative bubble, characterised by rising inflation rates and inflationary expectations, especially in capital stocks and real estate. When the real rate of interest was low in the latter part of the 1980s or even negative, the process created positive wealth effects, which in turn led to further strengthening of aggregate demand.

In many ways, the Finnish and Swedish deregulation processes and their outcomes were very similar (Jonung et al, 2008). In Finland, the system of financial governance changed significantly when capital movements were liberalised and interest rate controls were phased out in the mid-1980s. Households and companies, previously accustomed to living in a world of credit rationing, responded by increasing their debt significantly. Lending in foreign currency rose dramatically, too. In this situation, the demand for housing, real estate and stocks led to a rise in their prices. Furthermore, the rise in borrowing was also driven by the fact that expenses for interest payments were deductible from income taxation, causing low after-tax real rates of interest. All in all, the Finnish economy was characterised by a rapid growth in GDP and a boom in the labour market and the housing market.

In Sweden also, financial deregulation affected the behaviour of borrowers and lenders in a fundamental way. The banks were now facing more open and aggressive competition for market shares. They adjusted to the new situation by expanding credit as borrowers stood in line to increase their debt. The result, then, was the creation of a financial bubble in the economy, built on excessive indebtedness within the private sector and corresponding over-lending within the financial sector. The labour market too became overheated, with unemployment at less than 2%. As a consequence of the rapid domestic expansion, the export sector was squeezed, and this came to be one of the causes of the economic recession of the early 1990s (Jonung et al, 2008). During this boom phase, the pegged exchange rate was perceived as irrevocably fixed by investors. The expectation of a stable peg was the central prerequisite for the accumulation of financial imbalances that later fuelled the crisis. An interesting question is why the pegged rate was defended so stubbornly (Jonung et al, 2008); this calls for further research.

Towards the end of the 1980s, it became clear that the upswing was gradually turning into an overheating of both the Finnish and Swedish economies. The deregulation of the credit market resulted in a very rapid expansion of credit and a surge in real estate prices along similar lines in the two countries. For many, it was initially hard to judge to what extent the credit expansion was merely the result of a one-time adjustment from a previously 'underleveraged' situation in the household sector, or a migration of credit supply from the unrestricted 'grey' credit market into the regular banking system. As it later turned out, it was indeed a bubble, fed by a number of factors: leverage-friendly tax rules, lax supervision, low capital requirements, and a complete absence of risk culture in the banks, that is, the banks relied on the promise from the side of the state that if problems occur, the state would ultimately bail them out (Gylfason et al, 2010, pp 104-5).

Then, as usually happens, the boom ended, and as could have been expected, a *deep financial crisis* followed. By 1989, inflation was increasing in both economies. Declining competitiveness slowed exports and economic growth and this resulted in growing current account deficits. House prices also began to decline at the same time that European interest rates rose as a result of German reunification.

Problems in the housing market were exacerbated in Sweden with tax reforms that limited the deductibility of interest payments in 1990 at the same time that there was a strong and unexpected upturn in the real rate of interest adjusted for taxes. The *krona* was subject to several speculative attacks due to the falling credibility of the pegged exchange rate, which led to an inevitable increase in the level of interest rates to resist these attacks. And when the real interest rate rose, the price of assets declined in a downward spiral. The real interest rate shock created a sharp fall in aggregate demand. As a result, unemployment increased from the relatively low levels that had prevailed in Sweden for some time, to more than 8%. The banking crisis that came to characterise the period meant that emergency state support was required.

In Finland, export demand took a strong hit when all exports to the collapsing Soviet Union stopped in 1991 (Gylfason et al, 2010, pp 105-6). This, coupled with slowing exports to Western Europe, reduced the trade balance by more than 15%. Weak export performance together with sizeable current account deficits caused growing uncertainty in the foreign exchange market and speculative attacks against the *markka*. In response, the central bank raised interest rates in order to defend the pegged – and clearly overvalued – exchange rate. High real interest rates together with shrinking asset values depressed domestic demand and GDP fell 13% between 1990 and 1993. The result in the wider economy was a collapse in public finances and a massive increase in unemployment.

Jonung et al (2008, p 30) classify the 1990s crisis as a real interest rate crisis that spread to all parts of society via the balance sheets of companies and households. The value of assets fell as the real interest rate rose while the nominal value of debt remained unchanged. The losses of wealth became enormous. The more households and companies tried to improve their wealth position by selling assets, the deeper the crisis became. The difficulties encountered by both economies in their currency markets continued until they were forced to let their currencies float and depreciate during the autumn of 1992. This corresponded to 'old-style' devaluation (earlier devaluations had been decided by the central banks and the governments, but this time floating currencies operated at arm's length from governments). Then, as interest rates were reduced, the crisis was checked and recovery began, although slowly.

The Finnish and Swedish crisis, 1990-93: economic and social policies

The governments facing the challenge of recession were coalitions of bourgeois (centre-right) parties, led by Esko Aho (Finland) and Carl Bildt (Sweden). The challenge was to manage the crisis somehow, which proved to be difficult.

Since an essential element in the Finnish and Swedish crisis in the early 1990s was a banking crisis, systematic and comprehensive crisis management measures had to be taken (Gylfason et al, 2010, p 110). An initial policy approach was to prevent bank creditors from suffering any losses, so that funding of banks was secured, and domestic financial operations could continue with minimal disruption. To this end, both countries issued an unlimited 'blanket' guarantee of bank debts in the form of parliamentary resolution. It was also soon recognised that the banking systems could not be kept operational without extensive recapitalisation of the banks. In Finland, the government capital injection schemes were divided into two: a general precautionary offer of capital injection into all deposit banks assessed to be fundamentally sound, on the one hand, and capital injection into falling institutions, on the other. In Sweden, public capital injections were only made into banks that would otherwise have fallen. Thus, guarantees were given to the banks; in Finland and Sweden, banks received generous monetary support. All in all, the gross cost was some 3-4% of GDP in Sweden, but 9% of GDP in Finland. Since part of the support was paid back, the eventual cost was actually very small in Sweden, but some 5-6% of GDP in Finland.

Also important to the recovery, when it eventually came, was the depreciation of the *markka* and *krona* that followed the decision to let the two currencies float. Exports grew strongly and the surplus on the current account increased, making it possible to reduce the volume of foreign debt held by the public and private sectors. In both countries, financial deregulation led to changes in the stabilisation regime, causing an end to the pegged exchange rate regime. The countries adopted initially a floating rate and inflation targeting. Later on, Finland became a member of the eurozone, while Sweden remained outside, as did Denmark. In Denmark and Sweden, the euro issue created a hot political debate, and decisions were made only after the 'no' vote won in public referendums in both countries. The proposal to adopt the single currency proved to be unpopular and was rejected by opposing movements and votes, both from the rightist (nationalistic) forces and by the leftist forces, for very different reasons.

It has been argued that the Finnish and Swedish welfare states coped well with the recession and endured without drastic changes (see, for example, Kautto and Heikkilä, 1998). This means that despite decreases in benefit levels, the main institutional characteristics remained intact (the 'Nordic normative legacy'). While this may be true to some extent, some more structural and longstanding changes should be taken into account. First, even though unemployment started to decline from 1994, it remained at a higher level for a long time, and a new kind of long-term unemployment emerged. Moreover, the number of social assistance recipients continued to increase over an even longer period (Lehtonen et al, 2001). In addition, while income differences remained unchanged during the deepest recession, the differences started to increase during the following boom in the latter part of the 1990s, as well as after 2000.

Changes in economic structures and institutions occurred in the aftermath of the 1990s crisis. In both Finland and Sweden, a new kind of structural unemployment emerged. Moreover, the level of public debt increased, justifying changes and cuts in social entitlements, although the cuts also continued during the recovery under Social Democrat-led governments in both countries (Kautto, 2000). In Finland, earnings-related unemployment benefits were cut by 3% in 1992, and in 1993 the qualifying conditions were tightened. In 1994, the structure of unemployment security was renewed and work history was introduced as a precondition for obtaining the basic unemployment allowance. Those without a decent work history would henceforth receive low, flat-rate, labour market supports. Later, qualifying conditions for labour market support for the young were tightened and compensation rates of earnings-related sickness benefits were reduced. The housing allowance was also the target of major cuts in 1993. All in all, when the recession continued and proved deeper than expected, savings measures strengthened in 1993 and 1994. However, despite the change of government in 1995, the cutbacks continued under the Social Democrat-led government.

In Sweden, crisis measures came somewhat later than in Finland. While the centre-right government started cutbacks, these were strengthened after the re-election of the Social Democrats in 1994. Ending wage indexation was the most important way of reducing pension expenditure. The basic pension was reduced by 2% in 1993 and further in 1996. Sickness benefits also came under heavy attack. Coverage, compensation rates and length of recipiency were renegotiated. Housing allowances were cut considerably. Since severe cutbacks were implemented in both countries, they did not differ much, perhaps most in timing, Sweden coming later than Finland.

After the banking crisis in the early 1990s, a restructuring of the Nordic financial markets took place. In particular, the savings banks (small, local banks) largely disappeared. In Sweden, Första Sparbanken (a medium-sized bank) was first merged with other savings banks. In Finland, the central bank (Bank of Finland) took control of Skopbank, a savings bank, in September 1991. Afterwards, all saving banks more or less disappeared. In Sweden, during the crisis a separate, public resolution agency was set up (by the government), which offered public support to the banks. In Finland, this public support included awarding preferred capital certificates to banks. The government also set up a crisis management agency to restructure the banking system. In practice, this meant a reduction of the banks' personnel as staff numbers were halved. In the Finnish case, one big commercial bank (KOP) was merged with another (SYP) – and finally this remaining commercial bank merged with the Swedish Nordbanken. Thus, the leading commercial bank in the Nordics is Nordea, owned mostly the Swedes, the Finns, the Danes and the Norwegians, although in fact the biggest shareholders come from outside of the Nordics. As a result of these mergers and restructuring, a concentration process has happened in Nordic banking life. In addition, the commercial banks are closely linked to the insurance and housing sector.

All in all, in both Finland and Sweden, changes in social policies took place, while the main pillars of the welfare systems were maintained. The savings measures meant a decrease in most of the social entitlements, thereby also contributing to the widening income gaps. In addition to these quantitative changes, a new line of thinking emerged in labour market policies towards a more controlling attitude with regard to activation, in particular in the case of young unemployed persons.

Economic and financial crisis, 2008-10: Denmark, Finland and Sweden

The post–2007 crisis did not have an immediate impact in the Nordics. It occurred against a relatively sound macroeconomic position in all three nations: public debts (as a share of GDP) had been reduced, and economic prospects were quite optimistic. However, the Nordics did not escape the full impact of the crisis as it deepened. First, exports decreased dramatically as the global crisis extended to the most important export countries such as Britain, Germany and Russia and, since the Nordics are very dependent on export incomes, the slowing global economy hit them hard from late 2008. GDP levels dropped in 2009 by some 5% in Denmark and Sweden, and as much as 8% in Finland. Second, there have been difficulties in the banking sector, but these have been modest in relation to the early 1990s. However, bank support was necessary to support the three biggest banks in Denmark. In Sweden, there were big credit losses in 2009 due to events in the Baltic countries, which experienced serious economic problems. The Swedish-led banks such as Nordea and Swedbank had given loans to enterprises in Estonia and Latvia, where the economic downturn was severe. However, these Swedish-led banks could cope relatively easy with the credit losses. Compared to the previous financial crisis, the Finnish banking sector has fared relatively well.

In terms of the economic backcloth to the post-2007 crisis, the Finnish and Swedish economies were relatively stable, and key sectors, such as housing, were not overheated in the same way as they were elsewhere, partly as a result of the after-effects of the 1990s crisis. There was a housing bubble in Denmark, however, which had previously experienced rapid house price inflation. The result following the onslaught of the global crisis was that house prices crashed in Denmark by almost 30%.

Given the problems in currency exchange in the previous crisis, an interesting question in examining the current crisis as it has extended to the Nordics is whether or not the adoption of the euro has had an impact. Denmark has followed its own route: while retaining the *krone* it has been pursuing a policy of keeping its exchange rate fixed in terms of the euro. Sweden has maintained its floating *krona*, but Finland has joined the eurozone. As a result, Finland and Sweden have diverged during the current crisis. In 2008 to 2009, the Swedish currency weakened vis-à-vis the euro, without any central bank intervention and this had the effect of increasing the competitiveness of Swedish exports. Finland has not made the same gains and has experienced a tougher export position. To be sure, there are other factors at play such as the composition of exports (as Gylfason et al, 2010, p 187 point out), but the importance of exchange rate changes should not be denied. More recently in 2010, the euro has weakened vis-à-vis the dollar, and this is beneficial for Finnish industry because of improved price competitiveness.

What kind of macroeconomic measures have then been taken in the Nordics? Possible countercyclical measures include tax reductions, increasing public expenditure, or keeping expenditure levels the same by public debt. In addition, in countries with a large public sector, automatic stabilisers help during a recession. The size of the fiscal impulse is often measured by the change in the cyclically adjusted balance (a positive change indicating contracting policy, and vice versa). Using this measure, we find that fiscal expansion in 2009-10 was relatively strong in Denmark and Finland (stronger than in the eurozone), but somewhat weaker in Sweden (Gylfason et al, 2010, p 199). The fiscal expansion in these cases is almost completely based on the increase of public debt from international financial markets. This fiscal stimulus, however, does not automatically lead to economic growth and increasing employment. Thus, big changes are occurring in the Nordic economies. Industrial output has decreased, and lay-offs are general – thus leading to higher unemployment. All is not due to financial crisis, since there are underlying problems in the industrial sector, in particular in the forestry sector in Finland and Sweden. In forestry, the problem is on the demand side, that is, both Finland and Sweden have more production capacity than can be sold abroad, and many unprofitable units have been closed. This has created severe social problems, especially unemployment, in small towns that have been very dependent on one or few large employers.

Nordic employment and social developments during the current crisis

As yet, it is difficult to evaluate employment and social developments in the Nordics during and after the financial crisis. First, it is probable that – as the experiences of the early 1990s show – changes in these policy areas are still to come. Second, and this differs from the 1990s, drastic cuts and other measures have been postponed before parliamentary elections (autumn 2010 in Sweden, spring 2011 in Finland), because the ruling parties like to avoid unpleasant and unpopular decisions. However, the plans are still open. It seems likely that these measures will be taken soon after the elections, whatever the new coalitions will be. In Sweden, the old centre-right coalition is continuing in power, although somewhat weakened. As yet, savings plans have not been published, but in the light of increasing public debts, some measures are more than likely. In particular the only euro country among the Nordics, Finland, is facing the biggest pressure to rebalance its economy by reducing public expenditure.

Unemployment rates have increased in all three countries, albeit by relatively low amounts. In 2007 to 2009, unemployment increased from 7 to 8-9% in Finland and from 6 to 8-9% in Sweden. In particular in Finland, the increase has remained clearly smaller than in the 1990s. While comparatively low, however, these figures are in contrast to previous periods of full employment that characterised the Nordic states. In Denmark, in part due to its new labour market policies of the 1990s, unemployment remained quite low before the current crisis. Thus, the rise of the unemployment rate from 4% to some 7% has been relatively rapid. As a result, in the post-2007 period, the Nordics have come closer to the European averages, although on the basis of their traditional active labour market policies they are likely to fight rising unemployment (in particular long-term unemployment) more fiercely.

As mentioned above, Nordic *income differentials* have been on the increase since the mid-1990s. From the mid-1990s to the mid-2000s, this increase was most notable in Finland, but also in Sweden (OECD, 2008a). It is too early to say anything firm regarding recent developments, although problems related to income poverty seem to be increasing. Still, Denmark, Finland and Sweden belong to the group of countries with relatively even income distribution.

In the first half of the 1990s, the Nordics (especially Finland and Sweden) first experienced financial and economic crisis, then rising unemployment and later a rise in social assistance expenses, that is, in the last resort support to citizens. This seems also to be the model during the current crisis. As mentioned, unemployment rates have increased, but more slowly than during the previous crisis. Thus, the need for *social assistance* is rising, but it has not been expanding as much as in the 1990s.

The fact is that, in the name of stimulation of economies, the Nordic economies are more and more indebted. Moreover, demographic change is going on, and even more public resources are needed. Therefore, it is not difficult to predict that drastic measures in the public economy are ahead. It is important to evaluate the distributional impacts of the coming savings measures and taxation decisions and also challenge the prevailing truths about the work incentives.

Conclusions

The national systems of regulation in the Nordics have been undergoing change since the mid-1980s when deregulation of financial markets began, leading from boom to bust. The recession of the early 1990s was deep in Finland and Sweden, and only after a radical change in the stabilisation regimes could economic growth begin again. However, unemployment rates remained relatively high, and income differentials have been on the increase. The crisis of the 1990s can be referred to as homemade. In contrast to this, the current financial crisis is mainly global in nature. In the Nordics, the crisis is connected to problems in the export market, and due to this, GDP levels have fallen and unemployment rates have increased.

We can find similarities between the two crisis periods, but differences as well. One obvious difference is that before 2008, no overheating of economies was experienced as before the 1990 turn. This may explain why enterprises and households have faced much smaller problems than in the early 1990s. Second, in contrast to the radical savings measures in Finland and Sweden, fiscal policies have rather stabilised or stimulated economies this time. Third, a rise in unemployment has occurred, but clearly at a slower pace than in the previous crisis. The change in income distribution is, as yet, difficult to analyse.

THIRTEEN

Social policy and the recent economic crisis in Canada and the United States

Daniel Béland and Alex Waddan

Introduction

The economic crisis that manifested itself in 2008 in the United States (US) also had serious consequences in Canada, a country that has strong economic ties with its powerful southern neighbour. From a social policy standpoint, these countries also have a lot in common in as much as both are considered to be liberal welfare regimes featuring limited public support in at least some policy areas, with an extensive role for private benefits (Esping-Andersen, 1990). One consequence of the gaps in public coverage in policy areas such as unemployment and social assistance benefits is that both the Canadian and the US social welfare safety nets are ill-prepared to alleviate the social suffering stemming from economic hard times. On the other hand, there are important differences between the natures of the social policy systems in the two countries. Furthermore, the impact of the recent economic crisis differed in the two countries in terms of the severity of the recession, the political consequences and the public policy responses.[1]

Two differences between Canada and the US are especially striking. First, the Canadian welfare regime features universal social programmes that simply do not exist in the US, a country characterised by a strict dichotomy between social assistance and social insurance (Fraser and Gordon, 1992). Simply speaking, in Canada, there is a commitment to social citizenship and redistribution that is not as widely present in the US (Myles, 1998; Rice and Prince, 2000). Second, the recent recession did not affect these two countries in the same way. In part because of its better-regulated banking and housing sectors, Canada experienced a significantly milder economic crisis than the US, a situation that has had direct policy consequences. This chapter explores the politics of social policy reform in Canada and the US during the recent economic crisis in order to provide a better understanding of how, if at all, the crisis disrupted prevailing patterns of social policy development in the two countries.

The chapter starts by discussing the impact of the economic crisis on US politics and society before briefly assessing recent policy trends in the fields of unemployment benefits, Food Stamps, healthcare and old-age pensions. Next, looking at Canada we discuss the nature and the political and social impact of the economic crisis. The discussion here focuses on Employment Insurance and on old-age pensions, the two policy areas that witnessed the most activity at the federal level between 2008 and 2010 (there are no Food Stamp programmes in Canada and the impact of the crisis on healthcare reform is hard to assess at this point). The conclusion stresses the differences and the similarities between the two countries regarding their social policy response to the recent economic crisis.

The United States

Nature and scope of the economic crisis

The full extent of the financial crisis in the US was exposed in September 2008 as the Secretary of the Treasury, Henry Paulson, frantically devised a series of policy packages to rescue Fannie Mae and Freddie Mac, the failing investment banks (except Lehman Brothers) and the insurance giant AIG. For many Americans, however, there was already clear evidence by the summer of 2007 that serious economic trouble was brewing. One of the central narratives of suffering during the recession was the increasing number of Americans losing their homes because they were unable to keep up with financing their mortgage repayments. Between July and September 2007, the number of homes facing foreclosure activity rose by 100% on the same quarter the previous year (Veiga, 2007). By 2009, foreclosure filings were reported on 2.8 million properties – a 21% increase on 2008 and a staggering 120% up on 2007 (Armour, 2010).

The impact of the housing crisis on the finance industry was disastrous. 'When Bear Stearns, and later Lehman Brothers and Merrill Lynch, went broke, the failure of bonds backed by subprime loans was the biggest hole in their balance sheets' (Kuttner, 2010, p 47). As the leading US investment banks went into meltdown, it was inevitable that the problems would begin to afflict the wider economy. The contraction in Gross Domestic Product (GDP) caused by the recession, measured in constant US dollars, manifested itself in the third quarter of 2008 with a fall of 2.7%. The next quarter saw a drop of 5.4%. The annual figure for GDP change in 2009 was −2.4%. That represented the largest annual percentage decline in real terms US GDP since 1946 (US Bureau of Economic Analysis, 2010). Unsurprisingly, this led to a dramatic increase in the rate of unemployment. In March 2007, the official unemployment rate was 4.4%. This had climbed, but only to 5.1%, 12 months later. By March 2009, however, the figure had jumped to 8.6%. It then peaked at 10.1% in October 2009. In May 2010, unemployment remained at 9.7% (US Department of Labor, 2010a). When compared to the recessions of the early 1980s and early 1990s, the peak was lower than the rate of 10.8% in November and December of 1982 but notably higher than that of 7.8% in June 1992 (US Department of Labor, 2010b).

In addition to the numbers officially counted as unemployed were many millions more who were either underemployed or who had been so discouraged by the unavailability of work that they had effectively temporarily withdrawn from the labour market. In March 2010, an estimated 9.1 million workers, seeking full-time jobs, could find only part-time employment. The Department of Labor described another 2.3 million people as being 'marginally attached to the labour force', meaning that they wished to work but had not actively sought a job in the four weeks prior to the compilation of the unemployment figures (US Department of Labor, 2010c, p 2). Adding up all these numbers meant that in the autumn of 2009, 17.4% of American workers were either unemployed or underemployed (Peck, 2010).

Furthermore, in comparison to previous recessions, there was evidence that the downturn of 2008/09 had had a severe impact on those who had lost their jobs as spells of unemployment were lasting longer. The official unemployment tally for March 2010 included 6.5 million people, or 44.1% of the unemployed, who had been out of work for 27 weeks (US Department of Labor, 2010c, p 2). By the end of 2009, the average spell of unemployment lasted for over six months. This was the first time that dubious landmark had been exceeded since the Bureau of Labor statistics first tracked the longevity of unemployment spells in 1948 (Peck, 2010). In the circumstances, it is hardly surprising that the official US poverty rate rose from 12.5% in 2007 to 13.2% in 2008, meaning that an extra 2.6 million people lived in poverty (US Census Bureau, 2009). Given the diversity of the US economy and pre-existing rates of economic inequality, it is not surprising that the pain caused by the recession was unevenly spread. Unemployment rates have consistently been higher for the African-American and Hispanic communities than for whites and these trends were reinforced as the recession bit. In March 2010, the official unemployment rate for whites was 8.8%. For Hispanic workers it was significantly higher at 12.6% but for black Americans the unemployment rate stood at 16.5% (US Department of Labor, 2010c).

Political consequences

Unlike in Canada where the Conservative government led by Stephen Harper survived in the 2008 elections, in the US the Republicans were punished for the emerging crisis. Most significantly, the accumulating bad news in the autumn of 2008 reinforced the presidential candidacy of Democratic Senator Barack Obama. The Republican candidate, Senator John McCain, did not help his cause when he declared, in the immediate aftermath of the bankruptcy of Lehman Brothers, that the fundamentals of the US economy 'were strong' (Cooper, 2008, p A1). From that point in mid-September onwards, Obama took a lead in the polls that carried through to Election Day.

Having been elected in a time of crisis, the critical question for the incoming Obama administration was how to respond to the mounting problems. Given the extraordinary situation in January 2009 when Obama was sworn in and the manifest failure of prevailing institutions to either anticipate the crisis or respond coherently to its consequences, it appeared as if the new President might have an opportunity to declare the need for radical, path-breaking, reform. In Skowronek's (1997) terminology, Obama looked as if he might become a President of 'reconstruction'. During the transition, President-elect Obama's choice for chief-of-staff, Rahm Emmanuel, suggested that Obama understood that the moment was at hand to bring about substantive change: 'You never want a serious crisis to go to waste…. What I mean by that is that it's an opportunity to do things you could not do before' (Emmanuel, quoted in Leonhardt, 2009, p 23). Unlike the situation in Canada, where the impact of the recession was less far-reaching and where the Conservative Party remained in power with a minority government facing a weak opposition, there was, in the US, a sense that the political fallout of the economic downturn would lead to significant social policy change: and the first major piece of legislation enacted by the Obama White House in cooperation with the Democratic majorities in Congress was the American Recovery and Reinvestment Act 2009 (ARRA). ARRA's primary purpose was to create a stimulus for the economy but as part of its package of US$787 billion expenditure, ARRA bolstered some of the social policy programmes serving those hit hardest by the economic downturn. Thus, ARRA included extra funding for the Unemployment Insurance (UI) and Food Stamp programmes.

Unemployment Insurance and Food Stamps

In contrast to Canada where UI is administered by the federal government, UI in the US sees eligibility drawn up at state level within federal guidelines. In most states and in normal times, unemployed workers receive benefits for 26 weeks. When unemployment levels in a state reach a certain point, generally 6%, an Extended Benefits programme is factored in that normally provides a further 13 weeks of benefit. In exceptional circumstances when there is a period of high unemployment, there is a federally funded further period of benefit available under the Temporary Emergency Unemployment Benefits scheme (Dobelstein, 2009, pp 114-16). Problematically, however, access to UI is denied to many workers. Part-time and low-waged workers are particularly vulnerable to being deemed ineligible to claim UI after losing their jobs. The system was established during the Great Depression with the expectation that it would offer protection to people employed full-time in manufacturing and trade industries. As, however, the nature of employment and the workforce changed over subsequent decades, so a diminishing proportion of workers qualified for the benefit. In a study of unemployed workers between 1992 and 2003, the Government Accountability Office found that 'low-wage workers were almost two-and-a-half times as likely to be out of work as higher-wage workers, but half as likely to receive UI benefits' (US Government Accountability Office, 2007, p 12).

Consequently, in March 2009, while over 13 million Americans were registered as unemployed, fewer than six million were collecting UI (Hagenbaugh, 2009). In an effort to provide more protection to a greater number of unemployed people while pumping up the economy therefore, ARRA set aside US$7 billion for states if they revised their UI eligibility rules. ARRA provided incentives to states to expand UI eligibility to a greater number of people in part-time and low-waged work who would normally not receive benefits on losing their jobs. ARRA also offered more federal government money to help states pay for emergency-extended benefits for a further 20 weeks beyond that normally available. ARRA did not impose mandatory changes on the states, and a small number of Republican governors vociferously voiced their opposition; but in the first months of 2009, many states did adapt their rules to provide UI benefits to a greater number for a longer period (NELP, 2009).[2]

Another part of the safety net that was patched up by ARRA was the Food Stamp programme.[3] Unlike most other means-tested programmes in the US, all households with a low income and limited assets are eligible for Food Stamps, including childless adults. The federal government funds Food Stamps and administration costs are shared between federal and state governments. ARRA both provided extra funding to increase the amount of benefits a household could receive and also extended the eligibility for the programme. Thus, the maximum available to a household of four increased from US$588 to US$668 per month and ARRA temporarily suspended the rule that restricted unemployed workers to three months of Food Stamps' receipt. Finally, ARRA provided extra funds to states in order to help them pay the increased administrative costs associated with increased Food Stamp rolls (Pavetti and Rosenbaum, 2010, p 9). The administration also actively encouraged states to enrol all those eligible for the programme (DeParle and Gebeloff, 2009). At the end of 2008, a near record number of 30 million Americans were in receipt of Food Stamps; yet, a year later, that figure had risen to 37 million (Pavetti and Rosenbaum, 2010, p 5).

Healthcare and social security

While the extension of UI benefits and Food Stamps provided important relief to many households, these measures were temporary emergency responses to the economic crisis that did not change the basic structures of US social policy. A most profound change did come in March 2010 with the passage of comprehensive healthcare reform. The legislation does not mean that the US has adopted a United Kingdom (UK)-like, government-run health service; but through a series of complex measures, involving new rules and regulations for health insurance companies and government subsidies to low-income households, many millions of people previously unable to access health insurance will be able to do so over the next few years.

The failure of President Bill Clinton's effort at healthcare reform in 1993/94 apparently acted as a warning of the dangers of over-reaching in terms of social policy reform. President George W. Bush's failed effort at social security reform in 2005, while ideologically quite distinct from Democratic efforts at health reform, seemed further to reinforce the message that the institutional obstacles to comprehensive social change were overwhelming. Nevertheless, healthcare reform remained a key item on the Democratic agenda and, as the economic downturn worsened, the worry that people would lose not only their jobs but also their employer-subsidised health insurance increased liberal concerns about the inequity inherent in the US healthcare system.

During the Democratic primaries, candidate Obama had been slower to commit to health reform than the other leading candidates, notably John Edwards and Hillary Clinton (Balz and Johnson, 2009, pp 72-4). President Obama, however, pushed ahead and made health reform a top domestic priority. Two overriding problems were to be addressed: first, the high numbers of Americans, ineligible for government provision and unable to access the private market, left without health insurance; and second, the overall cost of healthcare. In 2006, 16% of the US population lacked health insurance, yet Organisation for Economic Co-operation and Development (OECD, 2010g) figures show that in 2005 the US spent 15.4% of GDP on healthcare compared to 11.1% in France, 10.7% in Germany and 8.3% in the UK. One problem in devising reform was that different constituencies prioritised different problems. Liberal Democrats worried about the number of uninsured, but centrists emphasised the need for cost control, arguing that health costs were undermining the finances of both government and employers. Initially, the administration was anxious to portray its efforts to find ways of reconciling these potentially conflicting objectives as being bipartisan. In the end, however, this proved a fruitless although time-consuming sideshow. The real issue was to get the congressional Democrats to agree on a plan.

In order to defuse interest group opposition, from the start of the process, Obama involved an array of stakeholders, including those who had opposed previous reform efforts (Pear and Stolberg, 2009). In the end, there was a pay-off to this strategy as opposition from the insurance industry, the pharmaceutical industry and the American Hospital Association was much more muted than had previously been the case. Republicans remained steadfast in their opposition, and public opinion, while supportive of reform in theory, remained sceptical of 'Obamacare'.[4] The Democratic majorities in Congress proved more disciplined than in 1993 when Clinton could not even force his proposals through the relevant congressional committees. In a seminal article about the failure of Clinton's plan, Steinmo and Watts (1995) argued that the institutional fragmentation of the US legislative process and party indiscipline had made reform impossible. That argument is perhaps too one-dimensional (Hacker, 1997) but certainly Congress had proved to be a graveyard for health reform (Peterson, 2005). It was therefore critical that the Democratic leadership in the House controlled just enough votes to let some Democrats stray and that, at least during 2009, the administration had a majority in Senate that could overcome a filibuster.

For all the undoubted potential significance of the reform, its long-term political and policy impact remains uncertain as it is being phased in over a number of years. In the circumstances, therefore, it is impossible to know what its institutional consequences will be. If it proves popular and successful then it will likely establish its own policy legacies. The delay in full implementation of the law means that it will be some time before its component parts are fully embedded.

It is also important to note that healthcare reform should not simply be seen as a direct consequence of the economic crisis. The problems with the healthcare system had long been recognised and various reform plans discussed. What the crisis did do was help Democrats win the presidency and more seats in Congress at the November election. In turn, this provided the White House and Democratic leaders in Congress with the institutional capacity to drive through the reform package. So the relationship between the economic crisis and healthcare reform is more about electoral outcomes than about the response to the crisis itself.

In contrast to the situation prevailing in the field of healthcare, no major reform has affected old-age pensions, another major area of federal social policy. Following the failure of George W. Bush's effort to partially privatise Social Security in 2005, there have not been further significant efforts at policy reform of this large, federal earnings-related pension scheme, which covers the vast majority of the older population. Concerns still persist about the long-term viability of the programme, but any retrenchment would be politically risky. During the 2008 presidential campaign, Barack Obama pledged to protect Social Security against potential Republican attempts at 'privatisation' while generating new revenues by forcing wealthy people to contribute more to this popular federal programme. Since the beginning of the Obama administration, nothing has been done to address the long-term fiscal challenges facing the programme. Regarding Social Security, it is thus possible to talk about the status quo. Elsewhere, however, there has been considerable turmoil in the pension system. First, state governments have seen the liabilities associated with benefits promised to public sector employees upon retirement grow (Bullock and Weitzman, 2010). Second, many private pension schemes have declined in value due to collapse of the stock market. Through 2008, for example, participation in 401(k) pension schemes[5] remained steady, but the average account lost 28% of its value (Healy, 2009). Thus far, nothing major has been done to address this crisis in private pension benefits, which could seriously undermine the economic security of future retirees.

Fiscal constraints

The passage of healthcare reform suggests that, whatever else happens during his tenure, President Obama and his administration will have left a significant mark on social policy. Two years into his presidency, however, it had become increasingly clear that further social policy expansion was likely to be limited as the US struggled to come to terms with its large federal deficit and accumulated debt. The White House, for example, found it increasingly difficult to persuade Congress to finance further stimulus efforts. In the end, in the lame duck session of Congress after the 2010 mid-term elections, Obama approved a controversial deal with Congress that extended the payment of benefits to the long-term unemployed as part of a package that continued the Bush-era tax cuts, including those for the wealthiest Americans, which had been due to expire at the end of the calendar year (Baker, 2010).

Perhaps under even more duress than the federal government, were many state governments, especially as nearly all states have some sort of balanced budget requirement (Maynard, 2010). In social policy terms, the programme most directly threatened was Medicaid, which provides health insurance to very low-income Americans and is jointly funded by the federal and state governments. By the summer of 2010, it was clear that many states would run into deep fiscal trouble if there was not further enhanced federal funding provided for Medicaid, but as deficit fever increasingly took hold in Washington, it was less evident that the states could rely on federal largesse (Luo and Wheaton, 2010).

Overall, these fiscal constraints threatened to undermine the Obama administration's efforts to further stimulate the economy and expand, or even maintain, the existing social safety net. In the spring of 2011, the major cuts and the privatization of Medicare proposed as part of the House Republican proposal known as the 'Ryan Budget' illustrate the recent rise of conservative retrenchment advocacy in Washington. On the other hand, the measures contained in ARRA and the healthcare legislation illustrate the importance and impact of Obama's presidency. The US has hardly become a social democratic welfare regime as there are many remaining holes in the safety net, but assuming that it is not repealed or watered down before full implementation, health reform in particular could have a significant redistributive effect. However, as stated earlier, in the case of the US, speaking of a strict causal relationship between the economic crisis and healthcare reform is problematic at best.

Canada

Nature and scope of the economic crisis

Due to the high level of economic integration between Canada and the US in the context of the North American Free Trade Agreement (NAFTA), the financial and economic crisis that hit the US in 2008 had a direct and immediate impact on the Canadian economy. In fact, the downturn struck Canada at a faster pace than during previous recessions. For instance, 'real GDP and employment posted faster and sharper declines early in the recent downturn than in 1981-1982 and 1990-1991. For GDP, nearly two-thirds (64.0%) of the decline occurred between November 2008 and January 2009, a 3-month period during which GDP fell 2.5% as Canada's exports tumbled 26%' (Cross, 2010).

The official unemployment rate increased from 6.1% in August 2008 to 8.7% in August 2009, which was the highest rate in more than a decade (Reuters, 2009). This rapid deterioration of the economy caught many Canadians and their politicians by surprise. For Prime Minister Stephen Harper, the timing of the 2008 financial crisis was especially bad, as stock fell dramatically during the federal electoral campaign, in which his Conservative Party attempted to gain enough seats to constitute a majority government. Echoing Republican presidential candidate John McCain, who at first denied the scope of the crisis facing his country, Harper repeatedly declared that '[t]he fundamentals of the Canadian economy are sound' (Harper, quoted in Taber, 2008). Facing much criticism from opposition leaders, Harper later modified his optimistic discourse to acknowledge the possibility of a major economic downturn in Canada. In the end, in the 14 October election, the Conservative Party gained seats but in insufficient number to form a majority government. One of the reasons why Harper's party gained more seats at the election amid the growing concerns about the economy is probably the lacklustre performance of the Liberal Opposition Leader, Stéphane Dion. However, the political tension kept increasing later in the autumn, as the opposition attempted to create a coalition government that would have removed the Conservatives from office. Partly because the 'biggest loser' at the October election, Stéphane Dion, would have become Prime Minister, the coalition proposal proved extremely controversial, especially in Conservative strongholds such as Alberta and Saskatchewan. In the end, Governor

General Michaëlle Jean sided with Harper by allowing him to prorogue Parliament and, as a consequence, save his minority government. Still under strong pressure from the opposition and the public, however, the Harper government put forward a CDN$30 billion stimulus package as part of the 2009 federal budget, which was tabled in late January (Department of Finance, 2009). Overall, there is a strong contrast between the political outcomes of the autumn 2008 federal elections in Canada; while the US witnessed a shift to the left and a change of the party controlling the White House, in Canada, the Conservatives found a way to remain in power, despite the emerging economic crisis.

Canada has long been characterised by important regional variations and inequalities and this was reflected in the way that the economic downturn had a stronger impact on some regions than on others. One of the hardest-hit places in Canada was Ontario, once the country's economic engine but now facing industrial decline in sectors such as the car industry. Across the country, the two provinces that fared considerably better on average were Manitoba and Saskatchewan, which largely avoided the downturn altogether. Importantly, as far as unemployment rates are concerned, significant variations existed within the same province, which points to the territorially fragmented nature of the Canadian economy (*CBC News*, 2009).

Another characteristic of the recent economic crisis in Canada is the fact that, although it hit the country suddenly, it proved milder than the economic downturn witnessed in the US. One reason behind the better overall shape of the Canadian economy compared to its 'big neighbour' was the absence of subprime crisis in Canada and the relative strength of the country's financial and banking sector, which is better regulated than in its US equivalent. Moreover, with public finances in better shape in Ottawa than in Washington, DC, Canada was in a stronger position to deal with the economic crisis than the US. A possible reason why Canada is in a better overall fiscal situation than the US is the budget-cutting and revenue-raising efforts of the 1990s, for instance the creation in 1991 of the federal Goods and Services Tax (GST), a national sales tax that has no direct US equivalent. Furthermore, if the recession proved milder in Canada than in the US, the recovery that began to materialise in early 2010 seemed more robust in Canada than south of the border. In the first quarter of 2010, for example, Canada's GDP witnessed a 6.1% growth and the Bank of Canada even increased the interest rate for the first time in nearly three years. But although unemployment rates began to decline, concerns about the slower recovery in the US and the problems within the eurozone following the 2010 Greek debt crisis created uncertainty that worried Canadian observers (Yew, 2010).

At the time we write this chapter, it is not yet clear how durable the Canadian recovery will be. If the global economy deteriorates once more due to failing demand, Canada could be seriously hit. Moreover, as of January 2011, the national unemployment rate was 7.8%, nearly two points higher than the average rate for the year 2007 (6%).

Despite these cautionary remarks, it is clear that the economic crisis in Canada has proved less profound than in the US and in many European countries. This reality helps explain why the social policy response to the economic crisis seemed modest in scope, at least as far as concrete reforms are concerned. Although there has been much talk about comprehensive reforms, by June 2011, relatively little had changed in the Canadian social policy landscape. This is notably true at the federal level, where the presence of a Conservative minority government throughout the recession made bold reforms unlikely for both ideological and political reasons. While opposition parties and labour unions called for major reforms in fields such UI and old-age pensions, the minority government only supported minor changes to existing programmes and frameworks. Instead, the government focused mainly on traditional, short-term economic stimulus measures such as infrastructure projects (for example road construction). Clearly, as the discussion below about Employment Insurance and old-age pensions suggests, the economic crisis helped push social policy reform onto the federal agenda but, thus far, it has failed to generate enough political momentum to force the Conservative government to embrace comprehensive reforms aimed at durably improving social protection.

Unemployment

In contrast to the US, Canada has a purely federal UI system. This programme was enacted in 1940 after Ottawa reached a constitutional deal with the provinces, a situation made necessary by the fact that a similar legislation had been struck down by the courts in 1937.[6] In 1971, a major expansion of UI took place, which led to quasi universal coverage and more liberal eligibility criteria. Six years later, in 1977, eligibility criteria became more stringent but they now varied according to the level of unemployment recorded in specific regions of the country. According to this logic, people living in high unemployment regions qualify more rapidly for benefits than people living in low employment regions. This territorially variable entry model remains in place to this day. Major austerity reforms took place in the 1990s, culminating in the Employment Insurance Act 1996, which changed the name of the programme to Employment Insurance (EI). Overall, these reforms made it harder on average for the unemployed to access benefits. As a result of the changes enacted between 1990 and 1996, many unemployed people could no longer qualify for benefits, and those who did received lower payments on average for a shorter period of time. Not surprisingly, when the economic crisis hit the country in late 2008, it did trigger a major debate about EI eligibility criteria and benefit duration. As the media ran stories about the many unemployed who did not qualify for benefits and about others who soon ran out of benefits due to seemingly short entitlement periods, federal opposition parties began to request changes to EI aimed at improving the protection offered to the unemployed (*CBC News*, 2009).

Responding to criticisms from opposition parties that something should be done to help the unemployed during the economic crisis, as part of the 2009 federal budget the Conservative government temporarily extended the maximum duration of EI benefits from 45 to 50 weeks. However, this modest change did not liberalise eligibility criteria in a country where more than half of the unemployed did not even qualify for EI benefits. In this context, opposition parties increased the pressure on the Harper government for bold actions on EI reform. For instance, the Liberals proposed the creation of a single national eligibility standard of 360 hours of work, which would be considerably more generous than the existing criteria that, depending on region, varied from 420 to 700 hours (*CBC News*, 2009). In June 2009, considering the Prime Minister's refusal to enact such bold changes, Opposition Leader Michael Ignatieff (Liberal Party) threatened to take down the Conservative government in the absence of reform. Finally, Ignatieff and Prime Minister Harper agreed to put together a bipartisan working group that was tasked to explore possible changes to the EI programme during the summer. Yet, in September, Ignatieff did not even wait for the report to withdraw his support to the Harper government. The government survived only because the two other opposition parties (the New Democratic Party and the Bloc Québécois) decided not to overthrow the government, since the Prime Minister pledged to increase by up to 20 weeks the duration of benefits for the unemployed who had contributed to EI during at least seven of the previous 10 years (Bourgault-Côté, 2009). Later in the autumn, the Harper government announced another change to EI: the voluntary inclusion of self-employed workers, who could now decide to pay contributions granting them access to parental and sickness benefits available under the programme. These changes provoked contrasting reactions: while the Left generally thought that the reforms were far too modest, the pro-market Right criticised them as wasteful (Veldhuis and Lammam, 2009). Overall, the modest nature of the changes put forward by Prime Minister Harper suggests that his government did not prioritise social policy reform, except when the opposition and the public forced them to react.

Pensions

Beyond the issue of EI reform, the recent economic crisis helped push the debate on the future of Canada's pension system onto the policy agenda. To understand the nature of that debate, a few general remarks about the structure of that system are necessary. First, the Canadian pension system is similar to the American one, in the sense that it is grounded in a close relationship between public benefits and voluntary private schemes and a strong reliance on the latter (Boychuk and Banting, 2008). Second, however, the public side of the Canadian pension system is quite different from its American counterpart. In Canada, citizens and permanent residents aged 65 and older meeting certain eligibility conditions are entitled to a flat pension called Old Age Security (OAS). Although the benefits are taken away from wealthier Canadians through a tax provision, the pension remains quasi universal. On the top of this flat pension lies the Canada Pension Plan (CPP) and the Quebec Pension Plan (QPP), which is the equivalent of the CPP for the province of Quebec. These two schemes were adopted in the mid-1960s to supplement the OAS pension, which was created in 1951. The replacement rate and the Yearly Maximum Pensionable Earnings of CPP and QPP are low by international standards (25% and CDN$47,200 in 2010, respectively). However, despite the modest nature of the OAS pension and the low replacement rate of the two earnings-related schemes, the Canadian pension system does well in the field of poverty alleviation, where a third programme plays a major role: the Guaranteed Income Supplement (GIS), which is available to low-income older people. Partly due to this federal programme, regarding the reduction of poverty among older people, Canada performs as well as countries such as Sweden and much better than the UK and the US (Béland and Myles, 2005; Wiseman and Yčas, 2008).

These public programmes are important but they should not hide the sheer scope of Canada's reliance on private pensions and personal savings even though coverage remains uneven (Boychuk and Banting, 2008). In common with the US, private coverage is voluntary and, as a result, pensions cover less than half of the workforce. In fact, between 1977 and 2008, workforce participation declined from 46% to 38% (Baldwin, 2010). Perhaps more importantly, Canada is witnessing a gradual decline in defined benefit pensions. As in the US, defined contribution schemes are gaining ground at the expense of these traditional pension plans. As a result, financial risks are being transferred from businesses to workers. In this context, it is not surprising that the 2008 financial crisis forced some Canadians to postpone their retirement due to negative returns that suddenly lowered the value of their invested savings. Additionally, the financial crisis exacerbated problems such as benefit reductions and plan terminations while hurting all existing pension funds. For instance, in 2008, Canadian private pension plans suffered losses varying between 10 and 25%, on average (Gold, 2008).

Overall, the well-known flaws of voluntary private pensions and personal savings thus became more apparent than before in the aftermath of the 2008 financial crisis, which in turn increased the level of public concern over old-age security. Thus, although the debate on the problems facing private pensions began long before the 2008 financial crisis, this debate intensified in the wake of the crisis. In this context, labour unions and other constituencies called for reforms that could increase public pension benefits to compensate for the problems facing private pensions. The Canadian Labour Congress, for example, has actively promoted a plan to double the CPP replacement rate (Canadian Labour Congress, 2009). Supported by the New Democratic Party, this plan calls for a substantial – and politically controversial – increase in payroll contributions (currently at 9.9% for the combined rate).

Although the Conservative government has not embraced this type of comprehensive reform, it reacted almost immediately to deal with growing concerns about retirement security. For instance, in an Economic Statement released on 27 November 2008, Finance Minister Jim Flaherty (2008) proposed 'a one-time change that will allow RRIF [Registered Retirement Income Fund] holders to reduce their required minimum withdrawal by 25 per cent for this tax year'. In the same statement, the Finance Minister promised to launch national 'consultations on issues facing defined benefit and defined contribution pension plans' (Flaherty, 2008). Considering the sheer complexity of the Canadian pension system and the lack of consensus about how to fix the challenges facing private pensions, however, these consultations remain an ongoing process that have not led to any meaningful reform yet. As for the idea of increasing the CPP replacement rate promoted by the Canadian Labour Congress and the New Democratic Party, it faces a major institutional challenge, as CPP reform requires the approval of at least two thirds of the 10 Canadian provinces, representing at least two thirds of the country's population. Moreover, CPP and QPP are closely related programmes, and the need to keep the institutional 'parallelism' between them further complicates the reform process (Tamagno, 2008). Perhaps more important, increasing CPP benefits is at odds with the ideological commitment of the ruling Conservative Party. This does not mean that CPP reform is impossible; simply, it suggests that the road to reform is treacherous at best. Finally, a widely discussed alternative to CPP reform is the creation of a voluntary supplementary savings scheme based on 'automatic enrolment' (that is, workers participate in the programme unless they decide to opt out of it), an approach meant to help more Canadians save for retirement (Newton, 2010). As it is, although the financial and economic crisis of 2008 intensified debate about old-age security, it remains unclear whether any significant policy change will result. In December 2010, at a meeting of the federal and the provincial finance ministers, the idea of a modest increase in CPP payroll tax and replacement rate, which the Conservative government had finally embraced earlier that year, was put on hold due to opposition from the governments of Alberta and Quebec. Instead, during the meeting, the finance ministers simply supported the development of new (private) pooled plans targeting smaller businesses and the self-employed, among others. Several months later, the government of Quebec announced modest hikes in QPP payroll contributions aimed only at improving the fiscal standing of the program, without any alteration to its 20% replacement rate, which remains identical to CCP's.

Fiscal constraints

Although less dramatic than in other countries, the economic crisis had a negative impact on federal public finances. In contrast to the US, Canada was in a good fiscal position before entering the economic crisis, as the federal government had been running budget surpluses for more than 10 consecutive years. However, starting in late 2008, the fiscal situation deteriorated. In 2009, large stimulus spending aggravated that situation as the federal governments ran large deficits for the first time in more than a decade (Whittington, 2009). For example, for the fiscal year ending in late March 2010, the federal deficit was an estimated CND$47 billion. This deficit was lower than expected due to the apparent recovery that had began to materialise by that date (*CBC News*, 2010) but it still poses a policy challenge, especially since the Conservative government tends to oppose tax increases that could help restore fiscal balance in Canada. In this context, future programme cuts are a possibility. As long as the Conservatives operated as a minority government they had relatively little room to manoeuvre as the three opposition parties are located to their left on the political spectrum, with the Liberal Party taking more centrist positions than the social democratic New Democratic Party and Bloc Québécois. As a consequence of the May 2011 election, a Conservative majority government in Ottawa is unlikely to trigger welfare state expansion. On the contrary, if fiscal problems remained, cutbacks in existing social programmes and perhaps in transfers to other provinces could move onto the federal agenda, just as they did during the 1980s and 1990s. Also, the fiscal situation of the provinces has deteriorated, which could favour the return of fiscal austerity traditionally associated with cuts in social programmes (Vieira, 2010). Considering that the provinces are in charge of major policy areas such as education, healthcare and social assistance, this fiscal situation is a potential source of concern in the field of social policy. Overall, from the fall of 2008 to the spring of 2011, a comparatively milder recession coupled with the presence of a Conservative minority government in Ottawa undermined the quest for bold social policy reforms.

Conclusion

This chapter shows both the similarities and the differences in the way the US and Canada dealt with the recent economic crisis. In both countries the recession drew attention to the limitations of the safety net, including, in both cases, significant gaps in UI coverage. Although the recession proved milder in Canada than in the US, the Harper government took some modest measures to improve the plight of the unemployed while pushing forward the idea of an increase in CPP benefits. In the US, in addition to extending access to unemployment benefits and increasing payments through the Food Stamps programme, the recession played a significant but indirect role in healthcare reform by helping Democrats make big gains at the 2008 federal election. From this perspective, the impact of the recession on electoral politics proved much greater in the US than in Canada, where the Harper government was re-elected even as the financial crisis struck the world in the early autumn 2008.

Overall, therefore, when dealing with the impact of economic crises, cross-national partisan and electoral differences are crucial. For instance, in Canada, although adjustments have been made to social programmes, the weaker nature of the crisis and the presence of a Conservative government in Ottawa favoured relatively modest and often temporary adjustments to social benefits rather than sweeping reforms. In the US, the depth of the 2008 financial crisis helped Democrats both win the presidency and increase their congressional majorities, thus empowering them to launch a major healthcare reform in 2009. Enacted in March 2010, the reform is important but it would be a mistake to describe it as a mere reaction to the economic crisis, as the problems of the US healthcare system had been known for decades. In general, despite the adoption of this reform in the US, in itself, the recent economic crisis has not led to a dramatic overhaul of the Canadian and US welfare regimes. Change has been much more significant in the US, but the welfare systems in both countries remain fragmented and characterised by a reliance on private benefits that provide limited or no economic security to a large portion of workers. Finally, in both countries, the economic crisis has led to a deterioration of the fiscal situation of both the federal and substate governments. Although the situation is more favourable in Canada than in the US, the fiscal challenges facing these two counties could lead to a return to the politics of austerity that became so central in both societies during the 1980s and, especially, the 1990s. From this perspective, in the long run, the economic crisis may well have paved the way for future conservative attacks against the welfare state. This was illustrated in the 2010 mid-term elections that saw significant gains for the Republican Party, as conservatives lambasted both the economic stimulus package and the healthcare reform as fiscally reckless examples of big government in an era of budget deficit.

Notes

[1] For a general discussion about the impact of economic crises on social policy, see Castles (2010).

[2] For a more detailed look at the measures taken to expand and extend the availability of UI, see US Committee on Ways and Means (2010).

[3] The programme's formal title is the *Supplemental Nutrition Assistance Program*.

[4] For a detailed list of poll results taken through 2009-2010, see Real Clear Politics, Obama and Democrats' Health Care Plan: www.realclearpolitics.com/epolls/other/obama_and_democrats_health_care_plan-1130.html

[5] 401(k) pension schemes are personal retirement accounts whereby workers invest in plans by choosing between different types of mutual

funds. Employers may well contribute to these accounts, but importantly they are defined contribution rather than defined benefit schemes.

[6] This paragraph draws extensively on Courchene and Allan (2009). On the history of UI in Canada, see Pal (1988), Porter (2003) and Campeau (2005). For a discussion of the reforms taking place in the 1990s, see Hale (1998) and Béland and Myles (2008).

Acknowledgements

The authors thank Kevin Farnsworth and Zoë Irving for their comments and suggestions. Daniel Béland acknowledges support from the Canada Research Chairs Programme.

FOURTEEN

From economic crisis to a new age of austerity: the UK

Kevin Farnsworth

As already noted in previous chapters of this volume (see especially Chapter One), the post-2007 economic crisis was a global economic event that had variable effects on national economies. How, and to what extent, it has had an impact depends on local circumstances: prevailing economic conditions and political responses. Thus, the global economic crisis can be better understood as a series of national economic crises, each being distinguished by the size of the initial economic hit and by the particular mix of political and economic weapons selected to defend national economies. And as we shift the focus to individual nations, the *politics* of the crisis become as, or even more, important than the economics.

For its part, the United Kingdom (UK) could scarcely have been in a worse position to mediate the effects of the global crisis as it took hold in 2007 and 2008. The UK's close economic relationship with the United States (US) meant that its financial sector experienced the repercussions of the initial collapse of the US sub-prime market earlier than many other economies and it was ultimately hit much harder. The knock-on effects on its housing market and manufacturing and services sectors have also been more prolonged. The particular confluence of UK political and economic factors prior to, and since, the onset of the crisis served to increase its effects; the UK economic crisis was especially deep and the early political response especially comprehensive (or to put it another way, especially financially costly). The crisis helped to unseat the Labour government in 2010 and paved the way for a new Conservative-led coalition government, which, in turn, introduced a more right-wing mode of crisis management (to which we will return later). This has been decisive in the evolution of the crisis and its impact on social policy in particular. In the UK, the crisis has ushered in a new age of welfare austerity.

Background to the UK crisis

Before we consider the UK crisis in detail, it is important to examine its context. As Chapter One made clear, the political economy of the crisis – its roots, how it took hold, where and how it has had an impact on economies and how it has been tackled and/or mediated – is hugely important (see Gamble, 2009; also Gough, this volume). The crisis that began in the US demonstrated at once the extent to which the UK and US economies were intrinsically tied together. The UK, like the US, is steeped in the liberal tradition, typified by adversarial industrial relations, competing economic interests, and relative short-termism, at least when compared with other 'varieties' of capitalism (Hall and Soskice, 2001). Coupled with this, the UK has suffered from two very British, and very interrelated, problems historically: declining relative competitiveness during the latter half of the 20th century and a politically, if not economically, dominant financial sector coexisting with a relatively weak industrial sector and a burgeoning service sector (Longstreth, 1979; Ingham, 1984; Gamble, 1990). Together, these challenges have encouraged economic oscillation between programmes that seek to variously boost manufacturing and financial interests. In most cases, finance has continued to shine on the global and national stages while industry has struggled and governments have variously viewed this as a problem or have accepted, or even welcomed, it as an inevitability of modern capitalism.

One of the key objectives of the post-1979 Conservative governments was to reduce the size and regulatory reach of the state. According to the neoliberal perspective that strongly informed the Conservatives' approach, the economic and social policies that underpinned the post-war welfare consensus in the UK had undermined entrepreneurialism, individual responsibility, business competitiveness and, in particular, the operation of labour markets. The economic problems that confronted the UK were pinned on big government and the welfare state and, most importantly, the 1970s economic crisis was blamed on the Left and the ruling Labour government. Indeed, the Conservatives' success in associating Labour policies with the economic problems of the 1970s proved to be decisive in keeping Labour out of power during the following decade and a half.

During this period of Conservative rule, the divisions between industrial and financial capital also continued to widen. The growing dominance of the finance industry was facilitated by what has come to be referred to as 'neoliberal globalisation'. The phenomenon of neoliberal globalisation facilitated and encouraged the expansion of international trade, the erosion of protectionism and the reduction of regulatory barriers to the international movement of capital and currency exchange in many nations, and the UK has progressed rapidly along this path under successive Conservative and Labour governments since the early 1980s. The UK was one of the first to open up its financial and currency markets and it has gone further than most in liberalising its economy. The 'big bang' relaxation of regulatory controls on share dealing, the internationalisation of share brokerage and the establishment of electronic share trading, brokered by then Trade and Industry Secretary Cecil Parkinson in 1986, allowed London to position itself as one of the major global players in international finance. Government and financiers viewed the liberalisation of finance markets as crucial to this. Nicholas Goodison, chair of the London Stock Exchange in 1986, argued that:

> Regulation must be as light as is compatible with nurturing trust.... Continuous assessment of the value of regulations is essential to make sure that they are not driving business away or reducing competition or damping innovation. Regulators must be prepared for coping with serious risks that might damage London's reputation.... Competition law and practice must keep up with the fast-changing scene. *Financial Times* (2006)

The injection of market discipline also meant that less-competitive industries were allowed to decline (where other governments have propped up such industries) and the government actively sought to attract new investment from more dynamic and more internationally competitive corporations and it has done so through a deliberate strategy to reduce labour costs, regulations and industrial unrest at the same time that it has invested in post-compulsory education and training. In other words, the UK has sought to compete internationally on the basis of low labour costs coupled with relatively high skills. But relations between the Conservative government and industry were also tense during the early 1980s because some of the key policies the Conservatives pursued in the name of competitiveness – high interest rates in order to quell inflation and cuts in industrial support in order to withdraw the dependence of old industries on government – had a direct negative impact on large manufacturers (Grant, 1993). The strengthening of financial interests and the growing dependence on the City during the 1980s and 1990s was a deliberate and inevitable outcome of government policy. There is a paradox here. Policies aimed at making industry leaner, meaner and more independent of government resulted in the relative demise of manufacturing and the growing importance of services and finance to the British economy and this did, indeed, reduce the size of the industrial props of old. The paradox is that the finance sector, which appeared to require very little from the state except its regulatory freedom, has ended up costing more in terms of state support than even the largest and most dependent industries would ever have required.

The relaxation of regulations regarding financial transactions was also extended to corporate mergers and acquisitions from the 1980s and continued by subsequent governments. One key policy decision that exacerbated the crisis was the deregulation of building societies from the mid-1980s, which enabled a large number to 'demutualise' by transferring ownership from their members to their shareholders. This also transformed their traditionally conservative lending arrangements, which were funded primarily by their members' deposits (Augar, 2008). Financiers spotted huge opportunities to capitalise on the transformation of these institutions and a series of rapid takeovers occurred to form huge financial institutions, which controlled ever larger shares of the UK mortgage market. Northern Rock demutualised in 1997 and engaged in ever-more risky lending practices before its collapse in 2008 (Augar, 2008). Birmingham Midshires and Cheltenham and Gloucester were acquired by Lloyds Banking Group.[1] By the time the crisis hit in 2008, Lloyds had also acquired HBOS (a previous merger between Halifax building society and the Bank of Scotland) in a deal partly brokered by the Labour government.

These various reforms implemented by a Conservative government that lost power more than a decade before the 2008 crisis are directly relevant here. The Conservatives transformed the debate on taxation, taking income tax out of rational political debate and hence limiting the ability of subsequent governments to put up income taxes; they shifted the tax burden and increased the income gap between rich and poor, which continued to widen long after they left office; they continued to promote the interests of financial and mobile capital against domestic industry and increased the UK's dependence on these sectors of the economy; and in order to facilitate this revolution, they tied the economy to a low-regulatory base, a policy that subsequent governments felt they had no choice but to follow if they were to retain the UK's, by then, relatively high levels of foreign investment. Together, these policy transformations were precisely those that helped to increase the impact of the crisis when it hit.

New Labour: same regulatory regime

The Labour government that assumed power in 1997 actually had more in common with the Thatcher government than with the Labour Party of the 1970s. It emphasised this difference by 'rebranding' itself 'New Labour' prior to, and following, the General Election (although the party name was not formally changed). As New Labour, the party gave an undertaking not to raise income taxes, in line with the perceived mood of the country, and to approach key decisions in an 'un-ideological' way, relying instead on evidence of 'what works'. In order to convince the electorate of its credibility in terms of the economy, it also sought to get business, and parts of the right-wing press, on board. As one of its first acts in office, Labour gave independence to the Bank of England. This was an important gesture to financial capital that government would play a more minimal role in regulating the City. Labour, and financial interests, had previously maintained that monetary policy had been too beholden to politics; that the latter had shaped the former, not in the interests of economic strength, but in the interests of the governing party. Under Labour, it became clear, the economy would continue to take precedence over most other decisions, as it had under the Conservatives, and Gordon Brown played this particular card with enthusiasm.

A number of key decisions taken by the Labour government are testament to such prioritisation. First, Labour honoured the previous government's spending decisions during its first two years in office. Second, the new government continued the light-touch regulatory regime put in place by the Conservative government in order to continue to bolster the interests of financial capital and facilitate the further growth of industrial globalisation. Gordon Brown, as Chancellor of the Exchequer, told the Confederation of British Industry (CBI) in 2006 that:

> "As well as promoting greater deregulation across Europe, we will stand up for an approach that is pro-Britain, pro-business and pro-European single market – for a Europe which is outward looking, reforming, liberalising and lighter touch in its regulation.... The risk-based approach of the future that Britain is now pioneering is founded on a different view of the world – trust in the responsible company, the educated consumer and the informed employee....And over time this new model of regulation should not only apply the concept of risk to the enforcement of regulation, but

also to the design and indeed to the decision as to whether to regulate at all." (Gordon Brown, speech to the CBI, 28 November 2006)

Ed Balls, then Economic Secretary to Gordon Brown, told the British Bankers Association in 2006, one year prior to the start of the economic crisis in the US, that:

"The Government's interest ... [is] to safeguard the light touch and proportionate regulatory regime that has made London a magnet for international business.... We do not view bank profits as undesirable. Profits are essential for any industry to survive let alone invest, grow and innovate. And in banking, profits, which are generally strongest at an advanced stage of the cycle, are an essential part of keeping the sector sound and stable over the whole cycle. Some have suggested that given their central role in the economy, it would be appropriate to treat banks just like utilities – to subject them to price-setting and onerous rules on how they interact with their customers. The alternative approach – and the one I favour – is to rely on market forces and competition policy to promote efficiency through open and competitive markets." (Ed Balls, speech to the British Bankers Association, 11 October 2006)

In January 2011, Ed Balls assumed the position of Shadow Chancellor and immediately accused the Conservative-led coalition of failing to properly regulate the banks and bank bonuses.

Third, Labour sought to ensure that the UK maintained its competitive corporate tax position, lowering corporate tax rates in 1997 from 32% to 30% and then again in 2007 to 28%. Fourth, the government increased massively the reliance on private sector-led investment within state services through the expansion of the private finance initiative. The key rationale for this latter policy was that it transferred the investment burden, and many of the risks associated with large-scale investment, from the public to the private sector. Fifth, in an attempt to shift public perception, Labour promised during its first and second terms of office not to increase income taxes, with the result that this reduced the party's options when it needed to raise taxation. It did raise direct taxation, but chose prior to the crisis to increase National Insurance contributions rather than income tax. Only once Gordon Brown had taken over as Leader, and as the crisis forced Labour into a rethink, did the government choose to put up income taxes to 50% for the highest earners.

This, coupled with the fact that Labour wanted to ensure that the wealthy continued to be rewarded, meant that the government struggled to tackle economic inequality and, where it did redistribute, it did so through targeted benefits rather than through the tax system. At the same time, Labour was committed to increasing investment in key services, even if it was keen to increase the role of the private sector in their delivery. Healthcare in particular received a significant injection of new spending, and spending as a percentage of Gross Domestic Product (GDP) increased by around 8 percentage points between 1997 and 2007 (Brewer et al, 2011). The pressure on Labour to increase public expenditure, tackle poverty but maintain low taxation rates began to unravel in the mid-2000s, however, especially as the economy began to slow. For this reason, while accumulated public debt was relatively low in 2007, the size of the annual deficit had been steadily rising from the mid-2000s (Chote et al, 2008).

A very British crisis

The crisis hit soon after Gordon Brown had taken over from Tony Blair as Prime Minister in 2007. Although occupying the centre-ground, Brown was positioned to the left of Blair and he was certainly more sympathetic to the ideas of Keynes and far less cautious on the question of state economic intervention. At the same time, like Blair, Brown was internationally and multilaterally minded. As the crisis began to hit, therefore, Brown strongly advocated an internationally coordinated response and, after the full depth of the crisis became clear, signalled a decisive break from neoliberalism towards Keynesianism. He accordingly campaigned for an internationally coordinated pump-priming of national economies to prevent a global meltdown. Brown was especially keen on this strategy as the depth of the UK crisis became clear. As one of the hardest-hit economies, the UK ran the risk that any intervention to boost the economy would simply result in increased sales for imported goods. Unless exports could also be protected, any effort at economic management would prove to have only limited success. Brown also proved decisive on the world stage, bringing together the new President of the US and the other G20 leaders (see Chapter One). Thus, he was able to pronounce in 2009 that '[t]he old Washington consensus is over' and reveal details of a US$1.1 trillion global rescue fund for the international banking system.[2] What Brown actually meant by this was that Keynes was back on the agenda and neoliberalism was off it. In some ways, therefore, the crisis gave purpose to the Brown government. Huge sums were directed at trying to save various financial institutions and kick-starting the economy and Brown made it his personal mission to rescue the UK, and even the world, economy.

Financial capital in the crisis

Chapter One highlighted one of the key causes of the crisis as the irresponsibility of banks and the failure of government and regulators. This has particular salience in the context of the UK since the power and dominance of the financial sector, coupled with the view that lower regulations were important to a strong UK economy, have prevailed in the era of globalisation. The fact that UK banks were both large by international standards and government and regulators have failed to properly regulate domestic and investment banking, both increased the impact of the crisis on British banks and increased the potential repercussions for the economy if the banks collapsed. By the time the crisis hit, a number of banks had simply become too big to fail. Northern Rock, Lloyds Banking Group and Bradford and Bingley (another former building society) had to be taken into public ownership in 2008 and 2009 in order to prevent their collapse. The combined cost of taking on these companies alone meant every UK taxpayer assuming the huge mortgage and debt liabilities of the nationalised banks.

The coalition government and the new cuts agenda

Labour's interventions to stem the crisis, through the various bank bailouts, industrial subsidies and tax reductions – most markedly a reduction in VAT from 17.5% to 15% for one year – were important stimulus measures, but together they contributed to mounting public debt. Added to this was pressure of the impending General Election, which had to be called before May 2010. Despite winning international praise for his decisive action on the economy, domestic opinion was less favourable. As Prime Minister, Gordon Brown appeared indecisive and the political Right, in a repeat of the post-1970s crisis, have been able to pin a great deal of the blame for the crisis in the UK on the previous Blair/Brown governments. As a result, Labour lost the General Election when it finally came.

Although the Conservatives were unable to form a government by themselves, they were able to form a coalition with the Liberal

Democrats. They inherited a heavily indebted economy, which they presented as fatally wounded. The new government argued that borrowing and spending were both out of control and the spectres of Greece, Iceland and Ireland were held up as examples of the path the UK would head in if drastic spending cuts were not imposed. The actual health of the British economy and the sustainability of its debt were, of course, matters of divided economic opinion. The coalition government diagnosed the problem and prescribed a solution based on a particular ideological position, as did the government before it, of course. The economic crisis in the UK has diverted attention away from questions of ideology. The direction of government policy has been presented as inevitable, unquestionable and un-ideological.

> I didn't come into politics to make cuts. Neither did Nick Clegg [Deputy Prime Minister]. But in the end politics is about national interest, not personal political agendas. We're tackling the deficit because we have to – not out of some ideological zeal. This is a government led by people with a practical desire to sort out this country's problems, not by ideology.[3]

The fact that the Conservatives' Liberal Democratic coalition partners eventually came to accept the need for deep and rapid cuts (after opposing this position during the election campaign), reinforced the impression that anyone with access to the full Treasury data would share the view that there was simply no alternative. And yet, if we consider the legislation so far introduced by the coalition, the key reforms have an unmistakably neoliberal flavour. Budget cuts mean inevitable reductions in the size of the state, but the primary direction of policy so far has been to shrink the state. The key slogan of the Conservative Party is the notion of the 'Big Society' and this has promoted the idea that individuals and communities should rely less on the state and more on each other. Voluntarism rather than statism is the order of the day. Thus, when asked whether the Conservative Party would seek to restore government to pre-crisis levels once it had reduced the deficit, David Cameron (*The Guardian*, 2010) replied: 'The direct answer to your question, should we cut things now and go back later and try and restore them later, I think we should be trying to avoid that approach'.

More generally for the Right, situated outside of party politics, the correct policy response to the crisis should be a return to the policies of the 1980s:

> People are nervous of world war-sized deficits when there
> isn't a war to justify them.... The remedy ... must be the
> kind of policy regime-change ... which the Thatcher and
> Reagan governments successfully implemented. Then, as
> today, the choice was not between stimulus and austerity. It
> was between policies that boost private-sector confidence
> and those that kill it. (Ferguson, 2010)

The Right have also sought to emphasise that the cuts do not go
far enough. Simon Heffer, a right-wing commentator for the *Daily
Telegraph*, argued that:

> The reduction of £83 billion sounds like a lot of money, but
> it still represents a £92 billion increase in public spending
> by 2014-15. It will leave a state that is still too large, that is
> too much of a drain on the productive areas of the economy,
> and that is undertaking functions that could be done more
> efficiently and cheaply if transferred to the private sector.
> (Heffer, 2011)

Moreover, it is important to note that, while public debt will top over
100% of GDP in many economies between 2010 and 2015, the UK is
not one of these economies. Whether 'acceptable' national accumulated
debt is 60%, 80% or 120% of GDP is quite arbitrary (see Gough, this
volume).

Viewed cynically, the Conservative-led coalition is determined to not
let a good crisis go to waste. The crisis has provided an opportunity to
impose swingeing cuts in excess of those proposed during the election
campaign. Although the Conservatives did not win an outright victory,
they did win a higher share of the vote than the other two parties and
they have taken this as a mandate to impose large cuts. The Liberal
Democrats have fallen into line behind this argument, stating that, had
they known the extent of the economic problems confronting the UK,
they would have campaigned prior to the election for immediate and
dramatic cuts (they actually campaigned against such measures in the
run-up to the General Election). The result was that the coalition held
an emergency Budget within weeks of taking office and promised five
years of unprecedented cuts that would begin with immediate effect.
The Conservative Chancellor, George Osborne, announced cuts in
June 2010 of up to 25% in the worst-hit government departments
and a projected cut of almost 5% of GDP between 2011 and 2015.
This represented, according to the *Financial Times* (23 June 2010, p 1),

'one of the most drastic spending squeezes of any advanced economy in recent times'. The enormity of the planned cuts announced in the emergency Budget of June 2010 was summed up by the Institute for Fiscal Studies: 'In total, the cut in central government public services spending as a share of national income now planned by the Coalition will more than reverse the entire increase we saw under Labour. We are looking at the longest, deepest sustained period of cuts to public services spending at least since World War II'.[4]

Given that it has taken one of the biggest hits from the crisis of the G7 countries, it would have been expected that the UK would take longest to balance its budgets. But, under the Conservatives' plans, the UK is seeking to pay back debt at a far faster rate than any of the other G7 countries, including Japan and the US, which faced similar-sized fiscal problems in 2010.[5] The extent of the austerity measures planned by the government was vividly contextualised by Hutton (2010), writing for *The Guardian*:

> It is as tough a package of retrenchment as the IMF [International Monetary Fund] imposed on Greece, a country on the brink of bankruptcy and twice as tough as the famously harsh measures Canada took between 1994 and 1997. It is three times tougher than Sweden's measures between 1993 and 1995. In British terms, it is immeasurably tougher than what we did after the IMF crisis in 1976 or after the ERM [exchange rate mechanism] crisis in 1992.... No country has volunteered such austerity.

Nor is the pain of these cuts likely to be evenly distributed. Analysis carried out by the Institute for Fiscal Studies (Crawford, 2010) of the impact of planned spending cuts in 2010, for instance, suggested that the pain of the cuts would fall disproportionately on the poorest. Moreover, research carried out by the IMF in 2010 (IMF, 2010d) suggested that the combined cuts being made by the majority of developed economies over the next few years will likely have a deeply depressing impact on economic growth overall, since home consumption will decline as demand is further squeezed out. The UK, in cutting expenditure so rapidly and so deeply, runs the risk of a long period of low or negative growth and it isn't difficult to find a swathe of opinion from opposite sides of the ideological spectrum to caution against the coalition's austerity measures.

George Soros, an international hedge fund owner, who has made millions speculating on the fortunes of various markets, argued during the 2011 World Economic Forum that: 'I don't think [the spending cuts] can possibly be implemented without pushing the economy into a recession.... My expectation is that it will prove to be unsustainable'.[6]

Paul Krugman, a Nobel Laureate winner for economics, writes: 'while the advocates of austerity pose as hardheaded realists, doing what has to be done, they can't and won't justify their stance with actual numbers – because the numbers do not, in fact, support their position. Nor can they claim that markets are demanding austerity'.[7]

David Blanchflower, economics editor for the *New Statesman* and former member of the Bank of England's Monetary Policy Committee, also cautioned against the 'madness' of the cuts:

> Despite the scale of the challenge [David Cameron] faces, he argues that there is no alternative to his policies. He argues that public spending cuts, and tax increases along with all this talking down of the economy will not push us back into recession despite the growing evidence to the contrary. Many of his supporters, especially his Chancellor, George Osborne, wanted the size of the state to shrink in the first place and this was a perfect excuse.[8]

Even the Confederation of British Industry (CBI) has been lukewarm in its assessment of the cuts agenda:

> This coalition Government has been single minded – some might even say ruthless – in its approach to spending cuts. Very unpopular decisions are being driven through on the argument that they are essential to the long-term stability of the economy. That policy is strongly supported by business, on the grounds that sound public finances are an essential foundation for a sound economy.... But my argument this morning is that the Government has not been nearly so consistent and focussed when it comes to policies that support growth. (Richard Lambert, CBI press release, 24 January 2011)

Even more worrying is the fact that the coalition is cutting capital expenditure faster than current expenditure (Inman, 2011). Between the General Election of 2010 and the following December alone, capital expenditure was cut by £6 billion and, on government spending plans, will fall by around 46% between 2010 and 2015 (Crawford, 2010). This will inevitably impact on jobs, consumer spending and the quality of other public buildings.

The early evidence on the impact of the cuts is that they may indeed be having a depressing impact on the UK economy. The economy was beginning to contract again by December 2010 after a year of modest growth. Prior to the coalition government, UK quarterly growth was running at 1.1%. In the third quarter of 2010, once the first of the coalition cuts had begun to bite, growth had shrunk to 0.7% and the fourth quarter figures had fallen still further to minus 0.5%. Larry Elliot's conclusion was that the government had 'killed the economy stone dead'.[9]

Social policy in the new age of austerity

This section considers the social policy implications of the UK crisis. As already noted, the political Right in the UK have capitalised on the opportunities provided by the economic crisis to cut welfare provision and reshape UK politics. It is important to remind ourselves that the cuts were deemed to be necessary because of the size of public debt. The key reasons why public debt increased so rapidly as a result of the crisis were: (a) the UK government had to pour billions of pounds into the economy in order to rescue the financial sector from collapse; and (b) it sought to boost demand in the economy in order to stave off recession. It is important to note that there was little opposition to these policies at the time. This massive increase in public spending represented public expenditure, funded primarily out of borrowing, which was designed to defend and boost the private sector more generally, and the financial sector specifically. Having accumulated huge public debt as a result of these measures, the coalition government now argues that it must repay debt by cutting public expenditure. But, in very stark terms, cutting expenditure on social welfare in order to pay for provision aimed at the private sector represents a major redistribution of resources, from the poorest to the wealthiest in society. To put it another way, cuts in social welfare are being made in order to pay for the increases in corporate welfare (Farnsworth, 2011).

The alternative to cutting expenditure would have been to increase taxation, especially on the corporations that created the crisis in the first place, and on higher earners who gained so much from tax cuts introduced since the 1980s. Economic inequality continued to widen in the UK under the Labour government and it is among the most unequal developed countries in the world (Wilkinson and Pickett, 2009). Increasing taxation on the wealthy would have helped to close the gap. However, the UK government is choosing to pare down the deficit through a 59:41 ratio of spending cuts to tax rises in the first year of cuts and this ratio will rise in favour of cuts to 77:23 by the end of this Parliament (in 2015/16). Labour's plans were for a ratio of 70:30. Public expenditure as a percentage of GDP is projected to fall from over 47% in 2010–11 to less than 40% by 2015–16. This is a massive transformation in the size of the state, especially when we consider the size of the private sector rescue that has been undertaken (and the resulting debt will continue to impose heavy additional expense beyond 2015). Such a heavy reliance on cuts, as opposed to tax rises, will inevitably mean deeper cuts in welfare services, in public sector pay and in benefit payments and state pensions than would have otherwise been necessary but this is, of course, an ideologically desirable outcome on the part of the political Right.

Meanwhile, amidst the 'unavoidable' spending cuts and tax increases, the government has announced a number of tax cuts, primarily aimed at businesses. Corporate income tax will be further reduced from 28% to 24%. Small businesses will also be given selective exemptions from National Insurance and corporation tax and their income tax rate will be cut from 21% to 20%.[10] As already noted, a higher rate of income tax of 50% had already been introduced by Labour, which brings the UK more into line with its international competitors although this is far lower than the 78% rate that prevailed in the 1970s. The coalition government has also maintained the planned increase in National Insurance, announced by Labour in 2009, although this is a far less progressive form of direct tax than income tax. The increase in the employers' rate of National Insurance has also been effectively wiped out by increases in the tax threshold, effectively taking 650,000 employees (and their employers) out of the tax altogether.[11] But the coalition has chosen to increase its revenues primarily through a large increase in VAT, the most regressive form of taxation (Murphy, 2010b), which has been raised from 17.5% to 20%. These changes in taxation will impact especially on the poorest groups who already pay the highest rate of taxation as a percentage of their income. The result will likely be a further widening of the gap between the wealthy and those on the the lowest incomes. It is important to note that the total value of tax cuts in 2014 will be worth around £12 billion, only slightly less than the £13 billion projected increase in VAT (from 17.5% to 20%). It is also worth noting here that George Osborne, the Chancellor of the Exchequer, announced in January 2011 that, although he did not propose to reverse the 50% income tax rate, he regarded it as 'a temporary feature of the tax system' (Osborne, 2011).

Growing inequality will also inevitably result from the large planned cuts in public sector pay and pensions and in cuts to social security benefits. In addition to the inevitable large number of job losses in the public sector, the government has commissioned a report to end the perceived 'generosity' of 'gold-plated public sector pensions'.[12] And despite the fact that each successive government since 1979 has promised to reduce the welfare bill and reduce dependence on the state, the current coalition plans to find further savings by targeting claimants and taking more 'undeserving' people off benefits. In June 2010, the coalition announced a plan to begin a comprehensive reassessment of those on Incapacity Benefit from April 2011 and to impose benefit cuts on those who subsequently fail to actively look for, or take up offers of, work.[13] In November 2010, the coalition announced plans to introduce a Universal Credit to replace all other out-of-work benefits and also promised tougher rules on claimants. Under the new scheme, benefits will be withdrawn at a slower rate for those finding work, so that everyone will be better off in work. Those who fail to actively look for work, however, will face more draconian measures. Benefits will be totally withdrawn for varying periods for those who fail to seek employment or make themselves available for work. A first offence would result in benefits being withdrawn for one month and 'serial' offenders could be shut out of benefits for up to three years.[14] The state pension age is also being increased to 66 for men from 2016 and for women from 2020 although the coalition has pledged to restore the link between pensions and earnings.

All this is despite the anticipated increase in the numbers claiming benefits as a result of the continued sluggishness of the economy. But the cuts will be made, not simply by reducing the number of claimants, but also by reducing the value of benefits. From 2011, benefits will be increased in line with the Consumer Price Index (CPI) rather than the Retail Price Index (RPI). The CPI excludes housing costs, hence it typically runs far behind the RPI. Through this simple switch, the government is seeking to take around £6 billion out of the benefits budget.[15] The rationale for the change is that most people on benefits do not have housing costs since most claim Housing Benefit. The implicit assumption is that the benefits received by claimants in the past were higher than they should have been.

The planned cuts to benefits will be difficult to realise without further changes since redundancies will continue to increase even if the economy does grow between 2010 and 2015. The massive cuts will increase public and private sector job losses. It is important to note here that, based on the Treasury's own data, tax increases would bring fewer job losses than spending cuts.[16] Unemployment rates in the UK were already running at 2.5 million when the coalition came to power. The cuts in public expenditure are projected to result in a further one million job cuts in the public sector and this will, the Institute for Public Policy Research estimates, lead to an additional one million job losses from the private sector (Cox and Schmuecker, 2010). This is on top of the two and a half million workers who were unemployed at the end of 2010. Because they are not fully counted in the figure, this figure masks a more worrying trend: a sharp increase in youth unemployment, especially among 16- to 19-year-olds, precisely those who are likely to be hit by changes in higher education funding.[17]

Essential services will also inevitably be withdrawn. The largest cuts, amounting to some 36% of their budget, will be imposed on local government. These cuts will result in reduced services, investment and/ or increases in local taxation (which tends to be relatively regressive).[18] They will also directly lead to job losses as already noted, but these losses will not be even across the country. The public sector job losses will impact much more heavily on the poorest regions of the country (Cox and Schmuecker, 2010). Much of the regional support that Labour provided to poorer areas will be abolished to the detriment of investment and growth in the north. One further factor that will impact on welfare services in the future but which has received very little attention is that the Private Finance Initiative deals agreed with the private sector in the past cannot be renegotiated or reneged on without large penalties. Thus, a large part of current expenditure cannot be reduced or changed, meaning that other categories of public spending will have to be reduced still further. This will mean that the UK government will have to continue to service the profits of private companies in order to maintain capital projects while making cuts in current expenditure on staff and service delivery (Shifrin, 2010).

In addition to this, the culture of the public sector will be further transformed, not just as a result of the cuts, but also as a result of a distinct approach to services. The coalition government has introduced changes in services that will not result in immediate savings, but which will transform their management and delivery dramatically. The role of the state is being curtailed and the role of the private sector and other players, under a 'Big Society' slogan, is being dramatically increased. In education, parents and other providers are being encouraged to set up 'Free Schools' independently of government and there are plans to free further education colleges from local authorities. The Education Maintenance Allowance (EMA), which supported students in further education, has also been scrapped. Universities, meanwhile, are effectively being privatised since they will no longer be funded by the state. Instead, graduates will be forced to pay market rates for their education. These changes will inevitably deter those from poorer backgrounds, who are already underrepresented in post-compulsory education, from participating in further and higher education. The removal of the EMA will, it is estimated, lead to a 30% reduction in further education participation rates among 16- to 19-year-olds.[19] A similar effect is likely to be seen in higher education as a result of the massive increase in graduate debt. In healthcare, while the coalition has not introduced immediate cuts, it has announced plans to introduce more competition into the health service, encouraging general practitioners to contract with private providers in competition with National Health Service hospitals, in selecting healthcare providers for their patients.

In terms of the effects of the proposed cuts on incomes, analysis by the Institute for Fiscal Studies has found that, on a simple measure of the impact of the coalition cuts announced in 2010, the budget will be regressive overall in its impact. Under the previous cuts planned by Labour, the richest 10% of the population were set to bear the biggest burden. Under the coalition's plans, the poorest 10% will lose 5% of their incomes between 2010 and 2015 compared with a loss of less than 1% for the richest 10%.[20] Moreover, this is based on the assumption that the cost of services reflects their full value. The actual value of public services, especially to lower-income families, may be many times their actual cost to the public purse.

Conclusions: what hope for welfare?

While the UK was hit by the global crisis particularly hard, the 'medicine' that has subsequently been prescribed by the coalition government is not justified. The planned cuts are unprecedented and, although they have been sold as necessary and unavoidable, they are deeply ideological. Moreover, the reforms follow a relatively clear trajectory from previous Conservative governments. Indeed, many of the policies and programmes introduced by the post-1979 Conservative governments, and carried on by Labour, secured the conditions that saw the UK hit so dramatically by the economic crisis in the first place. The planned austerity measures will have a huge cost in terms of economic equality and the future of the welfare state. The gap between rich and poor was already among the highest of any developed nation in the UK, thanks to the taxation and spending decisions of successive governments since 1979, and this gap is set to widen further as a result of the coalition's austerity measures. Where Labour did have an impact, on child poverty, steadying the income divide and investing in public services, these advances look set to be wiped out within a single term of the coalition government. However, the history of social policy teaches us that there are always (or nearly always) clear policy choices to be made. The coalition is simply viewing and reacting to a given set of economic challenges from a particular centre-right perspective. The hope for the future of social policy is that resistance will force the government to consider the alternatives before imposing the kinds of cuts that risk destroying the social fabric and undermining the fragile economy. What is clear is that, at some point, the UK economy will emerge from the current crisis. What is less clear is whether the UK welfare state will recover to quite the same extent.

Notes

[1] Lloyds had itself merged with the Trustee Savings Bank (whose shares were not, in common with building societies, traded on the stock market) in 1995.

[2] www.number10.gov.uk/Page18934

[3] www.number10.gov.uk/news/speeches-and-transcripts/2010/12/new-year-podcast-58413

[4] IFS, June 2010, www.ifs.org.uk/budgets/budgetjune2010/chote.pdf

[5] *The Economist*, www.economist.com/node/16791650

[6] *The Daily Telegraph* (2011) 'Davos WEF 2011: George Soros says UK risks slipping back into recession' *The Daily Telegraph* 6th July http://www.telegraph.co.uk/finance/financetopics/davos/8283995/Davos-WEF-2011-George-Soros-says-UK-risks-slipping-back-into-recession.html

[7] *The Guardian*, 18 June 2010, www.guardian.co.uk/commentisfree/2010/jun/18/merkel-1937-german-deficit-hawks

[8] *New Statesman*, 30 January 2011, www.newstatesman.com/blogs/david-blanchflower/2011/01/revised-chance-sight-economic

[9] *The Guardian*, 25 January 2011, www.guardian.co.uk/commentisfree/2011/jan/25/gdp-shock-quarter-shrinking-economy

[10] www.taxresearch.org.uk/Blog/2010/06/22/corporation-tax-the-ultimate-regressive-tax-in-the-uk-from-now-on/

[11] *The Guardian*, 22 June 2010, www.guardian.co.uk/business/2010/jun/22/budget-2010-small-business-tax-changes

[12] *The Guardian*, 14 June 2010, www.guardian.co.uk/business/2010/jun/14/clegg-obr-pensions-deficit-economy

[13] *The Guardian*, 30 June 2010, www.guardian.co.uk/politics/2010/jun/30/incapacity-benefit-tests-welfare-unemployment

[14] *The Guardian*, 11 November 2010, www.guardian.co.uk/politics/2010/nov/11/tories-hail-radical-benefits-overhaul

[15] www.economist.com/node/16791650

[16] *New Statesman*, Table C8, budget, www.newstatesman.com/blogs/the-staggers/2010/12/spending-cuts-tax-ideological

[17] *The Guardian*, 19 January 2011, www.guardian.co.uk/business/2011/jan/19/youth-unemployment-heads-towards-1-million

[18] www.bbc.co.uk/news/business-11595551

[19] *The Independent*, 18 January 2011, www.independent.co.uk/news/education/education-news/70-would-drop-out-if-ema-is-scrapped-2187309.html

[20] *The Guardian*, 25 August 2010, www.guardian.co.uk/uk/2010/aug/25/poor-families-bear-brunt-of-austerity-drive

Acknowledgements

Thanks to Lata Narayanaswamy and Zoë Irving for comments on an earlier draft of this chapter.

FIFTEEN

Responding to the challenges: some concluding remarks on welfare futures in changed circumstances

Kevin Farnsworth and Zoë Irving

The opening chapter to this volume drew attention to the significance of variance in understanding the nature and impact of the financial crisis that began in the United States (US) in 2007 and went 'global' in 2008. This theme was evident at the workshop held in 2009 that initially inspired this book, where optimists pointed to the opportunities for challenging failed neoliberal models of capitalism, which seemed to be surfacing in a range of contexts, and to the possibilities for pursuing more progressive welfarist agendas. Pessimists argued that the crisis would only squeeze welfare systems still further, making them less tenable in the future. With the benefit of some hindsight, gained over the period during which the chapters have been developed, it appears that both positions have been borne out, but not necessarily in the ways anticipated. What emerges from the analyses included here is a complexity of national outcomes, transnational relationships and global processes that remains as unpredictable as it is fluid. The crisis was *global* in the sense that its impact was felt in almost every country and the response to it involved multilateral engagement to a degree that has not been seen since the Second World War. But in terms of its impact on nation states and its implications for social policy, the global crisis can best be understood as related national crises, and although multilateralism of a sort was promised, entrenched national and economic interests have ascended at the expense of full international cooperation, and new differences and divisions have been created between states.

In coming to terms with the crisis, and subsequently understanding national crises then, what can assist in making sense of this complexity of changed circumstance? Drawing from a range of policy studies literatures (historical institutionalist, varieties of capitalism, welfare regimes, policy networks), all the contributions here demonstrate that the centrality of politics is manifest in explaining both the changed circumstance and the varieties of crisis. However, while all these theoretical frameworks would suggest that given their political and institutional differences, welfare systems would fare differently as a result of the crisis, none has completely reliable predictive capacity because the causes of specific crises reflect much more the differences rather than the similarities between states. Thus, in developing explanations it is necessary to look much more at the specific features, the hybridity and the exceptionalisms rather than the commonalities and essence.

For example, while it is broadly true that liberal market economies have been hit harder than managed market economies, closer inspection reveals that within these two groups, individual economies have actually been affected very differently and their responses to the crisis are not shared. Among the liberal market economies, the US and the United Kingdom (UK) have suffered similar effects, but their responses are at variance both with each other, and in the case of the US with its conventionally agreed 'type'. Ireland has experienced the most negative effects and, true to type, has adopted comprehensive austerity measures in the face of huge international pressure. Canada and Australia have been affected much less than the other liberal states, and although they have introduced cuts in order to reduce public debt, their response has been far more muted and they have returned to growth much more speedily. It is important therefore to separate out the dimensions of the crisis of the 2000s that have particular significance to this period in time. From the preceding country case studies, it appears that there are two important dimensions that lead to variation: the (selective) global collapse of the financial sector and the global economic slowdown (or the 'Great Recession' as it has come to be known).

While some nations such as Iceland, Ireland, the UK and US, have experienced the effects of both dimensions, others, including Finland, Germany and Sweden together with many less advanced economies have escaped a 'crisis' but have suffered the effects of the resulting economic slump. Iceland, Ireland and, to a lesser extent, the UK, have in common their heavy dependence on short-term financial capital. These countries have developed growth strategies around short-term and highly mobile capital investments since the 1990s, competing on the basis of low regulations and low rates of corporate taxation. The more rounded UK economy helped to protect it from the fate of Iceland and Ireland, however, and, compared with Ireland, its sovereign currency also helped it to stave off total collapse. In the countries where the crisis appears far less significant, Germany and Canada for example (despite the latter's embeddedness in the US economy), a combination of relatively small finance industries coupled with firmer regulations prevented an initial collapse of the same magnitude as that experienced by the UK and the US. Both countries have experienced a slowing of their economies, however, as a result of the recession. Germany in particular suffered a major downturn in its export markets, but in both countries, pre-emptive measures to boost demand appear to have staved off deep recessions. Similarly, the Nordic countries appear to have survived the worst of the crisis and are dealing with recession rather than crisis management. As Kosonen's chapter (Chapter Twelve) makes clear, these countries' crises in the early 2000s assisted in responding to post-2007 period since they had already learned some of the lessons of rapid bank deregulations. They were also better positioned to forestall economic slowdown given their already large public policy infrastructure, not to mention their interventionist histories. For these reasons, Finland, Germany and Sweden have adjusted far more painlessly to the changed circumstance than the countries where 'crisis' has occurred.

Chapters by many of the authors in this volume point to the role of past experience and the use of 'crisis' measures in informing and shaping the measures materialising in the post-2007 context but equally, in countries such as Iceland, Ireland and the UK, there is much about this crisis that lacks precedent. Thus, for these countries, it may be that the political choices and hence policy options it has created are far less constrained.

In thinking through the nature of welfare futures, then, it is clear that a systemic crisis such as that which has taken place in the 2000s requires both attention to what existing frameworks can provide in the way of explanation but also examination of what is missing from these frameworks and what contemporary developments can further reveal. In Part One, Michael Hill and Ian Gough (in Chapters Two and Three respectively) began this task with an attempt to deconstruct the notion of 'crisis' in politics. There is less agreement on the use of the term than we might expect, and as their chapters suggest, there is also a danger in over-using the term to describe any interruption to 'normal' times. If we focus on the post-2007 crisis, it is deeper and more global than previous economic events that have shared the label, but in common with previous 'crises' the present one has its first- and second-order effects. Economic crises tend to give way to political crises and both have repercussions for social policies.

Hill's chapter (Chapter Two) examines the tendency, or capacity, of economic crises to give birth to major transformations in political thinking – or paradigm shifts. The crisis of the 1930s gave birth to Keynesian ideas and so the post-2007 crisis may, in time, be regarded as having given way to a similar transformation – perhaps a shift back towards Keynesianism after a prolonged period of neoliberalism (as Deacon suggests in Chapter Five) or not (as several of the country case studies imply). Whether there will be a sustained global shift in ideas does remain to be seen, but at the level of nation states, political change has certainly occurred and renewed questions of state legitimation have come to the fore. The extent to which the response to threats to legitimacy favours welfare expansion (as in South Korea, the US, China and some lower-income countries), maintaining the status quo (as in Germany and, to some extent, Canada) or a return to growth (as in Ireland and the UK) clearly depends very much on the perceived causes of countries' economic troubles and the apportionment of blame. While in Iceland and the US the crisis initially engendered a more progressive social policy climate, in Sweden, particularly after the worst election result for the Social Democratic Party since the 1930s in 2010, the future of the 'Nordic normative legacy' is, as Kosonen suggests in Chapter Twelve, highly uncertain. Whether this kind of political change is permanent and will subsequently follow more predictable patterns of policy transformation depends on the battles over social investment that are still being played out, and how we make sense of the outcomes will undoubtedly be a matter of judgement in retrospect, or, as Hill (Chapter Two) puts it, interpretation after the event.

Above all, the economic crisis has emphasised the importance of government in economic management. Economic problems, as Gough reminds us in Chapter Three, tend to highlight the relationship between economic performance and social policies, which may be perceived as compatible or incompatible depending on one's ideological approach. But what is not in doubt is that economic crises tend to lead governments to draw upon social policies as one of their mechanisms to shield both individuals and businesses. Many of the internationally coordinated and nationally implemented interventions between 2008 and 2010 might be viewed as 'corporate welfare' – public provision to meet the needs of businesses, without which those businesses would perish. Of course, governments and individuals also required these interventions for the protection of their own interests, but the point here, emphasised by Sinfield and Farnsworth in Chapters Four and Fourteen respectively, is that the tendency to separate the needs and interests of state, individuals and corporations is artificial and only serves to undermine the welfare state. Thus, Sinfield's argument is an appeal to the collective; for state and fiscal structures that encourage common interests as opposed to individual risk taking and recklessness that, with unfortunate irony, visit huge costs upon society as a whole.

We conclude, then, with some final remarks on the ideological dimensions of the crisis (and crises) and how these interrelate with the distributive impact of crisis and recession post-2007. The varieties of crisis incorporate also a variety of politics that is given wider scope by both crisis and recession, as polities seek not only to respond to economic and (sometimes) social needs arising but also to use these events as 'policy windows' through which prior policy ideas, and more ideologically driven agendas, can be pursued. This latter is the case in France, as discussed in Chapter One, but is also more obviously apparent in developments in the US as Béland and Waddan observe in Chapter Thirteen, where this window led to the election of the Democrats in 2008. This strengthening of the Left helped to maintain the stimulus measures longer than in many other economies, including the UK, and enabled the Obama administration to push health reform through both houses. In Iceland, too, the election of the Left-Green coalition has paved the way for the pursuit of a Nordic social model, which, even if the coalition goes on to lose power, will have led to an extension of social rights that will be politically difficult to reverse. In contrast, in both Ireland and the UK the crisis has been seized upon by powers that are anti-pathetic to state welfare, as an opportunity to undertake just such a reversal under the 'no choice' guise. In terms of the basis of the welfare state, the crisis has, in fact, tended to reopen the conflicting arguments between Left and Right that have lain dormant in recent years. Alongside the chapters by Considine and Dukelow (Chapter Ten) and Farnsworth (Chapter Fourteen), both Gough (Chapter Three) and Deacon (Chapter Five) highlight the divide between those arguing for deep cuts in the public sector and those arguing for continued expansion (or at least a cautious and gradual withdrawal of public expenditure as the conditions permit). The divide between Left and Right is also clear when it comes to key questions regarding the repayment of government debt. For the Right, spending cuts are the order of the day, while the Left has argued for a greater emphasis on tax rises, especially on the better off and on the finance industry itself. It is telling, however, that governments have stepped back from earlier proposals to tax and regulate financial institutions at anything like the level that is required to quash speculative finance or to make a dent in public borrowing. In the global financial industry it is looking more like a return to normal.

While the ideological battles that will determine the long-term distributive impact take place, the immediate impact is yet another dimension of the varieties of crisis. In so far as there is a 'new' struggle over the redistribution of resources in many countries, it is one that is more easy to trace to political factors as opposed to economic realities in some. The alignment and dominance of economic and political interests within countries appear to be important to determining not just the impact of the crisis on nations, but also the chosen methods of mediating the crisis and alleviating the symptoms. And there are some nations, as Gough (Chapter Three), Sinfield (Chapter Four) and Farnsworth (Chapter Fourteen) point out in particular, that are utilising the crisis in order to further protect the interests of the most privileged in society. Evidence regarding the long-term distributive outcome of this has yet to be gathered but early indications are that what has been gained in terms of social equality will now regress. While the politics of the crisis is threatening to undermine social policies in some states, however, in others, such as China, social policy has become a matter of social investment rather than economic cost. A general expansionist programme in China to tackle economic slowdown has served to boost social policies, and without facing a fiscal crisis, China has actually benefited from the slowdown since it has gradually increased its holdings of US debt (further challenging the relative power of China and the US in the former's favour). In terms of redistribution, Cook and Lam (Chapter Eight) highlight new approaches and radical shifts in social policy towards meeting the needs of a wider range of groups, including migrants and the deliberate strategy of embracing social security as a tool to facilitate greater domestic demand. This latter policy is important in that it points to a change in Chinese economic strategy towards the greater pursuit of domestic, as opposed to foreign, demand. Within this model, Cook and Lam suggest, social policies are becoming part of a core strategy in the pursuit of sustainable growth.

In considering the global distributive impact, the chapters by Barrientos (Chapter Six), Lee-Gong (Chapter Seven) and Cook and Lam (Chapter Eight) highlight the impact of the crisis beyond wealthiest nations. Their analyses also point to a great deal of variability between crises and their impact on social policies in countries of the Global South, the 'BRIC' and the 'Next-11'.[1] As mentioned earlier, these countries are threatened more by the slowdown than its precipitating crisis, but as Barrientos (Chapter Six) suggests, this is no less a challenge in terms of preserving the fragile systems of social protection emerging from the 'quiet revolution' in the Global South. Differences between the prospects for social policy in these countries and China and South Korea are clearly also linked to the potential effects of the outcome of the global battle of ideas discussed by Deacon (Chapter Five). The lessons of crisis management in the South to which Barrientos (Chapter Six) also alludes are nevertheless prescient to the seemingly expansionist features of developments in the US (and Canada) as much as those in China and South Korea: that while the crisis highlighted some immediate limitations of existing provision that led to 'emergency measures' (US investment under Bush and then Obama in the extension of the Food Stamps programme or time limits on benefit claims, for example), these measures also have unintended consequences. Two in particular are worthy of note here: first, that 'crisis measures' do not have the capacity to provide 'effective and longlasting institutions to address poverty and vulnerability'; and second, that it is too easy in crisis situations to focus on the acute problems, (the 'downstream' symptoms in Sinfield's [Chapter Four] terms) at the expense of those that are chronic in nature (the upstream causes).

This leads to the question of 'solutions' to the crisis, and a number of the chapters here highlight possible steps. Deacon (Chapter Five), for example, suggests the need for multilateral solutions in order to combat entrenched interests within states that are an obstacle to reform. Sinfield (Chapter Four) argues that since inequality is an intrinsic part of the problem that led to the crisis, a first step in arriving at a solution would be proper recognition of inequality as the real problematic. Thus, the responsibilisation (to use an inelegant New Labour term) of society for the problem of riches has to be part of a stable welfare future. Alongside the recognition of public expenditure as a social investment rather than a luxury item, part of this long-term strategy, as Gough (Chapter Three) suggests, is fair taxation, which includes a systematic attempt to restrict avoidance and tackle evasion. More specifically, Gough also posits revisiting the entire basis on which debt is understood and calculated so that nations, as opposed to international capital and international governmental organisations, more transparently account for assets and public investment in their balance sheets. In the aftermath of the crisis, Gough reminds us, many governments have accrued debt, but they have also obtained assets that can be sold in due course (indeed, the US government has made a significant profit on some of the assets sold off to the private sector so far). For Gough, then, a stable welfare future depends on a new economic–social–ecological model.

The abovementioned solutions, then, are all possible roads to economic recovery and they, alongside many of the conclusions drawn in the other chapters in this book, reject the idea that, to use Katzenstein's (1985, p 20) powerful phrase, '[s]ocial fat must be cut to stop the atrophy of economic muscle'. Nevertheless, despite Gordon Brown's suggestion that neoliberal globalisation is dead, it appears to have been resuscitated in at least two of the countries that have suffered the greatest impact since 2008: the UK and Ireland, where, as Considine and Dukelow (Chapter Ten) comment, neoliberalism 'now informs the mainstream policy domain as the solution to the crisis'. However, in a third nation that has been especially hard hit – Iceland – the neoliberal project has been arrested and in the search for alternative futures, the unfolding story is a little more positive for social policy, couched as it is, in collective solutions. A key factor in these very different post-crisis trajectories is the level of mobilisation among those who oppose 'business as usual', and it is the strength of this opposition in both national contexts and at the global level that will counteract the logic of 'no choice'. What sets the 2008 crisis and its aftermath apart from its most recent predecessor in the 1970s is that then it was possible for the Right to focus attention and maintain ill-feeling towards the 'problem' of organised labour whereas post-2007 the blame patently lies elsewhere. Thus, despite attempts to demonise the public sector (through the pensions debate for example), the problem of the culpability of the banking sector and the unfairness of the many paying for the recklessness and greed of the few, is much more difficult to align with neoliberal orthodoxy. This sense of injustice has reawakened politics and galvanised action that governments dismiss at their peril.

We end here with a final remark on the question of whether it is 'too soon to tell' in regard to the impact of economic crisis on welfare systems. Clearly, the situation in 2011 is one where many countries remain in economic turmoil and the global recession looks set to continue for some time to come. However, in analysis of events such as the 2008 financial crisis there is a sense in which it will always be 'too soon to tell' since the decisions now will continue to reverberate down the years as those of the 1930s, 1890 (UK), 1873 (France), 1857 (US) and probably even the 1637 'Tulip mania' crisis still do today. What the contributions here demonstrate is not only that emergency events are crucial to both the shaping of social policy, and to the understanding of that process, but also that challenging times are as likely to widen the scope for progressive welfare state-building as they are to diminish it, and that how states respond is a matter of political struggle and political choice.

Note

[1] The 'Next-11' or 'N11' group includes Bangladesh, Egypt, Indonesia, Iran, Mexico, Nigeria, Pakistan, the Philippines, South Korea, Turkey and Vietnam, which were considered to be countries set to follow in the wake of development of the BRIC group – Brazil, Russia, India and China – in research undertaken by Goldman Sachs in 2005 (www.euromonitor.com/the-next-11-emerging-economies/article).

Bibliography

AABA (Association of Accountancy and Business Affairs) (2007) *Code of Conduct on Taxation*, Basildon: AABA, http://visar.csustan.edu/aaba/CODE%20OF%20CONDUCT%20FOR%20TAXATION.pdf

Adam, S. and Brewer, M. (2010) *Do the Poorest Really Pay the Most in Tax?*, London: Institute for Fiscal Studies.

Adonis, A. and Pollard, S. (1997) *A Class Act: The Myth of Britain's Classless Society*, London: Hamish Hamilton.

Alcock, P., Glennerster, H., Oakley, A. and Sinfield, A. (eds) (2001) *Welfare and Wellbeing: Richard Titmuss's Contribution to Social Policy*, Bristol: The Policy Press.

Allen, C. (2005) 'Ordo-liberalism trumps Keynesianism in the Federal Republic of Germany', in B. Moss (ed) *Monetary Union in Crisis: The European Union as a Neo-Liberal Construction*, London: Palgrave, pp 199–221.

Allen, K. (2009) *Ireland's Economic Crash: A Radical Agenda for Change*, Dublin: The Liffey Press.

André, C. (2010) *A Bird's Eye View of OECD Housing Markets*, OECD Economics Department Working Paper No. 746, Paris: OECD.

Andreß, H.-J. and Lohmann, H. (eds) (2008) *The Working Poor in Europe: Employment, Poverty and Globalization*, Cheltenham: Edward Elgar.

Antoniades, A. (2007) 'Examining facets of the hegemonic: the globalization discourse in Greece and Ireland', *Review of International Political Economy*, vol 14, no 2, pp 306–32.

Armour, S. (2010) 'Foreclosure jump in December after months of declines', *USA Today*, 14 January.

Ásgrímsson, H. (2005a) 'Globalisation: realising the opportunities', Prime Minister's speech, FIH Erhvervsbank, Denmark, 1 March, http://eng.forsaetisraduneyti.is/minister/Speeches_HA/nr/1732

Ásgrímsson, H. (2005b) 'The Icelandic economy', Prime Minister's speech, Landsbanki Islands, 14 March, http://eng.forsaetisraduneyti.is/minister/Speeches_HA/nr/1732

Athukorala, P.-C. and Kohpaiboon, A. (2010) 'China and East Asian trade: the decoupling fallacy, crisis and policy challenges', in R. Garnaut, J. Golley and S. Ligang (eds) *China: The Next Twenty Years of Reform and Development* Sydney: ANU E Press, http://epress.anu.edu.au/china_20_citation.html

Atkinson, A.B. (2007) 'Measuring top incomes: methodological issues', in A.B. Atkinson and T. Piketty (eds) *Top Incomes over the Twentieth Century: A Contrast between Continental European and English-Speaking Countries*, Oxford: Oxford University Press.

Atkinson, A.B. (2009) 'Factor shares', *Oxford Review of Economic Policy*, vol 25, no 1, pp 3-16.

Augar, P. (2006) *The Greed Merchants: How the Investment Banks Played the Free Market Game*, London: Penguin.

Augar, P. (2008) 'The big bang model that blew up in our faces', *Financial Times*, 28 September.

Baker, P. (2010) 'With new tax bill, a turning point for the President', *New York Times*, 17 December.

Baldwin, B. (2010) 'Workplace pensions: trouble in pillar 3', presentation to the 'Older and Wiser' conference, University of Saskatchewan (Johnson–Shoyama Graduate School of Public Policy), 8 March.

Balz, D.J. and Johnson, H. (2009) *The Battle for America 2008: The Story of an Extraordinary Election*, New York, NY: Viking.

Bank of England (2000) *Statistical Abstract*. London: Bank of England.

Bank of Korea (2007) *Economic Growth Statistics: 1953-2007*, Jung-gu, Seoul, http://ecos.bok.or.kr/jsp/use/koreco/KorEcoPopUp.jsp?tableId=T_ECO_GRO

Barkham, P. (2010) 'The victims of Ireland's economic collapse', *The Guardian*, 26 May.

Barnard, A. (2010) *The Effect of Taxes and Benefits on Household Income 2008-09*, Newport: ONS, www.statistics.gov.uk/taxesbenefits

Barrientos, A. (2009) 'Introducing basic social protection in low income countries: lessons from existing programmes', in P. Townsend (ed) *Building Decent Societies: Rethinking the Role of Social Security in Development*, London: Palgrave Macmillan and ILO.

Barrientos, A. and Hulme, D. (eds) (2008) *Social Protection for the Poor and Poorest: Concepts, Policies and Politics*, London: Palgrave.

Barrientos, A. and Santibañez, C. (2009a) 'New forms of social assistance and the evolution of social protection in Latin America', *Journal of Latin American Studies*, vol 41, pp 1-26.

Barrientos, A. and Santibañez, C. (2009b) 'Social policy for poverty reduction in low income countries in Latin America: lessons and challenges', *Social Policy and Administration*, vol 43, pp 409-24.

Barrientos, A., Nino–Zarazua, M. and Maitrot, M. (2010) *Social Assistance in Developing Countries Database Version 5*, Manchester: Brooks World Poverty Institute.

Basham, P. and Tupy, M. (2005) 'Thatcher again?', *nationalreview.com*, 16 September, http://old.nationalreview.com/comment/basham_tupy200509160900.asp

Baumer, E., Wright, R., Kristinsdottir, K. and Gunnlaugsson, H. (2002) 'Crime, shame and recidivism: the case of Iceland', *British Journal of Criminology*, vol 41, pp 40-59.

BBC (British Broadcasting Corporation) (2008) 'Honda, Swindon, closing for 50 days', *BBC News*, 21 November, http://news.bbc.co.uk/1/hi/business/7741269.stm

Beijing Review (2009) 'Can shopping vouchers boost consumption?' no. 2 (2 January), www.bjreview.com.cn/forum/txt/2009-01/05/content_173252.htm

Béland, D. (2005) 'Ideas and social policy: an institutionalist perspective', *Social Policy & Administration*, vol 39, no 1, pp 1-18.

Béland, D. (2009) 'Ideas, institutions, and policy change', *Journal of European Public Policy*, vol 16, no 5, pp 701-18.

Béland, D. and Myles, J. (2005) 'Stasis amidst change: Canadian pension reform in an age of retrenchment', in G. and T. Shinkawa (eds) *Ageing and Pension Reform around the World*, Cheltenham: Edward Elgar, pp 252-72.

Béland, D. and Myles, J. (2008) *Policy Change in the Canadian Welfare State: Comparing the Canada Pension Plan and Unemployment Insurance*, Research Paper No. 235, Hamilton: SEDAP, McMaster University.

Bell, B. and Van Reenen, J. (2010) *Bankers' Pay and Extreme Wage Inequality in the UK*, Special Paper No. 21, London: Centre for Economic Performance.

Beveridge, W.H. (1944) *Full Employment in a Free Society*, London: Allen & Unwin.

Bevins, V. and Cappitt, O. (2009) 'FT timeline: the history of finance', *Financial Times*, 10 November, www.ft.com/cms/s/0/334eea46-ce0d-11de-95e7-00144feabdc0.html

Birdsall, N. (2007) *Reflections on the Macro Foundations of the Middle Class in Developing Countries*, Working Paper 130, Washington, DC: Center for Global Development.

Birdsall, N. (2008) 'The development agenda as a global social contract; or, we are all in this development boat together', Lecture to the Dutch Scientific Council, Hague, December.

BIS (Bank for International Settlements) (2010) *The Future of Public Debt: Prospects and Implications*, Working Paper 300, Basel, Switzerland, www.bis.org/publ/work300.pdf

Blair, T. (1998) *The Third Way: New Politics for the New Century*, London: Fabian Society.

Blair, T. and Schröder, G. (1999) *Europe: The Third Way / Die Neue Mitte*, London: Labour Party.

Blyth, M. (2008) 'The politics of compounding bubbles: the global housing bubble in comparative perspective', *Comparative European Politics*, vol 6, no 3, pp 387–406.

Boas, M. and McNeill, D (2004) *Global Institutions and Development*, Basingstoke: Palgrave.

Boucher, G. and Collins, G. (2003) 'Having one's cake and being eaten too: Irish neo-liberal corporatism', *Review of Social Economy*, vol LXI, no 3, pp 295-316.

Bourgault-Côté, G. (2009) 'Pas d'élections cet automne', *Le Devoir*, 17 September.

Boychuk, G.W. and Banting, K.G. (2008) 'The public–private divide: health insurance and pensions in Canada', in D. Béland and B. Gran (eds) *Public and Private Social Policy: Health and Pension Policies in a New Era*, Basingstoke: Palgrave Macmillan, pp 92-122.

Boyes, R. (2009) *Meltdown Iceland, How the Global Financial Crisis Bankrupted an Entire Country*. London: Bloomsbury.

Brewer, M., Emmerson, C. and Miller, H. (2011) *The IFS Green Budget*. London: Institute for Fiscal Studies.

Brewer, M., Sibieta, L. and Wren-Lewis, L. (2008) *Racing Away? Income Inequality and the Evolution of High Incomes*, Briefing Note No. 76, London: Institute for Fiscal Studies.

British Academy (2009) *Letter to the Queen*, London: British Academy, www.britac.ac.uk/events/archive/forum-economy.cfm

Brittan, S. (2009a) 'Green shoots debate misleads policy makers', *Financial Times*, 26 June.

Brittan, S. (2009b) 'What is wrong with "slash and burn"', *Financial Times*, 15 September.

Brittan, S. (2010) 'Now is the time to ask: what crisis?', *Financial Times*, 20 May.

Brook, L., Hall, J. and Preston, I. (1996) 'Public spending and taxation', in R. Jowell, L. Brook and B. Taylor (eds) *British Social Attitudes: The 8th Report*, Aldershot: Gower.

Brook, L., Preston, I. and Hall, J. (1998) 'What drives support for higher spending', in P. Taylor-Gooby (ed) *Choice and Public Policy*, Basingstoke: Macmillan.

Brown, G. (2006) Gordon Brown's budget speech, 22 March, www.guardian.co.uk/uk/2006/mar/22/budget2006.budget

Bullock, N. and Weitzman, H. (2010) 'US state pensions becoming a federal issue', *Financial Times*, 19 May, www.ft.com/cms/s/0/b9d90504-6379-11df-a844-00144feab49a.html

Bundesagentur für Arbeit (2008) *Arbeitsmarkt in Zahlen*, Nuremburg: Bundesagentur für Arbeit.

Bundesagentur für Arbeit (2010) *The Labour Market in June 2010*, Nuremburg: Bundesagentur für Arbeit.

Busch, A. (2005) 'Globalisation and national varieties of capitalism: the contested viability of the "German model"', *German Politics*, vol 14, no 2, pp 125-39.

Butcher, T. (1995) *Delivering Welfare: The Governance of the Social Services in the 1990s*, Buckingham: Open University Press.

Buxton, N. (2009) *UN Mission Accomplished?*, Amsterdam: Transnational Institute.

Byun, Y.-C. (2009) 'Policy tasks for social integration in time of economic crisis: the case of Korea', *International Symposium: Beyond the Economic Crisis: Social Integration and Shared Prosperity*, 27-28 May, Seoul: Ministry of Health and Welfare.

Cable, V. (2009) *The Storm*, London: Atlantic Books.

Caijing Magazine (2010) 'Guangdong enterprises in shortage of 900,000 workers (guang dong qi ye que gong 90wan ren 广东企业缺工90万人)', 25 February, http://policy.caing.com/2010-02-25/100120680.html)

Caijing.com (2009) 'Facelift for China's economic stimulus plan', 6 March, http://english.caijing.com.cn/2009-03-06/110114405.html

Cameron, D. (2010a) 'Transforming the British economy: coalition strategy for economic growth', Speech, 28 May, www.number10.gov.uk/news/speeches-and-transcripts/2010/05/transforming-the-british-economy-coalition-strategy-for-economic-growth-51132

Cameron, D. (2010b) 'Prime Minister's speech on the economy', Open University, Milton Keynes, 7 June, www.number10.gov.uk/news/speeches-and-transcripts/2010/06/prime-ministers-speech-on-the-economy-51435

Campbell, J. (1998) 'Institutional analysis and the role of ideas in political economy', *Theory and Society*, vol 27, pp 377-409.

Campbell, J. and Pedersen, O. (2001) 'The rise of neoliberalism and institutional analysis', in J. Campbell and O. Pedersen (eds) *The Rise of Neoliberalism and Institutional Analysis*, Princeton, NJ: Princeton University Press, pp 1-23.

Campeau, G. (2005) *From UI to EI: Waging War on the Welfare State*, Vancouver: UBC Press.

Canadian Labour Congress (2009) *Security, Adequacy, Fairness: Labour's Proposals for the Future of Canadian Pensions*, Ottawa: CLC Discussion Paper.

Caporaso, J. and Levine, D. (1992) *Theories of Political Economy*, Cambridge: Cambridge University Press.

CASS (China Academy of Social Science) (2009) *The Blue Book of China's Society*, Beijing: CASS.

Cassidy, J. (2009) *How Markets Fail*, London: Allen Lane.

Castles, F.G. (2010) 'Black swans and elephants on the move: the impact of emergencies on the welfare state', *Journal of European Social Policy*, vol 20, no 2, pp 91-101.

CBC News (2009) 'A primer on the employment insurance debate', *CBC News*, 28 July, www.cbc.ca/canada/story/2009/05/29/f-ei-wait-times.html

CBC News (2010) 'Federal deficit estimate falls', *CBC News*, 28 May, www.cbc.ca/money/story/2010/05/28/deficit-projection-smaller.html

CCTV (2009) 'Consumption voucher: welfare or stimulus tool? [jin ri guan cha: xiao fei quan shi fu li hai shi jiu shi gong ju? 今日观察：消费券是福利还是救市工具]', 17 February, http://news.sina.com.cn/c/2009-02-17/113717231761.shtml

Center for Economic Policy Research (2009) 'IMF shouldn't get the money without reform', www.cepr.net/index.php/op-eds-&-columns/op-eds-&-columns/imf-shouldnt-get-money-without-reform/

CEPAL (2009) *La reacción de los gobiernos de las Américas frente a la crisis internacional: Una presentación sintética de las medidas de politica anunciadas hasta el 31 de Julio de 2009*, Santiago: CEPAL.

Chang, H.J. (1998) 'Korea: the misunderstood crisis', *World Development*, vol 26, no 8, pp 1555-61.

Chartier, D. (2011) *The End of Iceland's Innocence: The Image of Iceland in the Foreign Media during the Financial Crisis*, Ottawa: University of Ottawa Press.

Chen, S. and Ravallion, M. (2009) 'The impact of the global financial crisis on the world's poorest', www.voxeu.org

Chhibber, A., Ghosh, J. and Palanivel, T. (2009) *The Global Financial Crisis and the Asia-Pacific Region*, Colombo: UNDP Regional Center for Asia and the Pacific.

China Business Weekly (2009) 'Unemployment of migrant workers exposed as China's urban unemployment rate jump to 9.4% [zhong guo cheng zhen shi ye lu sheng zhi 9.4% nong min gong shi ye wen ti tu xian 中国城镇失业率升至9.4%农民工失业问题凸显]', 5 January, http://acftu.people.com.cn/GB/8621908.html

China Daily (2009a) 'Should China issue consumption coupons?' 19 January http://www.chinadaily.com.cn/bw/2009-01/19/content_7407506.htm

China Daily (2009b) 'Should China issue consumption coupons?' 19 January, http://www.chinadaily.com.cn/bw/2009-01/19/content_7407506.htm

China Economic Times (2009) 'Chengdu: how effective is the 37.91 million yuan consumption voucher [Cheng du: jiu shi meng yao 3791 wan xiao fei quan cheng xiao ji he 成都：救市猛药3791万"消费券"成效几何？]', 18 February, http://www.jjxww.com/html/show.aspx?id=143369&cid=133

China.com (2009a) '4900 enterprises closed down, go bankrupt and relocation in the crisis [Huang Hua-hua: jin rong wei j ixia guang dong guan bi po chan ban qian qi ye 黄华华：金融危机下广东·闭破产搬迁企业4900家]', 6 March, http://www.china.com.cn/news/2009-03/06/content_17390742.htm

China.com (2009b) 'Shenzhen mayor dismisses rumors of 2 billion yuan consumption voucher handouts [shen zhen shi zhang four en shen zhen ni fa fang 20 yi xiao fei quan chuan wen 深圳市长否认"深圳拟发放20亿消费券"传闻]', 17 February, http://news.022china.com/2009/02-17/35875_0.html

Choi, Y. and Chung, C.S. (2002) 'Social impact of the Korean economic crisis, EADN regional project on the social impact of the Asian financial crisis', www.eadn.org/Social%20Impact%20of%20the%20Korean%20Economic%20Crisis.pdf.

Chote, R., Emmerson, C. and Tetlow, G. (2008) *The UK public finances: ready for recession?* London: Institute for Fiscal Studies.

Chung, M.K. (2001) 'Rolling back the Korean state: how much has changed?', 2001 Meeting of the IPSA Section of Structure of Governance, University of Oklahoma, 30-31 March.

Clarke, P. (1988) *The Keynesian Revolution in the Making*, Oxford: Oxford University Press.

Clarke, P. (2009) *Keynes*, London: Bloomsbury.

Clasen, J. (2005) *Reforming European Welfare States: Germany and the United Kingdom Compared*, Oxford: Oxford University Press.

Clasen, J., Davidson, J., Ganßmann, H. and Mauer, A. (2006) 'Non-employment and the welfare state: the United Kingdom and Germany compared', *Journal of European Social Policy*, vol 16, no 2, pp 134-54.

Clemens, C. (2007) 'Two-steps forward, one step back: Merkel's CDU/CSU and the politics of welfare reform', *German Politics*, vol 16, no 2, pp 222-46.

Clemens, C. (2009) 'Modernisation or disorientation? Policy change in Merkel's CDU', *German Politics,* vol 18, no 2, pp 121-39.

Cohen, S. (2004) *Searching for a Different Future: The Rise of the Global Middle Class,* Durham, NC: Duke University Press.

Cohen, S. (2009) Paper for Moroccan Policy Conference, Journee d'Etude Sur la Class Moyenne, Rabat, April.

Cole, G.D.H. (1955) 'Socialism and the welfare state', *New Statesman and Nation,* 23 July, pp 88-9.

Commission on Taxation (2009) *Commission on Taxation Report 2009,* Dublin: The Stationery Office.

Conefrey, T. and Fitz Gerald, J. (2009) *Managing Housing Bubbles in Regional Economies under EMU: Ireland and Spain,* ESRI Working Paper No. 315, Dublin: ESRI.

Considine, M. and Dukelow, F. (2009) *Irish Social Policy: A Critical Introduction,* Dublin: Gill and Macmillan.

Conway, E. (2008) 'Fear of Iceland bail-out could signal new future for the IMF', *The Telegraph,* 6 April, www.telegraph.co.uk/finance/comment/edmundconway/2787581/Fear-of-Iceland-bail-out-could-signal-new-future-for-the-IMF.html

Cook, D. (1989) *Rich Law, Poor Law: Different Responses to Tax and Supplementary Benefit Fraud,* Milton Keynes: Open University Press.

Cook, S. and Gu, J. (2009) 'The global financial crisis: implications for China's South–South cooperation, *IDS Bulletin,* vol 40, no 5.

Cooper, M. (2008) 'McCain laboring to hit right note on the economy', *New York Times,* 16 September.

Cornia, G., Jolly, R. and Stewart, F. (1987) *Adjustment with a Human Face,* Oxford: Clarendon Press.

Courchene, T.J. and Allan, J. (2009) 'A short history of EI, and a look at the road ahead', *Policy Options,* vol 30, no 8, pp 19-29.

Cowen, B. (2008) Speech by the Taoiseach, Mr Brian Cowen TD, at the First Business Roundtable with the Government of Ireland, Dublin, 30 October, www.taoiseach.gov.ie/eng/Government_Press_Office/Taoiseach%27s_Speeches_2008/?pageNumber=4

Cowen, B. (2010) 'The Irish banking crisis – the mistakes, the responses and the lessons', Speech by the Taoiseach, Mr Brian Cowen TD, North Dublin Chamber of Commerce, Dublin City University, 13 May, www.taoiseach.gov.ie/eng/Government_Press_Office/Taoiseach's%20Speeches%202010/Speech_by_An_Taoiseach_North_Dublin_Chamber_of_Commerce_Dublin_City_University%2013%20May%202010.html

Cox, E., and Schmuecker, K. (2010) *Well North of Fair: The Implications of the Spending Review for the North of England.* London: IPPR.

CPC (Communist Party of China) (2006) Communique of the Sixth Plenum of the 16th CPC Central Committee, 11 October, http://english.peopledaily.com.cn/200610/12/eng20061012_310923.html

Crawford, R. (2010) *Where did the Axe Fall? Spending Review Briefing, 21 October* London: Institute for Fiscal Studies.

CRESC (Centre for Research on Socio-Cultural Change) (2009) *An Alternative Report on the UK Banking System: A Public Interest Report*, Manchester: CRESC, University of Manchester.

Cross, P. (2010) 'The accelerated pace of the 2008-2009 downturn,' *Statistics Canada*, 14 May, www.statcan.gc.ca/pub/11-010-x/2010005/part-partie3-eng.htm

CSO (Central Statistics Office) (2009) *Survey on Income and Living Conditions 2008*, Dublin: The Stationery Office.

Daly, M. and Yeates, N. (2003) 'Common origins, different paths: adaptation and change in social security in Britain and Ireland', *Policy & Politics*, vol 31, no 1, pp 85-97.

Danielsson, J. (2009) 'Waking up to reality in Iceland', *BBC News*, 26 January, http://news.bbc.co.uk/1/hi/world/europe/7852275.stm

Daunton, M. (2001) *Trusting Leviathan: The Politics of Taxation in Britain 1799-1914*, Cambridge: Cambridge University Press.

Davies, H. (2010) *The Financial Crisis: Who is to Blame?*, Cambridge: Polity Press.

Davies, M. (2002) 'Thatcher's famous speeches', *BBC News*, 22 March, http://news.bbc.co.uk/1/hi/1888158.stm

de Haan, A. (2007) *Reclaiming Social Policy*, Basingstoke, Palgrave.

Deacon, B. (2007) *Global Social Policy and Governance*, London: Sage Publciations.

Deacon, B. (2009) 'From the global politics of poverty alleviation to the global politics of welfare state (re)building', presented at a panel on the role of social research and social policy (CROP-CLASCO-CODESERIA), World Social Science Forum (WSSF), Bergen, 10-12 May.

Deacon, B., Hulse, M. and Stubbs, P. (1997) *Global Social Policy: International Organizations and the Future of Welfare*, London: Sage Publications.

Deacon, B., Jakobi, A.P. and Kaasch, A. (2009) 'International policy networks and basic social needs: shaping global social policy', paper presented at the RC19 Conference, Montreal, August.

Deacon, B., Macovei, M.C., Van Langenhove, L. and Yeates, N. (2010) *World Regional Social Policy and Global Governance: New Research and policy Agendas in Africa, Latin America and Asia*. London, Routledge.

Dearden, N. (2009) 'Rich nations shut out the UN', *The Guardian*, 22 June, www.guardian.co.uk/commentisfree/2009/jun/22/un-g8-rich-nations

DeParle, J. and Gebeloff, R. (2009) 'Food stamp use soars, and stigma fades', *New York Times*, 29 November.

Department of Finance (2009) *Budget 2009: Canada's Economic Action Plan*, Ottawa: Department of Finance, www.fin.gc.ca/n08/09-011-eng.asp

Department of Planning and Development (2004) *The Icelandic National Health Plan to the Year 2010*, Reykjavik: Ministry of Health and Social Security.

Department of the Taoiseach (2006) *Building on Success: International Financial Services Industry in Ireland*, Dublin: The Stationery Office.

Department of the Taoiseach (2008) *Building Ireland's Smart Economy: A Framework for Sustainable Economic Renewal*, Dublin: The Stationery Office.

Dervis K. (2009) 'The G-20 summits and the UN system: prospects and challenges', *UNESCO Futures Lecture*, Paris, 18 June.

DFID (Department for International Development) (2006) *Making Governance Work for the Poor*, White Paper, London: DFID.

DIW (German Institute for Economic Research) (2010) 'Armutsrisiko in Deutschland steigt: Kinder und junge Erwachsene besonders betroffen', Press Release, 18 February.

Dobelstein, A. (2009) *Understanding the Social Security Act: The Foundation of Social Welfare for America in the Twenty-First Century*, New York, NY: Oxford University Press.

Dommen, E. (1980) 'Some distinguishing characteristics of island states', *World Development*, vol 8, pp 931–43.

Downs, A. (1957) *An Economic Theory of Democracy*, New York, NY: Harper & Row.

Driver, S. and Martell, L. (1998) *New Labour: Politics after Thatcherism*, Cambridge: Polity Press.

DSFA (Department of Social and Family Affairs) (2009) *Statistical Information on Social Welfare Services 2008*, Dublin: DSFA.

DSP (Department of Social Protection) (2010) *Statistical Information on Social Welfare Services 2009*, Dublin: DSP.

Dunaway, S. (2009) *Global Imbalances and the Financial Crisis*, Council Special Report No. 44 (March 2009), Washington, DC: Council on Foreign Relations.

DWP (Department for Work and Pensions) (2010) *21st Century Welfare*, London: DWP, www.dwp.gov.uk/consultations/2010/21st-century-welfare/

EAPN Ireland (2009) *Social Welfare: How Ireland Compares in Europe*, EAPN Ireland Factsheet, Dublin: EAPN Ireland.

EC (European Commission) (2003) *Employment in Europe 2003*, Brussels: EC.

ECLAC (Economic Commission for Latin America and the Caribbean) (2008) *Social Panorama of Latin America 2008*, Washington, DC: ECLAC.

Economic Observer (2008) 'Basic pension for enterprise workers to increase to 110 yuan in next year [ming nian qi ye tui xiu ren yuan jib en yang lao jin ren jun jiang zeng jia 110 yuan 明年企业退休人员基本·老金人均将增加110元]', 20 November, http://www.cnr.cn/2008zt/sxcs/tbch/gsms/ws/200811/t20081120_505155692.html

Economic Observer (2009) '4 trillion yuan package scales down as 200 billion yuan central government investment sitting idle [jin nian zhong yang tou zi 2000 yi mei hua si wan yi ji hua suo shui 今年中央投资2000亿没花四万亿计划缩水]', 19 December, http://finance.qq.com/a/20091219/002076.htm

Egle, C. and Henkes, C. (2003) 'Später Sieg der Modernisierer über die Traditionalisten? Die Programmdebatte in der SPD', in C. Egle, T. Ostheim and R. Zohlnhöfer (eds) *Das Rot-Grüne Projekt: Eine Bilanz der Regierung Schröder 1998–2002*, Wiesbaden: Westdeutscher Verlag.

Eldridge, J. (1983) *C. Wright Mills*, London: Tavistock.

Elliot, L. (2010) 'G20 Accord: you go your way, i'll go mine', *The Guardian*, 28 June, www.guardian.co.uk/world/2010/jun/28/g20-summit-economics-global-imbalances

Esping-Andersen, G. (1990) *The Three Worlds of Welfare Capitalism*, Cambridge: Polity Press.

Esping-Andersen, G. (1996a) 'Welfare states without work: the impasse of labour shedding and familialism in continental European social policy', in G. Esping-Andersen (ed) *Welfare States in Transition: National Adaptations in Global Economies*, London: Sage Publications, pp 66-87.

Esping-Andersen, G. (1996b) *Welfare states in transition*, London: Sage Publications.

ESRI (Economic and Social Research Institute) (2010a) *Quarterly Economic Commentary*, Summer 2010, Dublin: ESRI.

ESRI (2010b) *Quarterly Economic Commentary, Summer 2010*, Dublin: ESRI.

Estévez-Abe, M., Iversen, T. and Soskice, D. (2001) 'Social protection and the formation of skills: a reinterpretation of the welfare state', in P. Hall and D. Soskice (eds) *Varieties of Capitalism: The Institutional Foundations of Competitive Advantage*, Oxford: Oxford University Press, pp 145-83.

Fanning, B. (2003) 'The construction of Irish social policy 1953-2003', in B. Fanning and T. McNamara (eds) *Ireland Develops: Administration and Social Policy 1953-2003*, Dublin: IPA, pp 3-18.

Farnsworth, K. (2006). 'Capital to the rescue? New Labour's business solutions to old welfare problems', *Critical Social Policy*, vol. 26, no. 4, pp 817-42.

Farnsworth, K. (2011) *Social Versus Corporate Welfare*. London: Palgrave.

FCIC (Financial Crisis Inquiry Commission) (2011) *Financial Crisis Inquiry Report*. Washington, FCIC.

Ferge, Zs. (1997) 'The changed welfare paradigm - the individualization of the social', *Social Policy and Administration*, vol 31. no 1, pp 20-44.

Ferguson, N. (2010) Today's Keynesians have learnt nothing. *Financial Times* 19 July.

Ferguson, T. and Johnson, R. (2010) 'When wolves cry "wolf": systemic financial crises and the myth of the Danaid Jar', paper presented at the INET Inaugural Conference, King's College, Cambridge University.

Financial Times (2006) 'Ask the Expert: Can London Stay at the Top', 25 October, www.ft.com/cms/s/2/4f281438-6455-11db-ab21-0000779e2340.html#axzz1RMmDB1yR

Financial Times (2010) 'Warning over sell-off in bond market', *Financial Times*, 27 January, www.ft.com/cms/s/0/f77dfe4a-0b82-11df-8232-00144feabdc0.html#axzz1E7G2QKzo

First Financial Daily (2010) 'Central government may need to increase investment as local governments found it hard to provide matching fund [di fang zi jin pei tao kun nan 4 wan yi hua jia da zhong yang tou zi bi li 地方资金配套困难 4万亿或加大中央投资比例]', 5 January, http://business.sohu.com/20100105/n269375818.shtml

Fiszbein, A. and Schady, N. (2009) *Conditional Cash Transfers: Reducing Present and Future Poverty*, Washington, DC: World Bank.

Flaherty, J.M. (2008) *The Economic and Fiscal Statement 2008*, Ottawa: Department of Finance, www.fin.gc.ca/ec2008/speech/speech-eng.html

Fleckenstein, T. (2008) 'Restructuring welfare for the unemployed: the Hartz legislation in Germany', *Journal of European Social Policy*, vol 18, no 2, pp 177-88.

Fraser, N. and Gordon, L. (1992) 'Contract versus charity: why is there no social citizenship in the United States?', *Socialist Review*, vol 22, pp 45-68.

Freud, D. (2007) *Reducing Dependency, Increasing Opportunity: Options for the Future of Welfare to Work*, London: DWP.

Freud, D. (2008) *Freud in the City*, London: Bene Factum.

Friedman, M. and Schwartz, A.J. (1963) *A Monetary History of the United States*, Princeton, NJ: Princeton University Press.

Friedman, T. (2005a) 'The end of the rainbow', *New York Times*, 29 June.

Friedman, T. (2005b) 'Follow the leapin' leprechaun', *New York Times*, 1 July.

Furlong, R. (2009) 'Unlikely activists fight Iceland woes', *BBC News Online*, 19 December, http://news.bbc.co.uk/1/hi/world/europe/7790264.stm

Gallie, D., Paugam, S. and Jacobs, S. (2002) 'Unemployment, poverty and social isolation: is there a vicious circle of social exclusion?', *European Societies*, vol 5, no 1, pp 1-32.

Gamble, A. (1990) *Britain in Decline: Economic Policy, Political Strategy and the British State*, London: Macmillan.

Gamble, A. (1995) 'The new political economy', *Political Studies*, vol 43, 516-30.

Gamble, A. (2009) *The Spectre at the Feast: Capitalist Crisis and the Politics of Recession*, Basingstoke: Macmillan

Giddens, A. (1998) *The Third Way: The Renewal of Social Democracy*, Cambridge: Polity Press.

Ginsburg, N. (2001) 'Globalization and the liberal welfare states', in R. Sykes, B. Palier and P.M. Prior (eds) *Globalization and European Welfare States: Challenges and Change*, Basingstoke: Palgrave, pp 173-91.

Glennerster, H., Power, A. and Travers, T. (1991) 'A new era for social policy: a new enlightenment or a new leviathan', *Journal of Social Policy*, vol 20, no 3, pp 389-414.

Glyn, A. (2006) *Capitalism Unleashed: Finance, Globalization, and Welfare*, Oxford: Oxford University Press.

GNDG (Green New Deal Group) (2010) *The Great Tax Parachute*, London: New Economics Foundation, GNDG, www.neweconomics.org/sites/neweconomics.org/files/The_Great_Tax_Parachute.pdf

Golbert, L. (2004) *Derecho a la inclusión o paz social? Plan Jefes y Jefas de Hogar Desocupados*, Santiago: CEPAL, División de Desarrollo Social.

Gold, M. (2008) 'Canada is facing a crisis in the private pension sector', *The Toronto Star*, 11 December, www.thestar.com/comment/article/551912

Goodman, R. and Peng, I. (1996) 'The East Asian welfare states: peripatetic learning, adaptive change, and nation-building', in G. Esping-Andersen (ed) *Welfare States in Transition: National Adaptations in Global Economics*, London: Sage Publications, pp 192-223.

Goodman, R. and White, G. (1998) 'Welfare orientalism and the search for an East Asian welfare model', in R. Goodman, G. White and H.J. Kwon (eds) *The East Asian Welfare Model: Welfare Orientalism and the State*, London: Routledge, pp 3-23.

Gorz, A. (1999) *Reclaiming Work: Beyond the Wage-Based Society*, Cambridge: Polity Press.

Gough, I. (1979) *The Political Economy of the Welfare State*, London: Macmillan.

Gough, I. (2000) 'The fiscal crisis of the state: the contribution of James O'Connor', in I. Gough (ed) *Global Capital, Human Needs and Social Policies: Selected Essays 1994-1999*, Basingstoke: Palgrave, pp 65-76.

Gough, I. (2010) 'Economic crisis, climate change and the future of welfare states', *Journal of the Academy of Social Sciences*, vol 5, no 1, pp 51-64.

Gough, I. and Olafsson, G. (eds) (1999) *Capitalism and Social Cohesion: Essays on Exclusion and Integration*, London: Macmillan.

Gould, J. (2005) *The New Conditionality: The politics of Poverty Reduction Strategies*, London: Zed Press.

Gov.cn (2009) 'State Council Standing Committee decides to raise pension for retired enterprise workers [guo wu yuan chang wu hui yi jue ding ti gao qi ye tui xiu ren yuan jib en yang lao jin 国务院常务会议决定提高企业退休人员基本 • 老金]', 22 December, www.gov.cn/ldhd/2009-12/22/content_1493887.htm

Government of Ireland (2010) *National Recovery Plan 2011-2014*, Dublin: The Stationery Office.

Graham, A. (2010) 'Beware calls for hasty cuts', *The Guardian*, 18 February.

Grant, W. (1993) *Business and Politics in Britain*. London: Macmillan.

Green, K. (2006) 'Foreword', in CPAG, *Welfare Benefits and Tax Credits Handbook*, London: CPAG.

Grosh, M., Del Ninno, C., Tesliuc, E. and Ouerghi, A. (2008) *For Protection and Promotion: The Design and Implementation of Effective Safety Nets*, Washington, DC: World Bank.

Guðnason, R. and Jónsdóttir, G. (2009) 'The impact of financial crises on the CPI', paper delivered at the 11th meeting of the International Working Group on Price Indices (The Ottawa Group), Neuchâtel, Switzerland, 27-29 May, www.statice.is/lisalib/getfile.aspx?itemid=9757

Gylfason, T., Holmström, B., Korkman, S., Söderström, H.-T. and Vihriälä, V. (2010) *Nordics in Global Crisis – Vulnerability and Resilience*. Helsinki: ETLA, www.etla.fi/eng/julkaisuhaku.php?type=details&id=1695

Habermas, J. (1975) *Legitimation Crisis*, Boston, MA: Beacon Press.

Hacker, J.S. (2002) *The Divided Welfare State: The Battle over Public and Private Social Benefits in the United States*, Cambridge: Cambridge University Press.

Hacker, J.S. (1997) *The Road to Nowhere: The Genesis of President Clinton's Plan for Health Security*, Princeton, NJ: Princeton University Press.

Hagenbaugh, B. (2009) 'Many of the jobless get no unemployment benefits', *USA Today*, 10 April.

Haldane, A.G. (2010) 'The $100 billion question: comments given at the Institute of Regulation & Risk, Hong Kong, Bank of England', 30 March, www.bankofengland.co.uk/publications/speeches/2010/speech433.pdf

Hale, G.E. (1998) 'Reforming employment insurance: transcending the politics of the status quo', *Canadian Public Policy*, vol 24, no 4, pp 429-51.

Hall, P.A. (1986) *Governing the Economy: The Politics of State Intervention in Britain and France*, Cambridge: Polity Press.

Hall, P.A. (1992) 'The movement from Keynesianism to monetarism: institutional analysis and British economic policy in the 1970s', in S. Steinmo, K. Thelen and F. Longstreth (eds) *Structuring Politics: Historical Institutionalism in Comparative Analysis*, Cambridge: Cambridge University Press.

Hall, P.A. (1993) 'Policy paradigms, social learning and the state: the case of economic policy making in Britain', *Comparative Politics*, vol 25, no 3, pp 275-95.

Hall, P.A. (2008) 'Comments', *Huffington Post*, 13 October.

Hall, P.A. and Soskice, D. (eds) (2001) *Varieties of Capitalism: The Institutional Foundations of Comparative* Advantage, Oxford: Oxford University Press.

Halsey, A.H. (ed) (1988) *British Social Trends since 1900*, Basingstoke: Macmillan.

Hanafin, M. (2009) 'Pensioners and vulnerable children protected despite budget cuts', Press Release, Department of Social and Family Affairs, Dublin, 9 December.

Hardarson, Ó. and Kristinsson, G. (2004) 'Iceland', *European Journal of Political Research*, vol 43, pp 1024-9.

Harford, K. (2010) '"When poverty flies in the window, love walks out the door": recessionary times for people experiencing poverty', *Irish Journal of Public Policy*, vol 2, no 1, http://publish.ucc.ie/ijpp/2010/01/harford/05/en

Hartmann, A.K. (2003), 'Patientennah, Leistungsstark, Finanzbewusst? Die Gesundheitspolitik der Rot-Grünen Bundesregierung 1998-2002' In: Egle, C., Ostheim, T. and Zohlnhöfer, R. (eds), *Das Rot-Grüne Projekt. Eine Bilanz der Regierung Schröder 1998-2002*. Westdeutscher Verlag, Wiesbaden.

Hartz, P. (2002) *Modern Services on the Labour Market: Report of the Commission* (Brochure A 306), Berlin: Ministry for Work and Social Security.

Haseler, S. (2008) *Meltdown*, London: Forum Press.

Hassel, A. and Williamson, H. (2004) 'The evolution of the German model: how to judge reforms in Europe's largest economy', paper prepared for the Anglo-German Foundation, Berlin.

Häusermann, S. (2010) *The Politics of Welfare State Reform in Continental Europe: Modernization in Hard Times*, Cambridge: Cambridge University Press.

Hay, C. (2006) 'Constructivist Institutionalism', in R.W. Rhodes, S. Binder and B. Rockman (eds) *The Oxford Handbook of Political Institutions*, Oxford: Oxford University Press, pp 56-74.

HIO (Health Insurance Organisation) (2008) 'Strategy', www.hio.org.cy/en/strategy.html

Healy, J. (2009) 'Cautiously, small investors edge back into stocks', *New York Times*, 11 September, B1.

Heffer, S. (2011) 'Spending Review 2010: £83 billion sounds a lot – but these cuts are nowhere near enough'. *The Daily Telegraph* 19 October. www.telegraph.co.uk/comment/columnists/simonheffer/8074390/Spending-Review-2010-83-billion-sounds-a-lot-but-these-cuts-are-nowhere-near-enough.html

Hepker, C. (2010) 'G20: Why we all want to be Canadian now', *BBC News*, 25 June, www.bbc.co.uk/news/10409354

Herbertsson, T. and Zoega, G. (2003) *A Microstate with Scale Economies: The Case of Iceland*, Working Paper 1-2003, Reykjavik: Centre for Small State Studies, University of Iceland.

Higginson, R. and Clough, D. (2010) *The Ethics of Executive Remuneration: A Guide for Christian Investors*, London: Church Investors Group.

Hills, J. (1989) 'Counting the family silver: the public sector's balance sheet 1957 to 1987', *Fiscal Studies*, vol 10, pp 66-85.

Hinrichs, K. (2003a) *Between Continuity and Paradigm Shift: Pension Reform in Germany*, ZeS Working Paper No. 14/03, Bremen: Centre for Social Policy Research, University of Bremen.

Hinrichs, K. (2003b) 'The politics of pension reform in Germany', paper presented to the 'Pension Reform in Europe: Shared Problems, Sharing Solutions?' conference, Hellenic Observatory/The European Institute, London School of Economics.

Hinrichs, K. (2008) 'Kehrt die Altersarmut zurück? Atypische Beschäftigung als Problem der Rentenpolitik', in G. Bonoli and F. Bertozzi (eds) *Les nouveaux défis de l'Etat social/Neue Herausforderungen für den Sozialstaat*, Lausanne/Bern: Presses polytechniques et universitaires romandes/Haupt, pp 19-36.

Hinrichs, K. (2010) 'A social insurance state withers away: welfare state reforms in germany – or: attempts to turn around in a cul-de-sac', in B. Palier (ed) *A Long Goodbye to Bismarck? The Politics of Welfare Reform in Continental Europe*, Amsterdam: Amsterdam University Press, pp 45-72.

HM Treasury (2010) *Spending Review 2010 – The Government's Approach*. http://www.hm-treasury.gov.uk/press_10_10.htm

HMRC Statistics, 'Tax expenditures and ready reckoners', *National Statistics*, http://www.hmrc.gov.uk/stats/tax_expenditures/menu.htm

Ho, K. (2009a) 'Disciplining investment bankers, disciplining the economy: Wall Street's institutional culture of crisis and the downsizing of "corporate America"', *American Anthropologist*, vol 111, no 2, pp 177-89.

Ho, K. (2009b) *Liquidated*, Durham, NC: Duke University Press.

Holliday, I. (2005) 'East Asian social policy in the wake of the financial crisis: farewell to productivism?', *Policy & Politics*, vol 33, no 1, pp 145-62.

Holzman, R., Robalino, D.A. and Takayama, N. (2009) *Closing the Coverage Gap: The Role of Social Pensions and Other Retirement Income Transfers*, Washington, DC: World Bank.

Hombach, B. (2000) *The Politics of the New Centre*, Cambridge: Polity Press.

Honohan, P. (2009) 'Resolving Ireland's banking crisis', *The Economic and Social Review*, vol 40, no 2, pp 207-31.

Honohan, P. (2010) *The Irish Banking Crisis: Regulatory and Financial Stability Policy, 2003-2008: A Report to the Minister for Finance by the Governor of the Central Bank*, Dublin: Central Bank.

Horton, T. and Reed, H. (2010) 'Don't forget the spending cuts', www.unison.org.uk/acrobat/B5131.pdf

Huaxia.com (2010) '11 provinces lift minimum range, with some over 10% [guang dong deng 11 sheng qu shi shang diao zui di gong zi iao zheng fu du jun chao 广东等11省区市上调最低工资 调整幅度均超10%]', 14 May, http://www.huaxia.com/xw/dlxw/2010/05/1885398.html

Hudson, J. Hwang, J. and Kühner, S. (2008) 'Between ideas, institutions and interests: analysing third way welfare reform programmes in Germany and the UK', *Journal of Social Policy*, vol 37, no 2, pp 207-30.

Hujo, K. and Mcclanahan, S. (2009) *Financing Social Policy: Mobilizing Resources for Development*, Basingstoke: Palgrave.

Hutton, W. (1995) *The State We're In: Why Britain is in Crisis and How to Overcome It*, London: Jonathan Cape.

Hutton, W. (2007) *The Writing on the Wall: China and the West in the 21st Century*, London: Abacus.

Hutton, W. (2009) 'Britain's no longer a world power, so let's be a better, fairer nation', *The Observer*, 26 April, www.guardian.co.uk/commentisfree/2009/apr/26/britain-super-power-will-hutton

Hutton, W. (2010) 'There is no logic to the brutish cuts that George Osborne is proposing', *The Guardian*, 20 June.

Hwang, R. (2009) 'Current status of health insurance and tasks ahead', presented at the International Symposium: Beyond the Economic Crisis: Social Integration and Shared Prosperity, Seoul, Ministry of Health and Welfare, 27-8 May.

ICSW (International Council on Social Welfare) (2009) 'UNESCO examines global financial crisis', *ICSW Global Cooperation Newsletter*, October, www.icsw.org

ICTU (Irish Congress of Trade Unions) (2009) *There is a Better, Fairer Way: Congress Plan for National Recovery*, Dublin: ICTU.

IFS (Institute for Future Studies) (2009) *What Future for Social Investment?*, Stockholm: IFS.

IFS (Institute for Fiscal Studies) (2010) 'The distributional effect of tax and benefit reforms to be introduced between June 2010 and April 2014: a revised assessment', *IFS Briefing Note BN108*, London: IFS.

ILO (International Labour Office) (2004a) *Economic Security for a Better World*, Geneva: ILO.

ILO (2004b) *A Fair Globalization: Creating Opportunities for All: Report of the World Commission on the Social Dimension of Globalization*, Geneva: ILO.

ILO (2008) *Can Low-Income Countries Afford Basic Social Security? Social Security Policy Briefings*, Paper 3, Geneva: ILO, Social Security Department.

ILO and WHO (World Health Organization) (2009) *The Social Protection Floor: A Joint Crisis Initiative of the UN Chief Executives Board for Co-ordination on the Social Protection Floor*, Geneva: ILO.

IMF (International Monetary Fund) (2000), *World Economic Outlook: Focus on Transition Economies*, Washington DC: IMF.

IMF (2003) 'When bubbles burst', *World Economic Outlook*, Washington, DC: IMF.

IMF (2008) *Iceland: Request for Stand-By Arrangement—Staff Report*, Country Report No. 08/362, November, Washington, DC: IMF, www.iceland.org/info/iceland-imf-program/

IMF (2009) *Global Financial Stability Report*, April. Washington: IMF

IMF (2009a) *Fiscal Implications of the Global Economic and Financial Crisis*, Staff Position Note, Washington, DC: IMF.

IMF (2009b) *Statement by the IMF Mission to Iceland*, Press Release 09/76, 13 March, Washington, DC: IMF, www.imf.org/external/np/sec/pr/2009/pr0976.htm

IMF (2010a) *Strategies for Fiscal Consolidation in the Post-Crisis World*, Washington, DC: IMF.

IMF (2010b) *Navigating the Fiscal Challenges Ahead: Fiscal Monitor*, Washington, DC: IMF.

IMF (2010c) *Restoring Confidence Without Harming Recovery: World Economic Outlook Update*, Washington, DC: IMF.

IMF (2010d) *Exiting from Crisis Intervention Policies*, Washington, DC: IMF.

IMF (2010e) *Ireland: 2010 Article IV Consultation—Staff Report; and Public Information Notice on the Executive Board Discussion*, IMF Country Report No. 10/209, Washington, DC: IMF.

IMF (2010f) *World Economic Outlook: Rebalancing Growth*. Washington DC: IMF.

IMF Direct (2010) *Taxing the Financial Sector*, http://blog-imfdirect.imf.org/2010/04/25/fair-and-substantial%E2%80%94taxing-the-financial-sector/, Washington, DC: IMF.

Ingham, G. (1984) *Capitalism Divided? The City and Industy in British Social Development*, London: Macmillan.

Inglehart, R. (1997) *Modernization and Postmodernization: Cultural, Economic and Political Change in 43 Societies*, Princeton, NJ: Princeton University Press.

Inman, P. (2011) 'Osborne's cuts strike at the roots of the British economy', *The Guardian*, 25 January.

INOU (Irish National Organisation of the Unemployed) (2010) 'Long term unemployment up to 5.3%', *Irish National Organisation of the Unemployed Press Release*, 15 June.

IPPR (Institute for Public Policy Research) (2010) *Financial Sector Taxes*, London: IPPR.

Irving, Z. (2006) 'Iceland', in T. Fitzpatrick, N. Manning, J. Midgely, H.-J. Kwon and G. Pascall (eds) *The International Encyclopedia of Social Policy*, London: Routledge.

Irving, Z. (2011) 'Curious cases: small island states' exceptionalism and its contribution to comparative welfare theory', in M. Benson and R. Munro (eds) *Sociological Routes and Political Roots*, Sociological Review Monograph Series, Oxford: Wiley-Blackwell.

Ísleifsson, S. (2009) 'Iceland: self-image after crisis', *Open Democracy News Analysis*, April, www.opendemocracy.net/article/iceland-self-image-after-crisis

Jackson, T. (2009) *Prosperity without Growth*, London: Earthscan.

Jacobsen, J. (1994) *Chasing Progress in the Irish Republic*, Cambridge: Cambridge University Press.

Jacobson, D. and Kirby, P. (2006) 'Globalisation and Ireland', in D. Jacobson, P. Kirby and D. Ó Broin (eds) *Taming the Tiger: Social Exclusion in a Globalised Ireland*, Dublin: tasc at New Island, pp 23-44.

Jonasdottir, M. (2007) *The Icelandic Pension System*, Reykjavik: Ministry of Finance, http://eng.fjarmalaraduneyti.is/pensions/

Jónsson, A. (2009) *Why Iceland? How one of the world's richest countries became the meltdown's biggest casualty*. New York, McGraw-Hill

Jonsson, G. (2001) 'The Icelandic welfare state in the twentieth century', *Scandinavian Journal of History*, vol 26, no 3, pp 249-67.

Jonung, L., Kiander, J. and Vartia, P. (2008) 'The great financial crisis in Finland and Sweden. The dynamics of boom, bust and recovery, 1985-2000', *European Economy, Economic Papers No 350*, December, Brussels, European Commission.

Kalecki, M. (1943) 'The political consequences of full employment', *Political Quarterly*, pp 322-31.

Kaletsky, A. (2010). *Capitalism 4.0: The birth of a new economy*, London, Bloomsbury.

Kampfner, J. (2009) 'A very British deference', *The Guardian*, 13 August.

Kapp, K.W. (1963) *Social Costs of Business Enterprise* (2nd edition), Bombay: Asia.

Karlsson, G. (2000) *Iceland's 1100 Years: The History of a Marginal Society*, London: Hurst and Company.

Katzenstein, P. (1985) *Small States in World Markets: Industrial Policy in Europe*, Ithaca, NY: Cornell University Press.

Katzenstein, P. (1987) *Policy and Politics in West Germany: The Growth of a Semi-Sovereign State*, Philadelphia, PA: Temple University Press.

Kautto, M. (2000) *Two of a Kind? Economic crisis, policy responses and well-being during the 1990s in Sweden and Finland. A report from the government commission A Balance Sheet for Welfare of the 1990s*. Stockholm: SOU 2000:83.

Kautto, M. and Heikkilä, M. (1998) Pohjoismainen selviytymistarina, *Yhteiskuntapolitiikka*, 63 (4), pp 301-16.

Kautto, M., Heikkilä, M., Hvinden, B., Marklund, S. and Ploug, N. (eds) (1999) *Nordic Social Policy, Changing Welfare States*. London, Routledge

Kay, J. (2009) 'What a carve-up', *Financial Times*, 1 August.

Keegan, W. and Brett, A. (2007) 'Mr Lamont's dark history', *The Observer*, 22 July.

Kelly, G., Kelly, D. and Gamble, A. (eds) (1997) *Stakeholder Capitalism*, Basingstoke: Macmillan.

Kelly, M. (2007) 'On the likely extent of falls in Irish house prices', in ESRI, *Quarterly Economic Commentary*, Dublin: ESRI, pp 42-54.

Kennedy, K.A., Giblin, T. and McHugh, D. (1988) *The Economic Development of Ireland in the Twentieth Century*, London: Routledge.

Keynes, J.M. (1936) *The General Theory of Employment, Interest and Money*, London: Macmillan.

KIHSA (Korea Institute for Health and Social Affairs) (2009) *A Survey on Welfare Status and Welfare Needs to Expand the Active Welfare Model: Policy Report 2009-82*, Seoul: KIHASA.

Kim, M.K., Kang, S.H. and Kim, T.W. (2008) *The extent of those Excluded from the NPS and Suggestions to Improve Management of Regional Participants*, Seoul: NPS.

Kim, S.W. (2009) 'Social changes and welfare reform in south korea: in the context of the late-coming welfare state', *International Journal of Japanese Sociology*, vol 18, pp 16-32.

Kim, T. (2008) 'The social construction of welfare control: a sociological review on state voluntary sector links in Korea', *International Sociology*, vol 23, pp 819-44.

Kim, T.S. and Son, B.D. (2004) *Poverty and Social Policy*, Seoul: Chongmok.

Kim, Y.S. (2007) 'The extent of non-regular workers: analysis of the 2007 KNSO statistics on the economically active population Aug 2008', *Labour and Society*, vol 137, November, pp 1-32.

King, S.D. (2010) *Losing Control: The Emerging Threats to Western Prosperity*, New Haven, CT and London: Yale University Press.

Kingdon, J.W. (1995) *Agendas, Alternatives and Public Policies* (2nd edition), New York, NY: Addison, Wesley, Longman (1st edition 1984).

Kirby, P. (2008) *Explaining Ireland's Development: Economic Growth with Weakening Welfare*, Social Policy and Development Paper No. 36, Paris: UNRISD.

Kohonen, M. and Mestrum, F. (2008) *Tax Justice: Putting Global Inequality on the Agenda*, London: Pluto.

Kollewe, J. (2010) 'German Parliament votes to share £650bn cost of protecting Eurozone', *The Guardian*, 21 May, www.guardian.co.uk/business/2010/may/21/germany-bundestag-vote-rescue-package

Korea National Statistics Office (various years) *Unemployment Rate*, Daejeon, Seoul: Korea National Statistics Office, http://kostat.go.kr/

Kosonen, P. (2000) 'Globalization and the Nordic Welfare States', in Sykes, R., Palier, B. and Prior, P. (eds.) *Globalization and European Welfare States. Challenges and Change*. Basingstoke: Palgrave, pp 153-72.

Kristmundsson, Ó. (2003) *Reinventing Government in Iceland: A Case Study of Public Management Reform*, Reykjavik: University of Iceland Press.

Krugman, P. (1997) 'Good news from Ireland: a geographical perspective', in A.W. Gray (ed) *International Perspectives on the Irish Economy*, Dublin: Indecon Economic Consultants, pp 38-53.

Krugman, P. (2008) *The Return of Depression Economics*, London: Penguin Books.

Krugman, P. (2010) 'The cruel bonds cult', *The Guardian*, 21 August.

Krugman, P. and Wells, R. (2010) 'Our giant banking crisis – what to expect', *New York Review of Books*, vol 57, no 8.

Kuttner, R. (2010) *A Presidency in Peril*, White River Junction, VT: Chelsea Green Publishing.

Kwon, H.J. (2003) 'Advocacy coalitions and the politics of welfare in Korea after the economic crisis', *Policy & Politics*, vol 31, no 1, pp 69-83.

Kwon, H.J. (2004), 'The economic crisis and the politics of welfare reform in Korea', in *Social Policy in a Development Context*, Thandika Mkandawire (ed.), Hampshire: Palgrave Macmillan.

Kwon, H.J. (2009) 'The reform of the developmental welfare state in East Asia', *International Journal of Social Welfare*, vol 18, pp S12-S21.

Kwon, S. and Holliday, I. (2006) 'The Korean welfare state: a paradox of expansion in an era of globalisation and economic crisis', *International Journal of Social Welfare*, vol 16, pp 242-8.

Lambert, R. (2010) RSA/Sky Sustainable Business Lecture, 30 March.

Lankester, T. (2009) 'The banking crisis and inequality', *World Economics*, vol 10, no 1, pp 151-6.

Lansley, S. (2006) *Rich Britain: The Rise and Rise of the New Super-Wealthy*, London: Politico's.

Lansley, S. (2008) *Do the Super-Rich Matter?*, London: Touchstone.

Lansley S. (2009) 'How soaring inequality fuelled the crash', www.taxpayersalliance.org/news/how-soaring-inequality-fuelled-the-crash

Le Grand, J. (1991) 'Quasi-markets and social policy', *Economic Journal*, vol 101, pp 1256-67.

Lee, H.K. (2005) 'Civil society and welfare reforms in post-crisis South Korea', presented to the Canada-Korea Social Policy Symposium II, Toronto, 27-28 January.

Lee, S.S. (2009) 'A shameful member of the OECD: Korea and the worst income inequality after the US', *The Pressian*, 20 September 20, www.pressian.com/article/article.asp?article_num=40090920134232

Lee-Gong, E. (2010) 'Contestations over rights: from establishment to implementation of the National Basic Livelihood Security System in South Korea', *International Journal of Human Rights*, vol 14, no 6, pp 880-95.

Legrain, P. (2010) *Aftershock*, London: Little Brown.

Lehtonen, H., Aho, S., Peltola, J. and Renvall, M. (2001) Did the crisis change the welfare state in Finland? In Jorma Kalela et al. (eds.) *Down from the Heavens, Up from the Ashes. The Finnish economic crisis of the 1990s in the light of economic and social research*. Helsinki: Government Institute for Economic Research, pp. 102-29.

Leibfried, S. and Obinger, H. (2003) 'The state of the welfare state: German social policy between macroeconomic retrenchment and microeconomic recalibration, *West European Politics*, vol 26, no 4, pp 199-218.

Lendvai, N. and Stubbs, P. (2010) '"Trans-nationalism, social policy and the crisis: revisiting post-structural theories in Central and Eastern Europe', presented at that World Congress of Sociology, Gothenburg, 11-17 July.

Lenihan, B. (2008a) 'Government and the financial services sector', minister's speech at the PAI Conference on Financial Regulation, 4 July 4, www.finance.gov.ie/viewdoc.asp?DocID=5352&CatID=54&StartDate=01+January+2008&m

Lenihan, B. (2008b) 'Financial statement of the Minister for Finance Mr Brian Lenihan TD', 14 October, www.budget.gov.ie/Budgets/2009/FinancialStatement.aspx

Lenihan, B. (2009a) 'Speech by Brian Lenihan, TD, Minister for Finance, Private Members Business 17th February 2009', www.finance.gov.ie/viewdoc.asp?m=&DocID=-1&CatID=54

Lenihan, B. (2009b) 'Financial statement of the Minister for Finance Mr Brian Lenihan TD', 9 December, www.budget.gov.ie/Budgets/2010/FinancialStatement.aspx

Lenihan, B. (2009c) 'Financial statement of the Minister for Finance Mr Brian Lenihan TD', 7 April, www.budget.gov.ie/Budgets/2009Supp/FinancialStatement.aspx

Lenihan, B. (2010a) 'Lenihan pledges "strong" action on banks', RTE.ie ExtraVideo, Dublin, 29 March, http://rte.ie/business/2010/0329/banks_av.html

Lenihan, B. (2010b) 'Financial statement of the Minister for Finance Mr Brian Lenihan TD, 7 December, www.budget.gov.ie/budgets/2011/FinancialStatement.aspx

Leonhardt, D. (2009) 'Theory and morality in the new economy', *The New York Times Book Review*, 23 August, p 23.

Levy, S. (2006) *Progress Against Poverty: Sustaining Mexico's Progresa-Oportunidades Program*, Washington, DC: Brookings Institution Press.

Levy, S. (2008) *Good Intentions, Bad Outcomes: Social Policy, Informality and Economic Growth in Mexico*, Washington, DC: Brookings Institution Press.

Lewis, M. (2009) 'Wall Street on the Tundra', *Vanity Fair*, April.

Lindblom, C.E. (1977) *Politics and Markets: The World's Political Economic Systems*, New York, NY: Basic Books.

Lindert, K., Skoufias, E. and Shapiro, J. (2005) *Redistributing income to the poor and the rich. Public transfers in Latin America and the Caribbean*, Social Protection Discussion Paper 0605, Washington, DC: World Bank.

Lisac, M. and Schlette, S. (2006) 'Health care reform in Germany: is Bismarck going Beveridge?', *Eurohealth*, vol 12, no 3, pp 31-2.

Liu, Cuixiao (2006) 'Social security system and the establishment of a harmonious society [she hui bao zhang zhi du yu gou jian he xie she hui 社会保障制度与构建和谐社会]', *Study and Exploration*, no 5, pp 104-9.

Liu, Ligang (2009) 'Impact of the global financial crisis on China: empirical evidence and policy implications', *China & World Economy*, vol 17, No 6, pp 1-23.

Lockwood, D. (1964) 'Social integration and system integration', in G.K. Zollschan and H. Hirsch (eds) *Explorations in Social Change*, London: Routledge & Kegan Paul.

Longstreth, F. (1979) 'The city, industry and the state', in C. Crouch (ed) *State and Economy in Contemporary Capitalism*, London: Croom Helm.

Luo, M. and Wheaton, S. (2010) 'Aid to states may be lost as jobs Bill stalls', *New York Times*, 26 June, p A8.

Lutz, S. and Kranke, M. (2010) *The European Rescue of the Washington Consensus? EU and IMF Lending to Central and Eastern European Countries*, LSE Europe in Question Discussion Paper Series (LEQS) Paper No. 22/2010, London: LSE.

Lynch, K. (2010) 'From a neo-liberal to an egalitarian state: imagining a different future', TASC Annual Lecture, Royal Irish Academy, Dublin, 17 June.

McArdle, P. (2009) 'Unambiguous document that makes for sobering reading' *Irish Times*, 5 November.

McCarthy, C. (2009a) *Report of the Special Group on Public Service Numbers and Expenditure Programmes, vol 1*, Dublin: Government Publications.

McCarthy, C. (2009b) '"Bord Snip" recommends €5.3bn in savings', *RTE News at One*, 16 July, www.rte.ie/news/news1pm/player.html?20090716,2581091,2581091,real,209

McCulloch N. and Sumner A. (2009) 'Will the global financial crisis change the development paradigm?', *IDS Bulletin*, vol 40, no 5.

McGee, H. (2009) 'IMF to have role if cuts not made, says Harney', *Irish Times*, 17 October.

McKinlay, J.B. and Marceau, L.D. (1999) 'A tale of 3 tails', *American Journal of Public Health*, vol 89, no 3, pp 295-98.

Main, B. (2004) 'A review of some questions on executive pay', presented to the NYU/LSE Corporate Governance Conference, LSE, London, 4-5 November.

Manow, P. and Seils, E. (2000a) 'The employment crisis of the German welfare state, *West European Politics*, vol 23, no 2, pp 137-60.

Manow, P. and Seils, E. (2000b) 'Adusting badly: the German welfare state, structural change, and the open economy', in F. Scharpf and A. Schmidt (eds) *Welfare and Work in the Open Economy Volume II: Diverse Responses to Common Challenges*, Oxford: Oxford University Press, pp 264-307.

Marmot, M. (2005) *The Status Syndrome*, London: Bloomsbury.

Marshall, T.H. (1950) *Citizenship and Social Class and Other Essays*, Cambridge: Cambridge University Press.

Marshall, T.H. and Bottomore, T. (1992) *Citizenship and Social Class*, London: Pluto.

Masson, P.R. (2007) 'The IMF', paper presented at the Centre for Global Governance, April, http://economics.ca/2007/papers/0999.pdf

Maynard, M. (2010) 'State budget cuts: across the board, and at cross-purposes', Stateline.org, 23 June, www.stateline.org/live/details/story?contentId=493525

Menz, G. (2005) 'Old bottles – new wine: the new dynamics of industrial relations', *German Politics*, vol 14, no 2, pp 196-207.

Mesa-Lago, C. (2007) *Reassembling Social Security: A Survey of Pensions and Healthcare Reforms in Latin America*, Oxford: Oxford University Press.

MGHA (Ministry of Government and Home Affairs), Ministry of Health and Welfare, Ministry of Planning and Budget and Presidential Committee on Social Inclusion (2005) *Social Welfare Delivery System Reform*, Seoul: Presidential Committee on Social Inclusion, http://pcsi.pa.go.kr/publish/chp05.asp?ex=v&ex2=1&seq=1264

Mills, C.W. ([1943] 1963) 'The professional ideology of social pathologists', *American Journal of Sociology*, vol 49, no 2, pp 165-180, reprinted in I.L. Horowitz (ed.) *Power, Politics and People*, New York: Ballantine, pp 525-552.

Mills, C.W. (1959a) *The Power Elite*, New York, NY: Oxford University Press.

Mills, C.W. (1959b) *The Sociological Imagination*, New York, NY: Oxford University Press.

Ministry of Finance (2009) Weekly web release, 14 May, http://eng.fjarmalaraduneyti.is/weekly-web-release/nr/12142

Ministry of Strategy and Finance, Ministry of Health and Welfare, Ministry of Land, Transport and Maritime Affairs and Ministry of Education, Science and Technology (2009) *Emergency Welfare Support Package*, Seoul: Ministry of Strategy and Finance, www.mosf.go.kr/_news/news01/news01a.jsp?boardType=general&hdnBulletRunno=60&cvbnPath=&sub_category=&hdnFlag=&cat=&hdnDiv=&&actionType=view&runno=4002182&hdnTopicDate=2009-03-12&hdnPage=1

Minsky, H.P. (2008) *Stabilizing an Unstable Economy*. McGraw Hill.

Mkandawire, T. (2004) *Social Policy in a Development Context*, Basingstoke: Palgrave.

[DW need to check dots]

MoF (Ministry of Finance) (2008) *A report on the implementation of fiscal budget of the central and local government in 2007 and the draft budget for central and local government in 2008* [˙ 于2007年中央和地方预算执行情况与2008年中央和地方预算草案的报告], Beijing: MoF.

MoF (2009) *A report on the implementation of fiscal budget of the central and local government in 2008 and the draft budget for central and local government in 2009* [˙ 于2008年中央和地方预算执行情况与2009年中央和地方预算草案的报告], Beijing: MoF.

MoF (2010) *A report on the implementation of fiscal budget of the central and local government in 2009 and the draft budget for central and local government in 2010* [˙ 于2009年中央和地方预算执行情况与2010年中央和地方预算草案的报告], Beijing: MoF.

MoHRSS (Ministry of Human Resources and Social Security) (2010) *Annual Statistical Report on the Development of Human Resources and Society Security in China 2009* (2009年度人力资源和社会保障事业发展统计公报), Beijing: MoHRSS, Ministry of Finance, and State Administration of Taxation, http://w1.mohrss.gov.cn/gb/zwxx/2010-05/21/content_382330.htm

MoHRSS, Ministry of Finance, and State Administration of Taxation (2008) *Notice Concerning Taking Proactive Measures to Reduce Burdens of Enterprises for Stabilising the Employment Situation* (《关于采取积极措施减轻企业负担稳定就业局势的通知》), Bejing: MoHRSS.

MoHW (Ministry of Health and Welfare) (1997) *Annual Statistics*. Available at: http://stat.mw.go.kr/

MoHW (2009) *Yearbook on Health, Welfare and Family Statistics*. Seoul: MOWH.

MoHW (2010) *NBLSS Yearbook 2009*, Seoul: MoHW, Available at: www.bokjiro.go.kr/data/statusView.do?board_sid=297&data_sid=212485&searchSort=REG_DESC&searchWrd=&searchCont=&pageUnit=10&searchProgrYn=&pageIndex=7

MoHW (no date) 'Introduction to the National Basic Livelihood Security System', http://team.mohw.go.kr/blss/contents/contentsView.jsp?no=1&menu_cd=B_02_01_01

Molina-Gallart, N. (2009) 'Bail-out or blow-out? IMF policy advice and conditions for low-income countries at a time of crisis', *Eurodad*, www.eurodad.org/uploadedFiles/Whats_New/Reports/Bail-out%20or%20blow-out.pdf

Moran, M. (1988) 'Crises of the welfare state', *British Journal of Political Science*, vol 18, pp 397-414.

Murphy, R. (2009) *The Missing Billions: The UK Tax Gap*, London: Touchstone.

Murphy, R. (2010a) *Tax Justice and Jobs: The Business Case for Investing in Staff at HM Revenue and Customs*, Downham Market: Tax Research LLP, www.taxresearch.org.uk/Documents/PCSTaxGap.pdf

Murphy, R. (2010b) 'Is VAT regressive and if so why does the IFS deny it?', 12 July, www.taxresearch.org.uk/Blog/2010/07/12/is-vat-regressive-and-if-so-why-does-the-ifs-deny-it/

Myles, J. (1998) 'How to design a "liberal" welfare state: a comparison of Canada and the United States', *Social Policy and Administration*, vol 32, no 4, pp 341-64.

Myners, Lord P. (2010) *Future of Banking Commission*, Evidence Session, 18 March, www.which.co.uk/documents/pdf/future-of-banking-commission---evidence-session-18th-march---lord-myners-209873.pdf

National Audit Office PRC (2009) *Audit Report*, no. 14. Beijing: National Audit Office PRC.

nef (New Economics Foundation) (2008a) *A Green New Deal*, London: nef.

nef (2008b) *Measuring Value: A Guide to Social Return on Investment*, London: nef.

NELP (National Employment Law Project) (2009) *Federal Stimulus Funding Produces Unprecedented Wave of State Unemployment Insurance Reforms*, New York, NY: NELP, www.nelp.org/page/-/UI/UIMA. Roundup.June.09.pdf?nocdn=1

NEP (National Equality Panel) (2010) *An Anatomy of Economic Inequality in the UK*, London: Government Equalities Office and CASE, LSE.

NESC (National Economic and Social Council) (2009) *Ireland's Five Part Crisis: An Integrated National Response*, Dublin: NESC.

Newton, M. (2010) *Canada's Pension Pillars in Need of Repair: Report of Provincial Finance Ministers*, Toronto: Heenan Blaikie.

NSBC (National Statistical Bureau of China) (2009) *China Statistical Yearbook 2008*. Beijing: NSBC.

NSBC (2010) *China Statistical Yearbook 2009*. Beijing: NSBC.

Ó Riain, S. and O'Connell, P.J. (2000) 'The role of the state in growth and welfare', in B. Nolan, P.J. O'Connell and C.T. Whelan (eds) *Bust to Boom? The Irish Experience of Growth and Inequality*, Dublin: IPA, pp 310-39.

O'Connor, J. (1973) *The Fiscal Crisis of the State*, New York, NY: St. Martin's Press.

ODI (Overseas Development Unit) (2009) *A Development Charter for the G-20*, London: ODI.

OECD (Organisation for Economic Co-operation and Development) (2005) *Economic Survey of Iceland, 2005*, Policy Brief, OECD Observer, Paris: OECD.

OECD (2006) *Recent House Price Developments: The Role of Fundamentals Working*, OECD Economics Department Working Paper No. 475, Paris: OECD.

OECD (2007) *Economic Surveys Korea 2007*, Paris: OECD.

OECD (2008a) *Growing Unequal? Income Distribution and Poverty in OECD Countries*, Paris: OECD.

OECD (2008b) *Economic Survey of Ireland*, Policy Brief, Paris: OECD.

OECD (2008c) *Economic Survey of Iceland 2008*, Policy Brief, Paris: OECD

OECD (2009a) *Economic Outlook Interim Report*, Paris: OECD.

OECD (2009b) *STAN Indicators*, Paris: OECD.

OECD (2009c) *Employment Outlook*, Paris: OECD.

OECD (2009d) *Economic Survey of Iceland 2009*, Policy Brief, September 2009, Paris, OECD.

OECD (2010a) *OECD Economic Outlook*, vol 2010/1, no 87, Paris: OECD.

OECD (2010b) *A Policy Brief: Economic Survey of China 2010*, Paris: OECD.

OECD (2010c) *OECD Factbook*, Paris: OECD.

OECD (2010d) OECD.stat database, http://stats.oecd.org/index.aspx

OECD (2010e) *OECD Economic Outlook*, vol 87, Paris: OECD, www.oecd. org/document/61/0,3343,en_2649_34573_2483901_1_1_1_1,00. html

OECD (2010f) *Economic Surveys Korea 2010*, Paris: OECD.

OECD (2010g) *Health Data 2010*, Paris: OECD.

OECD Observer (2009) *Iceland: A Deep Recession*, no 270/271, Dec 2008-Jan 2009, Paris: OECD.

Oelschläger, A. (2009) "Vom „Pensions-Sondervermögen" zur Riester-Rente – Einleitung des Paradigmenwechsels, in *der Alterssicherung unter der Regierung Kohl?*', ZeS-Arbeitspapier, No. 02/2009.

Ohmae, K. (2000) *The Invisible Continent: Four Strategic Imperatives of the New Economy*, London: Nicholas Brearley.

Ólafsson, S. (1993) 'Variations within the Scandinavian Model: Iceland in the Scandinavian perspective', *International Journal of Sociology*, vol 22, no 4, pp 61-88.

Ólafsson, S. (2001) 'The Icelandic pension system, characteristics and prospects', in J. Palme (ed) *Privata och Offentliga Pensionsreformer i Norden*, Stockholm: Pensionsforum 2001.

Ólafsson, S. (2003a) 'Welfare trends of the 1990s in Iceland', *Scandinavian Journal of Public Health*, vol 31, no 6, pp 401-4.

Ólafsson, S. (2003b) 'Contemporary Icelanders – Scandinavian or American?', *Scandinavian Review*, vol 91, no 1, pp 6-14.

Ólafsson, S. (2005a) 'Normative foundations of the Icelandic welfare state: on the gradual erosion of citizenship-based welfare rights', in S. Kuhnle and N. Kildal (eds) *Normative Foundations of the Nordic Welfare States*, London: Routledge.

Ólafsson, S. (2005b) 'Work and activation in the Icelandic welfare state: an international comparison', Presentation to the Nordic Conference on Innovation in Vocational Rehabilitation, Nordic Council of Ministers, Reykjavík, April, http://notendur.hi.is/olafsson/

ONS (Office for National Statistics) (2009) *Public Sector Interventions in the Financial Crisis*, London: ONS.

Orenstein, M (2005) 'The new pension reform as global policy', *Global Social Policy*, 5, pp 175-202.

Orenstein, M. (2008) *Privatizing Pension: The Transnational Campaign for Social Security Reform*. Princeton and Oxford: Princeton University Press.

Ortiz, I. (2009) *Recovery with a Human Face*, London: ODI–UNICEF conference.

Ortiz, I. (2007) *National Development Strategies: Policy Notes: Social Policy*, New York, NY: UNDESA.

Osborne, G. (2011) *Speech by the Chancellor of the Exchequer, Rt Hon George Osborne MP, at the British Business Leaders' Lunch, in Davos, 28 January*, London: HM Treasury.

Ott, D. (2000) *Small is Democratic: An Examination of State Size and Democratic Development*, New York, NY: Garland Publishing.

Pabst, A. (2010) 'G8 and G20 are deeply divided over European devotion to austerity', *The Guardian*, 25 June, www.guardian.co.uk/commentisfree/2010/jun/25/g8-g20-europe-deficit-hawks

PAC (Public Accounts Committee) (2008) *Tackling the Hidden Economy: Fifty-Fifth Report*, HC 712, London: The Stationery Office.

Pal, L.A. (1988) *State, Class, and Bureaucracy: Canadian Unemployment Insurance and Public Policy*, Kingston and Montreal: McGill-Queen's University Press.

Palan, R. (2009) *The History of Tax Havens*, London: Politico's.

Palier, B. (2006) 'Beyond retrenchment: four problems in current welfare state research and one suggestion on how to overcome them', in P. Pierson and F.G. Castles (eds) *The Welfare State Reader* (2nd edition), Cambridge: Polity Press.

Palier, B. and Martin, C. (eds) (2008) *Reforming the Bismarckian Welfare Systems*, Oxford: Blackwell.

Palmarsdottir, B. (1991) *Independence and Interdependence: Iceland and the EC*, Reading Papers in Politics, Occasional Paper No. 8, Reading: Department of Politics, University of Reading.

Pálsson, G. and Durrenberger, E.P. (eds) (1996) *Images of Contemporary Iceland: Everyday Lives and Global Contexts*, Iowa City, IA: University of Iowa Press.

Parsons, W. (1989) *The Power of the Financial Press*, Cheltenham: Edward Elgar.

Pavetti, L. and Rosenbaum, D. (2010) *Creating a Safety Net that Works when the Economy Doesn't: The Role of the Food Stamp and TANF Programs*, Washington, DC: Center on Budget and Policy Priorities.

Pear, R. and Stolberg, S.G. (2009) 'Obama says he is open to altering health plan', *New York Times*, 6 March 6, p A14.

Peck, D. (2010) 'How a new jobless era will transform America', *The Atlantic Online*, March, www.theatlantic.com/doc/print/201003/jobless-america-future

People's Daily (2009a) 'Central government to make new public investment of 1.18 trillion yuan to boost domestic consumption [zheng fu 4 wan yi kuo da nei xu tou zi zhong xin zeng gong gong tou zi 政府4万亿扩大内需投资中新增公共投资1.18万亿]', 27 June, http://finance.people.com.cn/GB/71364/9552276.html

People's Daily (2009b) 'Three central government units announce five delays measures to stabilize employment [zhong yang san bu men 'wu huan si jian san bu liang xie shang' wen ding jiu ye 中央三部门 "五缓四减三补两协商"稳定就业]', 24 December, http://gd.people.com.cn/GB/123946/8571086.html

People's Daily (2009c) 'Central government disburses 26.4 Billion yuan for rural and urban dibao subsidy [zhong yang cai zheng xia bo cheng xiang di bao bu zhu jin 264 yi yuan 中央财政下拨城乡低保补助金 264亿元]', 20 July, http://finance.people.com.cn/GB/9687083.html

People's Daily (2010), 'Central government disburses 75 billion yuan to local government for employment and social security subsidy [中央财政下拨地方就业和社会保障补助资金750亿元]', 2 July, http://politics.people.com.cn/GB/1027/12037291.html

People's Solidarity for Participatory Democracy (2010) 'Abolition of the family obligations: the only way to include those excluded', 22 April, http://blog.peoplepower21.org/Welfare/41283

Peterson, M. (2005) 'The congressional graveyard for health care reform', in J. Morone and L. Jacobs (eds) *Healthy, Wealthy and Fair: Health Care and the Good Society*, New York, NY: Oxford University Press, pp 205-34.

Pierson, P. (1994) *Dismantling the Welfare State*, Cambridge: Cambridge University Press.

Pierson, P. (2004) *Politics in Time*, Princeton, NJ: Princeton University Press.

Piven, F.F. and Cloward, P. (1977) *Poor People's Movements: Why they Succeed, How they Fail*, New York, NY: Pantheon Books.

Plant, R. (1986) 'Equality in hard times', in P. Bean and D. Whynes (eds) *Barbara Wootton: Social Science and Public Policy: Essays in her Honour*, London: Tavistock Press, pp 92-107.

Pochmann, M. (2006) *Protecção do Rendimento e Inclusão Social: Uma Abordagem Integrada, em São Paulo (2001-2004)*, Sao Paulo: Universidade de São Paulo.

Pollitt, C. and Bouckaert, G. (2009) *Continuity and Change in Public Policy and Management*, Cheltenham: Edward Elgar.

Porter, A. (2003) *Gendered States: Women, Unemployment Insurance, and the Political Economy of the Welfare State in Canada, 1945-1997*, Toronto: University of Toronto Press.

Powell, B. (2003) 'Economic freedom and growth: the case of the Celtic Tiger', *Cato Journal*, vol 22, no 3, pp 431-48.

PPI (Pensions Policy Institute) (2010) *Pension Facts*, London: PPI, https://www.pensionspolicyinstitute.org.uk/default.asp?p=165

Prime Minister's Office (2007) *Policy Declaration of the Government of the Independence Party and the Social Democratic Alliance 2007*, Reykjavik: Prime Minister's Office, http://eng.forsaetisraduneyti.is/news-and-articles/nr/2646

Prime Minister's Office (2009) *The First 100 Days Planned Actions*, Reykjavik: Prime Minister's Office, http://eng.forsaetisraduneyti.is/news-and-articles/nr/3702

Ramesh, M. (2009) 'Economic crisis and its social impacts: lessons from the 1997 Asian economic crisis', *Global Social Policy*, vol 9, supp, pp 79-99.

Ravallion, M. (2008) *Bailing Out the World's Poorest*, Washington, DC: World Bank.

Rawlings, L.B. and Rubio, L. (2005) 'Evaluating the impact of conditional cash transfer programs', *World Bank Research Observer*, no 20, pp 29-55.

Read, R. (2004) 'The implications of increasing globalization and regionalism for the economic growth of small island states', *World Development*, vol 32, no 2, pp 365-78.

Regling, K. and Watson, M. (2010) *A Preliminary Report on the Sources of Ireland's Banking Crisis*, Dublin: Government Publications.

Reinhart, C.M and Rogoff, K.S. (2009) *This Time is Different: Eight Centuries of Financial Folly*, Princeton, NJ: Princeton University Press.

Reuters (2009) 'Canada adds jobs but unemployment rate rises', *New York Times*, 4 September.

Reynolds, L.G. (1951) *The Structure of Labor Markets*, Westport, CT: Greenwood.

Rice, J.J. and Prince, M.J. (2000) *Changing Politics of Canadian Social Policy*, Toronto: University of Toronto Press.

Rieger, E. and Leibfried, S. (2003) *Limits to Globalization: Welfare States and the World Economy*, Cambridge: Polity Press.

Robinson, J. (1961) *Exercises in Economic Analysis*, London: Macmillan.

Roche, D. (no date) 'Why we cannot tax our way out of the recession', www.dickroche.com/taxrecession

Roh, D.M., Hong, K.J., Choi, S.A., Jeon, J.H. and Park, E.Y. (2009) *Study on Reform of Activation Policies in Korea*, Seoul: KIHASA, http://211.252.146.15/pub/docu/kr/AK/AA/AKAA2009AAU/ AKAA-2009-AAU.PDF

Romer, C.D. and Bernstein, J. (2009) *The Job Impact of the American Recovery and Reinvestment Plan*, http://otrans.3cdn.net/ ee40602f9a7d8172b8_ozm6bt5oi.pdf

Room, G. (2011) *Complexity, Institutions and Public Policy:Agile Decision-Making in a Turbulent World*, Cheltenham: Edward Elgar.

Ruane, F. and Görg, H. (1997) *Reflections on Irish Industrial Policy towards Foreign Direct Investment*,Trinity Economic Paper Series, Policy Paper No. 97/3, Dublin:Trinity College.

Rustin, M. (2009) 'Reflections on the present', *Soundings*, no 43. www. lwbooks.co.uk/journals/soundings/archive/soundings43.html

Saboia, J. (2009) 'Efeitos do Salário Mínimo sobre a Distribuição de Renda no Brasil no Período 1995/2005 – Resultados de Simulações', *Economía*, vol 11, no 1, pp 51-77.

Sachs, J.D. (1997) 'Ireland's growth strategy: lessons for economic development', in A.W. Gray (ed) *International Perspectives on the Irish Economy*, Dublin: Indecon Economic Consultants, pp 54-63.

Sampson, A. (2004) *Who Runs This Place? The Anatomy of Britain in the 21st Century*, London: John Murray.

Schmidt, M.G. (2003) 'Rot-Grüne Sozialpolitik (1998–2002)', in C. Egle,T. Ostheim and R. Zohlnhöfer (eds) *Das Rot-Grüne Projekt: Eine Bilanz der Regierung Schröder 1998–2002*,Wiesbaden: Westdeutscher Verlag, pp 239-58.

Schmidt, V. (2003) 'How, where and when does discourse matter in small states' welfare state adjustment?', *New Political Economy*, vol 8, no 10, pp 127-46.

Schmidt,V. (2008) 'Discursive institutionalism: the explanatory power of ideas and discourse', *Annual Review of Political Science*, vol 11, pp 303-26.

Schröder, G. (2003) 'Courage for peace and courage for change', Policy Statement to the German Bundestag, 14 March, Berlin.

Schröder, M. (2009) 'Integrating welfare and production typologies: how refinements of the varieties of capitalism approach call for a combination of welfare typologies', *Journal of Social Policy*, vol 38, no 1, pp19-43.

Secretaría de Desarrollo Social (2003) *Programa Institucional Oportunidades 2002-2006*, Mexico City: Secretaría de Desarrollo Social, Gobierno de Mexico.

Seeleib-Kaiser, M. (2002) 'A dual transformation of the German welfare state?', *West European Politics*, vol 25, no 4, pp 25-48.

Seeleib-Kaiser, M. (2003) *Continuity or Change? Red−Green Social Policy after 16 Years of Christian−Democratic Rule*, ZeS Working Paper No. 3/2003, Bremen: University of Bremen.

Seeleib-Kaiser, M. and Fleckstein, T. (2006) 'Discourse, learning and welfare state change: the case of German labour market reform', paper presented to the 2006 Social Policy Association Conference, University of Birmingham.

Sheng, Laiyun, Wang, Ran and Yan, Fang (2009) 'Impact of international financial crisis on flexible employment of peasant workers [guo ji jin rong wei ji dui nong min gong liu dong jiu ye de ying xiang 国际金融危机对农民工流动就业的影响]', 中国*Rural Economy* [nong cun jing ji 农村经济], no 9, pp 4-14.

Sherer, M. (1987) 'Welfare states: an overview of problems and prospects', in R. Friedman, N. Gilbert and M. Sherer (eds) *Modern Welfare States: A Comparative View of Trends and Prospects*, Brighton: Wheatsheaf

Shifrin, T. (2010) 'PFI to cost £40bn over next five years', *Public Finance Quarterly*, 11 February.

Shin, D.-C. and Rose, R. (1997) 'Koreans evaluate democracy: a new Korea barometer survey', *Studies in Public Policy*, no 292, Strathclyde: Centre for the Study of Public Policy, University of Strathclyde.

Shin, D-C. and Rose, R. (1998) *Responding to economic crisis: The 1998 new Korea barometer survey. Studies in Public Policy No. 311.* University of Strathclyde: Centre for the Study of Public Policy.

Shin, D.-M. (2000) 'Financial crisis and social security: the paradox of the Republic of Korea', *International Social Security Review*, vol 53, no 3, pp 83-107.

Shin, J.S. and Chang, H.J. (2005) 'The economic reforms after the financial crisis: a critical assessment of institutional transition and transition costs in South Korea', *Review of International Political Economy*, vol 12, no 3, pp 409-33.

Shin, Y.J. (2003) 'Poverty and health', in Korea Human Rights Foundation, *Human Rights Situation in Korea and Tasks for the Future II*, Seoul: Korea Human Rights Foundation, pp 108-33.

Siaroff, A. (1994) 'Work, welfare and gender equality: a new typology', in D. Sainsbury (ed) *Gendering Welfare States*, London: Sage Publications.

SIC (Special Investigation Committee) (2010) *Report of the SIC*, delivered to Althingi, 12 April, Reykjavic: SIC, http://sic.althingi.is/

Sigfússon, S. (2010) *Rising from the Ruins parts 1-6*, Reykjavik: Ministry of Finance, http://eng.fjarmalaraduneyti.is/minister/sjs/nr/13560

Sigmundsdóttir, A. (2010) *Living Inside the Meltdown*, Enska Textasmidjan, e-book, www.icelandweatherreport.com

Sigurardóttir, J. (2009) *Address Delivered at the AGM of the Central Bank of Iceland*, 17 April, http://eng.forsaetisraduneyti/minister/JS_speeches/nr/3669

Sikka, P. (2008) 'Economic warfare funded by taxes', *Chartist*, Nov/Dec, pp 12-13.

Sinfield, A. (1984) 'The wider impact of unemployment', in OECD, *High Unemployment: A Challenge for Income Support Policies*, Paris: OECD, pp 33-66.

Sinn, H. (1995) *A Theory of the Welfare State*, NBER Working Paper No. 4856, Cambridge, MA: National Bureau of Economic Research.

Skidelsky, R. (2009) *Keynes: The Return of the Master*, London: Allen Lane.

Skowronek, S. (1997) *The Politics Presidents Make*, Boston, MA: Harvard University Press.

Smith, A. ([1776] 1966) *The Wealth of Nations*, London: Dent.

Soares, F.V. and Britto, T.F.D. (2007) *Confronting Capacity Constraints on Conditional Cash Transfer Programmes in Latin America*, Brasilia: International Poverty Centre.

SPD (Sozialdemokratische Partei Deutschlands) (1998) 'Arbeit, Innovation und Gerechtigkeit: SPD-Programm für die Bundestagswahl 1998', Resolution of the Party Conference of the SPD, Lepizig, 17 April.

Standing, G. (2009) *Work after Globalization, Building Occupational Citizenship*, Cheltenham: Edward Elgar.

State Council (2010) *The Medium and Long Term Plan for Education Reform and Development (2010-2010)*, Beijing: State Council, http://politics.people.com.cn/GB/1026/12292564.html

Statistics Iceland (2009) *Migration Patterns 1988-2007*, Population 2009:2, issue date: 2009/03/26, Statistical Series, vol 94, no 19, Reykjavik: Statistics Iceland.

Statistics Iceland (2010) *Household Finances 2004-2010*, Wages, Income and Labour Market (2010-12), issue date 2010/11/19, Statistical Series, vol 95, no 68, Reykjavik: Statistics Iceland.

Statistics Iceland (2011) *Labour Market Statistics, 4th Quarter 2010*, Wages, Income and Labour Market 2011:1, issue date 2011/01/19, Statistical Series, vol 96, no 3, Reykjavik: Statistics Iceland.

Steinmo, S. and Watts, J. (1995) 'It's the institutions, stupid! Why the United States can't pass comprehensive national health insurance'. *Journal of Health Politics Policy and Law*, vol 20, no 2, pp 329-72.

Stevens, L. and Blackstone, B. (2010) 'Strong exports and weaker euro fuel a German rebound', *Wall Street Journal*, 30 April, http://online. wsj.com/article/SB10001424052748703572504575214464195560 050.html

Stewart, H. (2009) 'Can the IMF now feed the world?', *The Observer*, 26 April, www.guardian.co.uk/business/2009/apr/26/imf-g20-lending-global

Stiglitz, J. (2010a) *Freefall: Free Markets and the Sinking of the Global Economy*, London: Allen Lane.

Stiglitz, J. (2010b) 'Crisis policies were working – but now bankers are back in charge', *The Guardian*, 12 February.

Streeck, W. and Thelen, K. (eds) (2005) *Beyond Continuity: Institutional Change in Advanced Political Economies*, Oxford: Oxford University Press.

Streeck, W. and Trampusch, C. (2005) 'Economic reform and the political economy of the German welfare state', *German Politics*, vol 14, no 2, pp 174-95.

Sumarto, S., Suryahadi, A. and Bazzi, S. (2008) 'Indonesia's social protection during and after the crisis', in A. Barrientos and D. Hulme (eds) *Social Protection for the Poor and Poorest: Concepts, Policies and Politics*, London: Palgrave.

Sveinsson, J.R. (1992) 'The Scandinavianisation of Icelandic housing policy', in L. Lundquist (ed) *Policy, Organisation, Tenure: A Comparative History of Housing in Small Welfare States*, supplement 2, Oslo: Scandinavian University Press.

Sveinsson, J.R. (1996) 'Main trends of Icelandic housing in the 1980s and 1990s', *Scandinavian Housing and Planning Research*, vol 13, pp 215-20.

Taber, J. (2008) 'Canada's economy sound, Harper says', *Globe and Mail*, 29 September.

Tamagno, E. (2008) *A Tale of Two Pension Plans: The Differing Fortunes of the Canada and Quebec Pension Plans*, Ottawa: Caledon Institute of Social Policy.

Tang, J. (2010) 'Consumption promotion and social security [cu jin xiao fei he she hui bao zhang 促进消费和社会保障', *China Social Security* [zhong quo she hui bao zhang中国社会保障], no 4, www. zgshbz.com.cn/Article3581.html

Tang, Min, and Zhang, Cheng (2010) *The Global Financial Crisis's Impact on the Chinese Poor*, IPRCC Working Paper, Beijing: International Poverty Research Center in China.

Tawney, R.H. (1913) 'Poverty as an industrial problem', reproduced in *Memoranda on the Problem of Poverty*, London: William Morris Press.

Taylor-Gooby, P. (1997) 'In defence of second-best theory: state, class and capital in social policy', *Journal of Social Policy*, vol 26, no 2, pp 171-92.

Taylor-Gooby, P. and Stoker, G. (2011) The coalition programme: a new vision for Britain or politics as usual?, *The Political Quarterly*, vol. 82, no. 1.

Tett, G. (2009) *Fool's Gold: How Unrestrained Greed Corrupted a Dream, Shattered Global Markets and Unleashed a Catastrophe*, London: Little Brown.

The Argus (2008) 'Iceland crisis costs Sussex £21m', 10 October, www. theargus.co.uk/news/3746012.Iceland_crisis_costs_Sussex___21m/

The Economist (2010) 'Coming in from the cold', 16 December.

The Guardian (2008) 'If General Motors were to lose out, I think Detroit would go under', 14 November, /www.guardian.co.uk/ business/2008/nov/14/ford-chrysler-general-motors

The Guardian (2009a) 'US Senate waters down "buy American" clause amid trade war fears', www.guardian.co.uk/world/2009/feb/05/ buy-american-trade-war

The Guardian (2009b) 'Editorial: IMF as bad as ever', 27 April, www.guardian.co.uk/commentisfree/2009/apr/27/editorial-imf-international-financial-crisis

The Guardian (2009c) 'Bonuses warning as speeches reveal cracks between Treasury and Bank', 22 August, www.guardian.co.uk/ business/2009/oct/21/city-bonuses-rise

The Guardian (2010) 'Spending cuts – the fightback begins' 12 November. www.guardian.co.uk/politics/2010/nov/12/spending-cuts-fightback-begins

The Guardian (2011a) 'Financial crisis was "avoidable" says official US report', 27 January, www.guardian.co.uk/business/2011/jan/27/ financial-crisis-avoidable-fcic-report?INTCMP=ILCNETTXT3487

The Guardian (2011b) 'Mervyn King drawn into fresh row over Icesave collapse', 23 January.

The Hankyoreh (2010) 'Grey areas of social insurance: solutions?', 8 July, www.hani.co.kr/arti/SERIES/56/429478.html

The Ohmynews (2009) 'How many were excluded from the EIS?', 26 October, www.ohmynews.com/NWS_Web/view/ at_pg.aspx?cntn_cd=A0001244577

The Poor Can't Pay (2010) 'The poor can't pay – protect their incomes', statement for 2010, Dublin: The Poor Can't Pay, www.thepoorcantpay. ie/latest-news-1/draftmanifesto2010

The SBS News (2009) 'The revival of public work', 4 March, http:// news.sbs.co.kr/section_news/news_read.jsp?news_id=N1000554708

The Weekly GongKam (2010) 'Sharing society without class', 20 August, www.korea.kr/newsWeb/pages/brief/categoryNews2/view.do?newsDataId=148698096&toDate=2010.08.24&category_id=subject&out_site_id=&fromDate=2008.02.29&currPage=&call_from=rsslink

The Weekly Kyunghyang (2008) 'What is the "active welfare policy" of the new government?', 11 March, http://weekly.khan.co.kr/khnm.html?mode=view&artid=17042&code=113

The Welfare Watch (2010) *Report to the Althingi*, Reykjavik: Ministry of Social Affairs and Social Security.

Therborn, G. (1986) *Why Some Peoples are More Unemployed than Others*. London, Verso.

Thorhallsson, B. (2002) 'The skeptical political elite versus the pro-European public: the case of Iceland', *Scandinavian Studies*, vol 74, no 3, pp 349-78.

Titmuss, R.M. (1958) *Essays on 'the Welfare State'*, London: Allen & Unwin.

Titmuss, R.M. (1962) *Income Distribution and Social Change*, London: Allen & Unwin.

Titmuss, R.M. (1965) 'Poverty vs. inequality: diagnosis', *Nation*, February, pp 130-3.

Townsend, P. ([1958] 2009) 'A society for people', *Social Policy and Society*, vol 5, no 2, pp 147-58.

Townsend, P. (1975) *Sociology and Social Policy*. London: Allen Lane.

Townsend, P. (1979) *Poverty in the United Kingdom*, London, Allen Lane.

Townsend, P. (1981) 'Imprisoned in a casualty model of welfare', *Community Care*, 3 September, pp 22-5.

Townsend, P. (1993) 'Closing remarks at a conference to mark a retirement from the University of Bristol', Dartington Hall, 24 September.

Townsend, P., Davidson, N. and Whitehead, M. (1992) *Inequalities in Health*, Harmondsworth: Penguin.

Trampusch, C. (2003) 'Dauerproblem Arbeitsmarkt: Reformblockaden und Lösungskonzepte', *Aus Politik und Zeitgeschichte*, vol 18-19, pp 16-23.

Trampusch, C. (2005) 'Sozialpolitik in Post-Hartz Germany', *Welttrends*, vol 47, no 13, pp 77-90.

Trampusch, C. (2006) 'Sequenzorientierte Policy-Analyse: Warum die Rentenreform von Walter Riester nicht an Reformblockaden scheiterte', *Berliner Journal für Soziologie*, vol 16, no 1, pp 55-76.

Traynor, I. (2010) 'EU unveils tough proposal to curb public spending in member states', *The Guardian*, 30 June, www.guardian.co.uk/business/2010/jun/30/eu-tough-rules-to-ensure-auserity-budgets

TUC (Trades Union Congress) (2009) *Pensionswatch*, London: TUC, www.tuc.org.uk/pensions/tuc-16956-f0.cfm

Tucker, P. (2009) 'Regimes for handling bank failures: redrawing the banking social contract', British Bankers' Association Annual International Banking Conference: 'Restoring Confidence – Moving Forward', London, 30 June.

Turner, Lord A. (2009a) *The Turner Review: A regulatory response to the global banking crisis*. London: FSA.

Turner, Lord A. (2009b) *Mansion House speech*, FSA, 22 September, www.fsa.gov.uk/pages/Library/Communication/Speeches/2009/0922_at.shtml

UK (United Kingdom) (1979) *White Paper on Public Expenditure 1979*, London: HMSO.

UN (United Nations) (2009) *Report of the Commission of Experts of the President of the UN General Assembly (GA) on Reforms of the International Monetary and Financial System*, New York, NY: UN.

UN (2009a) Outcome of the UN Conference on the World Financial and Economic Crisis and its Impact Upon Development, Draft 18 May 2009.

UN (2009b) Outcome of the UN Conference on the World Financial and Economic Crisis and its Impact Upon Development, A/CONF.214/3*. Draft 22 June 2009.

UN (2009c) Outcome of the UN Conference on the World Financial and Economic Crisis and its Impact Upon Development, A/Res/63/303. 13 July.

UNCEB (United Nations Chief Executives Board for Coordination) (2009) *The Global Financial Crisis and its Impact on the Work of the UN System*, CEB Issue Paper, New York, NY: UN.

UNCTAD (United Nations Conference on Trade and Development) (2009a) *The Least Developed Countries Report 2009*, Geneva: UCTAD.

UNCTAD (2009b) *The Global Economic Crisis: Systemic Failures and Multilateral Remedies*, Geneva: UCTAD.

UNDP (United Nations Development Programme) (2008) *Human Development Report 2007-8*, New York, NY: UNDP.

US Bureau of Economic Analysis (2010) *National Economic Accounts: Gross Domestic Product, Percent Change from Preceding Period*, Washington, DC: Bureau of Economic Analysis, www.bea.gov/national/index.htm#gdp

US Census Bureau (1960) *Historical Statistics of the United States: Colonial Times to 1960*, Washington, DC: Census Bureau.

US Census Bureau (2009) 'Poverty status, by family relationship, race, and Hispanic origin', historical poverty tables, table 2, www.census.gov/hhes/www/poverty/histpov/perindex.html

US Committee on Ways and Means (2010) *Recently Enacted Unemployment Insurance Benefits Legislation*, Washington, DC: Committee on Ways and Means, http://waysandmeans.house.gov/media/pdf/111/UI_chronology.pdf

US Department of Labor (2010a) *Labor Force Statistics from the Current Population Survey*, Washington, DC: UDSL.

US Department of Labor (2010b) *Bureau of Labor Statistics, Databases, Tables and Calculators by Subject*, Washington, DC: Bureau of Labor Statistics, http://data.bls.gov/PDQ/servlet/SurveyOutputServlet

US Department of Labor (2010c) *The Employment Situation March 2010*, Washington, DC: Bureau of Labor Statistics, www.bls.gov/news.release/pdf/empsit.pdf

US Government Accountability Office (2007) *Unemployment Insurance: Low Wage and Part Time workers Continue to Experience Low Rates of Receipt*, Washington, DC: Government Accountability Office.

Utting, P., Razavi, S. and Buchholz, R. (eds) (2011) *The Global Crisis and Transformative Social Change*, Basingstoke: Palgrave Macmillan.

Vallance, C. (2010) 'Wikileaks and Iceland MPs propose "journalism haven"', *BBC News Online*, 12 February, http://news.bbc.co.uk/1/hi/8504972.stm

Van Hook, J. (2007) *Rebuilding Germany: The Creation of the Social Market Economy, 1945-57*, Cambridge: Cambridge University Press.

van Oorschot, W. (2008) *The Social Legitimacy of the European Welfare State*, annual conference plenary paper, Edinburgh: Social Policy Association.

Veiga, A. (2007) 'Number of U.S. homes facing foreclosure doubles', *USA Today*, 9 November.

Veldhuis, N. and Lammam, C. (2009) 'Reality checks needed on recent changes to employment insurance', Fraser Institute website (24 November).

Vieira, P. (2010) 'Austerity looms for Canada's provinces', *Financial Post*, 1 June.

Vision 2030 task force (2006) *Vision 2030*, www.mosf.go.kr/_upload/bbs/62/attach/060828_-_비전보고서2030.pdf

Walby, S. (2010) 'A social science research agenda on the financial crisis', *21st Century Society*, vol 5, no 1, pp 19-31.

Walker, D. (2009) *A Review of Corporate Governance in UK Banks and Other Financial Industry Entities*, London: HM Treasury.

Wang, D. (2010) *Can Social Security Boost Domestic Consumption in the People's Republic of China?*, ADBI Working Paper No. 215, Tokyo: ADBI.

Wang, Xiaogang, and Li Gang (2010) 'Discussion of insufficient consumption demand of urban residents [wo guo ju min xiao fei xu qiu bu zu when ti tan xi 我国居民消费需求不足问题探析]', *Lanzhou Academic Journal*, no 1, pp 55-8.

WDM (World Development Movement) (2010) *A Bank for the Future*, London: WDM.

Webb, B. and S. (eds) ([1909] 1974) *The Minority Report of the Poor Laws*, Clifton: Kelley.

Wen, Jiaobo (2009), *The government's work report 2009*, presented at the 2nd Plenary Meeting of the 11th NPC, Beijing, 5 March, http://www.gov.cn/english/official/2009-03/14/content_1259415.htm

Wen, Jiaobo (2010a) 'The government's work report 2010', presented at the 3rd Plenary Meeting of the 11th NPC, Beijing, 5 March, www.china.com.cn/policy/txt/2010-03/15/content_19612372.htm

Wen, Jiaobo (2010b) 'Several questions regarding social development affairs and the improvement of people's livelihoods [quan yu fa zhan she hui shi ye he gai shan min sheng de jig e wen ti 关于发展社会事业和改善民生的几个问题]', *Qiushi*, no 7, www.qstheory.cn/zxdk/2010/201007/201003/t20100326_25272.htm

Whittington, L. (2009) 'Federal deficit to top $50B', *The Toronto Star*, 26 May.

Wilkinson, R. and Pickett, K. (2009) *The Spirit Level: Why More Equal Societies Almost Always Do Better*, London: Allen Lane.

Wimann, R., Voipio, T. and Ylonen, M. (eds) (2006) *Comprehensive Social Policies for Development in a Globalising World*, Helsinki: Ministry of Foreign Affairs of Finland.

Wiseman, M. and Yčas, M. (2008) 'The Canadian safety net for the elderly', *Social Security Bulletin*, vol 68, no 2, pp 53-67.

Wolf, M. (2009) 'This crisis is a moment, but is it a defining one?', *Financial Times*, 19 May.

Wootton, B. (1962) *The Social Foundations of Wage Policy* (2nd edition), London: Unwin.

Work and Pensions Committee (2009) *Tackling Pensioner Poverty: Fifth Report, Session 2008-9, Volume 1*, London: The Stationery Office.

World Bank (2004) *Republic of Korea: Four Decades of Equitable Growth: A Case Study from Reducing Poverty, Sustaining Growth: What Works, What Doesn't, and Why: A Global Exchange of Scaling Up Success*, Washington, DC: World Bank, www-wds.worldbank.org/external/default/WDSContentServer/WDSP/IB/2004/12/06/000090341_20041206095700/Rendered/PDF/307810KOR0Poverty01see0also0307591.pdf

World Bank (2009a) *Argentina: Income Support Policies toward the Bicentennial*, Washington, DC: World Bank Publications.

World Bank (2009b) *Swimming against the Tide: How developing countries are Coping with the Global Crisis*, Washington, DC: World Bank.

Wu, Zhongmin (2009) 'Social policy to deal with financial crisis: short and long term effectiveness [yi she hui zheng ce ying dui jin rong wei ji: jin qi yu chang qi gong xiao 以社會政策應對金融危機：近期與長期功效]', *Economic Observer*, 13 August, http://theory.people.com.cn/BIG5/9848422.html

Xinhuanet (2009) 'Hu Jintao emphasis the promotion of social security system in a Politburo workshop [hu jin tao zai zheng zhi ju sue xi shi qiang diao tui jin she hui bao zhang ti xi jian she 胡锦涛在政治局学习时强调推进社会保障体系建设]', 23 May, http://big5.gov.cn/gate/big5/www.gov.cn/ldhd/2009-05/23/content_1322983.htm

Yang, Yiyong and Chi, Zhenhe (2009) 'Review and comment on China's social security policy [wo you she hui bao zhang zheng ce hui gu yu ping jia 我国社会保障政策回顾与评价', *Economic Review* [Jing ji zong heng 经济纵横], no 11, pp 20-3.

Yew, M.A.-T. (2010) 'Bank of Canada rate hike comes with a side of uncertainty', *Toronto Star*, 1 June.

Yun, S.M., Kwon, M.I., Bang, H.N., Sim, K.B., Yun, J.D., Lee, Y.H., Shin, H.Y. and Shin, H.Y. (2009) *Expanding Social Insurances for Vulnerable Groups: The Case of the National Pension*, Seoul: KIHASA.

Zahariadis, N. (2008) *State Subsidies in the Global Economy*, Basingstoke: Palgrave.

Zhang, Ming (2009) 'The impact of the global crisis on China and its reaction', *Real Instituto Elcano*, ARI 62, April.

Zheng, Bingwen (2010) '2009 financial crisis: new social security policy and boosting domestic consumption [2009 ji rong wei ji: she bao xin zheng yu kuo da nei xu 2009金融危机："社保新政"与扩大内需], *Academic Journal Graduate School Chinese Academy of Social Sciences*, no 1, pp 16-28.

Zheng, Gongcheng (2005) 'Social security – the basic protection of the development of a harmonious society [she hui bao zhang - she hui he xie fa zhan de jib en bao zhang 社会保障—社会和谐发展的基本保障]', *China.com*, 7 September, www.china.com.cn/chinese/zhuanti/sjlt/963892.htm

Zohlnhöfer, R. (2008) 'An end to the reform logjam? The reform of German federalism and economic policy-making', *German Politics*, vol 17, pp 457-69.

Index

Please note: 'n.' after a page number refers to notes